Ursula

love

Daniel & Helga

AN IRISH CHILDHOOD

AN IRISH CHILDHOOD

Edited by A. Norman Jeffares
and Antony Kamm

COLLINS
8 Grafton St, London, W1

William Collins Sons & Co. Ltd
London · Glasgow · Sydney · Auckland
Toronto · Johannesburg

BRITISH LIBRARY CATALOGUING IN PUBLICATION DATA

An Irish childhood: an anthology.
  1. Autobiography—Literary collections
  2. Children—Literary collections
  3. English prose literature—Irish authors
  I. Jeffares, A. Norman   II. Kamm, Antony
  828'.08   PR8887

ISBN 0–00–217788–9

First published 1987
Reprinted 1987

Copyright © in introduction and selection 1987 Jeffares and Kamm

Photoset in Linotron Old Style by
Ace Filmsetting Ltd, Frome
Made and Printed in Great Britain by
Biddles Ltd, Guildford and King's Lynn

Contents

5

Introduction

This is a collection of Irish memories and personal observations or impressions of childhood, arranged more or less in chronological order. The first inhabitants of Ireland, who built great stone passage graves in about 3000 BC, remain unknown. Called by some the Tuatha de Danaan, the tribes of the goddess Dana, their origins, their lives, their childhoods remain wrapped in mystery, their impressive tumuli in the Boyne Valley silent witnesses to their sophisticated skills. When the Celts came to Ireland about two thousand years after them, they were assimilated or destroyed. But the Celts, to be named Gaels by the Welsh missionaries, and to be generally known as Irish, have told us much about themselves. Theirs was an aristocratic civilization holding its poets and story tellers in high regard. In this tribally organized society highly trained poets celebrated the deeds of their kings and heroes and their tales provide a picture of recurrent warfare – the *Tain Bo Cualgne*, the cattle-raid of Cooley, being the best known of them – as well as of a society that had its own distinctive body of law (with elective not hereditary monarchies), its own established customs (such as fosterage), and its pagan religious rites and beliefs.

From this pre-Christian Gaelic civilization we have taken accounts of the childhoods of two of the best-known heroes, Cuchulain and Finn, translated by Lady Gregory and retold by Standish O'Grady respectively, perhaps to be contrasted with the poignant portrait of a modern hero in Fergus Allen's memories of a Dublin childhood in the 1920s, and providing a lead into an early real-life hero, Hugh Roe O'Donnell.

Military heroism has run through the history of Ireland ever since the Gaelic poets celebrated the deeds of the Red Branch in Ulster or the roving bands of the Fianna. We have selected some elements in the childhood of later military figures, of Wolfe Tone with his desire for a cockade, of the Duke of Wellington who did not know precisely where in Ireland he was born, of Viscount Wolseley who studied anything to do

9

with war with avidity and waged it with considerable success in later life, of Patrick Pearse with his cult of the hero and martyr-hero, and of Colonel Doyle, recently retired from the Irish Army, having served with the UN peacekeeping forces in the Congo, Cyprus and Lebanon and now actively involved in peace studies. Novelists and politicians, Charles Lever and Charles Stewart Parnell, for instance, had militant childhood experiences, Lever of gang warfare in the north side of Dublin, even to the extent of his genteel forces exploding a mine (by the means of a lighted cigar – a good fuse for sophisticated schoolboys to have used) under the enemy and subsequently appearing in court where they argued themselves, except for their commander, free. Parnell's army, though, was one of tin soldiers, and pea-shooting cannon the only heavy armament deployed.

Military action, however, is not what is associated with Irish Christianity so much as missionary activity. Christianity came to Ireland early in the fifth century. The story of Saint Patrick being captured as a boy in England by Irish slave-raiders is well known; after seven years as a slave in Antrim he escaped back to England, was ordained a Christian priest and returned to preach in Ireland, pre-eminent among many missionaries who began the conversion of the Irish. The effect of Christianity upon Irish childhoods has been recorded. Here we have included nineteenth- and twentieth-century reactions: those of William Allingham to church-going, of Lady Gregory to the Evangelical movement's threat that sinners would perish everlastingly – something that also affected John Millington Synge profoundly – of James Joyce, so shaped by his Catholic upbringing, to the contemplation of God, of Austin Clarke to the reading of the Douai version of the Bible, of Kate O'Brien, in her fiction, to a bullying nun, of Michael Farrell, as he recreated the emotional reactions of an altar-boy in *Thy Tears May Cease*, of Louis MacNeice remembering his father, then rector of Carrick in Co. Antrim, of Edna O'Brien capturing the nuances of an Irish convent school.

Christianity made sure if uneven progress and there ensued a great flowering of culture, nurtured by monastic centres over three hundred years. This was the period when Ireland was known as the Land of Saints and Scholars, when the magnificent books were written in the monasteries – copies of the Gospels such as the *Book of Kells*, and also versions of the pagan legends and tales – when Irish missionaries went overseas, teaching and acting as clerks at Charlemagne's court, establishing communities over a wide area of Europe, and teaching those who came to Ireland for instruction.

Outside forces, however, eventually intruded upon this civilization, this synthesis of Christian and pagan ideas. There were fierce Viking raids upon the monasteries and these incursions culminated in the Battle of Clontarf of 1014 when Brian Boru defeated a large force of Danes, himself being killed in the aftermath of the battle. Yet there had been another process at work, for the Norsemen established settlements along the coast – Dublin, Wicklow, Wexford, Waterford, Cork, Limerick – and thus began the urban life of Ireland. There was now a smattering of Scandinavian speech, and Christianity had introduced the Latin script into a county which had previously transmitted its knowledge orally (the inefficient Ogham script had not been widely used). And when the next wave of invaders arrived, the Normans who landed in Wexford in 1169, they brought French with them, and with it came the input of French chivalric literature. Though they – and the Irish Kings – accepted Henry II of England who was crowned King of Ireland in Waterford in 1171, those Normans who settled in Ireland, building stone castles as their strong points, soon came to be called more Irish than the Irish themselves. They supported Irish poets, as the Irish Kings did, they learned Irish and adopted Irish customs to such a degree that the English, deeply alarmed, had to legislate against this 'going native' two hundred years after the first landings, and again later. The English language itself was spoken largely in the Pale, the area around Dublin and Kildare controlled by Dublin Castle, the centre of English rule. The colonial process begun with the Norman landings continued; there were plantations of English settlers on land confiscated by Edward VI in the reign of Mary; the process accelerated under Elizabeth, to be followed by the plantation of Northern Ireland by Scots under James I and VI.

During Elizabeth's reign, the easy-going relationship which the Normans, Anglo-Normans and English – the 'old English' of Ireland – had with the Irish rulers vanished. The Elizabethan English did not approve of the Irish bards who kept alive the identity and traditions of the Gaelic Irish civilization. Edmund Spenser, for instance, one of those who took up a large share of the confiscated Desmond lands in Munster, thought Irish bards (whose work he described as having 'sweete witt and good invencion') should be put to death, since they had a dangerous desire to maintain 'their owne lewde libertie'. That liberty was nearly achieved by Hugh O'Neill, Earl of Tyrone, in a series of military actions, but then lost at the Battle of Kinsale in 1601. After it, Hugh Roe O'Donnell, Earl of Tyrconnel, who had been an effective partner in O'Neill's operations, lost heart and went to Spain, where he was poisoned. We have included an account of an earlier youthful escape from Dublin Castle, where he had been confined by the Lord Deputy, Sir John Perrott.

In 1607 there occurred the 'Flight of the Earls'; Tyrone and Hugh Roe O'Donnell's successor abandoned the struggle and left for the continent. The tough policies of Elizabeth's commander, Viscount Mountjoy, had succeeded. The effect was the collapse of the Gaelic civilization. The poets lost their munificent patrons and the Irish literary tradition became largely submerged, though the language survived.

However destructive the effects of her Irish wars, Elizabeth, in founding Trinity College in Dublin in 1591 as a counterbalance to the effects of the Counter-Reformation upon the Irish students who sought higher education in continental universities, created an institution which has educated many members of the Irish professional classes. Founded until recently upon the classics, its educational system nurtured many fine writers. Among them we find Jonathan Swift, the first great Irish writer in English, here lamenting the disappointments of his school-days, George Berkeley, the idealist philosopher, recording his early trust in his own imagination, Oliver Goldsmith, that versatile man of letters, portraying a village schoolmaster, Thomas Moore, most successful of song writers, evoking the spirit of childhood in hymning the minstrel boy, Charles Lever's childhood activities anticipating his rollicking novels of military life, W. R. Le Fanu describing the capacity of his novelist brother, Joseph Sheridan Le Fanu, for practical joking, John Butler Yeats the artist reminiscing about growing up in a rectory in Co. Down, John Millington Synge the dramatist recording how he was struck by the shock wave of Darwinian science, Oliver St John Gogarty, his wit in gentle mood, writing a poem about his daughter, and, of contemporary authors, J. P. Donleavy pinpointing some tensions of boarding-school life, and William Trevor revisiting the southern towns in which he grew up, doing it with an enjoyment of places and names, in the Irish *Dinschenchas* tradition, a fine recapturing of visual details, of an easy-going tempo and atmosphere.

To imaginative children school can often seem a prolonged prison sentence, to others it can offer a door of escape into a better world than that of their parents; yet to others, and perhaps the majority at that, it is something to be accepted, a mixture of good and bad, an inevitable episode in life. And schools, obviously, are vastly different in what they offer, from the bardic schools of Gaelic Ireland with their rigorous training to the Montessori principles animating the Waterford school

12

W. B. Yeats visited as a Senator, a sixty-year-old smiling public man, and about which as a passionate poet he wrote 'Among School Children', imagining how his beloved Maud Gonne had looked as a schoolchild until his heart 'was driven wild'. Here we have included John Banim's description of the great school at Kilkenny, set up by the Duke of Ormonde and still flourishing, where Swift and Congreve had their schooling. By way of contrast there is a vigorous description by the bilingual William Carleton of a hedge school, and Anna Maria Hall's recreation of the kind of lesson pupils might receive in one.

Many children got no education at all before the National Schools were set up in 1833, and we have therefore included a children's rhyme collected by Leslie Daiken to convey a touch of children's street wisdom. A poem by Cecil Frances Alexander reminds us of the poverty known by so many Irish children in the past, and Mary Leadbeater offers cautionary tales about what can happen to children who are left alone by those supposed to mind them.

Children's school experiences range widely. Here, for example, the sheer boredom of not being given interesting work is conveyed by George Tyrrell, who later became a Jesuit. A desire to conform to the norms of school life is put by Richard Brinsley Sheridan in a letter to an uncle asking for money to buy a new suit, and by Liam O'Flaherty in a story about the new suit made for a boy by a drunken tailor. The effects of religious bigotry are sharply drawn by Sir Charles Gavan Duffy, who emigrated and became Prime Minister of Victoria, Australia. Joyce's school-induced tension, his sense of guilt, his soul-searching over God can be balanced by the sorrow so movingly expressed by Peig Sayers at leaving school for a harsh adult world. C. S. Lewis recorded the traumatic experiences of going through unfamiliar and, to him, unpleasing country, to a school in England. This was something Lord Dunsany did not find disagreeable, however much it may have interrupted his shooting and boating at home in County Meath, and it did provide him with intelligent companions and plenty of cricket. The same school gave Cyril Connolly a stage on which to exhibit himself.

Disappearing, or mitching, was the resort of many pupils in Irish schools, a safety valve, an occasional opting out from what could be outrageously severe regimes, caricatured in the black comedy of Flann O'Brien's *The Poor Mouth*, with its account of the devastating physical effect of the Anglicizing National Schools upon Gaelic speakers. Discipline imposed upon a child can, however, sometimes be appreciated at a later age, as in Patrick Shea's description of a midland school and its

13

severe, at times terrifying, headmaster. Patrick Kavanagh's account of his early rural schooling also illustrates the power of the teacher, though in this case the omnipotence turned out to be relative. Brendan Kennelly recreates the sheer sadism of a teacher terrorizing and beating children as a matter of course, though Patrick Campbell's experience of bullying at the hands of fellow-pupils at a prep school is no less sombre. The similar experiences of Thomas Barnado, however, appear to have influenced his ultimate aspirations and helped the lives of countless children. Brendan Behan, of course, wrote about real confinement. Edna O'Brien's evocation of the tribulations of a convent school counterbalances the excesses, though Bob Geldof shows there are still trials to undergo in challenging, in confronting authority. The final piece by a teenager, Caragh Devlin, conveys the humour and sanity of a schoolgirl born in Belfast when the present troubles began in Northern Ireland.

A pleasing zaniness has entered into some Irish childhoods, sometimes caught by the contemplation of adults' oddities, as in M. Jesse Hoare's memories of eccentricities in and about Hoare Castle in County Cork. Macabre situations created by a drunken governess are sketched sharply in Molly Keane's nominally fictional account, while children's drunkenness itself is hilariously recreated by Father Peter Connolly, in a piece to be compared with Sir Aubrey De Vere's earlier account of the effect of alcohol.

Children are sharp observers of the social scene, and Anne Gregory's accounts of Shaw and Yeats at Coole Park have a nice – if somewhat resentful – objectivity about them. Brian Boydell, on the other hand, has recorded his Dublin grandparents with amused affection, while Richard Murphy recalled his mother's recreation of the Pleasure Ground in their west of Ireland estate and his grandmother's inability to maintain it once it was re-ordered. The Big House earlier shaped Sir Jonah Barrington's childhood, and Martin Ross portrays the fullness of her brother's life in a Big House family. Elizabeth Bowen's picture of the pleasures of an only child's life in Bowen's Court is overshadowed by her father's coming derangement. But a lighter side of Big House life emerges in Edith Somerville's lively description of a secret picnic, which illustrates how children and servants understood and appreciated each other in easy relationships – such as those suggested by Martin Ross and John Butler Yeats – something brought out also by Forrest Reid in his praise for his nurse, Emma, as devoted as any fairy nurse of the kind portrayed in Edward Walsh's poem could ever be.

The loss of a parent comes home in such accounts as those of Sir

Richard Steele, moving despite its being a somewhat formal eighteenth-century assessment, or of Katherine Tynan, when she remembers her father in a poem, or C. S. Lewis's reaction to the death of his mother. Cecil Day Lewis's later realization that his mother's death was probably the reason for a series of youthful panics gains emphasis from the sudden arrival of this thought in the middle of descriptions of his life in London, while T. R. Henn was haunted by his intense remembrance of the details of his father's death and funeral. This estranged him from his mother: some of the mothers described in the excerpts come off rather badly, while others are praised with discerning love. Samuel Beckett's lines on a mother's face 'seen from below' deserve pondering. And Valentin Iremonger's poem 'Elizabeth' shows clearly how the fact of death often etches details into a child's being.

Adults can fear the loss of childhood and its agelessness, as A.E. put it in his poem 'Upon an airy upland', but children's own varied fears are often not known at all, let alone understood by adults. They can become obsessions such as the fear of Simon the Jew so frighteningly evoked by Maria Edgeworth, or be a simple terror such as that triggered off by tinkers, though in describing this Patricia Lynch does involve an adult in the subsequent encounter to underline the menace which the contemporary liberal term 'travelling people' hardly conveys to anyone who has experienced similar terrorizing tactics deployed by tinkers in the past. Children's intensity of fear can take many forms: precisely centred, as in Seamus Heaney's poem 'Death of a Naturalist', or ranging widely, as in Sean Lucy's 'Night'. There can be fear of pain, as in Sean O'Casey's experience of what he called diseased eyes, or the gothic horror of Austin Clarke, seeing the eyes of a portrait pursue him.

Children's memories can indeed record with a passionate intensity. Love in all its forms affects them deeply, as in the case of young John Millington Synge, suddenly bereft of the close companionship of a cousin who transferred her close friendship to another boy cousin, of Christy Brown, the cripple, aware that pity motivated the girl who was his friend, of John Montague, sensing his father's unhappiness in exile in Brooklyn. And W. B. Yeats, who had thought that God brought calves or children into the world at night in a cloud, out of a burst of light, has told of the initial weeks of misery he suffered on hearing the facts of life from another boy and subsequently finding the pragmatic account confirmed in an encyclopaedia. He called it 'the first breaking of the dream of childhood'.

Childhood can be buoyed up by ambition and expectation, sometimes unduly, as in the case of Letitia Pilkington whose hopes, based as they were upon precocious poetic skills and personal charm, were dashed by her mother marrying her off to a clergyman whom she came to detest. Lola Montez, however, managed to escape the object of her mother's machinations, but by means of a runaway marriage which finished in the same way as that by which Mrs Pilkington's relationship with her husband was ended. There is a certain charm in the self-confidence bubbling out of a letter that George Henry Moore wrote to his mother from Oscott College telling her of the long poem about Lough Carra in County Mayo (on the shores of which Moore Hall was built) that he intended to publish 'right or wrong'. His son, George Moore the novelist, who had been elated by Shelley, whose dazzling stanzas he read by the shores of Lough Carra, was expelled from Oscott. For a time, back at Moore Hall where his father, in an interval of not being an MP, his boyhood dreams of writing long poems abandoned, was engaged in training racehorses, George dreamed of being a successful steeplechase rider, having his own hunter, riding to hounds every week, galloping every morning. The uncontrolled galloping of riderless horses, however, as Iris Kellett tells us, can be a potentially dangerous affair, and nearly debarred her altogether from her father's riding stables when she was a child, though now, among her other activities, she runs her own riding school most successfully.

Her contemporary and schoolfellow Adèle Crowder retails some of the many pranks indulged in by the pupils of a most respectable, indeed exclusive school established and run by the august – and sophisticated – classical scholar Dr Edith Badham and her sisters. Such indulgence of high spirits goes well back into the tradition. Charles Macklin, who teased his Scottish schoolmaster unmercifully, and was reputedly the first to leap off the old bridge into the Liffey – a foretaste of the famous Liffey swim – affords an early example of this exuberance which probably prompted Laurence Sterne's youthful experience of the stream of consciousness, when he fell into a mill stream near Annamoe and luckily survived the circuit of the wheel and the turbulence of the tail race. William Hickey, that wild eighteenth-century roué – whose wildness in his youthful sexual adventures was more than matched by the young Frank Harris, one of whose reflective memories we have included – was another to enjoy the risks of water play. And Daniel Griffin's jaunty account of shooting his sister is almost as melodramatic an event as those to be found in his brother's novels.

The legitimate drama has always found authors and actors in plenty

16

in Ireland. One of the most successful tragic actresses of the eighteenth century, George Anne Bellamy, the illegitimate child of Lord Tyrawley, here records her fond memories of her Irish nurse, her horror at finding herself in a continental convent where a nun was immured for breaking her vow of chastity, and her subsequent delight in being transferred to an Ursuline convent, 'an abode of tranquility and delight'. Micheál mac Liammóir, whose acting and directing career was such a feature of twentieth-century Dublin life, gives an account of a youthful audition which conveys a delightful self-confidence. And the pleasure of being a young member of the audience irradiates Con Curran's recollection of his Dublin childhood.

Poetry, singing and dancing attract large audiences in Ireland, which still has a living folk tradition, an oral culture – one of the main differences between the Irish and the English, not fully explored or understood by either. An oral tradition colours Irish attitudes to the past, to habits of speech and social attitudes. To reflect this, we include part of a recording made for us by Liam Weldon, a leading folksinger and musician; in this he remembers both good and bad moments in his youth in the Dublin tenements.

Children's games are for ever fascinating in their ingenuity, their deployment of imagination, their seeming more real than the apparent realities of life. James Stephens tells of his ability to empathize himself into other living creatures. And Bridget Boland's account of winning a prize in France for her sculptured tomb (which shocked the village) conveys the intensity of passion aroused by her loss of the bank note prize which had been destined to buy her a new kite.

Simple pleasures appeal to children as well as complex. Thus Adelaide O'Keeffe writes a poem about flying a kite, whereas Thomas Kinsella, a contemporary poet, describes a girl flying through the air on a swing. Sir Samuel Ferguson records the thrill of knieving trout, Sir William Orpen recounts whimsically the excitement of drawing a real, flesh and blood nude woman, and L. A. G. Strong transmits a boy's delight in the adventure of travelling on those magnificently fast Dalkey double-decked trams that swayed and rose and fell on their springs like some ship in a mild swell. And for readers there is another simple pleasure, in learning how others have grown up: there is Maurice O'Sullivan's limpidly written evocation of life on the Blasket Island, his fright at curraghs that seemed, upside down and covering over the heads and shoulders of the men carrying them, like moving black beetles; there is the account of Eamon de Valera's childhood in a cottage in Knockmore, his schooling at Bruree and Charleville; there is Sean O'Faolain's description of how their family lived in the attics of their house in Cork; and there is Joyce Cary's superb evocation of the Donegal scenery that was such a formative element in his childhood.

Some children seek a wider sphere for their activity, reacting against their parents. Shaw, as a child, for instance, had the example of his family to avoid, and developed in consequence a strong desire to escape the horror of genteel poverty. So, in his early 'teens, he refused promotion in his Dublin office and set off, in the classic manner, for the larger stage of London. Kate Cruise O'Brien, on the other hand, has, like Richard Murphy and his brother, sought to discover what it is like to be *echt* Irish – which virtually returns us to a view put forward by Michael McConville in *Ascendancy to Oblivion* (1986), that only pre-Celts, the builders of the passage graves, could 'have stood a chance of mounting a successful defence against charges of colonialism'. The Irish genetic admixture is a complex one, and no simplistic views about what constitutes Irishness can prevail. Kate Cruise O'Brien rightly shows it is all a matter of degree.

A matter of degree sometimes surprises children in other ways: when adults, for instance, react more sharply than might be expected, as Edward Stephens was surprised when he provoked his Uncle John, by simple childish repartee, into a violent reaction. But political tensions and the violence emanating from them are often accepted by children as part of the normal disorder of things. Something of this sang-froid can be noticed in Viscount Wolseley's account of his family. Sometimes, of course, children may, not unnaturally, feel threatened by political violence. Alice Milligan's poem records the bugaboo effect sought by her nurse:

> *Come in! Or when it's dark*
> *The Fenians will get ye.*

But children deal differently with things, contrary to adults' expectation, and she

> *Thought 'When the Fenians come*
> *I'll rise and go after.'*

Likewise Lady Gregory, youngest daughter of the Persse family in the Big House at Roxborough, would buy national ballads, *The Spirit of the Nation* and other Young Ireland literature in the little Loughrea bookshop, and this, surely, despite later orthodox reading more suited to the

Roxborough ethos – of Scott, Burns, Tennyson, Matthew Arnold, Montaigne and Malory – laid the foundations of that independence of mind that led her in late middle age to shout firmly, 'Up the rebels'.

Apart from the sheer excitement, stimulus and information books provide for children as well as adults, so attractively conveyed by Frank Delaney, there is the question of the effect of literature. Some of those who took part in the Easter Rising of 1916 might, Yeats thought in his old age, have been inspired by his patriotic play *Cathleen Ni Houlihan*. Certainly the Irish literary revival which he masterminded gave Ireland a lively interest in her Gaelic past, and an awareness of her heritage of mythology and history, while the Gaelic Athletic Association and the Gaelic League were developing towards the end of the century a new belief in the need – in Douglas Hyde's phrase – to de-Anglicize Ireland. In the political vacuum that occurred after Parnell's death, Yeats was able to press on with the creation of the literary movement. His own inspiration was founded initially upon the local poetry William Allingham wrote about the west of Ireland seaboard towns and scenery, then upon his reading of Gaelic literature in translations, notably those of Standish O'Grady and Sir Samuel Ferguson, followed by a careful study of the work of such scholars as Eugene O'Curry and Brian O'Looney, to whom he was introduced by the old Fenian leader John O'Leary. Yeats's driving impetus showed the way and encouraged many contemporary and younger writers. With the help and organizing skills of Lady Gregory, aided at first by George Moore and Edward Martyn, and then, after various not-unamusing clashes of temperament, with the Fays and John Millington Synge, he got the theatre movement into being, and in 1904, with the financial aid of Annie Horniman, into the actuality of the Abbey Theatre.

Though he was pondering the effect of his drama – and possibly the treatment he gave to the hero Cuchulain in his verse plays – upon young men, 'Certain men the English shot', there is a perennial question of how much literature influences children's nascent minds, and this comes across clearly in Frank O'Connor's account of how he was impressed by reading Eleanor Hull's retelling of the Ulster Sagas for children and finding what the youthful Cuchulain had done by the age of seven, and what he said when a druid prophesied a short life for him: 'Little I care though were I to live but a day and a night if only my fame and adventures live after me.' O'Connor, like Patrick Pearse before him, was deeply impressed by this attitude and followed up his interest in Cuchulain by trying to read the difficult Old Irish in Eugene O'Curry's

Lectures on the Manuscript Materials of Ancient Irish History and copying it out like a medieval scribe with coloured initial letters after the style of the *Book of Kells*. He then tried to emulate Cuchulain's killing of the hound of Culain, but could not bring himself to hit any dog on the head with a hurley, concluding that 'the Irish race has gone to hell since saga times' and that 'this was what had enabled the English to do what they liked with us'. We have begun this book with Cuchulain, but even though we have now returned to him, we can perhaps conclude this introduction by commending the concern of Florence Ross for her pigeons, in a letter that demands to be read aloud with almost breathless insistency – it seems an epitome of the spirit of childhood and it catches, too, the characteristic note of the English language as it is often spoken and sometimes written down in Ireland.

A.N.J. and A.K.

Boy Deeds of Cuchulain

It chanced one day, when Setanta was about seven years old, that he heard some of the people of his mother's house talking about King Conchubar's court at Emain Macha, and of the sons of kings and nobles that lived there, and that spent a great part of their time at games and at hurling. 'Let me go and play with them there,' he said to his mother. 'It is too soon for you to do that,' she said, 'but wait till such time as you are able to travel so far, and till I can put you in charge of some one going to the court, that will put you under Conchubar's protection.' 'It would be too long for me to wait for that,' he said, 'but I will go there by myself if you will tell me the road.' 'It is too far for you,' said Dechtire, 'for it is beyond Slieve Fuad, Emain Macha is.' 'Is it east or west of Slieve Fuad?' he asked. And when she had answered him that, he set out there and then, and nothing with him but his hurling stick, and his silver ball, and his little dart and spear; and to shorten the road for himself he would give a blow to the ball and drive it from him, and then he would throw his hurling stick after it, and the dart after that again, and then he would make a run and catch them all in his hand before one of them would have reached the ground.

So he went on until he came to the lawn at Emain Macha, and there he saw three fifties of king's sons hurling and learning feats of war. He went in among them, and when the ball came near him he got it between his feet, and drove it along in spite of them till he had sent it beyond the goal. There was great surprise and anger on them when they saw what he had done, and Follaman, King Conchubar's son, that was chief among them, cried out to them to come together and drive out this stranger and make an end of him. 'For he has no right,' he said, 'to come into our game without asking leave, and without putting his life under our protection. And you may be sure,' he said, 'that he is the son of some common fighting man, and it is not for him to come into our game at all.' With that they all made an attack on him, and began to throw their hurling sticks at him, and their balls and darts, but he escaped them all, and then he rushed at them, and began to throw some of them to the ground. Fergus came out just then from the palace, and when he saw what a good defence the little lad was making, he brought him in to where Conchubar was playing chess, and told him all that had happened. 'This is no gentle game you have been playing,' he said. 'It is on themselves the fault is,' said the boy; 'I came as a stranger, and I did not get a stranger's welcome.' 'You did not know then,' said Conchubar, 'that no one can play among the boy troop of Emain unless he gets their leave and their protection.' 'I did not know that, or I would have asked it of them,' he said. 'What is your name and your family?' said Conchubar. 'My name is Setanta, son of Sualtim and of Dechtire,' he said. When Conchubar knew that he was his sister's son, he gave him a great welcome, and he bade the boy troop to let him go safe among them. 'We will do that,' they said. But when they went out to play, Setanta began to break through them, and to overthrow them, so that they could not stand against him. 'What are you wanting of them now?' said Conchubar. 'I swear by the gods my people swear by,' said the boy, 'I will not lighten my hand off them till they have come under my protection the same way I have come under theirs.' Then they all agreed to give in to this; and Setanta stayed in the king's house at Emain Macha, and all the chief men of Ulster had a hand in bringing him up.

There was a great smith in Ulster of the name of Culain, who made a feast at that time for Conchubar and for his people. When Conchubar was setting out to the feast, he passed by the lawn where the boy troop were at their games, and he watched them awhile, and he saw how the son of Dechtire was winning the goal from them all. 'That little lad will serve Ulster yet,' said Conchubar; 'and call him to me now,' he said, 'and let him come with me to the smith's feast.' 'I cannot go with you now,' said Setanta, when they had called to him, 'for these boys have not had enough of play yet.' 'It would be too long for me to wait for you,' said the king. 'There is no need for you to wait; I will follow the track of the chariots,' said Setanta.

So Conchubar went on to the smith's house, and there was a welcome before him, and fresh rushes were laid down, and there were poems and songs and recitals of laws, and the feast was brought in; and they began to be merry. And then Culain said to the king: 'Will there be any one else of your people coming after you to-night?' 'There will not,' said Conchubar, for he forgot that he had told the little lad to follow him. 'But why do you ask me that?' he said. 'I have a great fierce hound,' said the

22

smith, 'and when I take the chain off him, he lets no one come into the one district with himself, and he will obey no one but myself, and he has in him the strength of a hundred.' 'Loose him out,' said Conchubar, 'until he keeps a watch on the place.' So Culain loosed him out, and the dog made a course round the whole district, and then he came back to the place where he was used to lie and to watch the house, and every one was in dread of him, he was so fierce and so cruel and so savage.

Now, as to the boys at Emain, when they were done playing, every one went to his father's house, or to whoever was in charge of him. But Setanta set out on the track of the chariots, shortening the way for himself as he was used to do with his hurling stick and his ball. When he came to the lawn before the smith's house, the hound heard him coming, and began such a fierce yelling that he might have been heard through all Ulster, and he sprang at him as if he had a mind not to stop and tear him up at all, but to swallow him at the one mouthful. The little fellow had no weapon but his stick and his ball, but when he saw the hound coming at him, he struck the ball with such force that it went down his throat, and through his body. Then he seized him by the hind legs and dashed him against a rock until there was no life left in him.

When the men feasting within heard the outcry of the hound, Conchubar started up and said: 'It is no good luck brought us on this journey, for that is surely my sister's son that was coming after me, and that has got his death by the hound.' On that all the men rushed out, not waiting to go through the door, but over walls and barriers as they could. But Fergus was the first to get to where the boy was, and he took him up and lifted him on his shoulder, and brought him in safe and sound to Conchubar, and there was great joy on them all.

But Culain the smith went out with them, and when he saw his great hound lying dead and broken there was great grief in his heart, and he came in and said to Setanta: 'There is no good welcome for you here.' 'What have you against the little lad?' said Conchubar. 'It was no good luck that brought him here, or that made me prepare this feast for yourself, King,' he said; 'for from this out, my hound being gone, my substance will be wasted, and my way of living will be gone astray. And, little boy,' he said, 'that was a good member of my family you took from me, for he was the protector of my goods and my flocks and my herds and of all that I had.' 'Do not be vexed on account of that,' said the boy, 'and I myself will make up to you for what I have done.' 'How will you do that?' said Conchubar. 'This is how I will do it: if there is a whelp of the same breed to be had in Ireland, I will rear him and train him until he is as good a hound as the one killed; and until that time, Culain,' he said, 'I myself will be your watchdog, to guard your goods and your cattle and your house.' 'You have made a fair offer,' said Conchubar. 'I could have given no better award myself,' said Cathbad the Druid. 'And from this out,' he said, 'your name will be Cuchulain, the Hound of Culain.' 'I am better pleased with my own name of Setanta, son of Sualtim,' said the boy. 'Do not say that,' said Cathbad, 'for all the men in the whole world will some day have the name of Cuchulain in their mouths.' 'If that is so, I am content to keep it,' said the boy. And this is how he came by the name Cuchulain.

From Cuchulain of Muirthemne (tr. by Lady Gregory)

The Childhood of Finn

'And now, O Finn,' said the old man, 'if it would not be irksome to thee,
I would gladly learn somewhat of thy boyish life. As long as I can
remember thou hast been famous and powerful, ruling in the midst of
thy unconquerable warriors and indefatigable hunters. But men tell
vaguely of a time, long ago, when thou wert solitary and surrounded
with peril of many kinds. They also say that the sons of Morna searched
the world for thee, to slay thee, when thou wert a young child. But of
these things they speak vaguely. If it would not weary thee, I would
gladly learn these things with more exactness from thy own eloquent
and correctly-speaking lips.'

'I will tell thee somewhat,' said Finn. 'It will not weary me, for I am by
nature eloquent, and speech flows from me without effort. I was a babe
in the cradle when that great battle was fought in which my father was
slain. The conquerors, the sons of Morna, forthwith spread themselves
over Ireland with the object of exterminating all my father's sons and
grandsons, and, in fact, our whole race. A fierce company came straight
from the battle to my mother's house to kill me. No news of the battle
had yet reached my mother, when two strange women entered the
house, snatched me from the cradle before her eyes, and fled. They were
leaving the palace by one door when my enemies were entering by the
other. The latter gave chase, but they might as well have chased the
wind as chased those women. The women brought me to the depths of
the forests which clothe the Slieve Bloom Mountains. There I was
weaned, and dwelt as a child with the two women in the forest, cower-
ing low before the wrath of the sons of Morna, whose trackers and
searchers continued seeking for me. That was how I survived the
slaughter of all my father's house.'

From FINN AND HIS COMPANIONS by Standish James O'Grady

———◦◦◦———

Standish James O'Grady (1846–1928), novelist, folklorist and historian, was born in Castletown Berehaven, Co. Cork.

The Escape of
Hugh Roe O'Donnell

When it seemed to the Son of the Virgin time that he should escape, he and some of his companions found the keepers off their guard in the very beginning of the night before they were taken to the refectory, and they took their fetters off. They went after that to the privy, having a long rope, and they let themselves down by means of the rope through the privy, till they came to the deep trench which was around the fortress [Dublin Castle]. After that they climbed to the opposite bank, till they were on the edge of the trench at the other side. The hostages who escaped with Hugh were Henry and Art, the two sons of Shane, son of Con Bacach, son of Con, son of Henry, son of Eoghan. There was a certain faithful servant who visited them in the castle, in the guise of a horseboy, to whom they imparted their secret, so that he met them face to face when need was, and became their guide. They went off after that through the crowded street near the fortress, without being known or overheard by any one, for they were no more noticed than any one else of the city people, as no one stopped to converse with or visit anyone in the houses of the stronghold at that hour, for it was the beginning of the night exactly, and the gates of the city were not yet closed. They went out beyond the city in that manner. They leaped over the rough and rugged parts of the huge moats and of the strong, firm palisades which were outside the city, until they came to the slopes of Slieve Roe, over which Hugh had crossed at the time he first escaped. The darkness of the night and hurry of the flight separated the oldest of the party from them. This was Henry O'Neill. Hugh was the youngest of the nobles. They were not pleased at the separation. They went on, however, their attendant leading the way. The night came on with a drizzle and downpour, and a venomous shower of rain and thick smooth snowflakes, so that it was not easy for the high-born nobles to walk on account of the storm and the scanty clothing, for they were without overmantles, having left them in the privy through which they had come.

This hurried journey, strange and unusual, was more severe on Art

26

than on Hugh, and his gait was feebler and slower, for he was corpulent, thick-thighed, and he had been a long time confined in prison. It was not so with Hugh, for he had not passed the period of boyhood, and he had not ceased to grow in size and strength then, and he was active and light on that account, and his gait was quick and nimble. When he perceived Art growing weak and his step heavy, what he did to him was to place one hand of his on his own shoulder and the other hand on the shoulder of the servant. They went on in this way across the upper part of the level mountain. They were tired and weary then, and they could not bring Art further with them. As they could not, they rested under the shelter of a lofty cliff on the moor which was in front of them. After halting there, they sent the servant with news of them to Glenmalure, the place where Fiach MacHugh was. This was a secure impregnable valley, and the English of Dublin were accustomed with their engines of war to besiege and assault it, in order to plunder and lay it waste. This Fiach maintained it valiantly against them, so that many heads were left behind with him, and they could do nothing against him; but though their attacks were many and various, and though there was valour in their champions of battle, he was not submissive to them so long as he lived. If any hostage or captive escaped from them, he would not pass him by, but would make tryst with him, and his first journey would be to Glenmalure, the place where Fiach was, as we have said, for it was his strong dwelling. So, too, the hostages aforesaid made a tryst with him, and sent their servant to him. When he came to where Fiach was, he told his story to him and the state in which he left the youths who had escaped from the city, and that they would not be found alive if he did not go to their assistance quickly.

Thereupon Fiach selected a party of his picked men, and bade them go with the servant to the youths. They rose up at once as they were ordered, and went off, one having food and another ale and beer, until they came to the mountain, the place where the men had been left. Alas! truly the state and position of these nobles was not happy or pleasant when the soldiers who had come to seek them arrived. They had neither coverlets nor plaids nor clothing about their bodies to protect them from the cold and ice of the sharp winter season, but the only bedclothes around their fair skins, and pillows under their heads, were high-fenced bedrails, white bordered of hail, freezing all round them, and attaching their light tunics and shirts of fine linen thread to their bodies, and their long shoes and sandals to their shins and feet, so that they seemed to the men that had come not to be human beings at all, but their shapes in sods of earth covered up by the snow; for they did not perceive a stir in their limbs, but just as if they were dead, and they were nearly so. Thereupon the soldiers raised them from where they lay and bade them take some of the food and ale, but they failed in this, for every drink they took they let it out of their mouths again. Even so, Art died at last and was buried in that place. As for Hugh, he retained the beer after that, and his strength was on the increase after drinking of it, except in his two feet, for they were like dead members without motion, swollen and blistered from the frost and snow. The men carried him to the valley of which we have spoken. He was put into a house hidden in a remote part of the thick wood. He had medical skill and care in every way he needed, until the arrival of a messenger in secret, to inquire and get news about him from his brother-in-law Hugh O'Neill. He made ready to set out after the messenger had come to him. It was painful to him to go on that journey, for the physicians could not heal his feet all at once after being pierced by the frost, as we have said, and some one else was needed to put him on horseback and to take him in his arms again whenever he alighted. He was so until the physicians cut off his two great toes later on when he came to his own country. Fiach sent a troop of horse with him in the night to escort him across the river Liffey. . . . There were ambuscades and watches from the English of Dublin on the shallow fords of the river and on their usual roads, since they heard that Hugh O'Donnell was in Glenmalure, that he might not escape by them to the province of Conchobhar, and that the rest of the prisoners who had fled with him out of the city might not escape; so that it was necessary for the youths for that reason to approach very near the city, over a difficult and deep ford which was on the river, and they came without being seen or overheard by the English till they were at the lawn of the castle, in the very beginning of the night.

From LIFE OF HUGH ROE O'DONNELL by Lughaidh O'Clery (ed. and tr. by D. Murphy)

———◦———

Hugh Roe O'Donnell (*c.* 1575–1602) was Earl of Tyrconnel. His escape was in 1592. After the Irish defeat in 1602, he fled to Spain, where he died by poison. Lughaidh O'Clery (*fl.* 1609), chronicler, succeeded his father as chief of his sept in 1595.

JONATHAN SWIFT

Childhood Disappointments

I formerly used to envy my own Happiness when I was a Schoolboy, the delicious Holidays, the Saterday afternoon, and the charming Custards in a blind Alley; I never considered the Confinement ten hours a day, to nouns and Verbs, the Terror of the Rod, the bloddy Noses, and broken Shins.

From Letter to Charles Ford, 12 November 1708

When I was a schoolboy at Kilkenny, and in the lower form, I longed very much to have a horse of my own to ride on. One day I saw a poor man leading a very mangy lean horse out of the town to kill him for the skin. I asked the man if he would sell him, which he readily consented to upon my offering him somewhat more than the price of the hide, which was all the money I had in the world. I immediately got on him, to the great envy of some of my school fellows, and to the ridicule of others, and rode him about the town. The horse soon tired, and laid down. As I had no stable to put him into, nor any money to pay for his sustenance, I began to find out what a foolish bargain I had made, and cried heartily for the loss of my cash; but the horse dying soon after upon the spot gave me some relief.

From THE LIFE OF THE REV. DR JONATHAN SWIFT by Thomas Sheridan

I never wake without finding life a more insignificant thing than it was the day before: which is one great advantage I get by living in this country, where there is nothing I shall be sorry to lose; but my greatest misery is recollecting the scene of twenty years past, and then all on a sudden dropping into the present. I remember when I was a little boy, I felt a great fish at the end of my line which I drew up almost on the ground, but it dropt in, and the disappointment vexeth me to this very day, and I believe it was the type of all my future disappointments.

From Letter to Viscount Bolingbroke and Alexander Pope, 5 April 1729

———•○•———

Jonathan Swift (1667–1745), author and Dean of St Patrick's Cathedral, Dublin, was born in Dublin. He is best known today for his satire, *Gulliver's Travels*, though he was also a very influential political journalist and pamphleteer in his time.

GEORGE BERKELEY

Memorandum

distrustful
Mem: that I was ~~sceptical~~ at 8 years old and consequently by nature disposed for these new Doctrines.

From PHILOSOPHICAL COMMENTARIES

———•◦•———

George Berkeley (1685–1753), Bishop of Cloyne, was born at Dysart Castle, Co. Kilkenny. He wrote a number of idealist philosophical works.

Kilkenny College

Kilkenny College was the most famous as well as the most ancient preparatory school of Ireland. It commenced as an appendage to the magnificent cathedral of St Canice, for the preservation of which, after Cromwell's spoliation, we are indebted to the classic Pococke, and was then situated, according to Stanihurst, 'in the weste of the church-yard' of that edifice, and had for its founder Pierce or Peter Butler, Earl of Ormond and Ossory. And 'out of this schoole,' continued Stanihurst, 'have sprouted such proper impes, through the painful diligence and laboursome industre of that famous lettered man, Mr Peter White, as generally the whole weale publicke of Ireland, and especially the south-ern parts of that island, are greatly thereby furthered.' We have a sure clue to the date of its first erection, by the same writer mentioning that fact as 'of late'; and also by his proceeding to inform us that (under Mr Peter White, the original master) 'it was my happie hap (God and my parents be thanked) to have been one of his crue; and I take it to stande with my dutie, sith I may not stretch mine abilitie in requiting his good turns, yet to manifest my good will in remembering his pains. And certes I will acknowledge myself so much bound, and beholden to him and his, as for his sake, I reverence the meanest stone cemented in the walls of that famous schoole.'

In 1684, the first Duke of Ormond, then Lord Lieutenant of Ireland, granted a new Charter to Kilkenny College, vesting in himself and his heirs male the appointment of masters, and the office and dignity of patrons and governors of the establishment. The statutes passed by him on this occasion, no less then twenty-five in number, are each of formid-able length, regulating everything, from the master's morals, religion, and salary, to the punishment to be inflicted upon an urchin for 'cutting or defacing the desks or forms, walls or windows of the school'. Under this new arrangement the college also changed its situation from 'the weste of the church-yard of St Canice', to a large building at the other extremity of the town of Kilkenny, which, together with a fine park, and the rectories and tithes of several parishes, near and distant, the patron granted, in trust, for its uses and advantage.

But during the short and inauspicious Irish reign of James II that soon after ensued, this endowment was frustrated. The first master, appointed by the Duke of Ormond, fled on account of his politics; and 'King James,' says Harris, 'by charter dated the 21st of February, 1689, upon the ruins of this school erected and endowed a royal college, consisting of a rector, eight professors, and two scholars in the name of more; to be called the Royal College of St Canice, Kilkenny, of the foundation of King James'; and then followed 'Articles conclus du consentement unanime des regents des ecoles de Kilkenny, sous le protection de l'illustrisseme et reverendissime l'evesque d'Ossory', as curious, at least, as the state laws previously passed for the same establishment under hand and seal of the representative of majesty. William triumphed, however, James sought the retirement of Saint Germains, Ireland once more rested beneath the reflux of Protestantism, and Kilkenny College, in common with every other public institution, reassumed its Protestant charter and arrangement, and to this day continues to enjoy both, with, we should perhaps mention, only one difference from the whole economy proposed by the first Duke of Ormond; and that is, remarkably enough, a lapse of the right of presentation to the school by the Ormond family, in consequence of the attainder of the duke in 1715, and the vesture of said right in the provost and fellows of Trinity, Dublin.

It has been said that Stanihurst was a 'proper imp' of the old establishment; Harris by his own acknowledgment too, was also educated in Kilkenny College, under the first master nominated by the Duke of Ormond; as also were, subsequently, Thomas Prior, George Berkeley, Bishop of Cloyne, and other celebrated characters, among whom, if our recollection does not fail us, we believe we may rank Swift. In fact, it was after its return to the hands of Protestant masters and governors that this seminary rose to the height of its fame, and that young Irish noblemen and gentlemen crowded its classes for the most approved preparation of university honours. It might be called the then Eton of the sister country.

We find it necessary to observe that the building to which the title 'College of Kilkenny' now applies is not the same endowed by the Duke of Ormond. The Irish tourist is at present shown, from an opposite bank of the Nore, a large, square, modern house, three storeys high, dashed

33

or plastered, and flaunting with gay and ample windows, and this, he is informed, is the college. Turning its back, in suitable abstraction, upon the hum and bustle of the small though populous city, it faces towards the green country, an extensive lawn spreading before it, and the placid river running hard by, and is, altogether, appropriately and beautifully situated. But the original edifice, that existed at the time of our story, was pushed farther back, faced to the street of the town, and was a gray reverend pile of irregular and rather straggling design, or we should perhaps say, of no design at all; having, partly, a monastic physiognomy, and partly that of a dwelling-house, and bearing, to its present gay successor, about the same likeness that the levee skirts of Anne's time bear to the smart swallowtail of the last summer but one. We surmise that, at a more remote period, it belonged to the old and beautiful Augustinian Abbey of St John, from which the main building was not more than three hundred yards distant, and which was richly endowed 'for the salvation of his soul, and those of his predecessors and successors' (as Ledwich abstracts its charter) by William Marshall the elder, Earl of Pembroke, in 1220. The entrance to the school-room was immediately from the street, through huge oak folding doors, arching at top, to suit the arched stone doorway, and gained by two grand flights of steps at each side, that formed a spacious platform before the entrance, and allowed under them a passage by which visitors approached the college. To the left was another gateway, where carriages had egress. The whole front of the building was of cut stone, with Gothic windows composed of numerous small panes of glass, separately leaded, and each of diamond form; giving the appearance of a side or back rather than of a front, on account of its grotesque gables, chimneys, and spouts, the last of which jetted into the street, to the no small annoyance, in rainy weather, of the neighbours and the passengers; while, from the platform before the school-room entrance, the lads of the college contrived, in all weathers, further annoyances of every description.

But in the past, as well as in the present time, the lawn of the college was devoted to the exercise and sports of the students, and had, for its left-hand boundary, 'the dark walk', a shrubbery so called to this day, though its appearance, and indeed identity, are changed, and for its right the crystal Nore, of which the opposite banks were flanked by a wall some forty feet high; and over this wall – its foundations on a level with the top – towered in uncouth grandeur, amid throngs of luxuriant trees, the old family castle of the all but regal Ormonds. Close by the dark walk, at the left of the lawn, there ran, too, as there at present runs,

34

an artificial, but deep, rapid, and sufficiently broad stream, conjectured to have been an aqueduct formed by the old monks of St John's Abbey, that, while it discharged its immediate agency of setting in motion the water-wheels of more than one grist-mill on its course, served, at the same time, to cut off the college grounds from the adjacent gardens of the poorer class of people who inhabited the near outlet.

If local fame errs not, however, neither the broad Nore, nor the mill-stream, nor yet the high front wall that ran from the side of the college to the brink of the latter, completely succeeded in keeping within proper bounds, at improper hours, the mettlesome race of young students, that, in the old time, frequented Kilkenny College. Stories are whispered on the spot of stolen orgies at midnight, in confidential taverns through the town; of ardent breathings at the windows of not the ugliest lasses in the suburbs; of desperate wars between the native youth and the fiery sojourners; and all the et ceteras that spring from proximity to a small town of such an establishment, and which Harrow at this day might illustrate.

From THE FETCHES

John Banim (1798–1842), novelist, was born in Kilkenny and educated at Kilkenny College. His main works were the series of *O'Hara Tales*, in some of which he was assisted by his brother Michael (1796–1874). The two historians cited in this account were also Kilkenny College pupils. Richard Stanihurst (1547–1618) became a Catholic after the death of his wife, and took Holy Orders. Walter Harris (1686–1761) was expelled from Trinity College, Dublin, for disturbance, but was awarded an Hon. LLD there in 1753.

SIR RICHARD STEELE

On Recollections of Childhood

There are those among mankind, who can enjoy no relish of their being, except the world is made acquainted with all that relates to them and think every thing lost that passes unobserved; but others find a solid delight in stealing by the crowd, and modelling their life after such a manner, as is as much above the approbation as the practice of the vulgar. Life being too short to give instances great enough of true friendship or good will, some sages have thought it pious to preserve a certain reverence for the *manes* of their deceased friends; and have withdrawn themselves from the rest of the world at certain seasons, to commemorate in their own thoughts such of their acquaintance who have gone before them out of this life. And indeed, when we are advanced in years, there is not a more pleasing entertainment, than to recollect in a gloomy moment the many we have parted with, that have been dear and agreeable to us, and to cast a melancholy thought or two after those, with whom, perhaps, we have indulged ourselves in whole nights of mirth and jollity. With such inclinations in my heart I went to my closet yesterday in the evening, and resolved to be sorrowful; upon which occasion I could not but look with disdain upon myself, that though all the reasons which I had to lament the loss of many of my friends are now as forcible as at the moment of their departure, yet did not my heart swell with the same sorrow which I felt at the time; but I could, without tears, reflect upon many pleasing adventures I have had with some, who have long been blended with common earth. Though it is by the benefit of nature, that length of time thus blots out the violence of afflictions; yet, with tempers too much given to pleasure, it is almost necessary to revive the old places of grief in our memory; and ponder step by step on past life, to lead the mind into that sobriety of thought which poises the heart, and makes it beat with due time, without being quickened with desire, or retarded with despair, from its proper and equal motion. When we wind up a clock that is out of order, to make it go well for the future, we do not immediately set the hand to the present instant, but we make it strike the round of all its hours, before it can recover the regularity of its time. Such, thought I, shall be my method this evening; and since it is that day of the year which I dedicate to the memory of such in another life as I much delighted in when living, an hour or two shall be sacred to sorrow and their memory, while I run over all the melancholy circumstances of this kind which have occurred to me in my whole life.

The first sense of sorrow I ever knew was upon the death of my father, at which I was not quite five years of age; but was rather amazed at what all the house meant, than possessed with a real understanding why nobody was willing to play with me. I remember I went into the room where his body lay, and my mother sat weeping alone by it. I had my battledore in my hand, and fell a beating the coffin, and calling Papa; for, I know not how, I had some slight idea that he was locked up there. My mother catched me in her arms, and, transported beyond all patience of the silent grief she was before in, she almost smothered me in her embraces; and told me in a flood of tears, 'Papa could not hear me, and would play with me no more, for they were going to put him under ground, whence he could never come to us again.' She was a very beautiful woman, of a noble spirit, and there was a dignity in her grief amidst all the wildness of her transport; which, methought, struck me with an instinct of sorrow that before I was sensible of what it was to grieve, seized my very soul, and has made pity the weakness of my heart ever since. The mind in infancy is, methinks, like the body in embryo; and receives impressions so forcible, that they are as hard to be removed by reason, as any mark with which a child is born is to be taken away by any future application. Hence it is, that good-nature in me is no merit; but having been so frequently overwhelmed with her tears before I knew the cause of any affliction, or could draw defences from my own judgment, I imbibed commiseration, remorse, and an unmanly gentleness of mind, which has since insnared me into ten thousand calamities; and from whence I can reap no advantage, except it be, that, in such a humour as I am now in, I can the better indulge myself in the softness of humanity, and enjoy that sweet anxiety which arises from the memory of past afflictions.

We, that are very old, are better able to remember things which befell us in our distant youth, than the passages of later days. For this reason it is, that the companions of my strong and vigorous years present themselves more immediately to me in this office of sorrow. Untimely and unhappy deaths are what we are most apt to lament; so little are we able to make it indifferent when a thing happens, though we know it must happen. Thus we groan under life and bewail those who are relieved from it. Every object that returns to our imagination raises different passions, according to the circumstance of their departure. Who can have lived in an army, and in a serious hour reflect upon the many gay and agreeable men that might long have flourished in the arts of peace, and not join with the imprecations of the fatherless and widow on the tyrant to whose ambition they fell sacrifices? But gallant men, who are cut off by the sword, move rather our veneration than our pity; and we gather relief enough from their own contempt of death, to make that no evil, which was approached with so much cheerfulness, and attended with so much honour. But when we turn our thoughts from the great parts of life on such occasions, and instead of lamenting those who stood ready to give death to those from whom they had the fortune to receive it; I say, when we let our thoughts wander from such noble objects, and consider the havock which is made among the tender and the innocent, pity enters with an unmixed softness, and possesses all our souls at once.

Here (were there words to express such sentiments with proper tenderness) I should record the beauty, innocence, and untimely death, of the first object my eyes ever beheld with love. The beauteous virgin! how ignorantly did she charm, how carelessly excel? Oh death! thou hast right to the bold, to the ambitious, to the high, and to the haughty; but why this cruelty to the humble, to the meek, to the undiscerning, to the thoughtless? Nor age, nor business, nor distress, can erase the dear image from my imagination. In the same week, I saw her dressed for a ball, and in a shroud. How ill did the habit of death become the pretty trifler? I still behold the smiling earth – A large train of disasters were coming on to my memory, when my servant knocked at my closet-door, and interrupted me with a letter, attended with a hamper of wine, of the same sort with that which is to be put on sale on Thursday next, at Garraway's coffee-house. Upon receipt of it, I sent for three of my friends. We are so intimate, that we can be company in whatever state of mind we meet, and can entertain each other without expecting always to rejoice. The wine we found to be generous and warming, but with such a heat as moved us rather to be cheerful than frolicksome. It revived the spirits, without firing the blood. We commended it until two of the clock

38

this morning; and having to-day met a little before dinner, we found, that though we drank two bottles a man, we had much more reason to recollect than forget what had passed the night before.

In *Tatler*, No. 181

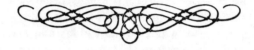

Sir Richard Steele (1672–1729), essayist and journalist, was born in Dublin. With his Charterhouse school friend, Joseph Addison, he founded the *Tatler* and later the *Spectator*.

Charles Macklin –
Schooling of an Actor

The choice of the person to whose tuition parents entrust their children is of the greatest consequence. It is not enough that such a man is a scholar: there are many of those deeply learned pedagogues, who fill the minds and hearts of their pupils with a thousand disgusting propensities, and even vices, for which no share of learning can atone.

How many have been made to abhor early rising and reading – how many to abhor their duty at church, by unreasonable rigour in those points, and inhuman chastisement for neglect of them. It was from the cruelty of a pedagogue, that Mr Macklin, almost in infancy, imbibed that invincible prejudice against the Scotch, which adhered to him through a long life, and is too glaringly avowed in his writings to have escaped the observation of any one who has read or seen them performed. The academy at which he was boarded was kept by a Scotchman, of the name of Nicholson – naturally morose, sour, and severe in his temper; the practice of a schoolmaster was not likely to improve it. Like too many of his profession, he was, in fact, a compendium of all those gloomy, brutal passions, which constitute the systematic tyrant; and only wanted power to be a perfect despot. A subject better calculated both for the indulgence and vexation of such a man could not have been found than in young Charles. If Nicholson was cruel, Macklin was arch, bold, resolute, and ingenious. Thus the tyranny and moroseness of the Scotchman, set off by a grotesque person, a ludicrous voice, and the most *outré*, whimsical deportment, were sufficient to recommend him to the boy's contempt and abhorrence. With such motives to hostility on both sides, it is not at all surprizing, that they soon declared war against each other, which they certainly continued for the space of nineteen months, till the boy passed his eighteenth year; a time truly astonishing for two human beings to remain wilfully inflicting and suffering. The one was content to undergo all the torment and confusion, which wit, archness, and ingenuity could devise for his annoyance, rather than forego the indulgence he felt in whipping the boy. The other was willing to purchase the luxury of tormenting his tyrant at the daily expence of a horsing – and if the talents of both be duly considered, it will remain doubtful to which of them the palm of persevering patience belonged. Charles, in his very infancy, disclosed strong marks of that temper, genius, and spirit, which marked his character in succeeding life – shrewd, keen, and penetrating beyond his years – bold, proud, and resolute, and even then inflexibly firm to his purpose; full of animation, fire and vivacity, with an heart which tenderness or persuasion might mould, but no tyranny depress or controul.

Upon such a vigorous, luxuriant stock, how many noble virtues might not have been ingrafted by the hand of skill. But it fell into the hands of a blockhead, who, though he could not marr its growth, contrived, perhaps, to distort its direction. The circumstances of this period of his life impressed themselves so deeply on Mr Macklin's mind, that he never forgot them, and frequently indulged his friends with humorous descriptions of his conflicts with, and machinations to tantalize, Nicholson.

He early possessed an extraordinary talent for mimickry, which he exercised to the continual annoyance of the pedant, by counterfeiting alternately the voices of him and his wife *Harriet*, and calling aloud upon either, in the voice of the other so exactly, as to baffle all their vigilance in guarding against his pranks; and a parrot which our young hero had taught not only to mimick both in the same style, but to call them by the most ridiculous names, compleated their mortification. Every week, a message was sent to Charles's mother, to request that either she or her husband would come and take the boy away, or silence him. She would come and threaten, and entreat. Charles would promise amendment – keep his word for a day or two – and again become as mischievous and troublesome as ever. Nor was his archness confined to *Nicholson*; every one who happened to have the least oddity or singularity was sure to become the subject of his mirth and humour – scarcely any one therefore escaped him – and he at last obtained the nickname of *Charles a Molluchth*; or, in English, *Wicked Charley*. While at school, he was celebrated for feats of prowess and valour. He was more than a match at boxing and cudgel-playing for any boy of his age – and excelled in swimming, even there, where that art has always been carried to a degree of perfection so great, as to surprise all foreigners, who have occasion to visit Dublin. The practice of leaping off the bridges of Dublin, and off the masts of ships into the river, was not then so common as it has since become. It was at that time deemed an act of

41

heroism, and Macklin was among the first, if not the very first, who undertook the seemingly hazardous feat of leaping from the Old Bridge into the Liffey.

From THE LIFE OF CHARLES MACKLIN by James Kirkman

———◆◇◆———

Charles Macklin (1692–1797), actor and dramatist, was probably born at Culdaff, Co. Donegal. He was much admired in his roles as Macbeth and Shylock. He wrote two good comedies, *The Man of the World* and *Love à la Mode*. James Thomas Kirkman (*fl.* 1799–1810) is said by some sources to have been an illegitimate son of Macklin.

LETITIA PILKINGTON

A Forward Miss

My mother being now in possession of a handsome fortune, and by the death of her grandmother entirely at her own disposal, for her father never enquired what became of her, did not, it may be supposed, want admirers, especially as she had a very graceful person, with abundance of wit, which was improved by reading and keeping the best company: however, none of them made any impression on her heart till she saw my father, who was the son of a Dutch physician that accidentally settled in Ireland, and who had no other fortune to boast of than a liberal education and a very amiable person and understanding – qualities which recommended him to my mother so powerfully that she had constancy enough to wait for him three years while he went to Leyden, where he studied physic under the late famous Dr Boerhaave; and, having taken his degree, he returned to Ireland, uniting himself in marriage to his faithful mistress. Her friends were at first much displeased with her; but my father's merit soon reconciled them to her choice; and there being then but one man-midwife in the kingdom, my father made himself of that useful art, and practised it with great success, reputation, and humanity.

I was their second child, and, my eldest brother dying an infant, for a long time their only one; being of a tender weakly constitution, I was by my father greatly indulged – indeed, I cannot say but it was in some measure necessary he should by this gentleness qualify my mother's severity to me: otherwise it must have broke my heart for she strictly followed Solomon's advice, in never sparing the rod: insomuch that I have frequently been whipped for looking blue on a frosty morning; and, whether I deserved it or not, I was sure of correction every day of my life.

From my earliest infancy I had a strong disposition to letters; but, my eyes being weak after the small-pox, I was not permitted to look at a book, my mother regarding more the beauty of my face than the improvement of my mind: neither was I allowed to learn to read. This restraint, as it generally happens, made me but more earnest in the pursuit of what I imagined must be so delightful. Twenty times a day have I been corrected for asking what such and such letters spelt; my mother used to tell me the word, accompanying it with a good box on the ear, which, I suppose, imprinted it on my mind. Had Gulliver seen her behaviour, I should have imagined he had borrowed a hint from it for his floating island, where, when a great man had promised any favour, the suppliant was obliged to give him a tweak by the nose or a kick on the rump, to quicken his memory. However, I do assure you, it had this effect on me, insomuch that I never forgot what was once told me; and quickly arrived at my desired happiness, being able to read before she thought I knew all my letters: but this pleasure I was obliged to enjoy by stealth, with fear and trembling.

I was at this time about five years of age; and, my mother being one day abroad, I had happily laid hold on *Alexander's Feast*, and found something in it so charming that I read it aloud – but how like a condemned criminal did I look when my father, softly opening his study-door, took me in the very fact! I dropped my book, and burst into tears, begging pardon, and promising never to do so again. But my sorrow was soon dispelled when he bade me not be frightened, but read to him, which, to his great surprise, I did very distinctly and without hurting the beauty of the numbers. Instead of the whipping of which I stood in dread, he took me up in his arms, and kissed me, giving me a whole shilling as a reward, and told me: 'He would give me another as soon as I got a poem by heart,' which he put into my hand, and it proved to be Mr Pope's sacred *Eclogue*; which task I performed before my mother returned home. They were both astonished at my memory, and from that day forward I was permitted to read as much as I pleased; only my father took care to furnish me with the best and politest authors; and took delight in explaining to me, whatever, by reason of my tender years, was above my capacity of understanding.

But chiefly was I charmed and ravished with the sweets of poetry; all my hours were dedicated to the muses; and from a Reader I quickly became a Writer; I may truly say with Mr Pope:

I lisped in numbers, for the numbers came.

My performances had the good fortune to be looked on as extraordinary for my years; and the greatest and wisest men in the kingdom did not disdain to hear the prattle of the little muse, as they called me, even in my childish days. But as I approached towards womanhood, there was a new scene opened to me; and by the time I had looked on thirteen years, I had almost as many lovers: not that I ever was handsome, farther than being very fair. But I was well-dressed, sprightly, and remarkably well-tempered, unapt to give or take offence; insomuch that my company was generally coveted; and no doubt but I should have been happily disposed of in marriage, but that my mother's capricious temper made her reject every advantageous proposal offered, and at last condemn me to the arms of one of the greatest villains, with reverence to the priesthood be it spoken, that ever was wrapped up in crape.

From MEMOIRS OF LETITIA PILKINGTON

————◦◦◦————

Letitia Pilkington (1712–50) was born in Dublin, the daughter of a Dutch doctor. She became a close friend of Jonathan Swift, about whose personal habits her *Memoirs* are a valuable source. She married Matthew Pilkington, a somewhat profligate Irish parson.

The Mill-Race

We lived in the barracks at Wicklow one year (one thousand seven hundred and twenty), when Devijeher (so called after Colonel Devijeher) was born; thence we decamped to stay half a year with Mr Fetherston, a clergyman, about seven miles from Wicklow; who, being a relation of my mother's, invited us to his parsonage at Animo.

It was in this parish, during our stay, that I had that wonderful escape in falling through a mill-race whilst the mill was going, and of being taken up unhurt: the story is incredible, but known for truth in all that part of Ireland, where hundreds of the common people flocked to see me. Hence we followed the regiment to Dublin, where we lay in the barracks a year. In this year (one thousand seven hundred and twenty-one) I learnt to write, etc. The regiment ordered in twenty-two to Carrickfergus, in the north of Ireland. We all decamped, but got no farther than Drogheda; thence ordered to Mullingar, forty miles west, where, by Providence, we stumbled upon a kind relation, a collateral descendant from Archbishop Sterne, who took us all to his castle, and kindly entertained us for a year, and sent us to the regiment at Carrickfergus, loaded with kindnesses, etc. A most rueful and tedious journey had we all (in March) to Carrickfergus, where we arrived in six or seven days. Little Devijeher here died; he was three years old: he had been left behind at nurse at a farmhouse near Wicklow, but was fetched to us by my father the summer after – another child sent to fill his place, Susan. This babe too left us behind in this weary journey. The autumn of that year, or the spring afterwards (I forget which), my father got leave of his colonel to fix me at school, – which he did near Halifax, with an able master; with whom I stayed some time, till, by God's care of me, my cousin Sterne, of Elvington, became a father to me, and sent me to the University, etc. etc.

To pursue the thread of our story, my father's regiment was, the year after, ordered to Londonderry, where another sister was brought forth,

Catherine, still living; but most unhappily estranged from me by my uncle's wickedness and her own folly. From this station the regiment was sent to defend Gibraltar, at the siege, where my father was run through the body by Captain Phillips in a duel (the quarrel began about a goose!); with much difficulty he survived, though with an impaired constitution, which was not able to withstand the hardships it was put to; for he was sent to Jamaica, where he soon fell by the country fever, which took away his senses first, and made a child of him; and then, in a month or two, walking about continually without complaining, till the moment he sat down in an arm-chair, and breathed his last, which was at Port Antonio, on the north of the island. My father was a little smart man, active to the last degree in all exercises, most patient of fatigue and disappointments, of which it pleased God to give him full measure. He was, in his temper, somewhat rapid and hasty, but of a kindly, sweet disposition, void of all design; and so innocent in his own intentions that he suspected no one; so that you might have cheated him ten times in a day, if nine had not been sufficient for your purpose.

My poor father died in March 1731. I remained at Halifax till about the latter end of that year, and cannot omit mentioning this anecdote of myself and schoolmaster: – He had the ceiling of the schoolroom new white-washed; the ladder remained there: I one unlucky day mounted it, and wrote with a brush, in large capital letters, LAU. STERNE, for which the usher severely whipped me. My master was very much hurt at this, and said, before me, that never should that name be effaced, for I was a boy of genius, and he was sure that I should come to preferment. – This expression made me forget the stripes I had received.

From MEMOIR

———•◦•———

Rev. Laurence Sterne (1713–68), novelist, was born at Clonmel, where his father's regiment was stationed, and spent part of his boyhood in Ireland. His most famous work, *Tristram Shandy*, was first published in nine volumes between 1759 and 1767.

OLIVER GOLDSMITH

The Village Schoolmaster

Beside yon straggling fence that skirts the way,
With blossomed furze unprofitably gay,
There, in his noisy mansion, skill'd to rule,
The village master taught his little school;
A man severe he was, and stern to view,
I knew him well, and every truant knew;
Well had the boding tremblers learned to trace
The day's disasters in his morning face;
Full well they laugh'd with counterfeited glee,
At all his jokes, for many a joke had he;
Full well the busy whisper circling round,
Conveyed the dismal tidings when he frowned;
Yet he was kind, or if severe in aught,
The love he bore to learning was in fault;
The village all declared how much he knew;
'Twas certain he could write, and cypher too;
Lands he could measure, terms and tides presage,
And even the story ran that he could gauge.
In arguing too, the parson owned his skill,
For even tho' vanquished, he could argue still;
While words of learned length, and thundering sound,
Amazed the gazing rustics ranged around,
And still they gazed, and still the wonder grew,
That one small head could carry all he knew.

From THE DESERTED VILLAGE

Oliver Goldsmith (1728–74), author of *The Vicar of Wakefield* and
She Stoops to Conquer, was born at Pallasmore, Co. Longford. *The
Deserted Village* was published in 1770. In spite of his reputation as
a writer, his excessive generosity led him into financial straits.

The Faithful Nurse

I was born on St George's day, 1733, some months too soon for Captain Bellamy to claim any degree of consanguinity with me. As soon as Lord Tyrawley had gained intelligence, after my mother's departure from Lisbon, of the place of her destination, he wrote to his adjutant, Captain Pye, who resided near Fingal, the town where she had settled, to request, if she should prove pregnant in time to conclude it was the effect of her visit to his lordship, that his lady would take the infant under her care as soon as it was born, without suffering my mother, if possible, to see it. This severe injunction of his Lordship proceeded from his entertaining a belief, that her sudden retreat from Lisbon was not in consequence of her having formed an honourable connection with Captain Bellamy, but through the natural depravity of her passions, and the fickleness of her disposition. I was, therefore, agreeable to his Lordship's directions, taken from my mother soon after my birth, and put under the care of a nurse, with whom I continued till I was two years old. At that time the regiment returning to barracks in Dublin, Mrs Pye, whose kindness I shall never forget, and whose memory I shall ever revere, took me from the nurse, and carried me with her.

Here, Madam, I must beg leave to entertain you with an anecdote of my nurse, which exhibits such a proof of the attachment and fidelity of the lower class of the Irish as does them infinite honour. It never occurs to my mind, but it excites the tenderest sensations; and I should deem myself ungrateful in the extreme, were I not always to mention her name with respect.

It happened that the summer, in the midst of which I was taken from the care of my foster-mother, was uncommonly hot. Notwithstanding this, so excessive was the good woman's affection for me that she walked *every day* from the village in which she lived, to the barracks, which were three miles distant, and with a child sucking at her breast. The intense heat, united with the affliction she felt at my being taken from

49

her, had such an effect upon her constitution, that it brought on an inflammatory fever, which put an end to her life. It is a custom in many parts of Ireland, to convey the remains of the dead to those for whom, whilst living, they appeared to have the sincerest regard; and the custom was not neglected upon the decease of my worthy nurse. Captain Pye's servants having risen one morning, upon some occasion or other, earlier than usual, and left the street door open; as I lay in bed, I heard my foster-father's voice audibly uttering what is vulgarly called the Irish howl. *Ah! why did you die?* with all its plaintive eloquence, distinctly reached my ear. Alarmed at the well-known sound, I hastily leaped out of bed, and ran almost naked into the street where, to my great grief, even at that early age, I found the lamentation now become universal around the body of my poor nurse, whose affection for me had cost her her life – Why, O thou great Disposer of events! why was I born to be the cause of unhappiness, and even death to those who really loved me; whilst thy inscrutable decrees have made me subservient to those whose vows 'were false as dicer's oaths', and whose views were only the promotion of their own pleasure or interest?

When I had nearly obtained the age of four years, Captain Pye received directions from Lord Tyrawley to send me to France for education. His Lordship had been intimate with the unfortunate Colonel Frazer in his youthful days. And though their political principles were diametrically opposite, humanity induced him to make some provision for the Colonel's only daughter, who was now left an orphan and destitute of support. True philanthropy will not suffer a difference either in political or religious principles to restrain its dictates.

This young lady, who was somewhat older than myself, and very amiable both in person and disposition, was fixed on by Lord Tyrawley to be my companion to France; and Mrs Pye attended us herself to London, in order to equip us with such necessaries as we wanted, and to enquire out the most eligible convent in which to place us.

Whilst we were in London, the maid-servant who had the care of me, seeing my mother's name in the play-bills of Covent-Garden-Theatre, imagined she should not be an unacceptable visitor, if she took me to pay my respects to her. She accordingly inquired where my mother lodged; and, without asking her mistress consent, led me to her. We were instantly ushered up stairs, where we found my mother in a genteel dress. Though I was too young to experience any attraction from her beauty, yet her fine clothes pleased me much, and I ran towards her with great freedom. But what concern did my little heart feel, when she rudely pushed me from her, and I heard her exclaim, after viewing me with attention for some moments, 'My God! what have you brought me here? this goggle-eyed, splatter-faced, gabbart-mouthed wretch is not my child! take her away!' I had been so accustomed to endearments, that I was the more sensibly affected at this unexpected salutation, and I went away as disgusted with my mother as she could be with me.

Mrs Pye having prevailed upon Mrs Dunbar, an Irish lady who lived at Boulogne, to take Miss Frazer and myself under her protection, we accompanied her to France. Strict orders were given that I should not be contradicted, and that if I disliked one convent, we should be removed to another. The money necessary for our support was to be remitted to Mr Smith, a wine-merchant in that town, to whom the same injuctions were given.

On our arrival at Boulogne, we were placed in the convent of the *Nunciats*, situated in the lower town. We had not been there long, before a nun was immured between the walls, the punishment usually inflicted on those of the sisters who unfortunately break their vow of chastity. The infliction of this horrid punishment affected Miss Frazer so much, and the dirtiness of the convent was so intolerably offensive, even to me, though but a child, that we determined to get removed. We accordingly applied to Mrs Smith for this purpose, who in a short time came and conducted us to the convent of the *Ursulines* in the upper town. On mentioning the name of the convent, even at this distant period, I cannot help exclaiming, 'Dear, happy, much-regretted mansion! thou sweet abode of tranquillity and delight! how supremely blessed should I have been, had I remained till this hour within thy sacred walls!'

Here I continued till I had attained the eleventh year of my age; when the mandate, the dreadful mandate arrived, which bid us prepare for our return. With what heart-felt pangs did I receive it! Having no knowledge of the nobleman to whom I was indebted for my being and subsistence; and the contemptuous manner in which my mother had treated me still dwelling on my remembrance; I had not the least desire to see either of them. To stay in the convent, and still be accompanied by my much-loved Maria, was the utmost of my wishes. The whole community, indeed, the sisters as well as the pensioners, treated me with great kindness. But one of the nuns perfectly idolized me. When I took my leave of her, my feelings were such as I am not able to describe. The pungency was far beyond what a girl of my age could be supposed to experience. I have often thought they were a pure presage of the miseries which have attended me through life; not only such as have arisen from my own indiscretions, but those which owe their foundation to the complicated machinations of the worst of men.

From APOLOGY FOR THE LIFE OF GEORGE ANNE BELLAMY

George Anne Bellamy (1733, according to her account, but more probably 1727–88), actress, was the illegitimate daughter of Lord Tyrawley and a Quaker schoolgirl from Kent. She first appeared at Covent Garden in 1742, and achieved great success in tragic roles. She ended her life in poverty.

WILLIAM HICKEY

Water, and Other, Sports

Whenever I was at Twickenham I passed much of my time upon the water, rowing about in a boat of my father's, and when I could get a companion – as I could not alone manage – sailing. In one of these excursions, having a Mr William Cane, (of whom I shall hereafter have occasion to speak much) and a first cousin of mine, John Edwards, then a Lieutenant of infantry, with me, we were running up against the stream at a quick rate, when the boat, from a sudden gust of wind, taking a deep heel, I tumbled overboard and down I went, but as I had the sheet of the sail in my hand at the time, on my quitting it upon falling into the water, the sail blew about loose, which kept the boat nearly stationary. Edwards, who swam tolerably well, jumped over to endeavour to recover me. I rose twice, as Cane said, and was just again sinking when my cousin caught hold of me by the hair, and with Mr Cane's assistance got me into the boat when nearly exhausted.

In consequence of this accident I was forbid going upon the water, but never very obedient to orders that I did not approve or considered tyrannical, I found frequent opportunities of taking a cruise, to put an end to which my father's next measure was securing the boat with an iron chain and padlock. This unjust step, as I pronounced it, only set my wits to work. I recollected that Mr Hindley, who possessed a house late the property of Lord Radnor, a short distance from ours, had a small canoe, which was kept in a narrow channel, or creek of the Thames, opposite his house, merely as a pretty object for the eye. This I conceived would answer my purpose, and I prevailed on the gardener not only to let me have the use of it, but to make me a double feathered paddle to work it with, which, when ready I began my manoeuvres, taking special care until I became used to my ticklish vessel, not to venture into deep water. This canoe was just my own length, only fifteen inches wide, and

53

of so tottering a nature that bending my body to the right or to the left would endanger the upsetting it. During my practice I got many a ducking, but in a few weeks I became so expert in the management of it that I with confidence ventured into deep water. Both ends were exactly of the same form, so that I could go either way without turning; it had no seat, I therefore placed myself as nearly in the centre as I could, and working the feathers of the paddle alternately, went on at a quick rate.

Having thus accomplished the perfect management of my little vessel, the next object I had in view was unexpectedly to exhibit myself in it, and thereby dreadfully to alarm my fond mother for the safety of her darling boy, to effect which cruel and ungrateful purpose, I fixed upon a day when company were to dine at our house, who being assembled and walking upon the lawn previous to dinner, I embarked at Lord Radnor's and going round an Island suddenly made my appearance in the middle of the Thames, opposite my father's, to the infinite terror and alarm of my dear mother, but even this did not satisfy me, for laying myself flat along in the canoe, the whole party concluded the bottom had given way and that I was gone, never more to appear. A loud and general scream ensued from the party; servants were dispatched in all directions to procure assistance; our own boat, Mr Hindley's, Sir William Stanhope's, Mr Hudson's, and two fishermen's punts were in a few minutes all in motion, pulling away to endeavour to recover my little carcase. When I heard their oars near my canoe, to the utter astonishment of those on board them, up I rose on my breech. My father was excessively angry at this prank, but my mother's joy was so great at seeing me safe that she proved a successful advocate in obtaining my pardon. My friend Mr Hudson took that opportunity of once more remarking there was not the least danger of my being drowned, fate having decreed me a very different end. . . .

The Coronation of His present Majesty being fixed for the month of September, my father determined that all his family should be present at the ceremony. He therefore engaged one of the Nunnery's, as they are called, in Westminster Abbey, for which he paid fifty guineas. They are situated at the head of the great columns that support the roof, and command an admirable view of the whole interior of the building. Upon this occasion they were divided off by wooden partitions, each having a separate entrance with lock and key to the door, with ease holding a

54

dozen persons. Provisions, consisting of cold fowls, ham, tongues, different meat pies, wines, and liquors of various sorts were sent in to the apartment the day before, and two servants were allowed to attend. Our party consisted of my father, mother, brother Joseph, sister Mary, myself, Mr and Miss Isaacs, Miss Thomas, her brother (all Irish), my uncle and aunt Boulton, and their eldest daughter. We all supped together in St Albans Street on the 21st of September, and at midnight set off in my father's coach and my uncle's, and Miss Thomas's chariot. At the end of Pall Mall the different lines of carriages, nearly filling the street, our progress was consequently tedious, yet the time was beguiled by the grandeur of the scene, such a multitude of carriages, with servants behind carrying flambeaux, made a blaze of light equal to day, and had a fine effect.

Opposite the Horse Guards we were stopped exactly an hour without moving onward a single inch. As we approached near the Abbey, the difficulties increased, from mistakes of the coachmen, some of whom were going to the Hall, others to the Abbey, and getting into the wrong ranks. This created much confusion and running against each other, whereby glasses and panels were demolished without number, the noise of which, accompanied by the screeches of the terrified ladies, was at times truly terrific.

It was past seven in the morning before we reached the Abbey, which having once entered, we proceeded to our box without further impediment, Dr Markham having given us tickets which allowed our passing by a private staircase, and avoiding the immense crowd that was within. We found a hot and comfortable breakfast ready, which I enjoyed, and which proved highly refreshing to us all; after which some of our party determined to take a nap in their chairs, whilst I, who was well acquainted with every creek and corner of the Abbey, amused myself running about the long gallery until noon, when notice being given that the procession had begun to move, I resumed my seat. Exactly at one they entered the Abbey, and we had a capital view of the whole ceremony. Their Majesties (the King having previously married), being crowned, the Archbishop of Canterbury mounted the pulpit to deliver the sermon, and as many thousands were out of the possibility of hearing a single syllable, they took that opportunity to eat their meal when the general clattering of knives, forks, plates, and glasses that ensued, produced a most ridiculous effect, and a universal burst of laughter followed.

The sermon being concluded, the anthem was sung by a numerous band of the first performers in the Kingdom, and certainly was the finest thing I had ever heard. The procession then began to move towards Westminster Hall, at which moment my father received a paper from Lord Egmont, enclosing four hall tickets, two of which he gave to Mr Thomas and me, desiring us to make the best of our way. We descended, and attempted to follow the procession, but were stopped by the soldiers, and told no one could be allowed to pass that way, and that we must go round to the Palace yard gate. Whilst endeavouring to prevail on the men to let us proceed, I spied my friend Colonel Salter, of the Guards, who was upon duty, and applying to him for assistance, he directly took us with him, and we reached the hall, which we otherwise never should have accomplished.

Upon getting into the raised gallery, it was so crammed that I could not see an inch before me, until some gentlemen kindly made way to let me forward, and then some ladies, who were in a part that was railed off, seeing a fine-looking boy (which at that time I was) in distress, they with the utmost good humour let me in, making room in the front row. Thus I found myself in the very best place in the hall, and within a few yards of their Majesties. I afterwards learnt that this situation belonged to the Duke of Queensbury, in right of some official post he held, they who occupied it being relations and friends of the Duchess. We were supplied abundantly with every kind of refreshment. Sitting perfectly at my ease, I saw the Dinner, the Ceremony of the Champion, and every particular, and was at a loss to decide which I thought the most magnificent, the Abbey scene, or that of the hall. About ten at night the whole was over, and I got home as fast as the crowd would permit, highly delighted at all I had seen, but excessively fatigued, not having had any sleep the preceding night, and having been so actively employed the entire day.

In the winter of this year I accidentally met in the park, Mr Murrough O'Brien, afterwards Earl of Inchiquin, and finally Marquis of Thomond. After questioning me about the school, he gave me a guinea, the first I believe I ever had possessed. Having just then discovered the residence of my wanton little bedfellow, Nanny Harris, I directly went to her lodgings which were in a court that ran out of Bow Street, Covent Garden. I told her the strength of my purse, and proposed going to the play, which she consenting to, there was I a hopeful sprig of 13, stuck up in a green box, with a disreputable woman*. From the theatre she took me home to supper, giving me lobster and oysters, both of which she knew I was very fond of, and plenty of rum punch; with my head full of which, at a late hour I went home, and as I would not tell where I had been, I received a smart flogging from the arm of my old operator, Doctor Lloyd.

From MEMOIRS OF WILLIAM HICKEY

William Hickey (1749–1830), attorney, was born in Dublin. His *Memoirs* describe his travels, his exploits and his loves.

* Another edition of these memoirs calls her a 'blazing whore'.

RICHARD BRINSLEY SHERIDAN

Letter to his Uncle

June 1766

Dear Uncle,

I hope you will not be surprised, when I tell you that the cause of my present letter is partly my want of cloaths, for my brown ones are quite gone, as I have had them almost a year, and those which I have now, being of a very light colour, and having mett with a few accidents, are not remarkably clean, though pretty decent. And as I have been some time obliged to wear them every day, I have two reasons for desiring new cloaths, first as I have lately got into the 5 form, which is the head form of the school I am under a necessity of appearing like the other 5 form boys, secondly as the sylver arrow is to be shot for next thursday sevennight and most of the boys having new cloaths at that time instead of August, I should be glad, if it is convenient to you, to have them likewise, and then I should be in a condition to save them very well, by having a pretty good suit at present, which I could not do, if I were to stay u[n]till these were almost wore out. I should be also very much obliged to you, if you would lett me have a hat at the same time. If you please I will writ[e] a line to Mr Riley how to send them to me. | Pray give my love to my Aunt. I am | Your affectionate Nephew | R B Sheridan.

Letter to Richard Chamberlain

———◆○◆———

Richard Brinsley Sheridan (1751–1816), dramatist, orator, politician and theatre manager, was born in Dublin and educated at Harrow. His best-known comedies are *The Rivals* and *School for Scandal*.

The Great House

Cullenaghmore, the mansion where my ancestors had resided from the reign of James the First, was then occupied by my grandfather, Colonel Jonah Barrington. He had adopted me as soon as I was born, brought me to Cullenaghmore, and with him I resided until his death.

That old mansion, the Great House, as it was called, exhibited altogether an uncouth mass, warring with every rule of symmetry in architecture. The original castle had been demolished, and its materials converted to a much worse purpose; the front of the edifice which succeeded it was particularly ungraceful – a Saracen's head, our crest, in coloured brickwork being its only ornament, whilst some of the rooms inside were wainscotted with brown oak, others with red deal, and some not at all. The walls of the large hall were decked, as is customary, with fishing-rods, firearms, stags' horns, foxes' brushes, powder-flasks, shot-pouches, nets, and dog-collars; here and there relieved by the extended skin of a kite or a king-fisher, nailed up in the vanity of their destroyers; that of a monstrous eagle, which impressed itself indelibly on my mind, surmounted the chimney-piece, accompanied by a card announcing the name of its slaughterer – 'Alexander Barrington' – who, not being a *rich* relation, was subsequently entertained in the Great House two years, as a compliment for his present. A large parlour on each side of the hall, the only embellishments of which were some old portraits, and a multiplicity of hunting, shooting, and racing prints, with red tape nailed round them by way of frames, completed the reception-rooms; and as I was the only child in the house, and a most inquisitive brat, every different article was explained to me.

I remained here till I was nine years old; I had no play-fellows to take off my attention from whatever I observed or was taught; and so strongly do those early impressions remain engraven on my memory, naturally most retentive, that even at this long distance of time I fancy I can see the entire place as it stood then, with its old inhabitants moving before me – their faces I most clearly recollect.

The library was a gloomy closet, and rather scantily furnished with everything but dust and cobwebs; there were neither chairs nor tables; but I cannot avoid recollecting many of the principal books, because I read such of them as I could comprehend, or as were amusing, and looked over all the prints in them a hundred times. While trying to copy these prints, they made an indelible impression upon me; and hence I feel confident of the utility of embellishments in any book intended for the instruction of children. I possessed many of the books long after my grandfather's death, and have some of them still. I had an insatiable passion for reading from my earliest days, and it has occupied the greater proportion of my later life. *Gulliver's Travels*, *Robinson Crusoe*, *Fairy Tales*, and *The History of the Bible*, all with numerous plates, were my favourite authors and constant amusement: I believed every word of them except the fairies, and was not entirely sceptical as to those good people either. . . .

Very few mirrors in those days adorned the houses of the country gentlemen – a couple or three shaving-glasses for the gentlemen, and a couple of pretty large dressing-glasses, in black frames, for the ladies' use, composed, I believe, nearly the entire stock of reflectors at my grandfather's, except tubs of spring water, which answered for the maid-servants.

A very large and productive, but not neatly dressed-up garden, adjoined the house. The white-washed stone images, the broad flights of steps up and down, the terraces, with the round fish-pond, riveted my attention, and gave an impressive variety to this garden, which I shall ever remember, as well as many curious incidents which I witnessed therein.

At the Great House all disputes amongst the tenants were then settled – quarrels reconciled – old debts arbitrated: a kind Irish landlord reigned despotic in the ardent affections of the tenantry, their pride and pleasure being to obey and to support him.

But there existed a happy reciprocity of interests. The landlord of that period protected the tenant by his influence – any wanton injury to a tenant being considered as an insult to the lord; and if either of the landlord's sons were grown up, no time was lost by him in demanding satisfaction from any gentleman for maltreating even his father's black-smith.

No gentleman of this degree ever distrained a tenant for rent: indeed, the parties appeared to be quite united and knit together. The greatest abhorrence, however, prevailed as to tithe-proctors, coupled with no great predilection for the clergy who employed them. These latter certainly were, in principle and practice, the real country tyrants of that day, and first caused the assembling of the White Boys.

I have heard it often said that, at the time I speak of, every estated gentleman in the Queen's County was *honoured* by the gout. I have since considered that its extraordinary prevalence was not difficult to be accounted for, by the disproportionate quantity of acid contained in their seductive beverage, called rum-shrub, which was then universally drunk in quantities nearly incredible, generally from supper-time till morning, by all country gentlemen, as they said, to keep down their claret.

My grandfather could not refrain, and, therefore, he suffered well; he piqued himself on procuring, through the interest of Batty Lodge (a follower of the family who had married a Dublin grocer's widow), the very first importation of oranges and lemons to the Irish capital every season. Horse-loads of these, packed in boxes, were immediately sent to the Great House of Cullenaghmore; and no sooner did they arrive than the good news of *fresh fruit* was communicated to the colonel's neighbouring friends, accompanied by the usual invitation.

Night after night the revel afforded uninterrupted pleasure to the joyous gentry: the festivity being subsequently renewed at some other mansion, till the gout thought proper to put the whole party *hors de combat* – having the satisfaction of making cripples for a few months such as he did not kill.

Whilst the convivials bellowed with only toe or finger agonies it was a mere bagatelle; but when Mr Gout marched up the country and invaded the head or the stomach, it was then called *no joke*; and Drogheda usquebaugh, the hottest-distilled drinkable liquor ever invented, was applied to for aid, and generally drove the tormentor in a few minutes to his former quarters. It was, indeed, counted a specific; and I allude to it the more particularly, as my poor grandfather was finished thereby.

From BARRINGTON'S RECOLLECTIONS

———•◦•———

Sir Jonah Barrington (1760–1834), lawyer, politician and historian, was born at Knapton, near Abbeyleix. He was a member of the Irish parliament and was appointed Judge in Admiralty, a post from which he was removed in 1830 for embezzlement.

MARY LEADBEATER

The Child-Minders

Rose, Nancy.

Rose. Nancy, Nancy, your mammy is looking for you. She wants you to hold the child, while she goes to dig the potatoes for the supper.

Nancy. I can't go indeed. If she asks you for me, tell her you did not see me.

Rose. That I won't. Don't you hear her calling, and didn't you hear her before?

Nancy. I did, but I was playing Jackstones with Judy, and I wanted to finish the game.

Rose. Oh, Nancy, how can you vex your poor mammy, who does every thing for you, and works early and late? Here she is – come in now – she saw us, and she is gone over the stile with the spade and the potato basket.

Nancy. Ay, little Bill is in the cradle asleep. I'll leave him there, and go out again.

Rose. No, upon my word you shan't. If you heard the frightful stories I did, you would never leave a child by itself.

Nancy. What frightful stories? Do tell them to me.

Rose. There was old Charley, the gingerbread-man, was left, when he was an infant, in the cradle by himself, and while he was asleep, an ugly brute of a pig came in, and ate off his poor little hand, as it hung over. And there was a sow and little pigs on the floor with a young child, and its mammy went out, and bid its daddy take care of it, and he bid another child watch it, while he took a nap, and when he wakened, he asked the child how the little one was; and she said he was very well, playing with the little pigs: then the man bounced up in the greatest fright that could be, and the poor little thing was all in a gore of blood, and its face so eat by the nasty sow, that the life was out of it, sure enough. And, like that, there was another child that was left by itself, and it got out of the cradle, and crawled to the hearth, and its little petticoat took fire, and it was burned to death.

Nancy.   O, indeed Rose, I will never leave the child again; often I have left it, and run home before my mammy came, for fear she would beat me. Sure it was great luck that nothing happened!

From Cottage Dialogues

Mary Leadbeater (1758–1826), author, was born and died at Ballitor, Co. Kildare. A quaker, she married a local landowner and kept the village post office.

Call of the Cockade

I was the eldest child of my parents, and a very great favourite. I was sent, at the age of eight or nine, to an excellent English school, kept by Sisson Darling, a man to whose kindness and affection I was much indebted, and who took more than common pains with me. I respect him yet. I was very idle, and it was only the fear of shame which could induce me to exertion. Nevertheless, at the approach of our public examinations, which were held quarterly, and at which all our parents and friends attended, I used to labour for some time, and generally with success; as I have obtained six or seven premiums in different branches at one examination, for mathematics, arithmetic, reading, spelling, recitation, use of the globes, &c. In two branches I always failed, writing and the catechism, to which last I could never bring myself to apply.

Having continued with Mr Darling for about three years, and pretty nearly exhausted the circle of English education, he recommended strongly to my father to put me to a Latin school, and to prepare me for the university; assuring him that I was a fine boy, of uncommon talents, particularly for the mathematics; that it was a thousand pities to throw me away on a business, when, by giving me a liberal education, there was a moral certainty I should become a fellow of Trinity College, which was a noble independence, besides the glory of the situation. In these arguments he was supported by the parson of the parish, doctor Jameson, a worthy man, who used to examine me from time to time in the elements of Euclid. My father, who, to do him justice, loved me passionately, and spared no expense on me that his circumstances would afford, was easily persuaded by these authorities. It was determined that I should be a fellow of Dublin College. I was taken from Mr Darling, from whom I parted with regret, and placed, about the age of twelve, under the care of the rev. William Craig, a man very different, in all respects, from my late preceptor.

As the school was in the same street where we lived (Stafford-street), and as I was under my father's eye, I began Latin with ardour, and continued for a year or two with great diligence, when I began Greek, which I found still more to my taste; but, about this time, whether unluckily for me or not, the future colour of my life must determine, my father, meeting with an accident of a fall down stairs, by which he was dreadfully wounded in the head, so that he narrowly escaped with life, found, on his recovery, his affairs so deranged in all respects, that he determined on quitting business and retiring to the country; a resolution which he executed accordingly; settling with all his creditors, and placing me with a friend near the school, whom he paid for my diet and lodging, besides allowing me a trifling sum for my pocket. In this manner I became, I may say, my own master, before I was sixteen; and as at this time I am not remarkable for my discretion, it may well be judged I was less so then.

The superintendance of my father being removed, I began to calculate, that, according to the slow rate chalked out for me by Craig, I could very well do the business of the week in three days, or even two, if necessary; and that, consequently, the other three were lawful prize; I therefore resolved to appropriate three days in the week, at least, to my amusements, and the others to school; always keeping in the latter three the day of repetition, which included the business of the whole week, by which arrangement I kept my rank with the other boys of my class. I found no difficulty in convincing half-a-dozen of my school-fellows of the justice of this distribution of our time, and by this means we established a regular system of what is called *mitching*; and we contrived, being some of the smartest boys at school, to get an ascendancy over the spirit of the master, so that when we entered the school in a body, after one of our days of relaxation, he did not choose to burn his fingers with any one of us; nor did he once write to my father to inform him of my proceedings, for which he most certainly was highly culpable.

I must do myself and my school-fellows the justice to say, that, though we were abominably idle, we were not vicious; our amusements consisted in walking to the country, in swimming parties in the sea, and, particularly, in attending all parades, field days, and reviews of the garrison of Dublin in the Phoenix park. I mention this particularly, because, independent of confirming me in a rooted habit of idleness, which I lament most exceedingly, I trace to the splendid appearance of the troops, and the pomp and parade of military show, the untameable desire which I ever since have had to become a soldier; a desire which has never once quitted me; and which, after sixteen years of various

65

adventures, I am at last at liberty to indulge. Being, at this time, approaching to seventeen years of age, it will not be thought incredible that *woman* began to appear lovely in my eyes, and I very wisely thought that a red coat and cockade, with a pair of gold epaulets, would aid me considerably in my approaches to the objects of my adoration.

From LIFE OF THEOBALD WOLFE TONE

Theobald Wolfe Tone (1763–98), fighter for a united Ireland, was born in Dublin. He was called to the Bar in 1789, but had to flee to America and France. His attempt to organize a French invasion failed. He was captured, condemned to death for treason, but committed suicide.

The Birth of
the Duke of Wellington

The Duke, who was born in 1769, used to celebrate his birthday on 1 May. Yet, from the register of St Peter's Church, Dublin, he was baptized on 30 April 1769. Accounts differ, too, as to where he was born. According to a letter published in *The Times* on 3 June 1926, the year before his death the Duke wrote in his own hand on the census form, which was preserved, in the space for 'place of birth', 'In Ireland – believe Athy'. Another theory is that he was born prematurely on the sea crossing between England and Ireland.

The Duke of Wellington (1769–1852) was born Arthur Wellesley, son of the Earl of Mornington. He defeated Napoleon at Waterloo in 1815, and later became Prime Minister.

The Minstrel Boy

The Minstrel Boy to the war is gone,
　　In the ranks of death you'll find him;
His father's sword he has girded on,
　　And his wild harp slung behind him. –
'Land of song!' said the warrior-bard,
　　'Though all the world betrays thee,
One sword, at least, thy rights shall guard,
　　One faithful harp shall praise thee!'

The Minstrel fell! – but the foeman's chain
　　Could not bring his proud soul under;
The harp he lov'd ne'er spoke again,
　　For he tore its chords asunder;
And said, 'No chains shall sully thee,
　　Thou soul of love and bravery!
Thy songs were made for the pure and free,
　　They shall never sound in slavery.'

Thomas Moore (1779–1852), poet, was born in Dublin, the son of a
grocer. He achieved enormous popularity through his Irish songs
and melodies, but had to spend the years 1819–22 abroad, having
been declared bankrupt through the dishonesty of his resident
deputy as Admiralty Registrar in Bermuda.

MARIA EDGEWORTH

Master Harrington's Obsession

When I was a little boy of about six years old, I was standing with a
maid servant in the balcony of one of the upper rooms of my father's
house in London – It was the evening of the first day that I had ever been
in London, and my senses had been excited, and almost exhausted by
the quick succession of a vast variety of objects that were new to me. It
was dusk, and I was growing sleepy, but my attention was wakened by a
fresh wonder. As I stood peeping between the bars of the balcony, I saw
star after star of light appear in quick succession, at a certain height and
distance, in a regular line, approaching nearer and nearer to me. I
twitched the skirt of my maid's gown repeatedly, but she was talking to
some acquaintance in the window of a neighbouring house, and she did
not attend to me. I pressed my forehead more closely against the bars of
the balcony, and strained my eyes more eagerly towards the objects of
my curiosity. Presently the figure of the lamp-lighter with his blazing
torch in one hand, and his ladder in the other, became visible; and, with
as much delight as philosopher ever enjoyed in discovering the cause of a
new and grand phenomenon, I watched his operations. I saw him fix
and mount his ladder with his little black pot swinging from his arm,
and his red smoking torch waving with astonishing velocity, as he ran
up and down the ladder. Just when he reached the ground, being then
within a few yards of our house, his torch flared on the face and figure of
an old man with a long white beard and a dark visage, who, holding a
great bag slung over one shoulder, walked slowly on straight forwards,
repeating in a low, abrupt, mysterious tone, the cry of *'Old-clothes!'* –
'Old-clothes!' – *'Old-clothes!'* I could not understand the words he said,
but as he looked up at our balcony my maid nodded to him; he stood still,
and at the same instant she seized upon me, exclaiming, 'Time for you to
come off to bed, Master Harrington.'

I resisted, and, clinging to the rails, began kicking and roaring.

'If you don't come quietly this minute, Master Harrington,' said she,

69

'I'll call to Simon the Jew there,' pointing to him, 'and he shall come up and carry you away in his great bag.'

The old man's eyes were upon me; to my fancy the look of his eyes and his whole face had changed in an instant. I was struck with terror – my hands let go their grasp – and I suffered myself to be carried off as quietly as my maid could desire. She hurried and huddled me into bed, bid me go to sleep, and ran down stairs. To sleep I could not go, but full of fear and curiosity I lay, pondering on the thoughts of Simon the Jew and his bag, who had come to carry me away in the height of my joys. His face with the light of the torch upon it appeared and vanished, and flitted before my eyes.

The next morning when day-light and courage returned, I asked my maid whether Simon the Jew was a good or bad man? Observing the impression that had been made upon my mind, and foreseeing that the expedient, which she had thus found successful, might be advantageously repeated, she answered me with oracular duplicity, *'Simon the Jew is a good man for naughty boys.'* The threat of *'Simon the Jew'* was for some time afterwards used upon every occasion to reduce me to passive obedience; and when by frequent repetition this thread had lost somewhat of its power, when the bare idea of the Jew would no longer reduce my rebel spirit, it was necessary to increase the terrors of his name. She proceeded to tell me, in a mysterious tone, stories of Jews who had been known to steal poor children for the purpose of killing, crucifying, and sacrificing them at their secret feasts and midnight abominations. The less I understood, the more I believed.

From HARRINGTON

———•◦•———

Maria Edgeworth (1767–1849), the first regional novelist, was born in England but returned to the family estate at Edgeworthstown, Co. Longford, in 1782 with her father, the eccentric inventor, educationalist and author Richard Lovell Edgeworth, where she died, unmarried. Her best-known works are *Castle Rackrent* and *The Absentee*.

ADELAIDE O'KEEFFE

The Kite

My kite is three feet broad, and six feet long;
   The standard straight, the bender tough and strong,
And to its milk-white breast five painted stars belong.

   Grand and majestic soars my paper kite,
   Through trackless skies it takes its lofty flight:
Nor lark nor eagle flies to such a noble height.

   As in the field I stand and hold the twine,
   Swift I unwind, to give it length of line,
Yet swifter it ascends, nor will to earth incline.

   Like a small speck, so high I see it sail,
   I hear its pinions flutter in the gale,
And, like a flock of wild geese, sweeps its flowing tail.

——◆◆——

Adelaide O'Keeffe (1766–1855) was born in London, daughter of the dramatist and actor John O'Keeffe, whom she looked after when he went blind.

SIR AUBREY DE VERE

Christmas Holidays

Our home life pursued the even tenor of its way. We, the three elder brothers, worked at our classics in the morning, and in the afternoon took a long walk or a long ride, for each of us boasted a horse, though we seldom rode together; and in the evening there was often music, especially when Lord Monteagle was with us, for he and his sister, my mother, had been used to play duets from Mozart in their youth, he on the flute, and she on the pianoforte, and they continued the habit in advanced life. At Christmas we used to visit at Adare Manor. It was a gay as well as a friendly and hospitable house; after dinner we had private theatricals, games of all sorts, dances, and, in the daytime, pleasant wanderings beside the beautiful Maique, which mirrored, in waters that even when swiftest seldom lost their transparency, as stately a row of elms, ninety feet high, as England herself can boast, and the venerable ruins of a castle which belonged to the Kildares – though islanded, as it were, in a territory almost all the rest of which belonged to the Desmond branch of the same Geraldine race. Adare, then as now a singularly pretty village, had for centuries been a walled town. It had seen many battles, and had been more than once burned down; but it was famous chiefly for the number of its monastic institutions, still represented by the ruins of a Franciscan convent, as well as by one of the Trinitarian and one of the Augustinian order, the churches of which have been restored, and are now used, one for Catholic and the other for Protestant worship. The Knights Templars once possessed a house at Adare; but its site cannot now be discovered.

Among our Christmas holidays at Adare there is one which I am not likely ever to forget. About eight miles from the village rises a hill eight hundred feet in elevation, with a singularly graceful outline, named 'Knockfierna', or the 'Hill of the Fairies', because in popular belief it abounded in the 'Good People', then universally believed in by the Gaelic race in Ireland. We set off to climb it one day soon after breakfast

–*we*, meaning my two elder brothers and I, and the son of our host, Lord Adare, afterwards well known as Earl of Dunraven, the author of two valuable works, 'Memorials of Adare' and an excellent book on Irish antiquities. Two other members of the exploring party were our tutor, and a friend of Adare's several years older than he. It was hard walking, especially after the ascent of the hill began; we had to climb many walls and ditches, and to force our way through many a narrow lane. We had brought no luncheon with us, and before we reached the summit the winter sun had sunk considerably.

We walked about the hill top for some time admiring the view, a very fine one, though, like many Irish views, somewhat dreary, from the comparative absence of trees, the amount of moorland intersected by winding streams, and the number of ruins, many of them modern. All at once we discovered that we were faint with hunger, and so much fatigued without refreshment we could hardly make our way home. Halfway down the hill stood a farmhouse. The farmer was most courteous, but, alas! there was not a morsel of food in his house. What he had he gave, and that was cider, for which, like the Irish peasant of that day, he would take no payment. Each of us drank only one cider glass of it, and we took our departure, cheered, but by no means invigorated. After the lapse of some ten minutes one of us became so sleepy that he could hardly walk, and his nearest neighbour at once gave him an arm. A little later the same complaint was made by another of us, and the same friendly aid was forced upon him. But in a few minutes more not only were we unable to walk, but we were unable to stand, the only exceptions being the two among us who were no longer boys – our tutor and Adare's friend.

Never shall I forget their astonishment first, and afterwards their vexation. They were in some degree in charge of us, and the responsibility seemed to rest upon them. The Christmas evening was closing around us; there was no help near, and apparently no reason why our sleep should not last till sunrise. They argued, they expostulated, they pushed us, and they pulled us; but all would not do. I was the last to give way, and my latest recollection was that my second brother had just succeeded in climbing to the top of a wooden gate, but could not lift his leg over it, and lay upon his face along it. Our tutor stamped up and down the road indulging largely in his favourite ejaculation 'Gracious patience! gracious patience!' to which my brother replied, with his last gleam of wakeful intelligence, 'There is one very amiable trait about you, Mr Johnstone: you are never tired of toasting your absent friends.'

73

The next moment he rolled over and slept beside us in the mud. The cider had affected our brains because our stomachs were empty. In about a quarter of an hour the trance was dissolved almost as suddenly as it fell on us; and we walked forward very mirthfully, reaching home just in time to hear the dressing bell ring. Only one light shone through the mullioned windows of the manor-house; and I remember Adare's remark as we drew near: 'Beside that light my little sister sits weeping. She is sure that I am dead.' At dinner we told the story of our adventures, and it excited much laughter. Lord Dunraven 'moralized the tale'. 'You see, young gentlemen, each of you undertook to support and guide his neighbour, though not one of you could take care of himself. That is the way of Ireland. You will help your neighbour best by taking care each of himself.' His advice was like that of another old Irish gentleman, a relative of mine, whose 'good-night' to his grandchildren often ended with this counsel, 'Take good care of yourself, child; and your friends will love you all the better.'

From RECOLLECTIONS OF AUBREY DE VERE

———◆◆———

Sir Aubrey De Vere (1788–1846) formerly Hunt, poet, was born and died at Curragh Chase.

WILLIAM CARLETON

The Hedge School

The reader will then be pleased to picture to himself a house in a line with the hedge; the eave of the back roof within a foot of the ground behind it; a large hole exactly in the middle of the *'riggin''*, as a chimney; immediately under which is an excavation in the floor, burned away by a large fire of turf, loosely heaped together. This is surrounded by a circle of urchins, sitting on the bare earth, stones, and hassocks, and exhibiting a series of speckled shins, all radiating towards the fire like sausages on a *Poloni* dish. There they are – wedged as close as they can sit; one with half a thigh off his breeches – another with half an arm off his tattered coat – a third without breeches at all, wearing, as a substitute, a piece of his mother's old petticoat, pinned about his loins – a fourth, no coat – a fifth, with a cap on him, because he has got a scald, from having sat under the juice of fresh hung bacon – a sixth with a black eye – a seventh, two rags about his heels to keep his kibes clean – an eighth crying to get home, because he has got a headache, though it may be as well to hint that there is a drag-hunt to start from beside his father's in the course of the day.

In this ring, with his legs stretched in a most lordly manner, sits, upon a deal chair, Mat himself, with his hat on, basking in the enjoyment of unlimited authority. His dress consists of a black coat, considerably in want of repair, transferred to his shoulders through the means of a clothes-broker in the country-town; a white cravat, round a large stuffing, having that part which comes in contact with the chin somewhat streaked with brown – a black waistcoat, with one or two 'tooth-an'-egg' metal buttons sewed on where the original had fallen off – black corduroy inexpressibles, twice dyed, and sheep's-gray stockings. In his hand is a large, broad ruler, the emblem of his power, the woful instrument of executive justice, and the signal of terror to all within his jurisdiction.

In a corner below is a pile of turf, where on entering, every boy throws his two sods, with a *hitch* from under his left arm. He then comes up to the master, catches his forelock with finger and thumb, and bobs down his head, by way of making him a bow, and goes to his seat. Along the walls on the ground is a series of round stones, some of them capped with a straw collar or hassock, on which the boys sit; others have bosses, and many of them hobs – a light but compact kind of boggy substance found in the mountains. On these several of them sit; the greater number of them, however, have no seats whatever, but squat themselves down, without compunction, on the hard floor. Hung about, on wooden pegs driven into the walls, are the shapeless 'caubeens' of such as can boast the luxury of a hat, or caps made of goat or hare's skin, the latter having the ears of the animal rising ludicrously over the temples, or cocked out at the sides, and the scut either before or behind, according to the taste or the humor of the wearer.

The floor, which is only swept every Saturday, is strewed over with tops of quills, pens, pieces of broken slate, and tattered leaves of *Reading made Easy*, or fragments of old copies. In one corner is a knot engaged at 'Fox and Geese', or the 'Walls of Troy' on their slates; in another, a pair of them are 'fighting bottles', which consists in striking the bottoms together, and he whose bottle breaks first, of course, loses. Behind the master is a third set, playing 'heads and points' – a game of pins. Some are more industriously employed in writing their copies, which they perform seated on the ground, with their paper on a copy-board – a piece of planed deal, the size of the copy, an appendage now nearly exploded – their cheek-bones laid within half an inch of the left side of the copy, and the eye set to guide the motion of the hand across, and to regulate the straightness of the lines and the forms of the letters. Others, again, of the more grown boys, are working their sums with becoming industry. In a dark corner are a pair of urchins thumping each other, their eyes steadily fixed on the master, lest he might happen to glance in that direction. Near the master himself are the larger boys, from twenty-two to fifteen – shaggy-headed slips, with loose-breasted shirts lying open about their bare chests; ragged colts, with white, dry, bristling beards upon them, that never knew a razor; strong stockings on their legs; heavy brogues, with broad, nail-paved soles; and breeches open at the knees. Nor is the establishment without a competent number of females. These were, for the most part, the daughters of wealthy farmers, who considered it necessary to their respectability, that they should not be altogether illiterate; such a circumstance being a considerable drawback, in the opinion of an admirer, from the character of a young woman for whom he was about to propose – a drawback, too, which was always weighty in proportion to her wealth or respectability.

From TRAITS AND STORIES OF THE IRISH PEASANTRY

William Carleton (1794–1869), novelist and writer of short stories, was born in Prillisk, Co. Tyrone, one of the large bilingual family of a small farmer. His works especially reflect the conditions and speech of the Irish peasantry.

ANNA MARIA HALL

The Spelling Lesson

Days, weeks, months, and years, went by; and Mary Ryan's daughter was fast merging from the girl into the woman. She had gleaned a little learning from a hedge schoolmaster, one of the clever political old fellows, who, in bygone times, taught the 'big boys' Law and Latin, Politics and the 'Read-a-made-aisy', in the same breath. He usually got up, every day, such a scene as the following:– 'Spell tyrant, James Sullivan. Now Jimmy, hould up yer head like a man, to show ye defy it.' 'T-i–' 'Och! murder, no. What spells Ty, besides T-i?' 'T-n, sir.' 'Och! my, ye're only fit for a slave, Jimmy; I'm sorry for ye, you poor craythur. Try *your* tongue at it, little Neddy.' – 'T-y-r-a-n-t!' spells out the young rogue, his bare foot placed firmly on the damp floor, and his eyes sparkling with triumph.

'There's my haro! – take the top of the class. Oh! not the Latin class, my boy; you're not up to that, Neddy, yet – but above Jimmy Sullivan. Now for the meaning: who was a tyrant?'

'Naro,' replies one. – 'Queen Elizabeth,' says another. – 'Oliver Crummel,' shouts a third. – 'My daddy's landlord,' observed Neddy, 'when he turned us to the wide world to starve!'

'That's bould spoken,' said the schoolmaster; 'I see you understand the word, little Neddy.'

'I have good right, sir,' answered the child.

'Spell mother, girls,' said the schoolmaster, who gave them, as he stated, 'word about', and managed to appropriate domestic phrases to the female class. 'I'm not in two syllables yet, sir,' said Mary Ryan's daughter, upon whom the schoolmaster's eye fell.

'M-u-d–' began one of the class. – 'No, that won't do. Sure you ought all to be able to spell it; for sorra a one that does not know what it is to have a good mother barring one or two. Mary Wright, poor child! your mother's in heaven since the day she gave you to a broken-hearted

78

world; and, indeed, yours' – and again his eye fell on Mary Ryan's daughter – never did much for you – so I'll excuse you.'

'If you please, sir,' said the girl, growing very red, 'I'll not be excused for that reason: my mother did the best she could for me'; and – she burst into tears – and then as suddenly checked her emotion, and spelt the cherished word correctly.

From Sketches of Irish Character

Anna Maria Hall (1800–81) née Fielding, novelist, was born in Dublin but spent most of her childhood in Co. Wexford, before being taken to London.

EDWARD WALSH

The Fairy Nurse

Sweet babe! a golden cradle holds thee,
And soft the snow-white fleece enfolds thee;
In airy bower I'll watch thy sleeping,
Where branchy trees to the breeze are sweeping.
          Shuheen, sho, lulo lo!

When mothers languish broken-hearted,
When young wives are from husbands parted,
Ah! little think the keeners lonely,
They weep some time-worn fairy only.
          Shuheen, sho, lulo lo!

Within our magic halls of brightness,
Trips many a foot of snowy whiteness;
Stolen maidens, queens of fairy –
And kings and chiefs a sluagh-shee airy,
          Shuheen, sho, lulo lo!

Rest thee, babe! I love thee dearly,
And as thy mortal mother nearly;
Ours is the swiftest steed and proudest,
That moves where the tramp of the host is loudest.
          Shuheen, sho, lulo lo!

Rest thee, babe! for soon thy slumbers
Shall flee at the magic koelshie's numbers;
In airy bower I'll watch thy sleeping,
Where branchy trees to the breeze are sweeping.
          Shuheen, sho, lulo lo!

Edward Walsh (1805–50), poet and folklorist, was born in Londonderry.
He died in Cork, having been forced by reduced circumstances to become
a teacher of convicts and then of workhouse inmates.

Daniel Griffin

Playing with Fire-arms

One Sunday Gerald and I with two younger sisters, having been left at home while the rest of the family were at their devotions at the chapel, were amusing ourselves together in the parlour. While playing about the room I don't know which of us first perceived a case of pistols that my father had very imprudently laid on the chimney piece before his departure. Such things are always an object of curiosity to children, and we eagerly seized on them. We must have been still very young at the time, for I remember we could only see them as we stood at the farther end of the room, and we were obliged to place a chair near the chimney piece to take them down. I was old enough, however, to know, that the length of the ram-rod was a measure of the barrel of the pistol when empty, and as the question at once arose whether they were loaded or not, I looked for this instrument to try, but they were screw-barrelled pistols and therefore had no ram-rod. I then threw back the pan – there was no priming – so with that common feeling which leads people to lean to what they most wish, where the circumstances are doubtful, we took it for granted in the absence of any positive proof to the contrary, that they were not loaded. It was immediately agreed that Gerald and I should fight a duel. The little girls were too young to take much interest in such things, and the amusement was therefore entirely our own. I cocked both pistols – my brother had not sufficient strength to cock his – and we took our stand at opposite corners of the room, took aim at each other, and snapped at a given signal, but no effect took place beyond a few sparks. This was repeated several times with the same result. At length we grew tired of it, and I began to cock and snap my own pistol without any other object than to watch the gay shower of sparks that sometimes arose from the pan. Gerald came over to look at me. It is an old and oft repeated remark, 'the mystery of the ways of providence'. I have often thought since how inscrutable is its course – what excessive dangers it sometimes permits, and what trifling circumstances the preservation of a life of some importance seems occasionally to depend upon. I had the stock of the pistol to my breast, holding the barrel in my left hand, and he stood opposite me in such a position that if it went off then, the ball could take no other direction than through the centre of his heart. From what took place immediately afterwards I have so often thought of this fearful moment that every circumstance connected with it has entered my mind with a force that time can never weaken. I see it all as if it occurred an hour ago. I could point out the very board of the floor he stood upon. I could almost tell the direction of every spark in the magnificent shower that flew upwards as I drew the trigger – but Heaven, in whose hands is the guidance of every one of those illuminated atoms, was then watching over him and decreed it otherwise. The constellation of fiery points that arose at that moment was so much more brilliant than usual that we both shouted with delight and I ran with extacy to repeat the experiment for one of my little sisters who was seated upon the end of a table near the window with her feet upon a chair, laughing and enjoying herself. – 'Oh, Anna,' said I, 'look at this!' I pulled the trigger and was immediately stunned by a loud and ringing report. We were both enveloped in smoke, and the pistol fell from my hand. The ball passed through both her thighs – she uttered a piercing cry, sprung from the chair, ran across the room and fell bleeding at the door. There was a military hospital opposite us, and one of the surgeons being there at the moment, the sentinel directed his attention to our house, saying he feared some accident had occurred, as he had just heard the report of fire arms and saw smoke in the parlour. The surgeon ran over, caught up the child in his arms, dressed her wounds, and had her placed quietly in bed by the time my father and mother returned. She was quite well in a month.

From LIFE OF GERALD GRIFFIN

———— ◆◇◆ ————

Gerald Griffin (1803–40), dramatist and novelist, was born in Limerick, and went to London in 1823. In 1838, he returned to Ireland and joined the Christian Brothers. He died of typhus. Daniel Griffin was his next of six older brothers, and became a doctor. Their sister Anna, perhaps not surprisingly, entered the order of the Sisters of Charity.

Charles Lever at the Front

The north side of Dublin was then noted for the escapades of vagabonds who played malign tricks on unoffending citizens. Party feeling ran high in those days. Lever's schoolfellows, who all represented families with unpopular sympathies, were more than once pelted as they passed. The roughs found allies in the pupils of another school in Grenville Street – one of inferior social caste. These boys were under the able generalship of a stripling not undistinguished in after life. Skirmishes took place, and at last it was agreed that a regular pitched battle should be fought in Mountjoy Fields, then a piece of waste ground on which Gardiner Street Church and Convent have since been built. Lever helped to organize the tiny troops. The little army had its companies, commander-in-chief, its outlying pickets, reserves, and even its sappers and miners. Mr Robert Mallet, a subsequent eminent engineer and F.R.S., first showed his talents by mining the ground on which the enemy were to be next day engaged. A small mine was worked, and some pounds of blasting powder laid. The opposite faction mustered at length in great force, and opened the fight by a brisk discharge of sharp stones, which was returned by Mr Wright's boys with shouts of defiance, and a fire of miniature cannon. A charge forward was then made by the roughs, some of whom were provided with black thorns, which, if applied to the skulls of the juvenile army, would have inflicted serious subsequent loss on letters, law, science, physic, and divinity. Dr Biggar is now almost the only survivor who took part in this conflict. He held a high rank in the command, and just as the enemy was about to fall upon them like an avalanche, word was given to fire the mine, which a lighted cigar promptly accomplished. The explosion scattered dismay, and inflicted some slight bodily wounds. Lever's company suffered quite as much as the enemy; the faces on both sides were scorched and scratched. The army of the north retreated in disorder, leaving Mr Wright's pupils in possession of the field – only to be scared, however, by the rapid approach of the police, who, with their glazed caps and side arms, the uniform of that day, entered Mountjoy Fields at every point.

Marlborough Street Police Office exhibited a scene of some excitement when the case came on next day. Hanging was still the penalty for incendiarism; and terrible forebodings of the gibbet or Botany Bay smote the small prisoners brought up before Mr Magrath, who, in his occasional ebullitions of temper, resembled Mr Fang, Oliver Twist's stern judge: and Fang, we know, was a veritable portrait. Some fussy matrons were in attendance to testify that the north side had been all but blown into the southern division by the shock, while the weak police seem to have regarded the whole affair very much as a god-send. The boy-prisoners, including Edward Dix, afterwards police magistrate, are described by Dr Biggar as tongue-tied. Mr Magrath said it was a bad case, and scowled. The police shook their heads, and a pin might be heard to drop.

At last a boy came forward as spokesman, and appealed to the bench. The magistrate declared that they were before him on a charge of riot and outrage, which it behoved him to suppress with a firm hand. Lever submitted that the provocation they received from a lawless gang justified them in inflicting condign punishment: that the vagabonds were the first aggressors; that self-defence was the first law of nature, and that a war of juveniles was not worse in principle than war waged by wiser heads.

MR MAGRATH. – 'But you are not to take the law into your own hands. Moreover, you use firearms and introduce gunpowder into a mine previously prepared, and with malice prepense.'

MASTER LEVER. – 'All sound and smoke, sir; our cannon were only toy-guns, and the mine a mimic mine. Most of us may take up arms yet in defence of our king and country; and might we not be worse employed than in learning the science at the most susceptible period of our lives?'

Mr Magrath's attitude of hostility relaxed: without complimenting Lever on his eloquence, he certainly seemed struck by it; and he brought the case to a close by imposing sundry small fines, which would suffice, he said, to satisfy offended justice.

This magistrate was himself soon after arraigned for much graver offences. He was proved guilty of embezzlement and banished. As for Master Biggar – the juvenile commander-in-chief – he was flogged five successive days because of the determination with which he refused to divulge the spot where Mallet had concealed his mining powder.

From LIFE OF CHARLES LEVER by W. J. Fitzpatrick

Charles Lever (1806–72), novelist, was born in Dublin. After working as a doctor and then a journalist, he spent the last twenty-five
years of his life on the Continent, latterly becoming British Consul
at Trieste. W. J. Fitzpatrick (1830–95) was a Dublin-born historian and biographer.

Knieving Trouts

'Knieving trouts' (they call it tickling in England) is good sport. You go to a stony shallow at night, a companion bearing a torch; then, stripping to the thighs and shoulders, wade in; grope with your hands under the stones, sods, and other harbourage, till you find your game, then grip him in your 'knieve' and toss him ashore.

I remember, when a boy, carrying the splits for a servant of the family, called Sam Wham. Now Sam was an able young fellow, well-boned and willing, a hard-headed cudgel-player, and a marvellous tough wrestler, for he had a backbone like a sea-serpent: this gained him the name of the Twister and Twiner. He had got into the river, and with his back to me was stooping over a broad stone, when something bolted from under the bank on which I stood, right through his legs. Sam fell with a great splash upon his face, but in falling jammed whatever it was against the stone. 'Let go, Twister!' shouted I; ''tis an otter, he will nip a finger off you.' 'Whisht!' sputtered he, as he slid his hand under the water; ' may I never read a text again if he isna a sawmont wi' a shouther like a hog!' 'Grip him by the gills, Twister,' cried I. 'Saul will I!' cried the Twiner; but just then there was a heave, a roll, a splash, a slap like a pistol-shot: down went Sam, and up went the salmon, spun like a shilling at pitch-and-toss, six feet into the air. I leaped in just as he came to the water; but my foot caught between two stones, and the more I pulled the firmer it stuck. The fish fell in a spot shallower than that from which he had leaped. Sam saw the chance, and tackled to again; while I, sitting down in the stream as best I might, held up my torch, and cried, 'Fair play!' as shoulder to shoulder, throughout and about, up and down, roll and tumble, to it they went, Sam and the salmon. The Twister was never so twined before. Yet, through cross-buttocks and capsizes innumerable, he still held on; now haled through a pool; now haling up a bank; now heels over head; now head over heels; now head and heels together; doubled up in a corner; but at last stretched fairly on his back, and foaming for rage and disappointment; while the victorious salmon, slapping the stones with his tail, and whirling the spray from his shoulders at every roll, came boring and snoring up the ford. I tugged and strained to no purpose; he flashed by me with a snort, and slid into the deep water. Sam now staggered forward with battered bones and peeled elbows, blowing like a grampus, and cursing like nothing but himself. He extricated me, and we limped home. Neither rose for a week; for I had a dislocated ankle, and the Twister was troubled with a broken rib. Poor Sam! he had his brains discovered at last by a poker in a row, and was worm's meat within three months; yet, ere he died, he had the satisfaction of feasting on his old antagonist, who was man's meat next morning. They caught him in a net. Sam knew him by the twist in his tail.

Note to THE WET WOOING

———❖———

Sir Samuel Ferguson (1810–86), poet and antiquarian, was born in Belfast. He was the first Deputy-Keeper of Irish Records. He translated the Gaelic epics.

Letter to his Mother

Oscott College
1st May, 1827

My Dearest Mother, – I have begun oil colour, and have sent a poem called 'Irene' of about five hundred lines to the London and Dublin magazine. I have no doubt of its being inserted, for after I sent them the first part, in the next number they requested their *'esteemed friend'* (pardon my vanity) to send them the rest of the communication; but that is nothing. The following is *entre nous*, so do not tell my father of the affair till after the accomplishment of the project. I am writing a poem which will be upwards of one thousand lines – I have written more than six hundred already – called the 'Legend of Lough Carra' which I intend, during the vacation, to offer to Murray or Colbourne for publication. I shall add a few of the best pieces of those I have already written, making up a tolerable volume. It often struck me that Lough Carra must have been the scene of much romantic incident, on account of the number of castles, forts, and churches on the shores and islands. I have chosen Church Island, Castle Carra, Castle Island and Castle Burke as the scenes of the plot; the time is the invasion of Cromwell and the hero is drawn from nature. I am at present very sanguine in my expectations, and oh! if I could get one hundred pounds from one of the booksellers for the child of my imagination, how happy I should feel in buying you a pair of handsome horses for the carriage. But these are, I fear, vapourings of air; however, prepare for rhyme – I'll publish, right or wrong.

———◦◦———

George Henry Moore (1811–70), politician, landowner (and land-lord), owner and breeder of racehorses, and father of the novelist George Moore, was born and died at Moore Hall, Co. Mayo.

W. R. Le Fanu

Practical Jokes

Joseph let no one see his poems but his mother, his sister, and myself. Whether he feared his father's criticism I cannot tell, but he never let him see them; still, he certainly had no great dread of my father, for whenever he had incurred his displeasure he would at once disarm him by some witty saying. One thing that much distressed the Dean was his being habitually late for prayers. One morning breakfast was nearly over and he had not appeared; and when he at last came in it was near ten o'clock. My father, holding his watch in his hand, said in his severest voice, 'I ask you, Joseph, I ask you seriously, is this right?' 'No, sir,' said Joe, glancing at the watch; 'I'm sure it must be fast.'

Practical jokes, I am glad to say, are seldom practised now, but in my early days they were much in vogue. Here is one my brother played on me:– I was in Dublin, and had a long letter from my father, who was at home at Abington, giving me several commissions. In a postscript, he said, 'Send me immediately *Dodd's Holy Curate*. If Curry has not got it you will be sure to get it at some other booksellers'; but be sure to send it, if possible, by return of post.' Curry had it not; in vain I sought it at other booksellers, so I wrote to my father to say that it was not to be had in Dublin, and that Curry did not know the book, but had written to his publishers in London to send it direct to Abington. By return of post I had a letter from my father saying he was utterly at a loss to know what I meant, that he had never asked me to get him *Dodd's Holy Curate*, and had never known of the existence of such a book. There is, in fact, no such book. What had happened was this: my father had gone out of the library for a few minutes, and had left his letter to me, which he had just finished, open on his writing-table; Joseph had gone into the library and took the opportunity of my father's absence to add the postscript, exactly imitating his writing, and on his return my father duly folded the letter and sent it to the post without having perceived my brother's addition to it.

Another, not so harmless – but boys are mischievous – he played on an elderly woman, whom he met near Dublin when he was staying on a visit with some friends. He had never seen the woman before, and never saw her after; but she looked at him as if she recognized him, stopped and stood before him looking earnestly at his face, when the following dialogue ensued:–

Woman. 'Oh, then, Masther Richard, is that yourself?'

Joseph. 'Of course it is myself. Who else should I be?'

Woman. 'Ah, then, Masther Richard, it's proud I am to see you. I hardly knew you at first, you're grown so much. Ah, but it's long since I seen any of the family. And how is the mistress and all the family?'

Joseph. 'All quite well, thank you. But why don't you ever come to see us?'

Woman. 'Ah, Masther Richard, don't you know I daren't face the house since that affair?'

Joseph. 'Don't you know that is all forgotten and forgiven long ago? My mother and all would be delighted to see you.'

Woman. 'If I knew that, I'd have been up to the house long ago.'

Joseph. 'I'll tell you what to do – come up on Sunday to dinner with the servants. You know the hour; and you will be surprised at the welcome you will get.'

Woman. 'Well, please God, I will, Masther Richard. Good-bye, Masther Richard, and God bless you.'

What sort of welcome the old lady (she had very probably been dismissed for stealing silver spoons) received on her arrival on the following Sunday has not transpired; but I dare say she was 'surprised' at it.

One morning, about this time, our family prayers were interrupted in a comical way. A Captain and Mrs Druid were staying with us for a few weeks. Having no child, their affections centred in a grey parrot, which they dearly loved, and on whose education most of their time was spent. And truly he was a wonderful bird. Amongst his other accomplishments, he sang 'God save the King' in perfect tune; but he never could get beyond 'happy and glorious'. The last word seemed so to tickle his fancy, that he couldn't finish it, but went on singing 'happy and glori-ori-ori-ori-ori-ori'. He would also say 'Have you dined? Yes, sir. And on what? Roast beef, sir.' Or, 'As-tu déjeuné, mon petit Coco? Oui, monsieur. Et de quoi? Macaroni, monsieur.'

For fear of accidents, he was not allowed into the breakfast-room till after prayers. One morning, however, by some mischance, he was there;

but behaved with becoming decorum until prayers were nearly over. My father had got to the middle of the Lord's Prayer, when, in a loud voice, Poll called out, 'As many as are of that opinion will say "aye"; as many as are of the contrary opinion will say "no". The "ayes" have it.' I need hardly say, prayers were finished under difficulties.

From SEVENTY YEARS OF IRISH LIFE

W. R. Le Fanu (1816–94), engineer, was born in Dublin. He became Commissioner of Public Works in 1863. His brother Joseph (1814–73) was the novelist and writer of ghost stories.

Schooling for a Patriot

An ardent youngster must have some outlet for his sympathies, and before patriotism awoke I was passionately religious. I can recall a time when I was despatched to bed at nightfall and took a coarse board with me to kneel upon under the blanket lest my prayers should be too luxurious; and for years after I read controversial books with avidity, and was ready on the shortest notice to defend the most abstruse mysteries of religion. But the first passion was superseded after a time by one which has lasted all my life – the determination to love, and, if possible, serve Ireland.

Some account of my early schools will help the reader to understand the social condition of Ulster at that time. The Ulster Catholics had been deprived by the Puritan Parliament in Dublin of their lands, their churches, and their schools at the beginning of the eighteenth century, and they were long forbidden by statute to obtain education at home or abroad, or to possess property in land. At the time I speak of their schools were still very often what were then known as 'poor schools'. The schoolroom was commonly a barn or a garret, the furniture rude and scanty, the walls and windows bare, and some of the pupils probably shoeless and unwashed. But these establishments were regarded as evidence of remarkable progress by those who remembered the 'hedge schools' of a previous generation, which had not even the shelter of a roof. My first schoolmaster was a one-handed man, named Neil Quin, who had probably become a teacher because this deficiency unfitted him for any other employment. He performed duties which were merely manual with marvellous dexterity – mending a pen, for example, as speedily and skilfully as a man with two hands. A long loop of twine passed through two holes in a table held the quill, flat, and was kept fast by his foot in the other end of the loop, while he trimmed it with his right hand, which happily remained. Of the elements of education Mr Quin did not teach us much, I fear, but he told us stories, generally little apologues or homilies, intended to impart a homely moral. His rudimentary science was taught with a scanty equipment of instruments, but he contrived to make it impressive. One day he let his hat fall from his head to the floor, and exclaimed, 'Now, boys, which of you will tell me why that hat fell down to the ground instead of falling up to the ceiling?'

My escape from this primitive institution was one of the most fortunate incidents of my life. My eldest sister, a girl of vigorous will, met me one day coming home from school in the midst of a clamorous swarm of urchins, some of them barefooted and ragged, and all riotous and undisciplined, and she interposed with a vigour worthy of our grandmother Judith. She peremptorily declared that I should never return to that society. But where was I to go? There was not a Catholic school in the county a whit better. There was, however, a classical academy in the town taught by a Presbyterian minister, the Reverend John Bleckley, where the boarders were sons of the small gentry and professional men of two or three neighbouring counties, and the day boys sons of the principal townspeople. There were about fifty pupils, all Protestants or Presbyterians, a Catholic boy never having been seen within the walls. It needed a considerable stock of moral courage to contemplate sending me to such an establishment, where I might be ill-received, or, if not ill-received, where I might be taught to despise the boys of my own race and creed whom I had quitted. The consent of my guardian, a parish priest living a dozen miles away, had to be obtained, and he had liberality and good sense enough to approve of the project. Mr Bleckley received me graciously, but during the first day one of the boys told me (what I soon learned had been muttered among many others) that it was unpardonable presumption for a Papist to come among them. But the bigotry of boys is mostly inherited from their elders, and has little root. This lad, Mat Trumble, son of a lieutenant in the British Army, but also grandson of a chaplain of the Volunteers, afterwards a notable United Irishman, soon became my close friend. He was a youth of good intellect, resolute will, and considerable reading, and with such aid I did not do badly in the strange society on which I had intruded. During the first year a boys' parliament, a boys' regiment, and a boys' newspaper were established, which I did something to initiate, and my connection with them was vehemently resisted in the name of Protestant ascendancy. But after a fierce debate the majority voted my emancipation, three years before the legislators of larger growth at St Stephen's made a similar concession to my seniors. I used to boast that I was the first Catholic emancipated in Ireland, but though tolerated I was never allowed altogether to forget that I belonged to the race who were beaten at the Boyne. A cynical lad, who afterwards became a noted local preacher, sometimes occupied the recreation hour with marvellous stories of Popish atrocities designed for my edification. . . .

Mr Bleckley was a careful and assiduous teacher, much devoted to his school, and for five years I profited by his instructions. We parted under circumstances which, as I have never since doubted, justified me in quitting him abruptly. One morning before the arrival of the head-master I had a contest with one of the boys about something I have altogether forgotten. He complained to an usher, but, as the ushers were not permitted to punish the boys, this one promised to report me for misconduct. On the arrival of the master he did so, and Mr Bleckley, who was perhaps disturbed by some personal trouble, immediately laid hold of me, stretched me over a desk, according to his practice, and administered a sharp discipline with a leather strap. When he had finished he faced me and demanded, 'Now, sir, what have you got to say for yourself?' Though the result proved a great inconvenience to me I can never regret what happened as a test of character. 'Say,' I roared, 'I say it is too late to ask for my defence after I have been punished; and that I will never suffer you to lay hands on me again.' I seized my cap and vanished out of the school. Mr Bleckley reported the facts to my mother, not ungenerously, I think, but I could not be induced to submit again to his authority. With the assistance of a student preparing for Maynooth, and in concert with my constant chum Mat Trumble, I read at home, to replace, as far as I could, the direction of a competent teacher. . . .

We did not know much of history, but we got what in recent times would be called 'object lessons', to keep it alive in our memory. The Orange drum was heard on every hill from June till August to celebrate the Boyne and Aughrim; Orange flags and arches adorned the town on party festivals; every office of authority in the province was held by Orangemen or their patrons and *protégés*, and to be a Protestant of any sort was a diploma of merit and a title to social rank not to be disputed. My comrade and I felt our present wrongs keenly, but we knew little of the remote causes from which they sprang. I had never seen a history of Ireland at that time. A few years earlier I had walked half a dozen miles to borrow a quasi history, Moore's *Captain Rock*, in a country parish which had the rare good fortune to possess a parish library. The Orange processions forbade us to forget the past, and there was a history transacted under our eyes of which it was impossible to be ignorant. The bench of magistrates who administered what was called justice was exclusively Protestant; the Grand Jury, who expended the rates paid by the whole population, were exclusively Protestant, and took care, it was alleged, that the improvements they projected should benefit only loyal citizens, themselves first of all. There had been a Corporation endowed out of confiscated lands, but the body had long ceased to exist, and its endowment had fallen to the local landlord, Lord Rossmore, who, to keep up the pretence of a Corporation, still named a town sergeant and other subordinate officials at his sole pleasure. There was a corps of Yeomanry receiving uniforms from the State, which was called out occasionally for inspection, and as the arms were left with the corps permanently, every Orange lodge had a liberal supply of guns, and used them freely at their annual festivity. One of my earliest recollections is to have seen a butcher named Hughes shot in the public street before my mother's door by a Government gun fired from an Orange procession. Hughes had probably used some offensive language, or perhaps thrown a stone at the procession, and for his offence, whatever it was, the immediate punishment was death. He was carried to the grave in a coffin festooned with red ribbons, to signify a murdered man, but there the incident ended. To indict any one for the murder would have been the idlest work of supererogation. His comrades in the procession would not have given evidence against him, and his comrades in the jury box would not have convicted him. The ordinary result of a party conflict at that time was that if a prosecution followed the Catholics were convicted, and the Orangemen escaped scot free, either by an acquittal or a split jury. On such juries a Catholic was not permitted to sit one time in a hundred.

From My Life in Two Hemispheres

———◆◇◆———

Sir Charles Gavan Duffy (1816–1903), journalist, poet and politician, was born in Monaghan. He emigrated to Australia in 1855, and later became Prime Minister of Victoria. His last years were spent at Nice.

Dublin Street Rhyme

Auld Granny Gray
She let me out to play
I can't go near the wa-ter
To hunt the ducks away.
Over the garden wall
I let the babby fall
Me mother came out
And gev me a clout
And knocked me over
A bottle of stout.

From OUT SHE GOES compiled by Leslie Daiken (1912–64), authority on children's games and toys, who was born in Dublin.

Child Bride

Daniel O'Connell used to be proud of being, as he said, 'the best-abused man in the world'. I do not know whether Lola Montez has been the best-abused woman in the world or not, but she has been pretty well abused at any rate; and has the honour, I believe, of having caused more newspaper paragraphs and more biographies than any woman living. I have, myself, seen twenty-three or twenty-four pretended biographies of Lola Montez; not one of which, however, came any nearer to being a biography of her, than it did to being an authentic history of the man in the moon. Seven cities claimed old Homer, but the biographers have given Lola Montez to more than three times seven cities. And a laughable thing is, that not one of all these biographers has yet hit upon the real place of her birth. One makes her born in Spain, another in Geneva, another in Cuba, another in India, another in Turkey, and so on. And at last, a certain fugitive from the gallows will have it, that she was born of a washerwoman in Scotland. And so of her parentage – one author makes her the child of a Spanish gipsy; another the daughter of Lord Byron; another, of a native prince of India, and so on, until they have given her more fathers than there are signs in the zodiac.

I declare, if I were Lola Montez, I should begin to doubt whether I ever had a father, or whether I was ever born at all, except in some fashion as Minerva was said to be – born of the brain of Jupiter.

Lola Montez has had a more difficult time to get born than even that, for she has had to be born over and over again of the separate brain of every man who has attempted to write her history.

Happily, however, I possess the means of settling this confused question, and of relieving the doubts of this unfortunate lady in relation to her parentage and birthplace; while I may at the same time gratify the curiosity of those who have honoured me with their presence here tonight.

Lola Montez was then actually born in the city of Limerick, in the

97

year of our Lord 1824. I hope she will forgive me for telling her age. Her father was a son of Sir Edward Gilbert; and his mother, Lady Gilbert, was considered, I believe, one of the handsomest women of her time. The mother of Lola was an Oliver, of Castle Oliver, and her family name was of the Spanish noble family of Montalvo, descended from Count de Montalvo, who once possessed immense estates in Spain, all of which were lost in the wars with the French and other nations. The Montalvos were originally of Moorish blood, who came into Spain at the time of Ferdinand and Isabella the Catholic. So that the fountain-head of the blood which courses in the veins of the *erratic* Lola Montez is Irish and Moorish-Spanish – a somewhat combustible compound, it must be confessed.

Her father, the young Gilbert, was made an ensign in the English army when he was seventeen years old; and before he was twenty he was advanced to the rank of captain in the 44th Regiment. He was but little more than twenty at the time of his marriage, and her mother was about fifteen. Lola was born during the second year of this marriage – making her little *début* upon this sublunary stage in the midst of the very honeymoon of the young people, and when they had hardly time to give a proper reception to so extraordinary a personage.

She was baptized by the name of MARIE DOLORES ELIZA ROSANNA GILBERT. She was always called DOLORES, the diminutive of which is LOLA.

Soon after the birth of this DOLORES, the 44th Regiment, of which her father was a captain, was ordered to India. I have heard her mother say that the passage to India lasted about four months – that they landed at Calcutta, where they remained about three years, when the Governor-General, Lord Hastings, ordered the 44th Regiment to Dinapore, some distance in the interior, upon the Ganges. Soon after the army arrived at this spot, the cholera broke out with terrible violence, and her father was among its first victims. There was a young and gallant officer by the name of Craigie, whom her father loved, and when dying and too far gone to speak, he took his child and wife's hand and put them in the hand of this young officer, with an imploring look, that he would be kind to them when death had done its work.

The mother of Lola Montez was thus left a widow before she was eighteen years old; and she was confided to the care and protection of Mrs General Brown. You can have but a faint conception of the responsibility of the charge of a handsome, young European widow in India.

The hearts of a hundred officers, young and old, beat all at once with such violence for her, that the whole atmosphere for ten miles round fairly throbbed with the emotion. But in this instance the general fever did not last long, for Captain Craigie led the young widow Gilbert to the altar himself. He was a man of high intellectual accomplishments, and soon after this marriage his regiment was ordered back to Calcutta, and he was advanced to the rank of major.

At this time the child Lola was little more than six years old, when she was sent to Europe to the care of Major Craigie's father at Montrose, in Scotland. This venerable man had been provost of Montrose for nearly a quarter of a century, and the dignity of his profession, as well as the great respectability of the family, made every event connected with his household a matter of some public note, and the arrival of the queer, wayward, little East Indian girl, was immediately known to all Montrose. The peculiarity of her dress, and I dare say not a little eccentricity in her manners, served to make her an object of curiosity and remark; and very likely the child perceived that she was somewhat of a public character, and may have begun, even at this early age, to assume airs and customs of her own.

With this family, however, she remained but a short time, when her parents became somehow impressed with the idea that she was being petted and spoiled, and she was removed to the family of Sir Jasper Nichols, of London, Commander-in-chief of the Bengal forces. His family remained in Paris for the sake of educating their daughters. After several years in Paris, Miss Fanny Nichols and the young Lola were sent to Bath for eighteen months to undergo the operation of what is properly called finishing their education. At the expiration of this finishing campaign, Lola's mother came from India for the purpose of taking her daughter back with her. She was then fourteen years old; and from the first moment of her mother's arrival, there was a great hubbub of new dresses, and all manner of extravagant queer-looking apparel, especially for the wardrobe of a young girl of fourteen years. The little Dolores made bold enough one day to ask her mother what this was all about, and received for an answer that it did not concern her – that children should not be inquisitive, nor ask idle questions. But there was a Captain James of the army in India, who came out with her mother, who informed the young Lola that all this dressmaking business was for her own wedding clothes; that her mother had promised her in marriage to Sir Abraham Lumly, a rich and gouty old rascal of sixty years, and Judge of the Supreme Court in India. This put the first fire to the magazine. The little madcap cried and stormed alternately. The mother was determined, so was her child – the mother was inflexible, so was her child; and in the wildest language of defiance she told her that she never would be thus thrown alive into the jaws of death.

Here, then, was one of those fatal family quarrels, where the child is forced to disobey parental authority, or to throw herself away into irredeemable wretchedness and ruin. It is certainly a fearful responsibility for a parent to assume of forcing a child to such alternatives. But the young Dolores sought the advice and assistance of her mother's friend, Captain James. He was twenty-seven years of age, and ought to have been capable of giving good and safe counsel. In tears and despair she appealed to him to save her from this detested marriage – a thing which he certainly did most effectually, by eloping with her the next day himself. The pair went to Ireland, to Captain James's family, where they had a great muss in trying to get married. No clergyman could be found who would marry so young a child without a mother's consent. The captain's sister put off for Bath, to try and get the mother's consent. At first she would not listen, but at last good sense so far prevailed as to make her see that nothing but evil and sorrow could come of her refusal, and she consented, but would neither be present at the wedding, nor send her blessing. So in flying from that marriage with ghastly and gouty old age, the child lost her mother, and gained what proved to be only the outside shell of a husband, who had neither a brain which she could respect, nor a heart which it was possible for her to love. Runaway matches, like runaway horses, are almost sure to end in a smash-up.

My advice to all young girls who contemplate taking such a step is, that they had better hang or drown themselves just one hour before they start.

From AUTOBIOGRAPHY

———◆○◆———

Lola Montez (1818–61), dancer, was born in Limerick, married in Meath, and divorced in 1842. She learnt Spanish dancing and captivated the King of Bavaria, who made her Countess of Landsfeld and a power in his land. She espoused the caused of Liberalism against the Jesuits, and after an exotic life, and two further marriages, died of paralysis, a penitent and helper of women less fortunate than herself.

Church Diversions

I was probably about four years old when they began to take me to church on Sundays. The edifice appeared to me spacious, lofty, and venerable. It was cruciform, with round-topped windows, the ground floor filled with high pews. There were three galleries – 'the Singing Gallery' over the west door; 'the Soldiers' Gallery' in the north transept; 'the Country Gallery' in the south transept, used mostly by small farmers and their families. The townsfolk and the country gentry had pews in the body of the church; some very poor people sat on benches in the aisle, and, at the other end of the scale, two families had notably large and comfortable pews, the Conollys in the right-hand corner as you came in by the west door, the Tredennicks of Camlin in the left. The Tredennick pew was a place of mystic and luxurious seclusion to my fancy, a sort of *imperium in imperio*. Its woodwork completely partitioned it off from the aisle, but chance peeps showed a snugly cushioned and carpeted interior, and even a special little fireplace with its special little bright fire on winter Sundays. In later days I knew a high lady who deemed it proper to go regularly to church once a week, but evaded part of the tedium by taking with her a novel or other amusing book, decently veiled in a dark cover. With such a pew as this she could have made herself very comfortable; but if anything of the kind occurred there (which probably never did) I had no suspicions of it.

Essentially, neither service nor sermon had the very slightest interest or meaning for me, but the sense of a solemn stringency of rule and order was deeply impressed, and the smallest infraction, it was felt, might have unimaginable consequences. A child's prayer-book falling from the gallery astounded like an earthquake; and once, I remember, when the congregation suddenly started up in the midst of the service, pew doors were thrown open, and people ran out into the aisles (a lady had fainted) – it was really as if the Day of Judgment had come. Connected with Church and churchyard was a thought, vague, vast, unutterably awful, of that Last Day, with Eternity behind it: yet it was definitely localized too, and it seemed that not only the Rising but the Judging of our particular dead must be in our own Churchyard.

A terrible thought of Eternity sometimes came, weighing upon me like a nightmare – on and on and on, always beginning and never ending, never ending at all, for ever and ever and ever – till the mind, fatigued, fell into a doze as it were and forgot. I suppose this was connected, though not definitely, with the idea of a state of punishment. The suggestion of eternal happiness took no hold upon my imagination; my earliest thought of Heaven pictured it as a Sunday street in summer, with door-steps swept and the shutters of the shops closed. Later, there was a vague flavour of Church and psalmody.

Our Pew, painted like the rest a yellowish colour supposed to imitate oak, was half-way up the Church, on the right-hand side of the central aisle, and had the distinction of a tall flat Monument of wood (or it seemed tall), painted black in George the Second taste, rising on the wall behind it. Atop was a black urn with faded gold festoons; at each side a pilaster with faded gold flutings; and there was a long inscription in faded gold letters.

It seems to me very curious that, after sitting so many an hour, so many a year, in that Pew, and recollecting numberless little things around me there, I cannot find in my memory one word of that inscription, except 'SACRED' in a line by itself at the top, in Old English letters – not even the chief name, which was a lady's (a remote and very slightly interesting relation or connection of ours, she must have been) nor the import of those Roman symbols which so ingeniously disguise a date to modern eyes. The wording no doubt was highly conventional, as nearly as possible meaningless, and felt by the child to be a sort of dull puzzle which after some attempts it was better to avoid. Had it been *verse*, of even moderate quality, it would have fixed itself in my memory; with point, it would have stuck there for ever.

My usual place in the Pew (habitude, or customariness, or whatever it may be called, being naturally strong in me) was the left-hand corner next the door as you went in. Standing on the seat, I could look up and down the aisle, and sometimes rest my arms and head on a little triangular shelf that fitted into the corner. When I had, against the grain, to sit down, I kept looking at the faces of the people near to me in the Pew, and the countenance of a certain half-pay Army Lieutenant, ruddy, swarthy, with a longish nose somewhat bulbous at the end, holds a very disproportionate place in my memory, because he generally sat in full view. The tedium of the service was also mitigated by the interest which I acquired in watching for the reg•ılar recurrence of its various stages, with the attitudes – of sitting, standing, or kneeling – appropriate to each. Certain phrases were greeted as milestones upon the journey; and at the end of the sermon (usually the most trying part of all, and of indefinite length) the words, 'Now to God the Father', etc., caused an unfailing gush of inner satisfaction. There was something curious and amusing in the Litany with its responses, but it was mostly meaningless to me, as indeed was the Service as a whole (both at this time and later in life). The mystic phraseology had of course its effect, as any other such would have had, and the regular recurrence and solemn repetition of the performance. The gathering together, too, of neighbours, rich and poor, old and young, as in the presence of the Universal Father and Ruler, has an impressiveness different from anything else in daily life. If it could indeed be done simply and purely 'in spirit and in truth'! But here, in our small community, a section only of the neighbours drew together at the set solemn seasons; another section, though animated by the same motives, drew together in different place and manner, drew *apart* from the former gathering, many of whom came from the same households; and in the very act of worship both sections displayed and emphasized feelings of mutual suspicion, contempt and animosity.

Once or twice I was taken clandestinely to mass by a nurse, on some Saint's Day most likely, and stood or sat for a while while just inside the Chapel door. It felt like a strange adventure, with some flavour of horror, but more of repulsiveness, from the poverty of the congregation and the intonation of the priests. I remember arguing with my nurse Kitty Murray (who only died this year, 1883, at the supposed age of ninety-three – but I don't think it was she who took me to the chapel), for the superiority of Protestantism because 'the Catholics, you see, are poor people'; to which Kitty replied, 'It may be different in the next world.' A good answer, I felt, and attempted no retort; being indeed at no time of my life addicted to argue for argument's sake, or for triumph.

103

Although very brisk in body and mind, my health from the first was considered delicate. I was thin and pale, and for several years – between my fifth and eighth, perhaps – there was a swallowing of nauseous doses to be gone through several times a day. But this was nothing to the Surgeon's frequent visits with his horrible lancet, in consequence of a swelling on the middle finger of the right hand (which remains contracted), and even in memory the bitter pain of the repeated cuttings makes me wince. My Aunt Bess used to 'dress it', a disagreeable operation for both of us. She was the Maiden Aunt of the family, at this time between forty and fifty, very charitable and helpful from an unwavering sense of duty, and inflexibly 'low-church' in her religious opinions and practices. She did her duty by me, as by everybody, with firmness, regularity, and a general good sense; what was missing in her ministrations was that soothing personal atmosphere of love and sympathy which does everybody good without effort, and especially children. This blessing I should doubtless have enjoyed from my dear Mother, had her short married life been more fortunate. At my grandmother's, besides my Aunt Bess, lived two younger Aunts, Maryanne and Everina. Aunt Everina glides through my memory little more than a mild pale shadow, straight and slender, and low-voiced. She had by nature a pictorial gift, and painted in water-colour – flowers, landscapes, portraits of friends and neighbours – as well as one might be expected to do who had no training and never saw any examples of good work. Aunt Everina's health was delicate, and she was perhaps about twenty-eight years old when she died.

Aunt Maryanne, the youngest, or youngest but one, of my Grandmother's large family was, both in person and temper, short and brisk with *nez retroussé* and lively gray eyes. She was quick and excitable, spoke fast, and a troublesome child would pretty soon feel her hands as well as her tongue. She was a Poetess, and wrote much on local and family subjects, but her simple ambition never even dreamed of actual print, and contented itself with sheets of note-paper, and little stitched books, neatly written out in something like printing letters, and given away to her friends. I have in my desk a ballad of hers on my father's approaching wedding – 'Will's to be married to Maggie,' etc. – O Time!

Aunt Maryanne was a voracious novel-reader. The winter evenings come clearly before me; my Grandmother in her arm-chair by the fire, with close cap, knitting incessantly, her snuff-box on a little table, an old cat called 'Norway' snoozing on the hearthrug and sometimes jumping into her lap; Aunt Bess also knitting, grave and silent; Aunt Maryanne reading aloud a Waverley Novel. I used to sit with paper and pencil, 'drawing' and also listening to the story. At any thrilling crisis ejaculations of interest or excitement were heard, and the end of a chapter often gave rise to comments, always on the incidents and characters, just as though they were real, never on the literary merits of the work or the abilities of the author. Criticism of the latter kind was all but unknown in our circle.

From A DIARY

William Allingham (1824–89), poet and journalist, was born in Ballyshannon, Co. Donegal, and started his working life as a customs officer. He was editor of *Fraser's Magazine* 1874–9.

The Beggar Boy

When the wind blows loud and fearful,
  And the rain is pouring fast,
And the cottage matron careful
  Shuts her door against the blast;

When lone mothers as they hearken,
  Think of sailor sons at sea,
And the eve begins to darken,
  While the clocks are striking three;

When the pavement echoes only
  Now and then to passing feet;
Still the beggar boy goes lonely,
  Up and down the empty street.

On his brow the wet hair bristles,
  And his feet are blue with cold,
And the wind at pleasure whistles
  Through his garments torn and old.

You can hear the plaint he utters,
  Standing dripping at your door,
Through the splashing in the gutters,
  When the wind has lulled its roar.

Little children playing gladly,
  In the parlour bright and warm,
Look out kindly, look out sadly
  On the beggar in the storm.

Speak ye softly to each other,
  Standing by the window pane;
'Had he father, had he mother,
  Would they leave him in the rain?

'In our home is peace and pleasure,
  We are loved and cared about,
We must give from our full measure,
  To the wanderer without.'

Cecil Frances Alexander (1818–95) née Humphreys, poet, was born
in Co. Wicklow. Her husband became Bishop of Derry and Raphoe
in 1867. She wrote the hymns, 'Once in Royal David's City', 'All
Things Bright and Beautiful', and 'There is a Green Hill Far
Away'.

JOHN BUTLER YEATS

Upbringing of an Artist

Why I became an artist is a question which every artist must sometimes put to himself. It was my father who made me an artist, though his intention was that I should become a barrister, and I did become a barrister, but soon left it to follow my destiny and be an artist. Had I remained a barrister, in all probability both my sons would have taken to the law and would not now be one a poet and the other a painter.

When I was a little child, like other children I took to drawing, and my father being very appreciative of his children admired what I drew. In those days there was a heavy tax on paper as a defence against cheap journalism, & the radical movements which it was bound to foster, and my mother, being, as are most mothers, careful of expenditure, and not very sympathetic toward my artistic strivings, was always reluctant to give me paper on which I could draw. However, my father was an Irish gentleman of the old school and not at all thrifty; from him I could always get as much paper as I wanted. At that time there were no illustrated magazines and only one illustrated paper which I saw very occasionally at a friend's house. The only newspaper which came into my father's house was the London *Times* and it had a picture of a clock. It was I think a rough wood-block. There is no child who will not really subscribe to Aristotle's doctrine that art is imitation, and in this case the imitation was roughly rendered so that it might be described as imitation with selection.

I was the eldest of the family and my brothers were much younger, for which reason my childhood was without companionship. Ah, the loneliness of such a childhood and the blessedness of it! Whether inside the house or out in the grounds I was always by myself, therefore I early learned to sustain myself by revery and dream. Years afterwards I suffered a good deal from the reproofs of my elders, for my habit of absentmindedness. Of course I was absentminded and am so still. In those childhood days I discovered the world of fantasy, and I still spend all my spare moments in that land of endearing enchantment.

I think as a child I was perfectly happy; my father my friend and counsellor, my mother my conscience. My father theorized about things and explained things and that delighted me, not because I had any mental conceit but because I delighted then as I still do in reasoning. My mother never explained anything, she hadn't a theoretical faculty; but she had a way of saying 'Yes darling' or 'No darling', which, when put out, she would change into a hasty 'Yes dear' or 'No dear' that was sufficient for all purposes. There was a servant in the house whose name was Sam Matchett. As is the way in the country, he was butler and coachman, land steward and gardener. He had been in the army and he several times told me that he had been the strongest man in the regiment. I admired him more than I did anybody else, and he enjoyed my admiration as much as Achilles did that of Patroclus. I think he did very much as he liked with my father, but my mother was made of firmer material. My mother had a great belief in exercise in the open air, and when Sam wanted to do a little shooting on his own account, he would approach her artfully and say that he knew where there was a pheasant or a hare and that he thought of going to get it, and that he would like to take 'Master Johnny' with him; and off we two would go. My father was six feet two inches in his stocking feet and well-built, famous in his college days as an athlete and racket player, and Sam Matchett to excite the admiration of the women servants would induce my father to stand on the palm of his hand, and he would raise him with arms outstretched to the level of the kitchen table. It was no wonder that I admired Sam, and it helped no doubt in my artistic education and started an appreciation, which still exists, for muscular well-made men. Of course I picked up all Sam's words and modes of expression, and my mother didn't quite like it; but as these referred to horses and cattle and fields and game, in my own mind I was convinced that Sam knew a good deal more about it than she did. I remember he used to wonder that I did not prefer my father to my mother. I think he was an exceedingly good influence upon my life. He bestowed a great deal of care on my manners, which is not surprising when one remembers that however it be with the upper classes, the Irish peasant has the instincts of a gentleman. My father was a Rector of a very large parish in County Down, Ireland, & there were no boys' schools anywhere within reach. A village school-master taught me to read, after which I read *Robinson Crusoe* diligently. In the evening after dinner my father would sit beside his candle reading, and my mother would sit by her candle sewing, and I would nestle beside her reading *Robinson Crusoe*, and I can remember that at certain critical passages in this history I would tremble with anxiety, and that I was most careful lest my elders should discover my excitement and laugh at me. These candles needed to be snuffed incessantly, and it was my ambition to be allowed to snuff them; but when I tried I snuffed the candle out, and never again got the chance, my mother was inexorable.

We were a large family, boisterous, full of animal spirits & health, sometimes very friendly together while at other times we would quarrel. Yet I never remember a single instance of corporal punishment or indeed any kind of punishment but once, and then I was the victim. My mother induced my father to commence my education, and he began by something in arithmetic, and I failed miserably as I would at the present moment. Up to that moment I had been the pride of my father: not only was I his eldest son and the heir to the family property, but he was convinced I was exceedingly like his brother Tom, who in his course at Trinity College, Dublin, had never been beaten in mathematics. When therefore I failed in arithmetic the blow was too much for his fond hopes, and he gave me a box on my ear. He had no sooner done so than he shook hands with me and hoped I was not offended, and then glided out of the room. I was not offended but very much astounded. I wonder if he told my mother. At any rate, years afterwards when I was a full grown man, I heard her regretting that she could never induce my father to teach any of us. He said he had no patience.

From EARLY MEMORIES

———◆◦◆———

John Butler Yeats (1839–1922), artist, conversationalist and father of W. B. Yeats and the painter Jack B. Yeats, was born at Tully-lish, Co. Down. He went to New York in 1908, and lived there until his death.

Soldier's Boy

During the rebellion of 1798, our house at Tullow was attacked and burned by the Irish. In some amusing letters to her people in England, my grandmother describes the sudden approach of the rebels and the panic which ensued, for they seemed bent upon ridding Ireland of at least one family of the hated Saxon settlers. Every one ran, some on horseback, others in any wheeled conveyance they could secure, all making for Carlow, about nine miles off, where there was a small English garrison. A very plain aunt, to whom as a boy I was much attached, was forgotten in the hurry and confusion. Finding herself left behind she set out on foot, but being soon overtaken by a Yeomanry trooper, he kindly took her up behind him. She did very well thus until about half-way to Carlow, when, unfortunately for her, they overtook a very pretty girl out of breath and much frightened. The trooper said she was his cousin, and insisted upon my ugly aunt giving up her place behind him to his handsome kinswoman. My poor aunt had to finish her flight on foot.

The rebels were not content with burning our house, but, being short of ammunition, they stripped the Church spire of its lead, and also smelted into bullets the leaden coffin in which my great-grandfather had been recently buried.

My father and his younger brother entered the Army. Both served for many years in the King's Own Borderers, then quartered in the West Indies. When other regiments were engaged in winning fame under Wellington in Spain, theirs was left to fight the French in Martinique, Guadeloupe, and other French West India Islands. I remember many a story about these encounters with the French, but will not inflict them upon my reader. The life led by our troops in the West Indies then was odious in every sense, and my father hated it. The officers, as well as the men, drank hard and often quarrelled over their wine. Duels were common occurrences, but, strange to say, they seldom ended fatally.

When either my father or uncle was so 'engaged in the morning', and it was often, one was always the other's second.

My father was by no means clever, and having entered the Army when extremely young, he was badly educated, a misfortune he never ceased to deplore. I often heard my mother say that my father spent his fourteenth birthday as an ensign in Gibraltar. He was very poor and very proud. Nothing could have induced him to do a mean action of any sort. Hot-tempered, and perhaps prone to quarrel, he was chivalry itself in thought, word and action. Full of charity, he felt much for the Irish poor, with whose misery, in those days of high rents and high prices, he had the most real sympathy. Very punctilious in manner and bearing, and particular about his clothes and general appearance, he looked a soldier all over. He was a very religious man in later years, and a strong Protestant, as all the family had been since the Reformation, until his cousin, the English Baronet, Sir Charles Wolseley – the curious, clever, half-cracked Chartist, who had taken part in the assault of the Bastile – joined the Church of Rome.

My father married late in life, my mother being twenty-five years his junior. She was the daughter of William Smith, Esq., of Golden Bridge House, County Dublin, and another daughter married my father's cousin, Sir Richard Wolseley, Bart. My maternal grandfather was a typical spendthrift Irish landlord, who lived recklessly beyond his means. His great-grandfather, a Mr de Herries, had fled from England during the plague in Charles II's reign, and, having bought the Golden Bridge property, built himself a house upon it. Why he assumed the homely name of Smith, I know not. Most of us have acquaintances who have sunk the patronymic 'Smith' into what sounded more imposing. But here was a well-born old gentleman who deliberately did the reverse.

My father sold out as a major, shortly after his marriage, and rented Golden Bridge House from his father-in-law, who had settled in England. There I was born, June 4, 1833, just 101 years after my paternal grandfather had come into the world at Mount Wolseley, in the County of Carlow. I was thus the third generation that had been born in Ireland. It is always pleasant to me to remember that the year of my birth was that in which we abolished 'that execrable sum of all villanies, commonly called the "Slave Trade"'.

Golden Bridge House was a red brick mansion of the King William or early Queen Anne period. Like most of the old country houses near Dublin, it is now a convent, and a dirty slum has grown up in and around what was once its undulating and well-watered little park.

I should like to record here my earliest recollections of my mother, but it is not easy to describe one so loved, and round whose memory there clings, as a halo, the holiest and loftiest of my childish thoughts and aspirations. As a boy I always thought hers the fairest and sweetest face in the world, and she still looms before my memory a beautiful, gracious, tall and stately woman, full of love and tenderness for all about her. Her smile was most fascinating, and the poor and sorrowful of heart never came to her in vain for help and sympathy. Her white, well-shaped teeth, very regular features, dark, nearly black, hair, and an almost southern complexion, made her more Spanish than English in appearance. She was very clever, capable, tactful, of sound judgment, and as a girl had read much. In my daily walks with her, when a boy, I drank in from her teaching much that I have now forgotten. Her religion – devoid of everything approaching to priest-craft – was the simplest Bible form of worship. She was indeed one of the pure in heart, of whom, we are told, 'they shall see God'.

I will pass rapidly over the story of my boyhood, for I know by the memoirs of others how uninteresting are the tales of early youth. As a boy, I was very active, ran and jumped well, was fond of boxing, single-stick, rowing, shooting, and all out-of-door amusements. I read much, and crammed my head with Hume's *History of England*, Alison's *History of Europe*, and Napier's *Peninsula War*. Devoted to mathematics, I disliked the 'Classics', especially Greek, and always loathed the ancient gods of Greece, and all the absurd myths and stories about them. My exact and mathematical mind revolted against the unreal nonsense taught me as the history of these mean and contemptible deities, about most of whom there was nothing good, wholesome, or manly. Horace and Juvenal, however, amused, and Virgil's description of the games excited me. Later on I read Caesar for my Army examination; his commentaries and Xenophon's *Anabasis* were the only classics I ever thoroughly enjoyed. I was taught drawing, the use of the pocket sextant and prismatic compass, and I devoured every work on the theory and practice of war that I could beg, borrow, or afford to buy.

From THE STORY OF A SOLDIER'S LIFE

Garnet Wolseley (1833–1913), soldier, was born at Golden Bridge House, Co. Dublin. He had distinguished service in Burma, the Crimea, India, China and Canada, before commanding the British forces in the Ashanti War. He was commander-in-chief of the expedition to Egypt in 1882, made viscount in 1885 and field marshal in 1894. He was commander-in-chief of the entire army 1895–1900.

THOMAS BARNARDO

The Making of a Philanthropist

As I look back upon my own schooldays, I cannot but wonder at the marvellous change which has come over boys and their treatment since that time. I remember one school that I went to (and indeed it would be impossible to forget it) where we were under the thraldom of one of the biggest and most brutal of bullies. The Principal was a clergyman and a Doctor of Divinity, possessing many claims to consideration and distinction; he was nevertheless, the most *cruel* man as well as the most *mendacious* that I have ever in all my life met. He seemed to take a savage delight in beating his boys, and there were two or three unfortunate lads in the school who were the special subjects of his unceasing persecution.

Public schools were not the fashion in Ireland then, and mine was a great day-school, from which most of the scholars went direct to the University, or to the various Queen's Colleges. But I often wondered why these unhappy lads, having an opportunity to go home, ever had the courage to return day after day. I am sure if I had been one of his victims (which happily I was not) I never could have returned to school and awaited the torture which he was so ready to apply.

I have often wondered concerning myself why it was that such cruelty did not beget in me a similar passion, as was, I know, the result with some of my companions, for cruelty begets cruelty. But I think I can understand now the reason. The fact was that such intense loathing and disgust for his brutality were awakened in my heart and in the hearts of many others that we went to the very opposite extreme in our detestation of anything having the least appearance of cruelty or harshness. This, however, was not so in all cases. A few of the older boys imitated their master, and I happen to know that in their subsequent careers some of my school-fellows have suffered from the terrible example which our pedagogue set us.

Dr Thomas John Barnardo (1845–1905), founder of the Dr Barnardo Homes, was born in Dublin of a Jewish father and a Quaker mother. He became a converted Protestant in 1862 and then, instead of pursuing his chosen career as a medical missionary, established the East End Mission in London for destitute children, which grew into the international organization which still bears his name.

Mrs Twopenny

My first recollection of Charley was when he was about two or three years old, and an inmate of the nursery, from which I had not long been promoted. I faintly remember him toddling about in his baby clothes.

When he gew a little older they wanted to put him into petticoats, but he created such an uproar that special breeches, made of the thinnest material, were provided for him, and also for myself. This was to make us hardy, as our father wanted to give each of us his own iron constitution. However, in the very cold weather our nether garments were plentifully coated with frost and icicles.

Charley was immensely proud of his victory, and then refused to wear boots once he was clear of the house, kicking them off and walking barefoot, especially in the snow. I'm afraid I usually followed his example.

One of poor Charley's most poignant griefs in his tender years was the frequent loss of his night-cap. His roars were incessant until it was found and safely fixed on his head.

Charley once had a very narrow escape of having his career cut short before he had even learned how to talk. Our mother was nursing him one day, when a visitor was suddenly announced. She hastily stowed away the future Irish leader in the drawer of a large press, which she closed without thinking, and hurried to the drawing-room. When the visitor left, about half an hour later, she found that she had clean forgotten what she had done with Charley, and a frantic search was made, until muffled yells from the drawer where he was imprisoned resulted in his release.

His nurse, Mrs Twopenny (invariably pronounced by us 'Tupny'), was a tall, buxom Englishwoman, with dark hair and fine hazel eyes. She was very fond of the scenery around Avondale, and instilled a love of the country into me, which Charley, however, did not show until later years.

Mrs Twopenny, who was a most respectable woman, quite different from the succession of uneducated nurses who had charge of us elder children, was very firm with Charley, but at the same time very kind to him. She used to lead him by the hand on her favourite rambles through the woods. When he was naughty, which was pretty often, she gave him a few slaps, but not very hard ones, and he never was whipped. Even later, when he had indulged in some special piece of mischief, he was never actually castigated by our father, but only shut in a room by himself, where he howled himself to sleep.

When we got a little older, he, I, and Fanny, were always fond of playing with tin soldiers. We each had a regiment set up on the floor, and, once ready, opened a furious fusilade on one another's forces with little pea-shooters fashioned in the form of cannon. Charley entered into the game with the greatest spirit, and was determined to win at all costs. Once, I remember, he reached the field of battle before us, and carefully gummed down his army to the floor, much to the disgust of Fanny, who did not detect the ruse until her own forces were annihilated, while his stood their ground.

Fanny, by the way, was always Charley's special chum, and they often used to go up to an old loft under the roof and shut themselves in, even from me. There they would discuss their pet schemes and have furious tin-soldier battles. In these battles, it is curious to relate, Fanny who even at that early period was a thorough little rebel at heart, used to consider her army as one composed of Irish patriots fighting for their freedom; while Charley had to be content with an English army, doomed by consent to defeat, but often, owing to his hatred of being beaten, proving victorious.

I certainly think that Fanny's impassioned patriotism had a great influence on Charley's convictions in after-life.

'I spy' and 'Follow my leader' were favourite games with us, and we used to play them all over the house, and out on to the lawn, and through the shrubberies.

Charley was also an expert at the ancient, if somewhat plebeian, game of marbles.

When Delia came back from school in France, she brought with her a new game, which consisted in her hiding her presents all over the house and getting us to search for them. The result was, as might be expected, pandemonium, followed frequently by punishment, seeing that the presents were generally hidden in ornaments, in the lining of chairs and sofas, up disused chimneys, and behind books.

I learnt billiards at a very early age, and used often to play with my father. Charley was always fond of sitting on the edge of the billiard-table and throwing the balls about. He often attempted to do this when we were actually playing, and, when lifted off the table, yelled vociferously, indignant as ever that his slightest whim should be thwarted.

Emily, who was always full of originality, started a little mint of her own in her room. She used to make her money out of gun-wads, and distribute it to the rest of us. I forget the exact nature of the currency, but it did quite well enough for our childish games.

Cricket, in after-life his favourite pastime, as I shall relate, had attractions for Charley even in his nursery days, for he used to toddle down to our private cricket-ground, generally hand in hand with Mrs Twopenny, and watch with the keenest interest every phase of the game.

As far as I can carry my mind back, his earliest form of recreation was riding a rocking-horse, and I can just remember him, a very small creature indeed, being held on a big wooden steed in the nursery by Mrs Twopenny.

From CHARLES STEWART PARNELL

----◦○◦----

Charles Stewart Parnell (1846–91), politician, was born at Avondale, Co. Wicklow. Leader of the Home Rule Party in the House of Commons, he fell from grace through his appearance as co-respondent in a divorce case. John Howard Parnell (1843–1923) was his elder brother.

A Different World

It was not only that tale of the landing of the French at Killala that led the youngest daughter of the house to her country's history. She would often finger the lichen-grown letters cut on a stone of the bridge near the avenue gates:

> *Erected by William Persse*
> *Colonel of the Roxborough Volunteers*
> *in the year* 1782
> *in memory of Ireland's Emancipation*
> *from foreign Jurisdiction*

when those Volunteers had gained for at least a while the freedom of the Irish Parliament to make its own laws. So it came about that she would bring out the sixpences, earned if memory held good, by repeating on the Sunday evenings Bible verses learned during the week; and standing on tiptoe at the counter of the little Loughrea book-shop would purchase one by one the paper covered collections of national ballads, *The Harp of Tara*, *The Irish Song Book*, and the like. It was perhaps because of the old bookseller calling attention to this by saying in his shop one day, 'I look to Miss Augusta to buy all my Fenian books,' that led to a birthday present of *The Spirit of the Nation*, a shilling copy, bound in green cloth, from the sister next in age to her, with Dr Johnson's sarcasm written in it, 'Patriotism is the last refuge of a Scoundrel'. It is not likely that the idea of her having any thoughts of sympathies different from their own had ever entered the mind of any of the elders of the house.

Childhood had thus slipped away, and it was perhaps some fifteen years after that midnight arrival in the world when religion in that Evangelical form in which it had always been set before the child, drove all other thoughts from the mind of the growing child. The theology taught had been that of the hymn 'There is a dreadful hell, With everlasting pains', 'Where sinners must with devils dwell in darkness, fire and chains'. To escape it even if you had been absolutely sinless would be impossible, and were it possible there would still be the guilt of Adam's disobedience, for which as one of his descendants, you were responsible; there was no escape except being washed in the Blood of the Lamb, and that could not be unless you were converted, unless you believed while still in this earthly life; there was no place for repentance, no Purgatory. It was before Disestablishment, and the difficult Athanasian Creed was still given out two or three times in the year by the Archdeacon 'which faith except everyone keep whole and undefiled, without doubt he shall perish everlastingly'. And to this others besides the Clerk would give a whole hearted 'Amen'.

So it was no wonder that she was troubled. Was she a believer? Lacking it, what must she do to be saved? What was the wall between her and heaven; the closed door between her and Christ? She would break it open by prayer; she would earn its unclosing by a blameless day. But belief, like Queen Vashti, was shy and would not come to order, and before the day was over a moment's forgetfulness of this high task would seem a crime, and prayer itself a vanity. The matter must be fought out alone, it is not in a large and critical family that such a secret of the heart could be made common property. The restlessness of the mind increased. Then of a sudden one morning in the cottage on Lough Corrib her father had taken as a fishing lodge, she rose up from her bed at peace with God. All doubts and all fears had gone, she was one of His children, His angels were her friends. The ballads, and poems and patriotic songs had become as ashes; His word, the Bible was her only book. She need no longer strive to do His will, it was her delight to do it. She was a little ashamed of this ecstasy, a little shy, unwilling to have it known. Yet it came to be accepted, without words, little by little, that she was not as it were quite in the same world as the others, that it was by a different table of values that she lived. 'I am not like Augusta who grew into religion from her childhood,' one married sister wrote, long after to another, Adelaide Lane. She was very happy.

For what might have been a long time the Bible and religious books, the only ones of which there were a plenty in the house, satisfied her. Then she began to discriminate. George Herbert's poems, given to a brother as a school prize, stayed more comfortably in the mind than the hymns of doctrine held to in the first fervour, as did the monk's vision of the jewel decked city, the sardius and amethyst of the New Jerusalem. The sermon books gave way to à Kempis's *Imitation of Christ*. As to novels, she had been taught to consider them food unfit for the use of Christ's flock; and indeed the daughters of the house were forbidden to read even the Waverleys until they attained the age of eighteen. And for this she was afterwards grateful, for coming later they never won her heart and all her romantic sympathies were kept for Ireland.

Although the books that had lain on the table at stated times, the *Ballads* and the yet unopened Shakespeare, had been taken away, the centre table was not quite unfurnished. Each Christmas a box of books would arrive to be chosen from, children's books chiefly, and religious ones, the *Sunday at Home*, the *Leisure Hour*. But from one of these boxes an elder sister, Gertrude, saying frankly she did not care for reading but would choose the biggest, took and laid on the drawing-room table the two volumes of Chambers' *Encyclopaedia of English Literature*.

That was to the younger sister the breaking of a new day, the discovering of a new world. She looked forward to those evening hours when she could read those volumes, first straight through, then over and over, a page here and there, till some of the poems given were known almost off by heart. The Bible had its appointed hours but was no longer everything, it may be its own beauty of words and imagination had spoiled her for common books; or she had become aware that there was other beauty and other poetry that might come near it, and had learned to know under what names this might be found. She knew now what to ask for at Christmas or from a brother in good humour, for the boys had more money in their pockets than the girls, given for the shooting of mischievous pests, and they were glad to give the sister who was their companion and favourite a share in this now and again, and would let her make her own choice. In this way there came into her possession by degrees Scott's poems, and Tennyson's (the Pre-Raphaelite edition), and even the excitement of each new volume of his as it came out, Scott, Burns, Montaigne, Matthew Arnold's essays, and Clough and Hood and Keats; and above and beyond all, most enduring of joys, Malory's *Morte D'Arthur*.

From SEVENTY YEARS

———•◦•———

Lady Gregory (1859–1932) née Isabella Augusta Persse, folklorist, dramatist and literary patron, was born in Roxborough, Co. Galway. She was a co-founder of the Irish Literary Theatre and with J. M. Synge and W. B. Yeats established the Abbey Theatre. Her translations of Irish material in *Cuchulain of Muirthemne* and *Gods and Fighting Men* were written in what came to be known as a Kiltartan style of English, after a village in Co. Galway near her home of Coole Park.

A Mis-spent Youth

My soul, so far as I understand it, has very kindly taken colour and form from the many various modes of life that self-will and an impetuous temperament have forced me to indulge in. Therefore I may say that I am free from original qualities, defects, tastes, etc. What is mine I have acquired, or, to speak more exactly, chance bestowed, and still bestows, upon me. I came into the world apparently with a nature like a smooth sheet of wax, bearing no impress, but capable of receiving any; of being moulded into all shapes. Nor am I exaggerating when I say I think that I might equally have been a Pharaoh, an ostler, a pimp, an archbishop, and that in the fulfilment of the duties of each a certain measure of success would have been mine. I have felt the goad of many impulses, I have hunted many a trail; when one scent failed another was taken up, and pursued with the pertinacity of instinct, rather than the fervour of a reasoned conviction. Sometimes, it is true, there came moments of weari-ness, of despondency, but they were not enduring: a word spoken, a book read, or yielding to the attraction of environment, I was soon off in another direction, forgetful of past failures. Intricate, indeed, was the labyrinth of my desires; all lights were followed with the same ardour, all cries were eagerly responded to: they came from the right, they came from the left, from every side. But one cry was more persistent, and as the years passed I learned to follow it with increasing vigour, and my strayings grew fewer and the way wider.

I was eleven years old when I first heard and obeyed this cry, or, shall I say, echo-augury?

Scene: A great family coach, drawn by two powerful country horses, lumbers along a narrow Irish road. The ever-recurrent signs – long ranges of blue mountains, the streak of bog, the rotting cabin, the flock of plover rising from the desolate water. Inside the coach there are two children. They are smart, with new jackets and neckties; their faces are pale with sleep, and the rolling of the coach makes them feel a little sick.

It is seven o'clock in the morning. Opposite the children are their parents, and they are talking of a novel the world is reading. Did Lady Audley murder her husband? Lady Audley! What a beautiful name! and she, who is a slender, pale, fairy-like woman, killed her husband. Such thoughts flash through the boy's mind; his imagination is stirred and quickened, and he begs for an explanation. The coach lumbers along, it arrives at its destination, and Lady Audley is forgotten in the delight of tearing down fruit trees and killing a cat.

But when we returned home I took the first opportunity of stealing the novel in question. I read it eagerly, passionately, vehemently. I read its successor and its successor. I read until I came to a book called *The Doctor's Wife* – a lady who loved Shelley and Byron. There was magic, there was revelation in the name, and Shelley became my soul's divinity. Why did I love Shelley? Why was I not attracted to Byron? I cannot say. Shelley! Oh, that crystal name, and his poetry also crystalline. I must see it, I must know him. Escaping from the schoolroom, I ransacked the library, and at last my ardour was rewarded. The book – a small pocket edition in red boards, no doubt long out of print – opened at the 'Sensitive Plant'. Was I disappointed? I think I had expected to understand better; but I had no difficulty in assuming that I was satisfied and delighted. And henceforth the little volume never left my pocket, and I read the dazzling stanzas by the shores of a pale green Irish lake, comprehending little, and loving a great deal. Byron, too, was often with me, and these poets were the ripening influence of years otherwise merely nervous and boisterous.

And my poets were taken to school, because it pleased me to read 'Queen Mab' and 'Cain', amid the priests and ignorance of a hateful Roman Catholic college. And there my poets saved me from intellectual savagery; for I was incapable at that time of learning anything. What determined and incorrigible idleness! I used to gaze fondly on a book, holding my head between my hands, and allow my thoughts to wander far into dreams and thin imaginings. Neither Latin, nor Greek, nor French, nor History, nor English composition could I learn, unless, indeed, my curiosity or personal interest was excited – then I made rapid strides in that branch of knowledge to which my attention was directed. A mind hitherto dark seemed suddenly to grow clear, and it remained clear and bright enough so long as passion was in me; but as it died, so the mind clouded, and recoiled to its original obtuseness. Couldn't and wouldn't were in my case curiously involved; nor have I in this respect ever been able to correct my natural temperament. I have always remained powerless to do anything unless moved by a powerful desire.

The natural end to such schooldays as mine was expulsion. I was expelled when I was sixteen, for idleness and general worthlessness. I returned to a wild country home, where I found my father engaged in training racehorses. For a nature of such intense vitality as mine, an ambition, an aspiration of some sort was necessary; and I now, as I have often done since, accepted the first ideal to hand. In this instance it was the *stable*. I was given a hunter, I rode to hounds every week, I rode gallops every morning, I read the racing calendar, stud-book, latest betting, and looked forward with enthusiasm to the day when I should be known as a successful steeplechase rider. To ride the winner of the Liverpool seemed to me a final achievement and glory; and had not accident intervened, it is very possible that I might have succeeded in carrying off, if not the meditated honour, something scarcely inferior, such as – alas! I cannot now recall the name of a race of the necessary value and importance. About this time my father was elected Member of Parliament; our home was broken up, and we went to London. But an ideal set up on its pedestal is not easily displaced, and I persevered in my love, despite the poor promises London life held out for its ultimate attainment; and surreptitiously I continued to nourish it with small bets made in a small tobacconist's. Well do I remember that shop, the oily-faced, sandy-whiskered proprietor, his betting-book, the cheap cigars along the counter, the one-eyed nondescript who leaned his evening away against the counter, and was supposed to know some one who knew Lord —'s footman, and the great man often spoken of, but rarely seen – he who made 'a two-'undred pound book on the Derby'; and the constant coming and going of the cabmen – 'Half an ounce of shag, sir.' I was then at a military tutor's in the Eastern Road; for, in answer to my father's question as to what occupation I intended to pursue, I had consented to enter the army. In my heart I knew that when it came to the point I should refuse – the idea of military discipline was very repugnant, and the possibility of an anonymous death on a battle-field could not be accepted by so self-conscious a youth, by one so full of his own personality. I said Yes to my father, because the moral courage to say No was lacking, and I put my trust in the future, as well I might, for a fair prospect of idleness lay before me, and the chance of my passing any examination was, indeed, remote.

From CONFESSIONS OF A YOUNG MAN

George Moore (1852–1933), novelist, was born at Moore Hall, Co. Mayo. He became a writer after failing as a painter, and established himself with *Esther Waters* (1894), based on his father's interest in horse-racing. His *Hail and Farewell* is an amusing and often mischievous account of his life in Dublin during the period of the Irish literary revival.

FRANK HARRIS

Calf Love

When I was between four and five, I was sent with Annie to a girls' boarding school in Kingstown kept by a Mrs Frost. I was put in the class with the oldest girls on account of my proficiency in arithmetic, and I did my best at it because I wanted to be with them, though I had no conscious reason for my preference. I remember how the nearest girl used to lift me up and put me in my high-chair and how I would hurry over the sums set in compound long division and proportion; for as soon as I had finished, I would drop my pencil on the floor and then turn around and climb down out of my chair, ostensibly to get it, but really to look at the girls' legs. Why? I couldn't have said.

I was at the bottom of the class and the legs got bigger and bigger towards the end of the long table and I preferred to look at the big ones.

As soon as the girl next to me missed me she would move her chair back and call me. I'd pretend to have just found my slate pencil which, I said, had rolled; and she'd lift me back into my high-chair.

One day I noticed a beautiful pair of legs on the other side of the table near the top. There must have been a window behind the girl, for her legs up to the knees were in full light.. They filled me with emotion, giving me an indescribable pleasure. They were not the thickest legs, which surprised me. Up to that moment I had thought it was the thickest legs I liked best but now I saw that several girls, three anyway, had bigger legs; but none like hers, so shapely, with such slight ankles and tapering lines. I was enthralled and at the same time a little scared.

I crept back into my chair with one idea in my little head: could I get close to those lovely legs and perhaps touch them – breathless expectancy! I knew I could hit my slate pencil and make it roll up between the files of legs. Next day I did this and crawled right up till I was close to the legs that made my heart beat in my throat and yet give me a strange delight. I put out my hand to touch them. Suddenly the thought came that the girl would simply be frightened by my touch and pull her legs back and I should be discovered and – I was frightened.

I returned to my chair to think and soon found the solution. Next day I again crouched before the girl's legs, choking with emotion. I put my pencil near her toes and reached round between her legs with my left hand as if to get it, taking care to touch her calf. She shrieked and drew back her legs, holding my hand tight between them, and cried: 'What are you doing there?'

'Getting my pencil,' I said humbly. 'It rolled.'

'There it is,' she said, kicking it with her foot.

'Thanks,' I replied, overjoyed, for the feel of her soft legs was still on my hand.

'You're a funny little fellow,' she said. But I didn't care. I had had my first taste of paradise and the forbidden fruit – authentic heaven!

I have no recollection of her face – it seemed pleasant, that's all I remember. None of the girls made any impression on me but I can still recall the thrill of admiration and pleasure her shapely limbs gave me.

I record this incident at length because it stands alone in my memory and because it shows that sex feeling may manifest itself in early childhood.

One day about 1890 I had Meredith, Walter Pater and Oscar Wilde dining with me in Park Lane and the time of sex-awakening was discussed. Both Pater and Wilde spoke of it as a sign of puberty. Pater thought it began about thirteen or fourteen and Wilde to my amazement set it as late as sixteen. Meredith alone was inclined to put it earlier.

'It shows sporadically,' he said, 'and sometimes before puberty.'

I recalled the fact that Napoleon tells how he was in love before he was five years old with a schoolmate called Giacominetta, but even Meredith laughed at this and would not believe that any real sex feeling could show itself so early. To prove the point I gave my experience as I have told it here and brought Meredith to pause. 'Very interesting,' he thought, 'but peculiar!'

'In her abnormalities,' says Goethe, 'nature reveals her secrets.' Here is an abnormality, perhaps as such, worth noting.

From My Life and Loves

Frank – real names James Thomas – Harris (1856–1931), author, editor, literary critic and biographer, was born of Welsh parents, probably in Galway, and spent most of his early years in Ireland. After many travelling and, by his own account, amorous adventures, he settled in London, becoming successively editor of the *Evening News*, *Fortnightly Review*, and *Saturday Review*, of which George Bernard Shaw was his dramatic critic.

No Business Calling

My uncles had an impression that the Government should give them employment, preferably sinecure, if nothing else could be found; and I suppose this was why my father, after essaying a clerkship or two (one of them in an ironworks), at last had his position recognized by a post in the Four Courts, perhaps because his sister had married the brother of a law baron. Anyhow, the office he held was so undeniably superfluous that it actually got abolished before I was born, and my father naturally demanded a pension as compensation for the outrage. Having got it, he promptly sold it, and set up in business as a merchant dealing wholesale (the family dignity made retail business impossible) on flour and its cereal concomitants. He had an office and warehouse in Jervis-street in the city, and he had a mill in Dolphin's Barn on the country side of the canal, at the end of a rather pretty little village street called Rutland-avenue. The mill has now fallen to pieces, but some relics of it are still to be seen from the field with the millpond behind Rutland House at the end of the avenue, with its two stone eagles on the gateposts. My father used to take me sometimes to this mill before breakfast (a long walk for a child), and I used to like playing about it. I do not think it had any other real use, for it never paid its way; and the bulk of my father's business was commissioned: he was a middleman. I should mention that as he knew nothing about the flour business, and as his partner, a Mr [George] Clibborn, having been apprenticed to the cloth trade knew if possible less, the business, purchased readymade, must have proceeded by its own momentum, and produced its results, such as they were, automatically in spite of its proprietors. They did not work the industry: it worked them. It kept alive, but did not flourish. Early in its history the bankruptcy of its customers dealt it such a blow that my father's partner broke down in tears, though he was fortified by a marriage with a woman of property, and could afford to regard his business as only a second string to his bow. My father, albeit ruined, found the magnitude of the catastrophe so irresistibly amusing that he had to retreat hastily from the office to an empty corner of the warehouse, and laugh until he was exhausted. The business struggled on and even supported my father until he died, enabling him to help his family a little after they had solved a desperate financial situation by emigrating to London: or, to put it another way, by deserting him. His last years were soothed and disembarrassed by this step. He never, as far as I know, made the slightest movement towards a reunion, and none of us ever dreamt of there being any unkindness in the arrangement. In our family we did not bother about conventionalities or sentimentalities.

Our ridiculous poverty was too common in our class, and not conspicuous enough in a poor country, to account wholly for our social detachment from my father's family, a large and (for Ireland) not unprosperous one. . . .

And now you will ask why, with such unexceptional antecedents and social openings, was I not respectably brought up? Unfortunately or fortunately (it all depends on how you look at it), my father had a habit which eventually closed all doors to him, and consequently to my mother, who could not very well be invited without him. If you asked him to a dinner or to a party, he was not always quite sober when he arrived; and he was invariably scandalously drunk when he left. Now, a convivial drunkard may be exhilarating in convivial company. Even a quarrelsome or boastful drunkard may be found entertaining by people who are not particular. But a miserable drunkard – and my father, in theory a teetotaler, was racked with shame and remorse even in his cups – is unbearable. We were finally dropped socially. After my early childhood I cannot remember ever paying a visit at a relative's house. If my mother and father had dined out, or gone to a party, their children would have been much more astonished than if the house had caught fire. . . .

I decided, at thirteen or thereabouts, that for the moment I must go into business and earn some money and begin to be a grown-up man. There was at that time, on one of the quays in Dublin, a firm of cloth merchants, by name Scott, Spain, and Rooney. A friend of ours knew Scott, and asked him to give me a start in life with some employment. I called on this gentleman by appointment. I had the vaguest notion of what would happen: all I knew was that I was 'going into an office'. I thought I should have preferred to interview Spain, as the name was more romantic. Scott turned out to be a smart handsome man, with moustachios; and I suppose a boy more or less in his warehouse did not matter to him when there was a friend to be obliged: at all events, he said only a few perfunctory things and was settling my employment, when, as my stars would have it, Rooney appeared. Mr Rooney was much older, not at all smart, but long, lean, grave, and respectable.

The last time I saw the late Sir George Alexander (the actor) he described to me his own boyhood, spent in a cloth warehouse in Cheapside, where they loaded him with bales, and praised him highly for his excellent conduct, even rewarding him after some years to the extent of sixteen shillings a week. Rooney saved me from the bales. He talked to me a little, and then said quite decisively that I was too young, and that the work was not suitable to me. He evidently considered that my introducer, my parents, and his young partner had been inconsiderate; and I presently descended the stairs, reprieved and unemployed. As Mr Rooney was certainly fifty then at least, he must be a centenarian if, as I hope, he still lives. If he does, I offer him the assurance that I have not forgotten his sympathy.

A year later, or thereabouts, my uncle Frederick, an important official in the Valuation Office, whom no land agent or family solicitor in Dublin could afford to disoblige, asked a leading and terribly respectable firm of land agents, carrying on business at 15 Molesworth-street, to find a berth for me. They did so; and I became their office boy (junior clerk, I called myself) at eighteen shillings a month. It was a very good opening for anyone with a future as a land agent, which in Ireland at that time was a business of professional rank. It was utterly thrown away on me. However, as the office was overstaffed with gentlemen apprentices, who had paid large fees for the privilege of singing operatic selections with me when the principals were out, there was nothing to complain of socially, even for a Shaw; and the atmosphere was as uncommercial as that of an office can be. Thus I learnt business habits without being infected with the business spirit. By the time I had attained to thirty shillings a month, the most active and responsible official in the office, the cashier, vanished; and as we were private bankers to some extent, our clients drawing cheques on us, and so forth, someone had to take his place without an hour's delay. An elder substitute grumbled at the strange job, and, though an able man, in his way, could not make his cash balance. It became necessary, after a day or two of confusion, to try the office boy as a stopgap whilst the advertisements for a new cashier of appropriate age and responsibility were going forward. Immediately the machine worked again quite smoothly. I, who never knew how much money I had of my own (except when the figure was zero), proved a model of accuracy as to the money of others. I acquired my predecessor's very neat handwriting, my own being too sloped and straggly for the cash book. The efforts to fill my important place more worthily slackened. I bought a tailed coat, and was chaffed about it by the apprentices. My salary was raised to £48 a year, which was as much as I expected at sixteen and much less than the firm would have had to pay to a competent adult: in short, I made good in spite of myself, and found, to my dismay, that Business, instead of expelling me as the worthless impostor I was, was fastening upon me with no intention of letting me go.

From Preface to IMMATURITY

George Bernard Shaw (1856–1950), dramatist and critic, was born in Dublin and emigrated to London, where he was an effective member of the Fabian Society. His best-known plays today are *Saint Joan* and *Pygmalion*, on which the musical *My Fair Lady* is based.

First School

From Rathgar Villa it was that I first went to Sunday-school at Zion Church, and fell under the dominion of a certain Miss Rose, whom I revered with the peculiar worship which a small boy often renders to a pretty woman old enough to be his mother. Later I was transplanted to a higher plane of religious culture, under a Miss Duner or Dooner. Here I became familiar with the books of Samuel and Kings, with all their very dubious morality, and carried off my first prizes at the yearly examination – *Jessica's First Prayer*, by Hesba Stretton – a book I would gladly re-read; and *First Lessons in Kindness to Animals* – a very superfluous reinforcement of my zoophilist propensities.

It was now judged fit I should go to school. So far I had got to read tolerably for my years; to write a laborious round hand; and to perform operations in Long Division with very uncertain results. I was certainly not one of those studious children, who have been through Scott before the age of seven and are deep in their Virgil at nine. As soon as lessons ceased to be a privilege and became an obligation I took the attitude of a minimizer and did as little as I could.

Dr North, to whose school my brother went, had a preparatory class taught by a Miss Segar (we called her Miss Cigar, of course), and later by a Miss Ball; and there I first faced the world in the form of some dozen little brats, whose names and natures I remember but need not retail. We sat on three forms, making a broken square; and Miss Segar or Miss Ball was enchaired where the fourth side should have been. We screamed footy little hymns and songs; repeated columns of Mavor's spelling-book with tin edges; read 'Little Arthur's History' and similar rubbish; chanted our tables, scratched on our slates and smudged our copy-books. Thanks to my mother's teaching I easily passed as a 'good boy', and was only once in jeopardy of Miss Ball's cane, owing to my holding my pen as I hold it at this moment, close to the point, between index and thumb. Do writing masters never reflect that hands are constructed differently? When I held it in the orthodox fashion my hand shook and large blobs of ink defiled the virgin page, for which I got scolded. Hence I learned to keep my eye on Miss Ball, and when she looked at me I held my pen correctly and affected abstraction, as it were pausing in my labour; when she looked away I produced satisfactory results in my own unorthodox way. My God! how like my present methods!

Every Saturday the best boy got a silver medal, which he wore gloriously on a piece of blue ribbon till the next week; and as I carried off this trophy time after time I became a sort of Joseph among my brethren, though I retained three or four friends in spite of my success.

Later I was advanced to male tuition, under a certain Mr Johnson, for whom I entertained an enormous and uncritical veneration. Now it was that I entered the thorny ways of the five Latin declensions and exercises in the same, and was advanced to Sullivan's spelling-book, with 'words pronounced exactly alike but different in meaning and spelling' – a rude awakening to the unnecessary complications of life – and to Anderson's geography, with its barren lists of names and brutal disregard of the needs of the young imagination. Those books, and others like them, had much to do with making me the idler I eventually became.

It was not my mother's fault if I did not know my lessons. Every morning, after breakfast, she drilled me in my declensions and other tasks, which I was piously believed to have prepared the night before. But I was fond of play and hated books, and, to avoid my mother's anger, I would often pretend that the appointed lesson was a repetition of the previous one which I knew. Hence catastrophes at school and bad marks in my Judgment Book, which of course perplexed my mother. Then I would leave the Judgment Book at home or else at school, or would lose it altogether. But, being a clever child, I applied to deceit the industry I should have applied to my books, and was rarely detected if at all. I could usually pick up from other boys, as we walked to school together, enough to pass muster; and, in short, the struggle for existence soon evolved my scheming capacities to a very surprising degree of perfection. My mother began to resign herself to the fact that I was rather a stupid boy, little knowing that my cleverness had simply been directed into a wrong channel. I never had the brains of my brother Willie, but had I been *interested* in books I should have done very well, if not brilliantly. But no attempt was made to get me interested, whereas my plays and diversions gave scope for my natural inventiveness and imagination. Thus it was, I think, that I began to cut myself off and lead a secret scheming life of my own.

To make, construct, produce, was then, as ever since, the dominant

135

need and desire of my life. My mother always considered me destructive, for my few weekly pence (2d. a week, later raised to 3d.) always went in toys, which were soon subjected to a searching analysis and reduced to their primitive elements. These and like purchases, for years after, were classified opprobriously as Crickle-Wockle, in reference to a wooden steam-engine which I secured at this time, which made a mysterious sound not inaptly so represented. But my interest was to know how that sound was made, and to deny mystery as long as it was possible to do so. To make the like and improve on it was really the motive of all my destruction. If my educators had only understood this propensity, and made it the basis of my mental training, what wasted years would have been saved! Even at that age I began to be referred to by my mother in domestic emergencies requiring mechanical and practical suggestion, and to this day, when my mind is turned in so different a direction, I pride myself on meeting such difficulties in the simplest and readiest way; if possible without going out of the room, for there is always something within reach that will do, if one will but think. This element was quite wanting in my brother, who could no more put a nail in straight than save his soul.

Extemporized games and plays, that involved invention, were part of my idleness, but rule-governed games I never cared for, for many reasons of which I may speak later. Climbing trees and walls, and walking on narrow ledges and getting out of the house and into it by non-natural and illegitimate ways, were all congenial diversions at this time.

I remember a good many passionate outbursts of blind animal anger in these days, chiefly over my morning repetition of lessons; and how my mother, rather cruelly perhaps, wrote an account of my misdeeds to my hero and divinity, Mr Johnson, who spoke to me solemnly about Our Lord's obedience to His Mother, and made me horribly mortified and ashamed, and therefore much worse instead of much better. To have lost caste in the eyes of one's deity is always a source of moral weakening.

From AUTOBIOGRAPHY

———◦◦———

George Tyrrell (1861–1909), theologian and philosopher, was born in Dublin and became a Jesuit in 1880. Because of his 'modernism' he was expelled from the order in 1906, and died before he could justify his stance.

KATHERINE TYNAN

A Memory

This is just the weather, a wet May and blowing,
  All the shining, shimmering leaves tossing low and high,
When my father used to say: ''Twill be the great mowing!
  God's weather's good weather, be it wet or dry.'

Blue were his eyes and his cheeks were so ruddy,
  He was out in all weathers, up and down the farm;
With the pleasant smile and the word for a wet body:
  'Sure, the weather's God's weather. Who can take the harm?'

With a happy word he'd silence all repining
  While the hay lay wet in field and the cattle died,
When the rain rained every day and no sun was shining:
  'Ah, well, God is good,' he'd say, even while he sighed.

In the parched summer with the corn not worth saving,
  Every field bare as your hand and the beasts to feed,
Still he kept his heart up, while other folk were raving:
  'God will send the fodder: 'tis He that knows the need.'

A wet May, a wild May; he used to rise up cheery
  In the grey of the morning for market and for fair.
Now he sleeps the whole year long, though days be bright, be drea
  In God's weather that's good weather he sleeps without a care.

Now, 'tis just the weather, a wild May and weeping,
  How the blackbird sang and sang 'mid the tossing leaves!
When my father used to say: ''Twill be the great reaping:
  God send fine weather to carry home the sheaves!'

137

Katherine Tynan (1861–1931), poet and novelist, was born in Dublin. She always had to contribute to the family income and when her lawyer husband, H. A. Hinkson, died in 1919 she increased her output, which in total included over a hundred novels and eighteen volumes of verse.

W. B. YEATS

The Facts of Life

Because I had found it hard to attend to anything less interesting than
my thoughts, I was difficult to teach. Several of my uncles and aunts had
tried to teach me to read, and because they could not, and because I was
much older than children who read easily, had come to think, as I have
learnt since, that I had not all my faculties. But for an accident they
might have thought it for a long time. My father was staying in the house
and never went to church, and that gave me the courage to refuse to set
out one Sunday morning. I was often devout, my eyes filling with tears
at the thought of God and of my own sins, but I hated church. My
grandmother tried to teach me to put my toes first to the ground because
I suppose I stumped on my heels, and that took my pleasure out of the
way there. Later on when I had learnt to read I took pleasure in the
words of the hymn, but never understood why the choir took three times
as long as I did in getting to the end; and the part of the service I liked,
the sermon and passages of the Apocalypse and Ecclesiastes, were no
compensation for all the repetitions and for the fatigue of so much
standing. My father said if I would not go to church he would teach me
to read. I think now that he wanted to make me go for my grandmother's
sake and could think of no other way. He was an angry and impatient
teacher and flung the reading-book at my head, and next Sunday I
decided to go to church. My father had, however, got interested in
teaching me, and only shifted the lesson to a week-day till he had
conquered my wandering mind. My first clear image of him was fixed on
my imagination, I believe, but a few days before the first lesson. He had
just arrived from London and was walking up and down the nursery
floor. He had a very black beard and hair, and one cheek bulged out
with a fig that was there to draw the pain out of a bad tooth. One of the
nurses (a nurse had come from London with my brothers and sisters)
said to the other that a live frog, she had heard, was best of all. Then I
was sent to a dame-school kept by an old woman who stood us in rows

and had a long stick like a billiard cue to get at the back rows. My father was still at Sligo when I came back from my first lesson and asked me what I had been taught. I said I had been taught to sing, and he said, 'Sing, then', and I sang –

> *Little drops of water,*
> *Little grains of sand,*
> *Make the mighty ocean*
> *And the pleasant land*

high up in my head. So my father wrote to the old woman that I was never to be taught to sing again, and afterwards other teachers were told the same thing. Presently my elder sister came on a long visit and she and I went to a little two-storeyed house in a poor street where an old gentlewoman taught us spelling and grammar. When we had learned our lesson well, we were allowed to look at a sword presented to her father who had led troops in India or China and to spell out a long complimentary inscription on the silver scabbard. As we walked to her house or home again we held a large umbrella before us, both gripping the handle and guiding ourselves by looking out of a round hole gnawed in the cover by a mouse. When I had got beyond books of one syllable, I began to spend my time in a room called the library, though there were no books in it that I can remember except some old novels I never opened and a many-volumed encyclopaedia published towards the end of the eighteenth century. I read this encyclopaedia a great deal and can remember a long passage considering whether fossil wood despite its appearance might not be only a curiously shaped stone.

My father's unbelief had set me thinking about the evidences of religion and I weighed the matter perpetually with great anxiety, for I did not think I could live without religion. All my religious emotions were, I think, connected with clouds and cloudy glimpses of luminous sky, perhaps because of some Bible picture of God's speaking to Abraham or the like. At least I can remember the sight moving me to tears. One day I got a decisive argument for belief. A cow was about to calve, and I went to the field where the cow was with some farm-hands who carried a lantern, and next day I heard that the cow had calved in the early morning. I asked everybody how calves were born, and because nobody would tell me, made up my mind that nobody knew. They were the gift of God, that much was certain, but it was plain that nobody had ever dared to see them come, and children must come in the same way. I made up my mind that when I was a man I would wait up till calf or child had come. I was certain there would be a cloud and a burst of light and God would bring the calf in the cloud out of the light. That thought made me content until a boy of twelve or thirteen, who had come on a visit for the day, sat beside me in a hay-loft and explained all the mechanism of sex. He had learnt all about it from an elder boy whose pathic he was (to use a term he would not have understood) and his description, given, as I can see now, as if he were telling of any other fact of physical life, made me miserable for weeks. After the first impression wore off, I began to doubt if he had spoken truth, but one day I discovered a passage in the encyclopaedia that, though I only partly understood its long words, confirmed what he had said. I did not know enough to be shocked at his relation to the elder boy, but it was the first breaking of the dream of childhood.

My realization of death came when my father and mother and my two brothers and my two sisters were on a visit. I was in the library when I heard feet running past and heard somebody say in the passage that my younger brother, Robert, had died. He had been ill for some days. A little later my sister and I sat at the table, very happy, drawing ships with their flags half-mast high. We must have heard or seen that the ships in the harbour had their flags at half-mast. Next day at breakfast I heard people telling how my mother and the servant had heard the banshee crying the night before he died. It must have been after this that I told my grandmother I did not want to go with her when she went to see old bed-ridden people because they would soon die.

From AUTOBIOGRAPHIES

———◦◦———

W. B. Yeats (1865–1939), poet and dramatist, was born in Dublin and studied to be an artist before determining to write about Irish subjects, and to express his nationalism in cultural rather than political ways. He founded the Abbey Theatre with Lady Gregory and J. M. Synge, and was a senator of the Irish Free State. He was awarded the Nobel Prize for Literature in 1923. Though his *Collected Poems* were published in 1933, and *Collected Plays* in 1934, he was writing vigorously up to his death.

Command Performance

Robert was a nervous, warm-hearted boy, dark-eyed and romantic-looking; the sensitive nature that expanded to affection was always his, and made him cling to those who were kind to him. The vigorous and outdoor life of Ross was the best tonic for such a nature, the large and healthful intimacy with lake and woods, bog and wild heather, and shooting and rowing, learned unconsciously from a father who delighted in them, and a mother who knew no fear for herself and had little for her children. Everything in those early days of his was large and vigorous; tall trees to climb, great winds across the lake to wrestle with, strenuous and capable talk upstairs and downstairs, in front of furnaces of turf and logs, long drives, and the big Galway welcome at the end of them. One day was like another, yet no day was monotonous. Prayers followed breakfast, long prayers, beginning with the Psalms, of which each child read a verse in due order of seniority; then First and Second Lessons, frequently a chapter from a religious treatise, finally a prayer, from a work named 'The Tent and Altar', all read with excellent emphasis by the master of the house. In later years, after Robert had matriculated at Trinity College, I remember with what youthful austerity he read prayers at Ross, and with what awe we saw him reject 'The Tent and Altar' and heard him recite from memory the Morning Prayers from the Church Service. He was at the same time deputed to teach Old Testament history to his brothers and sisters; to this hour the Judges of Israel are painfully stamped on my brain, as is the tearful morning when the Bible was hurled at my inattentive head by the hand of the remorseless elder brother.

Robert's early schoolroom work at Ross was got through with the ease that may be imagined by anyone who has known his quickness in assimilating ideas and his cast-iron memory. As was the case with all the Ross children, the real interests of the day were with the workmen and the animals. The agreeability of the Galway peasant was enthralling;

even to a child; the dogs were held in even higher esteem. Throughout Robert's life dogs knew him as their friend; skilled in the lore of the affections they recognized his gentle heart, and the devotion to him of his Gordon setter, Rose, is a thing to remember. Even of late years I have seen him hurry away when his sterner sisters thought it necessary to chastise an offending dog; the suffering of others was almost too keenly understood by him.

Reading aloud rounded off the close of those early days at Ross, Shakespeare and Walter Scott, Napier and Miss Edgeworth; the foundation of literary culture was well and truly laid, and laid with respect and enthusiasm, so that what the boy's mind did not grasp was stored up for his later understanding, among other things to be venerated, and fine diction and choice phrase were imprinted upon an ear that was ever retentive of music. Everyone who remembers his childhood remembers him singing songs and playing the piano. His ear was singularly quick, and I think it was impossible for him to sing out of tune. He learned his notes in the schoolroom, but his musical education was dropped when he went to school, as is frequently the case; throughout his life he accompanied himself on the piano by ear, with ease, if with limitations; simple as the accompaniments were, there was never a false note, and it seemed as if his hands fell on the right places without an effort.

A strange feature in his early education and in the establishment at Ross was James Tucker, an ex-hedge schoolmaster, whose long face, blue shaven chin, shabby black clothes, and gift for poetry have passed inextricably into the annals of the household. He entered it first at the time of the Famine, ostensibly to give temporary help in the management and accounts of the school which my aunt Marian had started for the tenants' children; he remained for many years, and filled many important posts. He taught us the three Rs with rigour and perseverance, he wrote odes for our birthdays, he was controller-in-chief of the dairy; later on, when my father received the appointment of Auditor of Poor Law, under the Local Government Board, Tucker filled in the blue 'abstracts' of the Auditor's work in admirably neat columns. Robert's recital of the multiplication table was often interrupted by wails for 'Misther Tucker' and the key of the dairy, from the kitchen-maid at the foot of the schoolroom stairs, and the interruption was freely cursed, in a vindictive whisper, by the schoolmaster. Tucker was slightly eccentric, a feature for which there was always toleration and room at Ross; he entered largely into the schoolroom theatricals that sprang up as soon as Robert was old enough to whip up a company from the ranks of his brothers and sisters. The first of which there is any record is the tragedy of 'Bluebeard', adapted by him at the age of eight. As the author did not feel equal to writing it down, it was taught to the actors by word of mouth, he himself taking the title *rôle*. The performance took place privately in the schoolroom, an apartment discreetly placed by the authorities in a wing known as 'The Offices', beyond ken or call of the house proper. Tucker was stage manager, every servant in the house was commandeered as audience. The play met with much acceptance up to the point when Bluebeard dragged Fatima (a shrieking sister) round the room by her hair, belabouring her with a wooden sword, amid the ecstatic yells of the spectators, but at this juncture the mistress of the house interrupted the revels with paralysing suddenness. She had in vain rung the drawing-room bell for tea; she had searched and found the house mysteriously silent and empty, till the plaudits of the rescue scene drew her to the schoolroom. Players and audience broke into rout, and Robert's first dramatic enterprise ended in disorder, and, if I mistake not, for the principals, untimely bed.

It was some years afterwards, when Robert was at Trinity, that a similar effort on his part of missionary culture ended in a like disaster. He became filled with the idea of getting up a cricket team at Ross, and in a summer vacation he collected his eleven, taught them to hold a bat, and harangued them eloquently on the laws of the game. It was unfortunate that its rules became mixed up in the minds of the players with a game of their own, called 'Burnt Ball', which closely resembles 'Rounders', and is played with a large, soft ball. In the first day of cricket things progressed slowly, and the unconverted might have been forgiven for finding the entertainment a trifle dull. A batsman at length hit a ball and ran. It was fielded by cover-point, who, bored by long inaction, had waited impatiently for his chance. In the enthusiasm of at length getting something to do, the recently learned laws of cricket were swept from the mind of cover-point, and the rules of Burnt Ball instantly reasserted themselves. He hurled the ball at the batsman, shouting : 'Go out! You're burnt!' and smote him heavily on the head.

The batsman went out, that is to say, he picked himself up and tottered from the fire zone, and neither then nor subsequently did cricket prosper at Ross.

From Memoir of her brother Robert

Martin Ross was the pen-name of Violet Florence Martin (1862–1915), novelist, who was born at Ross House, Co. Galway. With her cousin Edith Somerville she wrote many books, including *Some Experiences of an Irish R.M.* and *The Real Charlotte*. Her brother Robert died in 1905.

EDITH SOMERVILLE *and* MARTIN ROSS

The Picnic

The first picnic in which I clearly recall taking part was, like many that succeeded it, illicit. It unconsciously adhered to the great and golden precept that picnics should be limited in number and select in company. It consisted, in fact, of no more than four, which, with a leggy deerhound, a turf fire, and the smoke from the turf fire, were as much as could be fitted in. Why a ruinous lime-kiln should have been chosen is not worth inquiring into. It probably conformed best with those ideals of cave-dwelling, secrecy, and rigorous discomfort that are treasured by the young. We were, indeed, excessively young, and should have been walking in all godliness with the governess; two of us at least should. The other two were turf-boys, who should have been carrying baskets of turf on their backs into the kitchen, and submitting themselves reverently to the innumerable oppressions of the cook, who, they assured us, had already pitched them to the Seventeen Divils three times that same day. The lime-kiln was sketchily roofed with branches, thatched with sedge and was entered by the hole at which the smoke came out. It was a feat of some skill to lower oneself through this hole, avoid the fire, grope for the table – a packing-case – with one toe, and thence fall on top of the rest of the party. Except in the item of sociability I do not think that the deerhound can have enjoyed himself much; he spent most of the time in dodging the transits of the kettle, and it was our malign custom to wipe the knives on his back, in places just beyond the flaps of a tongue as long and red as a slice of ham. What we ate is best forgotten. Something disgusting with carraway seeds in it, kneaded by our own filthy hands, lubricated with lard, and baked in a frying pan in the inmost heart of the turf smoke. The drink was claret, stolen from the dining-room, and boiled with a few handfuls of the snow that lay sparsely under the fir trees round the lime-kiln. Why the claret should have been boiled with snow is hard to explain. I think it must have been due to its suggestion of Polar expeditions and Roman Feasts; subjects both of them, that lent themselves to learned and condescending explanation to the turf-boys. Afterwards, when the elder turf-boy, Sonny Walsh, produced a pack of cards from a cavity in his coat that had begun life as a pocket, and dealt them out for 'Spoilt Five' it was the turf-boys' turn to condescend. 'Spoilt Five' is not in any sense child's play; its rules are complicated, and its play overlaid with weird usages and expressions. For the uninitiated it was out of the question to distinguish kings from queens, or the all-important 'Five-Fingers' from any other five, through the haze of dirt with which all were befogged. The turf-boys knew them as the shepherd knows his flock, and at the end of the game had become possessors of our stock-in-trade, consisting of a Manx halfpenny, a slate pencil with plaid paper gummed round its shank, two lemon drops, and a livery button.

This was a good and thoroughly enjoyable picnic, containing within itself all the elements of success, difficult as these may be to define, and still more difficult as they are to secure.

From Some Irish Yesterdays

———◦◦———

Edith Somerville (1858–1949), artist, novelist and cousin of 'Martin Ross', was born in Corfu, where her father was stationed, but spent most of her life at Drishane, the family home in Co. Cork, where she was Master of the West Carbery Foxhounds.

ALICE MILLIGAN

When I Was a Little Girl

When I was a little girl,
In a garden playing,
A thing was often said
To chide us delaying:

When after sunny hours,
At twilight's falling,
Down through the garden walks
Came our old nurse calling.

'Come in, for it's growing late,
And the grass will wet ye!
Come in! or when it's dark
The Fenians will get ye.'

Then, at this dreadful news,
All helter-skelter,
The panic-struck little flock
Ran home for shelter.

And round the nursery fire
Sat still to listen,
Fifty bare toes on the hearth,
Ten eyes a-glisten.

To hear of a night in March,
And loyal folk waiting,
To see a great army of men
Come devastating.

An army of Papists grim,
With a green flag o'er them,
Red-coats and black police
Flying before them.

But God (Who our nurse declared
Guards British dominions)
Sent down a deep fall of snow
And scattered the Fenians.

'But somewhere they're lurking yet,
Maybe they're near us,'
Four little hearts pit-a-pat
Thought 'Can they hear us?'

Then the wind-shaken pane
Sounded like drumming;
'Oh!' they cried, 'tuck us in,
The Fenians are coming!'

Four little pairs of hands
In the cots where she led those,
Over their frightened heads
Pulled up the bedclothes.

But one little rebel there,
Watching all with laughter,
Thought 'When the Fenians come
I'll rise and go after.'

Wished she had been a boy
And a good deal older –
Able to walk for miles
With a gun on her shoulder.

Able to lift aloft
The Green Flag o'er them
(Red-coats and black police
Flying before them).

And, as she dropped asleep,
Was wondering whether
God, if they prayed to Him,
Would give fine weather.

———◆◆◆———

Alice Milligan (1866–1953), poet, novelist, dramatist and cam-
paigner for Irish independence, was born in Omagh.

J. M. SYNGE

The Nature of Life

Before I went to school I used to go out to walk every day with my maid or my relations. Even at this time I was a worshipper of nature. I remember that I would not allow my nurses to sit down on the seats by the River Dodder because they were man-made. If they wished to sit down they had to find a low branch of a tree or a bit of rock or bank. I do not seem to have lacked a certain authority, for they all obeyed. My brother also had this idea about 'made' things, perhaps he gave it to me. I had a very strong feeling for the colour of locality which I expressed in syllables of no meaning, but my elders checked me for talking gibberish when I was heard practising them.

My brother and I had several elaborate games which were not, I think, usual. There was a legendary character we called 'Squirelly' who was a sort of folk-lore creation. We would spend hours inventing adventures for him to pass through. I was a sort of poet with the frank imagination by which folk lore is created. I imagined myself half human monsters that went through series of supernatural adventures of which I kept a record. . . . I do not think this legendary instinct was suggested by fairy tales. We knew Grimm's alone, and our myths had no relation with the domestic instincts of the Germans. Then we had a number of 'Men' – spools with red flannel belts sewed round them – who lived a most complicated life with war and commerce between our opposite settlements. I sometimes gained in the war but at the commerce I was rarely successful.

I was then about seven, and soon afterwards I made an attempt at literary composition, a poem intended to be a satire on an aunt who had slightly offended me. I remember walking into the drawing-room and telling the company that I had 'invented' a poem. I was proud of the achievement and wanted to read it aloud, but got very nervous in the middle and had to give it up. This was the first time I remember feeling nervous, apart from direct fear*. . . .

---

* His elder brother, Rev. Samuel Synge, remembered a few lines and later quoted them in a letter to his daughter: She called me a greasy pig/And over her greasy wig/She put on her Sunday cap/And gave me a terrible rap.

Although I had the usual affection for my near relations I began while still very young to live in my imagination in enchanted premises that had high walls with glass upon the top where I sat and drank ginger-beer in a sort of perpetual summer with one companion, usually some small school-fellow I hardly knew. One day the course of my class put me for a moment beside my temporary god, and before I could find a fit term of adulation he whispered an obscene banality which shattered my illusions.

Soon afterwards – when I was about ten – my real affections and imagination acted together in a friendship with a girl of my own age who was our neighbour. . . . We had a large establishment of pets – rabbits, pigeons, guinea pigs, canaries, dogs – which we looked after together. I was now going to school, but I had many holidays from ill health – six months about this time especially which were recommended on account of continual head-aches that I suffered from – which gave us a great deal of time to wander about among the fields near our houses. We were left in complete liberty and never abused it. . . . She was, I think, a very pleasant-featured child and must have had an excellent character as for years I do not remember a single quarrel – with brothers, of course, I had plenty, sometimes of considerable violence. She was handy with her pencil and on wet days we used to draw animals from Vere Foster's copy books with great assiduity. . . .

About this time an aunt of mine died in our own house. My mother asked me the day after if I was not sorry. I answered with some hesitation – at this time I was truthful to an almost morbid degree – that I feared not. My mother was much shocked and began telling me little things about my aunt till I wept copiously. In reality the death impressed me with a sort of awe and wonder, but although I was fond of my aunt it did not grieve me – I suppose I did not realize what death meant. The days when the house was darkened – it was August – I spent in some woods near Rathfarnham with my little friend. They were wonderfully delightful, though I hardly remember what we did or talked of.

The sense of death seems to have been only strong enough to evoke the full luxury of the woods. I had never been so happy. It is a feeling like this makes all primitive people inclined to merry making at a funeral.

We were always primitive. We both understood all the facts of life and spoke of them without much hesitation but a certain propriety that was decidedly wholesome. We talked of sexual matters with an indifferent and sometimes amused frankness that was identical with the attitude of folk-tales. We were both superstitious, and if we had been allowed . . . we would have evolved a pantheistic scheme like that of all barbarians. . . . I never spoke of religion with my companion, although we were both well-versed in Christianity. The monotheistic doctrines seem foreign to the real genius of childhood in spite of the rather maudlin appeal Christianity makes to little children. . . .

As I grew older I became more interested in definite life, and I used to hide in bushes to watch with amorous fellowship the mere movements of the birds. People said I had an interesting taste for natural history and gave me books. My girl friend took fire at my enthusiasm and we devoted a great deal of our spare time to observation and reading books on ornithology. Further we clubbed our resources and bought a ten-shilling telescope, which led to trouble afterwards. This period was probably the happiest time of my life. It was admirable in every way.

The following summer, however, I had a horrible awakening. Our two families joined in a large country house in June where some Indian cousins of mine were coming to spend the later months with us. This June was absolutely delightful. I had my friend now under the same roof, and we were inseparable. In the day-time we played tennis or watched the birds . . . and we wandered arm in arm about among the odours of the old-fashioned garden till it was quite dark watching the bats and moths. I loved her with a curious affection that I cannot pretend to analyse and I told her, with more virile authority than I since possess, that she was to be my wife. She was not displeased. My cousins arrived, a small boy and a girl of my own age. My friend threw me over completely, apparently without a shadow of regret, and became the bosom friend of her new companion, my accursed cousin. I was stunned with horror. I complained to no-one, but I fretted myself ill in lonely corners whistling 'Down in Alabama', the only love-song I knew. My mother knew what was in my mind, and contrived occasionally to get me a walk with my old comrade, but our friendship was at an end, for the time at any rate. Thus I learned very young the weakness of the false gods we are obliged to worship. . . .

Before I abandoned science it rendered me an important service. When I was about fourteen I obtained a book of Darwin's. It opened in my hands at a passage where he asks how can we explain the similarity between a man's hand and a bird's or bat's wings except by evolution. I flung the book aside and rushed out into the open air – it was summer and we were in the country – the sky seemed to have lost its blue and the grass its green. I lay down and writhed in an agony of doubt. My studies showed me the force of what I read, and the more I put it from me the more it rushed back with new instances and power. Till then I had never doubted and never conceived that a sane and wise man or boy could doubt. I had of course heard of atheists but as vague monsters that I was unable to realize. It seemed that I was become in a moment the playfellow of Judas. Incest and parricide were but a consequence of the idea that possessed me. My memory does not record how I returned home nor how long my misery lasted. I know only that I got the book out of the house as soon as possible and kept it out of sight, saying to myself logically enough that I was not sufficiently advanced in science to weigh his arguments, so I would do better to reserve his work for future study. In a few weeks I regained my composure, but this was the beginning. Soon afterwards I turned my attention to works of Christian evidence, reading them at first with pleasure, soon with doubt, and at last in some cases with derision.

My study of insects had given me a scientific attitude – probably a crude one – which did not and could not interpret life and nature as I heard it interpreted from the pulpit. By the time I was sixteen or seventeen I had renounced Christianity after a good deal of wobbling, although I do not think I avowed my decision quite so soon. I felt a sort of shame in being thought an infidel, a term which I have always used as a reproach. For a while I denied everything, then I took to reading Carlyle, Leslie Stephen and Matthew Arnold, and made myself a sort of incredulous belief that illuminated nature and lent an object to life without hampering the intellect. This story is easily told, but it was a terrible experience. By it I laid a chasm between my present and my past and between myself and my kindred and friends. Till I was twenty-three I never met or at least knew a man or woman who shared my opinions. Compared with the people about me, compared with the Fellows of Trinity, I seemed a presumptuous boy, yet I felt that the views which I had arrived at after sincere efforts to find what was true represented, in spite of my immediate surroundings, the real opinion of the world.

From AUTOBIOGRAPHY (ed. Alan Price)

———•◦•———

J. M. Synge (1871–1909), dramatist, was born in Rathfarnham, Co. Dublin. He was the first major Irish dramatist to write about Ireland, yet when *The Playboy of the Western World* was originally performed at the Abbey Theatre it caused riots because of its frank nature. Two years later he was dead, of Hodgkin's disease.

Letter to J. M. Synge

July 1st
2 *Fortfield Terrace*

Dear Johnnie,

I am very sorry that you are sick, it is a great pity just as you got down there [Co. Wicklow]. I hope the hens and everything arrived all right and that nothing was smothered this time. I suppose you have heard about that wretched pigeon by this time, she does not care a scrap about her young ones or anything. I am afraid there is not much chance of her coming back for on Sunday evening when Papa was coming home from church he said he was nearly sure he saw her flying about with other pigeons. We are going to try and find out where they live, and perhaps we will be able to get her back that way. It will be an awful sell if we can't get her because she was such a good one. I am afraid we wont be able to get another as good. I don't know how to manage at all because I cant get another pigeon yet because I am afraid she would kill the young ones and then when they are old enough to shift for themselves I suppose another hen would not touch them. If this hen does not come back I will have to keep in the other for a good while after I get her and then the young ones won't be able to learn to fly, and I will have to keep the cock in also. When I am able to let them all out perhaps he will go away and the rest with him. If the young ones had no other pigeons with them when first they got out, I don't suppose they would be likely to go away because they were never in any other place but this. I wonder if I let the cock out now would he go away, he looks so lonely sitting there all day, I don't like to try and yet I hardly think he would, he seems so fond of his young ones and still perhaps he might go to look for the hen and if I wait till they are older and fledged he won't have anything to keep him here and perhaps he will be more likely to go away. Write as soon as you are able and try to solve some of my difficulties. When we are down on Saturday we can have a good talk over them. The little ones are getting on grandly. Their feathers are beginning to grow. I find a good difference in the way my wheat goes now that the youngsters are all getting older. Give my love to Aunt H, Annie, Mary and all, ever yr loving cousin F. A. R. I have not told you all my grievances yet – the cock's feet seem rather sore, they are very dirty but I suppose I can't do anything.

Florence Ross (1870–1949) was a first cousin to J. M. Synge, being the daughter of his mother's sister.

EDWARD STEPHENS

J. M. Synge and the Outside Slice

At this time, Charles Stewart Parnell had been dead six years . . . and his
mansion house was empty. When I asked my mother who had lived
there, she told me that the owner had been a Protestant who had joined
the nationalists and had come to a bad end. Her voice deprecated
further questions. . . .

Near the garden gate of Casino ran a path over which there was a
right-of-way from the Avoca road to the avenue of Avondale. My sister
and I used to watch women walking home that way from Rathdrum
wrapped in black shawls and carrying large baskets. One day a big
merry-looking woman put down her basket and, shaking us by the
hands, said, 'Welcome to Casino.' We were very shy but she, not
seeming to notice it, gave us smooth sugar sweets of which she had a
little bag in her basket. Just then our mother came out and said 'Good
evening' rather stiffly. The woman walked on, and our mother told us
that we must never eat sweets given to us by strangers: this was a very
hard saying because we were very rarely given any by people whom we
knew.

Our mother had a piece of green silk which she used to crimp with her
fingers as a centre-piece in the middle of the dining-room table, and
about this time she gave it to us as a plaything because our father had
splashed it with gravy. Somehow we had heard that the following year
was to be the centenary of the rebellion of 1798. We thought it would be
fun to honour the centenary by waving a green flag, so we mounted the
silk on a long stick and ran with it round the little garden in front of the
house shouting, 'Who fears to speak of '98.' Our mother stopped us and
said that we must be more quiet for fear that people passing the gate
might hear what we were shouting and think that we meant it. I replied:
'But we do mean it,' and she said: 'If I thought you did mean it, I should
not allow you to play that game at all.' We crept quietly away without
pushing the matter further. . . .

My father did not like staying at the steward's house instead of the mansion house of Avondale and his visits, which created a sense of unrest in the family party, were not long. In his absence, the days passed as tranquilly for its members as was usual when they stayed in Co. Wicklow for the summer. My brother and I spent much of our time fishing and on fine days, if we were tired, lay in the grass among innumerable grasshoppers trembling their legs in the sun on a steep bank above the river. On wet days we listened to our grandmother reading *King Solomon's Mines* aloud.

Once, when I had just come up to tea from the river, I unexpectedly threw John into one of those sudden passions which occasionally seized him and then left him amused by his own indignation. I had sat down next him and he had cut himself an outside slice from the loaf. At that time I did not know that he hotly resented remarks about anything he was eating. Just as I began my tea he accused me, whether justly or not I cannot remember, of having come to the table without washing my hands after baiting hooks with worms. I retorted: 'You are eating the microbe parade off the loaf.' He jumped round furiously on his chair and hit me a slap on the head. Partly from surprise and partly, I suspect, to stop myself crying, I put out my tongue at him with the reflex action of a jack-in-the-box, and his temper vanished in a roar of laughter.

From MY UNCLE JOHN (ed. Andrew Carpenter)

Edward Stephens (1888–1955), lawyer and nephew of J. M. Synge (John, in the extract above), was born in Dublin. The original unpublished manuscript of his biography of Synge contained over 750,000 words.

AE (GEORGE RUSSELL)

Upon an Airy Upland

Upon an airy upland
Within me and far away
A child that's ageless dances
All delicately gay.
A dance that is like sunshine
While I am old and grey.

Art thou gone before me
Unto that high air,
Youth that was in my youth?
And shall I meet thee there,
Leaving this weight behind,
Blurred mind and whitening hair?

O do not wander far
Before I too may go,
I have need of thy sunshine
As a lamp here below,
Of thy youth as a staff to lean on
Where the weary mind would go.

———◆◦◆———

George William Russell (1867–1935), artist, journalist, poet and
mystic, was born in Lurgan, Co. Armagh. After studying art, he
worked in a Dublin drapery store, and then for the Irish Agricultural Organization Society. He was editor of the *Irish Homestead*
1905–23, and of the *Irish Statesman* 1923–30.

Farewell to Youth

The following day was a Sunday and everybody was doing his best to get ready for Mass, but when I got out of bed my father was nowhere to be seen. After we came home from Mass, dinner was ready, but there was still no trace of my father nor did anyone know where he had gone to. About six o'clock in the evening he strolled in the door.

'May the morning hoarseness catch you!' said my mother, 'Where were you all day?'

'In Dingle.'

'What did you want there for?'

'To get some place that'd suit that chubby lassie there!'

'And did you get it?'

'There's a place for her in Séamas Curran's house. Don't be a bit uneasy: Nell will be as good as a mother to her.'

'And God help me,' said my mother in a troubled tone of voice, 'what will *I* do?'

'The very best you can, my good woman,' said my father. 'And if there's peace when she's gone so much the better for everyone.'

My mother said no more but put down her head and cried bitterly.

Young as I was, my heart almost broke when I realized what she would have to go through when I was far away from her. I slipped out of the house and went back to the garden; there I sat down and cried my fill. I wasn't thinking of sport nor of play at that time but of the time that lay before me. I was jealous of Cáit-Jim and of the other girls who were as happy as the days are long, playing away for themselves. I thought that the turns of the world are very strange: some people sorrowful and others full of joy. At that particular moment the heart in my breast was broken with sorrow and dissatisfaction. I told myself that if everyone who had a brother's wife in the house was as heart-scalded as I was, then they were all very much to be pitied. My brother, Seán, was a good man but he wore only one leg of the britches.

It was getting late and I came in home; the food was on the table but I

160

didn't eat much of it. Not a syllable out of anyone! They were all subdued, but when the time came for Muiris to arrive he came right in the door and Jim with him. They were chatting and making conversation for a while but they made no great delay because Muiris had a cold.

When my father got the house to himself and the rest were asleep: 'Go to school in the morning, child,' he told me, 'I have to talk to the schoolmaster about you.'

I didn't say a word but drew a sigh. I said my prayers and went to bed. But alas! I didn't get much sleep as I was weighing up the pros and cons of things the whole night long.

Apparently, I must have fallen asleep some time during the night, for it was bright morning when I awoke. I lifted the bedclothes from my head and looked directly in front of me. A sunbeam was coming through the window and a thousand midges were flitting here and there. I kept watching them and before long I saw a spider spinning a thread of slender silk out of his own body and lowering himself from the tie-beam of the rafters. On the bushes outside the little birds were singing sweetly. I heard the cock crowing gaily; he reminded me of the little tale my mother used to tell me some time previously. She had asked me: 'What does the cock say when he crows?'

'I haven't the faintest idea,' I answered.

This is what she said then: 'When Christ's body was placed in the grave the Jews told each other that the Joiner's Son, when He was alive, had boasted that He would rise on the third day. "Maybe," they told each other, "His followers will steal His body and then claim that He has risen from the dead!" "Go," said the President, "and secure the flagstone at the mouth of the tomb." When they had the flagstone well secured they came back and then made a feast and had a celebration. A pot of cockerels was boiling over the fire. "Did you do your business properly?" the President asked and one of the men concerned answered, "Never will He rise until the bird now boiling at the bottom of the pot rises from the dead." This was no sooner said than the cock rose to the edge of the pot, clapped his wings together and called out to the Son of Mary, "*Mac na hÓighe slán!* The Son of the Virgin is safe!" That's what the cock says when he crows,' my mother said.

I recalled that little story as I listened to the cock crowing.

'The High King of Creation be praised and thanked,' I said, 'Who ordained a livelihood for every creature according to nature! Whatever God has in store for me – that will come to pass!' With that I jumped out of bed.

When I was dressed, I washed my face and hands. I hadn't broken my fast but that made no difference for it wasn't the first time I had gone to school on an empty stomach. When I was ready I took my little bag of books and went down the road. I was only barely in time for school as the Rolls were being called as I went in. The Master looked at me out of a corner of his eye but never said a word.

An hour afterwards the latch on the door was lifted and my father came in. I knew well that the time had come and cold sweat broke out through me. My schooldays were over.

My father had a chat with the Master; after a while the teacher came over to me.

'Your father wants you,' he said in a kindly tone. 'Good luck to you, girl!'

I couldn't speak a word because I was too lonely. My father went off out and I followed him. I'm telling you no lie when I say that there was a lump in my throat as I went home.

As soon as I went in – 'Put on your clothes now,' my father said.

'Wait until I eat a bite anyway!' I answered.

I took some food and then put on my clothes. I caught my shawl and looked up towards the corner at my mother who was seated by the fire. Her body was huddled up and she was crying softly. I ran towards her and put my two arms around her.

My father had to come and take me away.

From PEIG (tr. by Bryan MacMahon)

Peig Sayers (1873–1958), story-teller and folklorist, was born at Vicarstown, Co. Kerry, and spent her early life in service. After her marriage, she lived for forty years on Great Blasket Island.

162

Emma

Emma had nursed us all, but none of the others had been so exclusively her property as I was. This arrangement suited me admirably, for I had conceived for her an affection which neither my mother nor anybody else in later life was to oust. Emma came first, and she remained first. In those days I don't suppose I thought about her at all: she was simply there, an essential part of my existence, like the air I breathed or the sun that warmed me. She was even mentioned after everybody else in my 'prayers' – that old parrot song she had taught me, and which, from her knee, I nightly offered up to a deity more drowsy than myself. Certainly her care for me was far beyond any that deities are wont to practise. It had a beautiful quality of mingled tenderness and wisdom, so that I cannot remember the slightest cloud darkening the happiness of those earliest years.

A brother and a sister shared to some extent the day nursery with me, but they were my seniors by several years, and hardly counted in my scheme of things. Of far more immediate interest was the personality of a sagacious old tabby, who would stroll into the nursery and lie on the floor in the sun, and was good-natured enough to purr when I used her as a pillow. I was aware that she timed these visits, and that if she did not find me alone (by which I mean alone with Emma) she would not stay. Not that she was, so far as I recall, a particularly affectionate animal. Cats are never sentimental; they treat you exactly as you treat them; and it was simply that she had marked me down, with unerring instinct, as 'safe' – a person who could be trusted to amuse the kittens while one dozed and dreamed.

Nearly all animals possess this instinct, this gift of divining an innate sympathy or its opposite. I have heard a benevolent old dog growl at the approach of some toddler of three, and have known he had a reason for doing so which bore no resemblance to that suggested either by his astonished master or the indignant parents of the child. Such a sympathy, indeed, can never be acquired; it has nothing to do with a habit of treating animals fairly, which *can* be acquired; it is a thing implanted at birth, a temperamental bias. It was just this bias, I dare say (to take a very ancient instance), which gave its peculiar form to the teaching of Empedocles, and lay behind all that philosopher's hatred of blood sacrifice and of the eating of flesh. In my own case it was broad enough to include even the battered stone lions in University Square, creatures I fed daily in my morning walks. Later on, my mother discouraged this sympathy, believing it exaggerated. She would not allow me to keep a dog, and even a cat was only tolerated because cats were preferable to mice. She herself had no liking for animals. They were all right in their proper place, and of course one must not ill-treat them, but their proper place, I gathered, was at a considerable distance from our house. Emma, though for all I know to the contrary she too may have been indifferent to animals, as usual understood; and so each morning we sallied out with our little parcel of provisions.

And thus I seem to see, as if at the end of an immense vista, these two figures moving sedately through the sunshine, the smaller with his hands clasped behind his back, a habit he clung to even when running. He is dressed each day in a fresh blue or brown or white or even pink sailor suit, and on his head a wide-brimmed straw hat is held firmly by an elastic band that passes under his chin. Beside this figure walks (though never holding his hand) the figure of Emma, clad in a long dark green double-breasted coat, and carrying in one black-gloved hand a parcel of bread, and in the other an umbrella. Their destination is the Botanic Gardens *via* University Square and the stone lions, and when they reach the Gardens they keep severely to themselves. Emma never talks to the other nurses, the little boy never talks to the other little boys. They may stop for a minute or two if they should chance to meet lovely Mrs Gerrard or some other of mamma's friends, and the beauty of Mrs Gerrard alone among these friends, the sweetness of her smile, and the soft southern music of her voice, awaken deep down in the little boy a curious thrill. She, too, somehow belongs to his happy world – that most bizarre garden of Epicurus, which includes the Wesleyan Emma, and three such frank pagans as Mrs Gerrard, tabby, and himself. I don't know that I am very successfully concealing the fact that I have a weakness for this little boy. He is shy, and at times, it may be, a little odd in his behaviour, but I cannot help thinking him a not unpleasant person. It is indeed a pity this chronicle should have to take note shortly of a rapid deterioration which set in during the years after Emma had gone home to England – years through which the words 'that odious child!' seem to me now to sound like a perpetual refrain. The words reach me, it is true, always in the voice of my eldest sister, but even comparative strangers recognized their aptness – recognized, at all events, to whom they referred.

From APOSTATE

Forrest Reid (1875–1947), novelist and critic, was born in Belfast, where he lived all his life.

Golden Stockings

Golden stockings you had on
In the meadow where you ran;
And your little knees together
Bobbed like pippins in the weather
When the breezes rush and fight
For those dimples of delight;
And they dance from the pursuit,
And the leaf looks like the fruit.

I have many a sight in mind
That would last if I were blind;
Many verses I could write
That would bring me many a sight.
Now I only see but one,
See you running in the sun;
And the gold-dust coming up
From the trampled butter-cup.

—◆◦◆—

Oliver St John Gogarty (1878–1957), surgeon, politician (he was a
senator of the Irish Free State 1922–36) and poet, was born in
Dublin. During the Civil War he escaped execution by the Republic-
ans by swimming the Liffey under a shower of bullets.

LORD DUNSANY

Cricket and the Shoot

Then came the summer holidays, spent at Dunsany. My preferences were those of most boys, if not all: I preferred cricket, boating and riding, to anything that could be offered indoors; and was lucky enough to have all those pastimes to hand. Shooting I had not yet taken to with the keenness that my father expected, and he was rather disappointed that I did not, though Joseph Reid, the old game-keeper, told him that I would soon take to it and then care for nothing else, a prophecy that was completely fulfilled very soon after it had been uttered. Meanwhile I was learning about the sights of a rifle in an unusual way, which to my father, an excellent shot with rifle and shot-gun, seemed worse than not shooting at all. Nevertheless I learned to shoot with a rifle that way. I used to shoot snails. They were on a wall from which I was separated by several yards by another wall, and I shot them with an air-gun. I could have got nearer, but I never did, and used to shoot the snails at what I thought a fair distance. My father tried to discourage this amusement by comparing it to lion-hunting with all the force of his wit. Nothing he said was unjust; and yet, when I look back on the two pursuits, I will say that I have never seen a lion or a rhinoceros crumple as those snails crumpled. If you hit them fair they simply vanished, whereas a rhinoceros would merely go on charging, and is of course a great deal easier to hit.

It was in these holidays that a cousin, John Hawksley, a boy of my own age, first came to stay at Dunsany. When we were not playing cricket we spent a good deal of time on the river, a river not much known to maps, for its width is artificial, where it runs through the place, nature having only intended it for a stream. The boats were made by the estate carpenter, and were flat-bottomed, and suited therefore to navigation above or below the points at which the stream was widened and deepened to look like a river. Our explorations with these boats would be no aid to geography, our scores at cricket at that time would not be worth recording, even if memory had not forsaken them long ago, but there began for me then a friendship with John Hawksley that lasted till August 8th, 1916, when he was commanding a brigade of artillery on the Somme and, hearing a wounded man calling from Nomansland, went out to him and was killed.

Other friends I had among the young cricketers of Meath, and for many summers we had a team called the Colts, most of whom played for the county when we grew up.

The long shadows of the old towers of my home slanted to the left at evening, touching the dun after which the place is named, a sign to us that summer is ending, and I went back to Eton. That half I was up to Mr Austen Leigh, the Lower Master. Like the family of a mediaeval executioner, dwelling unharmed in his house, but with the dreadful axe in full sight of them leaning against the wall, so we studied in the old schoolroom with the block before us, at which it was the Lower Master's peculiar duty to minister in the interests of the discipline of the whole of the Lower School. But, although he sometimes made grim jokes about his work, the boys who were up to him seem to have been immune.

This was the half in which we played football, coming back when white mists were rising, to warmth and tea. It was at one of these games that I first met George Brooke, a friend from that time until early in the Great War, which ended so many friendships. He came up to me, where I was keeping goal, and touched his cap, with the words: 'And how is your honour today?' I did not know who he was, but he talked to me for about five minutes, while the game had gone to the other end of the ground, entirely in the dialect of an Irish tramp. I was accustomed to people who smiled when they made jokes, and this intensely solemn boy rather puzzled me. The next time that I saw him was in the street at Eton, and he said to me: 'Come here, you boy! It is no use trying to run away; I know your name. And now; what is your name, and who is your house-master? Write me out a hundred lines and bring them to my pupil-room tomorrow.' At this he gravely walked away. A day or two later he was stopping a few of us to preach us a sermon, with a solemnity well suited to the subject, for he had a devilish gift of mimicry.

Cornish's got into the ante-final that year, chiefly owing to one boy, Muntz, who on three occasions got the ball and ran the whole length of the field with it alone and kicked a goal. I remember the present Lord Donoughmore, who was captain of the House XI, putting his own cap on Muntz's head at the end of the game, before they left the ground, giving him the house colours that he had so well earned. Muntz had been some time absent from Eton on account of ill-health, in spite of his robust frame; and so he was still only a lower boy. One day, near the time of Trials, when we all worked anxiously, he asked me to do some work on the Odyssey with him; and working with this heroic figure probably helped to give me a better interest in one of the greatest stories in the world. Muntz drew from between his mantelpiece and the over-mantel a volume of forbidden lore, or, to describe it more briefly, a crib; though I don't remember that we used it, except when we came to passages where it seemed that the gods were against us, and we saw no other way by which to defeat them. Very soon after he left Eton Muntz died, leaving a name that Fame had never known, and yet in that portion of the Eton sky that was visible from Cornish's house, he appeared for a while like a comet.

Trials came, and the half ended, and, as my parents were wintering in Egypt, I went to stay for the holidays with my aunt, Mrs Ponsonby, at Kilcooley Abbey in Tipperary. Her family consisted of two boys and two girls, and one of the boys was already at Eton with me. At Kilcooley one felt that one was far deeper into Ireland than in County Meath, which the Normans with their semi-circle of castles had been civilizing for seven hundred years; though, if one came to search into origins, I believe one would find that the tall Tipperary men were many of them descended from Cromwell's soldiers. Driving from the station, the eleven miles in an outside car, one saw, as one so often sees in Ireland, ruined towers here and there, splendidly built, and showing that here, too, men had had their dreams of a noble civilization, long since, and had failed. That was a passing dream, even if the towers were peopled for a few centuries; then came the eternal thing, the Irish bog, compared to which the road, and all roads, were things of a day. The talk at Kilcooley was much of these bogs, and of widgeon and teal, and of woodcock, which were more taken for granted, and of geese. Indeed I have myself sat up there till late, planning with one of my cousins how best to get at a goose in a few square miles of bog, and what shot to give him when met; but he never got any of that shot into him in those days, remaining much too elusive, a mere cry in the clouds, until I was some years older. Here first I saw an Irish bog and, what was almost as important as equipment for a writer, I was told by my aunt how in Galway these heathery wildernesses stretched away for miles and miles, so that in my imagination these strange lands lay ready to be used, if ever my fancy turned homeward from remote places in which it used to travel to find the gods and men of my earlier books and plays. And other literary encouragement she gave me by introducing me to William

169

Morris's Earthly Paradise and, better still, being the first person that ever showed me a book of poems by Kipling; but when I wrote myself I think it was a shock to her, although I think she might not have minded that if I had not had my plays acted, or allowed my books to be publicly sold. One of my cousins believed in me as a writer, though starting that faith on the terribly insecure foundation of my earliest poems, and another of them became my principal ally in plans for the overthrowing of snipe, which spread their ramifications through many years.

From PATCHES OF SUNLIGHT

Edward John Moreton Drax Plunkett (1878–1957), writer and sportsman, was born in London. He succeeded to the title of Lord Dunsany in 1899.

SIR WILLIAM ORPEN

Life Class

My general appearance, and especially my face, have always been a source of depression to me, even from my early days. I remember once, by mistake, overhearing a conversation between my father and mother about my looks – why it was that I was so ugly and the rest of the children so good looking. It was indeed a question difficult to explain, and I remember creeping away and worrying a lot about the matter. I began to think I was a black blot on the earth, and when I met people on the country roads I always used to cross to the other side to let them pass, and by so doing save them the pain of having a 'close-up' view of me. Later on I had a great chance of improving my looks, but, alas! it never came off. Everyone surely has noticed how like a husband and wife become after some time of living together, even if they are not deeply attached, or a dog and his master whether they are devoted to each other or not, as long as they depend on mutual agreement for peace of mind and body.

My opportunity came this way. When I went to the Art School in Dublin I noticed that the students, who were drawing figures from the antique, were without doubt growing like their subjects; and they had plenty of time to do so, as they worked at one figure, drawing every day, for one year. I remember one lady drawing the 'Venus de Milo'. My word, she was great! Now my chance would certainly come when I was promoted to draw an antique figure. Surely it would be some wonderful Apollo or Hermes, or perhaps the 'Fighting Gladiator'! Then my features would quickly change, my body would develop, I would gradually become pure classical Greek. After months of waiting, I was brought up to the room by the master and led to an easel, and said he, 'There is your place. Kindly make the drawing exactly twenty-eight inches high.' I looked up, and there, facing me, was the 'Dancing Faun', as ugly as you please. So my chance was missed, and after looking at the 'Dancing

Faun' for a year, I gave up worrying about my short-comings. After all, they were worse for others than for me.

> '*For beauty, I am not a star,*
> *Others are handsomer by far;*
> *But my face, I don't mind it,*
> *For I am behind it.*
> *It's the people in front get the jar.*'

So I just feel a mild pity for the rest of humanity who happen to cross my path in this world. That's all there is to it now. I hope they will be charitable enough to forgive me.

When I was about twelve years old a great innovation took place in the Dublin Art School – a real live woman was allowed to pose naked! I remember vaguely that when this great step had at last been decided on, there were further objections about my little self, whether I should be allowed to work from her, my tender years, etc. However, the head-master persuaded the powers that were – the Church, and the 'Department of Agriculture and Technical Instruction for Ireland' (who managed art matters in that country!) – that it would do no real harm to the lady or myself, and this I think proved correct. The great evening arrived for the first sitting. We learnt that she was an Italian, Signorina Angelina Esposito by name. Our excitement was intense. The head-master arrived to 'pose' the lady. While he was doing this, we all had to wait in the passage outside the 'Life Class' room; indeed, the door was locked on us. I suppose he thought we might rush it! Then we drew lots, and were allowed in, to take our places in the order in which we received them. Angelina, I fear, would never be chosen as an example of the perfect female form. But that worried us little then. Her extremities – head, neck, hands and feet – were exceedingly dirty; the rest of her beauty was marred by countless spots, as if she had been in an altercation with a wasp's nest. However, there she was, a woman in all her glory – an Italian – that nation renowned for its glorious development of the human figure. For an hour we worked in a frenzy, then Atty McLean, the head student, bowed low and made signs for her to rest; and this she promptly did, wrapping some old black piece of stuff round herself. We talked together in low tones. Atty said he thought we should try to speak to her. 'Perhaps she would like a glass of water or something.' We agreed. So Atty braced himself, braved it, and, walking over to where she sat, said, 'Signorina, pardon me, can you speak English?' The lady raised her head, and, in the worst Dublin accent I have ever heard, said, 'Oh, indeed I can. Me father tried to teach me Italian, but I couldn't take the trouble to learn the b—— language.' That remark made us feel on safer ground. After all, this 'goddess' was mortal, one of us. The Olympian clouds dispersed, and we saw her clearly under the blaze of electric light, of the earth earthy.

From STORIES OF OLD IRELAND AND MYSELF

———•◦•———

Sir William Orpen (1878–1931), artist, was born at Stillorgan, Co. Dublin. During World War I he was an official war artist, in which capacity he also attended the Versailles Peace Conference. He painted over six hundred portraits and was regarded as the most successful British artist of his day.

JAMES JOYCE

After the Universe?

He sat in a corner of the playroom pretending to watch a game of dominos and once or twice he was able to hear for an instant the little song of the gas. The prefect was at the door with some boys and Simon Moonan was knotting his false sleeves. He was telling them something about Tullabeg.

Then he went away from the door and Wells came over to Stephen and said:

—Tell us, Dedalus, do you kiss your mother before you go to bed?

Stephen answered:

—I do.

Wells turned to the other fellows and said:

—O, I say, here's a fellow says he kisses his mother every night before he goes to bed.

The other fellows stopped their game and turned round, laughing. Stephen blushed under their eyes and said:

—I do not.

Wells said:

—O, I say, here's a fellow says he doesn't kiss his mother before he goes to bed.

They all laughed again. Stephen tried to laugh with them. He felt his whole body hot and confused in a moment. What was the right answer to the question? He had given two and still Wells laughed. But Wells must know the right answer for he was in third of grammar. He tried to think of Wells's mother but he did not dare to raise his eyes to Wells's face. He did not like Wells's face. It was Wells who had shouldered him into the square ditch the day before because he would not swop his little snuffbox for Wells's seasoned hacking chestnut, the conqueror of forty. It was a mean thing to do; all the fellows said it was. And how cold and slimy the water had been! And a fellow had once seen a big rat jump plop into the scum.

The cold slime of the ditch covered his whole body; and, when the bell rang for study and the lines filed out of the playrooms, he felt the cold air of the corridor and staircase inside his clothes. He still tried to think what was the right answer. Was it right to kiss his mother or wrong to kiss his mother? What did that mean, to kiss? You put your face up like that to say goodnight and then his mother put her face down. That was to kiss. His mother put her lips on his cheek; her lips were soft and they wetted his cheek; and they made a tiny little noise: kiss. Why did people do that with their two faces?

Sitting in the studyhall he opened the lid of his desk and changed the number pasted up inside from seventyseven to seventysix. But the Christmas vacation was very far away: but one time it would come because the earth moved round always.

There was a picture of the earth on the first page of his geography: a big ball in the middle of clouds. Fleming had a box of crayons and one night during free study he had coloured the earth green and the clouds maroon. That was like the two brushes in Dante's press, the brush with the green velvet back for Parnell and the brush with the maroon velvet back for Machael Davitt. But he had not told Fleming to colour them those colours. Fleming had done it himself.

He opened the geography to study the lesson; but he could not learn the names of places in America. Still they were all different places that had those different names. They were all in different countries and the countries were in continents and the continents were in the world and the world was in the universe.

He turned to the flyleaf of the geography and read what he had written there: himself, his name and where he was.

Stephen Dedalus
Class of Elements
Clongowes Wood College
Sallins
County Kildare
Ireland
Europe
The World
The Universe

That was in his writing: and Fleming one night for a cod had written on the opposite page:

Stephen Dedalus is my name,
Ireland is my nation.
Clongowes is my dwellingplace
And Heaven my expectation.

He read the verses backwards but then they were not poetry. Then he read the flyleaf from the bottom to the top till he came to his own name. That was he: and he read down the page again. What was after the universe? Nothing. But was there anything round the universe to show where it stopped before the nothing place began? It could not be a wall but there could be a thin thin line there all round everything. It was very big to think about everything and everywhere. Only God could do that. He tried to think what a big thought that must be but he could think only of God. God was God's name just as his name was Stephen. *Dieu* was the French for God and that was God's name too; and when anyone prayed to God and said *Dieu* then God knew at once that it was a French person that was praying. But though there were different names for God in all the different languages in the world and God understood what all the people who prayed said in their different languages still God remained always the same God and God's real name was God.

From A PORTRAIT OF THE ARTIST AS A YOUNG MAN

———•◦•———

James Joyce (1882–1941), novelist and poet, was born in Dublin but left Ireland in 1902. *A Portrait of the Artist as a Young Man* is largely autobiographical. His major work *Ulysses* was published in France in 1922, but was not freely available in the USA or Britain until the mid-1930s. It was followed by *Finnegans Wake* (1939).

Into Bird, Into Bush

When I was a youngster I used to do an odd trick: maybe we all do it. I used to squat beside the dog or the cat, or beside a cow or a bird, and try to 'be' myself into the being of that creature. I used to moo at the cow and whistle at the bird and they always answered back. You could see them listening to the sounds you made, and you could see them being highly pleased at being taken notice of. The way all things love to be loved, and also love to kill each other is very strange.

I discovered that I didn't have to become cows or cats, for they were me already. There wasn't a scrap of difference between any of these creatures and myself. There was nothing whatever they did that I didn't do, and there was not one emotion open to them that wasn't part and parcel of the truck and stuff that I was filled with. They were all capable of being very happy, and they were all capable of being very frightened. So was I; and they were all living the life I was living.

I still think it curious that there should be conflicting capabilities anywhere, and that we should be capable of a joy or of a horror within merely a matter of seconds.

Then, one day I thought that I had come upon an happiness that had no contrary whatever in its nature. I sat beside a small bush that day, and tried to 'bush' myself into it. I vegetated at it.

The bush was about four feet high, and it had got itself up regardless. It had covered itself all over with new green; then it had covered its greenness all over with an outbursting of the very gum and glue of health; thereupon it had rioted itself into an exuberance of blossom, and added to that an excess and splendour of scent. It was full of life, it was full of power, it was full of joy. It was a very extravagance and lust of living. It was all the daintiness that dared be, and it was all the life that anything could stand without dropping dead of it. I thought that not God in his heaven could be happier or as happy as this plant was that was living like lightning and that hadn't got a care or a doubt or a shade in all its being, and I conceived that nothing whatever could surpass the ease and beauty and lavishness of life that was in that thing.

There are people who will say that a plant knows nothing about these things. They say! Let them say! But the plant knows, all right, and it couldn't bother to live if it didn't know just these things, and act according.

From LIVING – WHATEVER THAT IS

James Stephens (1882–1950), poet, essayist and broadcaster, was born in Dublin. He was Registrar of the National Portrait Gallery in Dublin 1915–24. He is best known today for the philosophical fairy-tale *The Crock of Gold*.

Glimpses of Patrick Pearse

I began straight away to people our house with the creatures of that book, and to see myself going into the perils that were pictured there. This was my way with every book that was read to me; with every picture that I saw; with every story or song that I heard. I saw myself doing or suffering all the things that were dared or suffered in the book, or story, or song, or picture: toiling across deserts in search of lost cities; cast into dungeons by wicked kings; starved and flogged by merciless masters; racked with Guy Fawkes; roasted on a gridiron with St Laurence; deprived of my sight with the good Kent. When I heard of anyone's sorrow or of anyone's triumphs, I suffered the sorrow and enjoyed the triumph myself.

Paddy passed through school a grave, sweet, silent boy. He never joined in the ordinary games at playtime. He often climbed up on the high window-ledge of the school-room and sat there reading. He did, however, play some school football. On one occasion we were challenged to play a 'frelden match' (I remember well the spelling of the challenge) by a team of working boys from City Quay. Pearse was on the school team. It was anything but a friendly match and we schoolboys were kicked and bruised and badly beaten and my recollection is that only five or six of us were able to continue to the end. Among this few I well remember Paddy who played with a fierce tenacity we had not given him credit for. He was hot-tempered too. At another match he missed the ball badly and someone sitting on the ditch laughed at him. He left the ball, walked across and struck the lad on the ditch a resounding blow on the jaw.

From Pearse Family Papers

Patrick Pearse (1879–1916), educationist and writer, was born in Dublin. At the Easter Week Rising in 1916, he was commander-in-chief of the Republican forces and had been appointed President of the Provisional Government. He was captured, court-martialled and executed.

Eamon de Valera –
Boyhood of a President

The Coll house at Knockmore was a typical survivor of pre-famine times. Consisting of one large room, it was mud-walled and thatched, with the fire at one end and a window nearby facing west. The child's bed was in the end furthest from the fireplace. The household consisted of his grandmother, an energetic woman who was not yet fifty, his Uncle Pat, just twenty-one, and Aunt Hannie, a slender fifteen-year-old.

The day after his arrival the whole household moved into one of the first agricultural labourers' cottages built by the Liberals. De Valera always remembered his single night in the old house because he woke up in the morning to find the whole place deserted. Everyone had gone to the new house nearby leaving him behind while they did the work of changing. He was very proud to have been the last occupant of his family home.

The new house was a palace compared with the old, but by that standard only. The kitchen occupied more than half the floor space. It had no ceiling but the slated roof. The rest of the floor space was occupied by two small rooms with a loft above, reached by a ladder. This ladder was nearly young Eddie's downfall. One morning his grandmother left him upstairs with his uncle who was still in bed. Then she went off to deliver the milk. Coming back a little later she prepared to give the little boy a bath. She found Eddie crumpled up at the bottom of the ladder. As he descended his attention had been diverted by the bloody end of a goosewing used for dusting and he had crashed to the ground. He came to, to hear his grandmother saying, 'Is he dead?'

He grew particularly fond of his young Aunt Hannie. She used to lace his boots for him, and on special occasions dressed him up in the velvet suit he had brought with him from America. But soon she, too, like her sister and her brother, had to go to America. So she laced Eddie's boots for the last time, warned him he would have to do it for himself in future and departed from Bruree station. Grandmother and child waved her goodbye, tearfully.

America must have seemed no further away than Dublin to a child in Bruree, for the next year there was another arrival off the boat from New York. It was Kate de Valera home for a visit. There were a few glorious weeks and a trip to Limerick and then she went back again. Soon after her return she married Charles Wheelwright – Uncle Charlie to her son.

By now, 1888, Eddie was old enough for school. Earlier efforts to send him had failed; it was difficult to find a companion to take him to Bruree and back. But now he was six and could walk the mile or so by himself. His first day at the National School was May 7th. The teacher was a dapper little man who dressed as befitted the 'master' in an Irish rural community. He was elderly and walked about with his head stuck in the air. His name was John Kelly; he wished de Valera's was as easy. But Uncle Pat wrote it in the boy's exercise books, which resolved the difficulty.

To the boys at school, John Daly, Tim Hannon, Paddy Horgan, Paddy Ruddle, he was Eddie Coll. So there was no difficulty over the name de Valera here. It was Uncle Pat's name that was the problem. He had to compete with 'Big Pat', 'Black Pat' and 'Foxy Pat' who all lived round about. But when the boys took to calling him 'the Dane Coll' it was too much. Related to the Norse invaders who had ravaged Ireland? Never. De Valera fought many a battle by the pump at the Bruree crossroads. The loose stones which filled the pot-holes were telling ammunition. Later de Valera heard that the name 'Dane Coll' (Dean) was bestowed upon his grandfather by some local wags because he used to give out the rosary in chapel. Or was it because his grandfather Coll was the nephew of Dean Coll of Newcastle West?

The rural village of Bruree was still a very self-sufficient community. The railway had opened it up to industrial goods but it still had its fascinating craftsmen. The most interesting of the houses in the village were the forge and the cooper's yard, producing an endless supply of firkins and barrels. There were three bootmakers, though Connors was only for fine boots, and there was Rourkes further down where a big blackbird was being trained to whistle 'Harvey Duff'. Then, of course, the barracks where Sneider carbines and bayonets hung forbiddingly, but beautifully polished.

The barracks was by no means a popular place. De Valera's first political memory is of the attitude towards the police after three people had been shot in Mitchelstown in 1887. The issue came nearer home. In order to extend his meagre grazing area, Uncle Pat allowed his cattle on to 'the long acre', the grass at either side of the road. One of Eddie's jobs was to keep a look-out for the police.

Politics ranged around the national issues in the 1880s. The Parnell split had not yet embittered feelings and de Valera remembers his joy at hearing his uncle announce to his grandmother that Parnell's name was cleared and later that the forger Pigott had shot himself. The walls of the loft were covered with political cartoons from the *Weekly Freeman*. Soon there would be a new one to record the discomfiture of the *Times* and of the Tories, both of whom had believed the worst of Parnell.

Uncle Pat's politics spread beyond the national issues to other problems. He became a member of the Land and Labour League, the first organization of rural workers, and was for a time on the Kilmallock board of poor law guardians.

One land dispute made a deep impression on Eddie, though not in precisely a political sense. A local landowner and horse-breeder John Gubbins was to be boycotted, i.e. ostracized. Eddie, in petticoats, watched from an upstairs window as the people assembled in the village. On a wagonette the Fedamore brass band had left the biggest drum he had ever seen. De Valera never forgot the pomp and glory which that drum represented for him.

Bruree village church was a centre of much excitement, for the parish priest was Father Eugene Sheehy whose support of the Land League had earlier landed him in prison. The well-to-do in the galleries or pews and the poor standing or kneeling on the tiled floor listened to a variety of fiery sermons.

Occasionally on St Munchin's Day, a parish holiday, he delivered his most famous sermons based on local Bruree history. Little de Valera sat with the other servers on the side steps of the altar drinking in every historic detail. Father Sheehy, eyes closed and long nose reaching his lips, retailed the golden exploits of bygone days, as if in ecstasy. By the time he checked his gold watch for the last time, Bruree seemed not only the capital of Limerick but of Munster and of Ireland. Who knows what seeds of patriotism he sowed?

For eight years Eddie walked the mile or so to Bruree, carrying with him a couple of quarts of milk for customers in the village. He had many jobs to do round the house, and with the cows, particularly after his grandmother's death in 1895, and also with neighbouring farmers in the summer time. Years later he claimed that the only farm work which he did not learn while growing up was how to handle a plough.

Partly because of these duties Eddie's attendance at school was never very regular. In class II he was present on thirty-six fewer days than the most regular boy. In his last year, as his home tasks became heavier, he was away even more often. Nevertheless, he was always passed for promotion each year. One year he rose from his bed of measles to be there when the inspector held the examination and drew up the promotion list.

Uncle Pat was quite severe with his nephew; he disapproved of wasting time with such games as hurling. He thrashed Eddie when he went 'on the slinge' (played truant) or, as he did once, used the donkey's Sunday pair of reins to make a swing. But Eddie's pleasures were not all stolen. The race-meeting at Athlacca with its 'thimble riggers', 'three-card tricksters', the man in the barrel who kept bobbing his head up and down while people tried to hit him with a thrown wattle, 'pigs crubeens', more sweets and cakes and, of course, the races themselves – all this was top entertainment.

At school, teacher succeeded teacher, although three of the four were from the Kelly family. They were helped by an assistant and 'monitors', boys who had just left school and hoped to become teachers themselves later. Uncle Pat occasionally sent Eddie's writing exercise books to his mother in America. In these hand-writing books he assiduously copied out such bald statements as that 'Queen Victoria was born on 24th May, 1819.' He had to depend on Father Sheehy's sermons for his Irish history. In 1892 he received his first communion and two years later was confirmed by the Bishop of Limerick, Dr Edward Thomas O'Dwyer. Soon the question of Eddie's future arose. Uncle Pat, who was a determined man, felt that he should become a school monitor. But de Valera thought this a dead end unless he had enough money to pay for his teacher's training later. The return of Aunt Hannie to nurse her mother had given him some support. After she went back to America again they continued to correspond. In the spring of 1896 he wrote her a firm letter. Would she persuade his mother to arrange for him to come to America? Bruree could never satisfy him. His closest friend had moved out of the neighbourhood and his uncle was about to get married. In fact this last development should have been good news for de Valera as he did most of their bachelor housekeeping; he even cooked his uncle's wedding breakfast. Nevertheless ahead of him was the life of a monitor or a farm labourer. Neither was at all attractive.

But there was a third plan which he tried to persuade his uncle to accept. Paddy Shea, who was a few years older than de Valera, and had been at the National School in Bruree with him, had gone to the Christian Brothers School in Charleville and had won a junior grade exhibition which paid for his further education at St Munchin's College, Limerick. Could he not do the same? But he forgot that Paddy Shea lived about three miles nearer to Charleville than Knockmore and there was no suitable transport; the Colls could not even afford a bicycle. At length Uncle Pat agreed to the scheme since de Valera was willing to walk the seven miles there when necessary.

De Valera started at the school on November 2nd, 1896, despite an unfortunate interview with the head brother at which Uncle Pat protested his nephew's ability to do arithmetic, algebra and geometry, but de Valera failed to give to the brother correctly the factors of $a^3 - b^3$. At Charleville he took Latin and Greek; arithmetic, geometry and algebra; and English and French. No history. He progressed quickly and was allowed to take the junior grade examination the following June. Though it was considered a trial attempt, he passed with honours but was young enough to take it again the next year. Often on the long walk home to Knockmore he would rest exhausted against a fence, longing to throw away the heavy pile of school books. But he persisted as so often later in life.

One day, as he and another boy were leaving the town to walk home, a race-horse passed them being ridden by a tipsy rider. It looked as if he might fall off but there was nothing they could do. Further down the road they found he had been stopped by the aforementioned horse-breeder John Gubbins who asked de Valera to take the rider's place. Gubbins later owned two horses that won the Derby. Thus originated the story that de Valera had ridden Galtymore, one of the two. In fact it was neither.

From Eamon de Valera by the Earl of Longford and Thomas P. O'Neill

——•○•——

Eamon de Valera (1882–1975), politician, was born in New York and brought up on his uncle's farm in Limerick. He formed the first Fianna Fail government in 1932, was re-elected (1933–48) and was Taoiseach (Prime Minister) yet again 1951–4 and 1957–9. He was President 1959–73.

C. P. CURRAN

From the Gallery

The Gaiety pantomime never lost its attraction. Once a year the family piled into a cab and rattled over the 'half-sets' to the magical chiaroscuro outside the theatre where bare-footed urchins were selling their broadsheets with 'all the pantomime songs one penny'. This was the vestibule of paradise. Already at mid-summer we hungrily looked out for the announcement of its name and long accounts in the *Freeman's Journal* of the glories to come; of busy scene-painters and stage-carpenters in preparation, and of Mrs Gunn and her army of needle-women already at work on the costumes. We hoped the lot would fall on Sinbad or Robinson Crusoe, wrecked ships, rafts and desert islands. Incongruously La Loie Fuller might also be there dancing her flame dance, limelit in multi-coloured draperies, a miracle of colour. The vision did not hide Lauri, the Pantomime Cat, or the funny man George Graves, all leading up to the ever more splendid kaleidoscope of the transformation scene, veil after ethereal veil lifting to disclose the triumphal entry and parade of the entire company. The harlequinade followed. We saw, though we did not know it, the last days of what once had been beginning and end of pantomime; we neither understood nor approved the conduct of so many of the audience who began to stand up between us and our view of the stage foolishly to adjust their wraps, as if they did not know that the best, or nearly the best, was still to come, with glittering Harlequin and Columbine, the pantaloon and strings and strings of sausages.

After St Patrick's Day came the family's regular visit to the Royal Hibernian Academy in Abbey Street – an impressive entertainment, but not to be compared with Pepper's Ghost and Vesuvius in eruption at Poole's Myorama in the Rotunda, nor even with what the National Museum had to offer. There we were let loose freely to wander and wonder at the magnificence of Lord Clare's coach and the yet more splendid coach of the Lord Mayor, and then to pick out the curiosities of the Bayeux tapestry which hung in replica in a now abolished corridor. It led to our last delight as with expected terror we passed under the belly of a suspended whale, into the natural history section, vicious sharks in attendance, and birds, to where in its isolated glory our Irish elk stood with far branching horns.

These things filled one's eyes in satisfactory measure, and could be collated with half understood books at home. So too, with actuality with history. Though the Parnell split might be tactfully avoided, the talk I listened to ran chiefly on the land agitation and the prospects of Home Rule. These vital issues engrossed everyone's attention. My mother was a farmer's daughter. With her passionate and retentive memory, before my schooldays were over there was little or nothing I had not learned from her of the iniquitous land system that prevailed in her parents' day and in her own youth. Coming of a long-lived stock and herself in due course an octogenarian, her memory to the end lost nothing of what she had heard or seen, and her recitals were in the plainest black and white – or, since she was an Ulster woman, should one rather say orange and green? She had little time for books, though it should also be said that a family connection and namesake McGahan was once a well-known traveller and correspondent, and had a statue erected to him in Sofia in recognition of his efforts on behalf of Bulgarian education. I was told he awakened Gladstone's conscience in the days of the Bulgarian atrocities as earlier Byron aroused Europe against the Turks and was similarly rewarded by his statue in Athens.

My father, as I have already suggested, was more historically minded and less agrarian. Though a Dublin man, his early schooling was in Mallow in the company of William O'Brien and Canon Sheehan, the one a Land Leaguer and Member of Parliament, the other the novelist whom I was later to meet, finding this friend of Judge Wendell Holmes a sad and, as I thought, a disillusioned man, but none the less eager to know what the young men of my generation were thinking about. With them at school was the more dubious figure whom I was to know as Sergeant Moriarty and later a Lord Justice in the old Court of Appeal.

My father laid claim to no such distinctions – nothing more than a bronze medal for third place in these islands in some technical examination in the South Kensington examinations. He was merely a technician in the telegraph service where my mother told me he invented some improvement in apparatus which was quietly adopted, but without any recompense.

From UNDER THE RECEDING WAVE

C. P. Curran (1883–1970), critic and writer, was born in Dublin, and became Registrar of the High Court.

186

On the Boards

I had discovered that in Cork it was only in a series of sensuous pictures that memories came to me, so that it is still a faint surprise in certain unforgotten places there not to see ladies wearing the bell-shaped skirts of 1905, the silver net-purses fastened to the waist, the princess blouses, and tilted blossoming hats I remembered in my early days. But here in London memory came sidling through every pore of my being. I had never dared, on those flat and cheerful days that preceded our Westminster Season, to take a bus to the suburb where I had travelled from childhood to adolescence, for I had dreaded that shrinking sense of confinement and ugliness that descends on places we have known in the days when a penny could open the gates of paradise, and one tasted all the heavens in a currant bun. But the West End, now that one was going to work so near – a stone's throw away through the park – and was no longer a fleeting passer-by hurrying to Paris or Madrid, the West End was full of ghosts, and the obvious physical changes could not dispel them.

Here was Charles Street at the corner of His Majesty's, still veiled in the dim yellow sunshine, still tingling with traffic and theatre bills. The maroon-and-white pillars of the Haymarket across the street were as gaunt and uncompromising as ever; it was difficult to believe that one had played there when the town was darkened against Zeppelins, and a-buzz with talk of the Kaiser and Edith Cavell and Violet Loraine. Charles Street was little changed; the white-tiled entrance to the stage of His Majesty's was exactly as I remembered it on the day when I had been taken for my first interview with Tree and recited both parts in the wooing scene from *The Taming of the Shrew*, and been engaged to play an apparition and Macduff's son in the autumn production of *Macbeth*.

I had acted in front of a mirror for years and had developed for myself a character that was melodramatic, self-centred, humourless, and obstinate. I was a born show-off, though at ten years old I was convinced that I had a simplicity of soul like that of the Infant Samuel whose picture I had admired in some shop window. But my poses threw no dust in the eyes of my father, a born adventurer and teller of wonderful tales, who had, as well as many ambitions for me, a friend who held some clerical position at His Majesty's Theatre, and one morning, before I had dreamed of Miss Lila Field and her children's play, he had said to me, 'Put on your best clothes and get mother to smarten you up. We're going to see Beerbohm Tree, the most famous actor in London.'

I had heard of Tree as one hears of the Great Wall of China, but it had never occurred to me that he really existed, and it was in a sort of stupefaction that, holding my father's hand, I was taken through the white tiles of the stage-door in Charles Street and then into a pale impersonal room full of red and gilt furniture where, after innumerable poppings in and out on the part of some elderly nervous-looking men, one of whom was my father's friend, the door opened for the twentieth time, and a big blond man floated eerily into the room, impeccably dressed and with a strange malicious grace in every movement he made, like some great soft cardinal who had decided momentarily to abandon his red robe. Fixing upon me two burning disks of light-blue fire, he bent down to shake hands and said, 'Can you stand on your head?'

'No,' I answered with a certain suspicion.

'Oh, what a pity! Can you turn somersaults?'

'No.'

'Can you jump through a hoop? Or play on a comb? Can you dance the hornpipe?'

'No.'

'Then, good God, boy, what can you do?'

'Oh, I can act,' I answered, and really believed what I said. That, I thought, would show him. It seemed to. He was silent for a moment, and then he said in a thrilling whisper, 'Ah, but are you sure of that?'

I was perfectly certain. He looked at my father.

'Irish people can do so much, but acting is difficult,' he murmured, and presently I was led away to recite for him and found myself alone in an enormous room that had no paper on the walls, no carpet on the floor, no tables or chairs, nothing but a vast, dim, echoing space with myriads of unlit electric bulbs hanging in long rows from a ceiling taller and darker than the sky at night, with hanging ropes and dangling sandbags and high iron lamps that gave no light. Suddenly then I saw that one of the walls of the room was missing; there was nothing there but a big black pit, and out of this the voice of the actor rose, warm and powerful as a wind laden with spices, and it said:

'Light! Give the child light! Oh, my God, where's Dana? Dana, tell them to give the boy some light.'

And a long line of yellow fire sprang suddenly from the edge of the floor at my feet and another and another overhead, and I looked round blinking and dazzled. I was on the stage.

And when I had had my ramping roaring way with the dual roles of Catherine and Petrucio, playing it I thought with the roll of the Cantos of the Inferno, tearing it to tatters, to very rags, I paused for breath and was surprised when he came on to the stage and said, 'Did you know, did no one ever tell you, that this is a comedy scene? It is meant to be funny, boy, to make people laugh. Never mind, you were quite funny in your own way. We must see about *Macbeth* in the autumn. Would you like to be the Drunken Porter, boy?'

'I'd rather be Macbeth,' I said, and was furious when my father snorted with laughter.

'Then we must put it on specially for you,' Tree said gravely, 'but, oh, do you think you could ever join your wig?'

He had a talk with my father and I could see them laughing together and thought they were laughing at me, and the feeling that I had acted beautifully went out like a candle in the wind, and I did not know for certain whether he would let me play in *Macbeth* or not, and looked enviously at the posters as we passed out of the theatre. They read: 'Herbert Tree in Shakespeare's *Henry VIII*. Violet Vanbrugh, Arthur Bourchier, Laura Cowie', in letters of scarlet and black on a subtle yellow ground. It was the memory of that colour scheme that thrilled me the most when I heard months later that I was engaged – I was going to play in that enchanted place with black and red and yellow pictures all over the walls.

From ALL FOR HECUBA

———•◦•———

Micheál mac Liammóir (1899–1973), actor, theatrical director and dramatist, was born Alfred Willmore, in Cork. He was a co-founder of the Dublin Gate Theatre. He is particularly remembered for his one-man performance, *The Importance of being Oscar*.

The Portrait

For many years I could never hear without a momentary feeling of uneasiness the name of Shakespeare mentioned by anyone. The very syllables had a sinister ring for me because of the dread that name caused me in childhood. There was an empty room at the top of our house and on the wall, between the fireplace and the window, almost hidden in the gloom, hung a small portrait in oils. Dim and yellowed by time, that picture showed the head of a man of strange appearance, for he had long hair and below his pointed beard was some kind of wide collar brim. His face was melancholy and yet it always seemed to me that there was a sneer upon those bearded lips. I cannot remember when the portrait first stirred my curiosity, but one day I asked the name of the man and I was told in jest or ignorance, that it was Shakespeare. The very name was foreign and had an inimical sound – who could be this moody stranger shaking a spear when he was angry? Children rarely look up when they are playing with toys on the floor, for they are too busy with their own imaginings, but one day, when I had strayed into that vacant room and was amusing myself, I happened to glance towards the portrait and saw, to my astonishment, that the eyes of the man were watching me. I turned away, then looked up, and once more his eyes met mine. I got to my feet and, as I did so, those eyes turned to watch every movement I made. I backed towards the door and that look still followed me, half mournful, half accusing. I did not tell anyone what had happened but I did not venture into the room again for more than a few seconds at a time except when I was with grown-ups. Emboldened by their company, I learned to play a fearful but exciting game. I moved slowly here and there about the room, knowing that wherever I went, those eyes followed me. I pretended not to look, I talked to my elders, then swung around sharply. I was still being watched. The searching gaze was always the same, so melancholy and accusing that I began to feel a sense of guilt, began to wonder what evil I could have committed. Guilt and fear mingled in my mind and I was certain, because of his name, that the stranger was treacherous, that his anger could be terrible when it was aroused. Sometimes, greatly daring, I crept up the stairs and opened the door very quietly, very quickly, and peeped in. Every time I did so, his eyes were looking straight at me.

But soon that daylight game of hide-and-seek had dire consequences. At night, before I went to sleep, I could not help thinking of the portrait in the empty room upstairs, for I was certain by now that it was alive. The faint glow of the altar light in the colza bowl was powerless to protect me from the mystery of the canvas. Stories of witches, ogres and magicians were fearful enough, but they were remote and, when I thought of the picture books from which they emerged, my anxiety could be dispelled. But this danger was different, for there were only two short flights of stairs between it and me. Children can enact in their little way the primary myths, find for themselves the ancient ritual of fear. So, night after night, my mind was drawn in obedient horror towards that room upstairs. It had become the forbidden chamber of legend, dreadful in darkness, and I was as powerless to resist it as Bluebeard's youngest wife when she turned the key in the lock. Were it not for the childish alarms which all of us remember so well, we would forget the power of our earliest imaginings, forget those first years when the mind seemed to part so readily from the body. Night after night I thought that I was actually climbing those two flights of stairs, compelled by the presence of that man in the frame. But the moment I got to the door of the forbidden room, the real struggle began. It is easy to forget not only the workings of our early imagination, but also the power of the will when we first discover its use, that determination shown by children when they are crossed or in the sulks. The struggle between my will and imagination was a mighty one. I seemed to be dashing down the stairs, but in a second or two, found myself on the top landing again. I fought my way back, step by step, a score of times, down those stairs. I raced, scrambled, slithered, but in the end my will always won and I was back in safety, my head under the bedclothes.

A night came, however, when my will failed me and I was drawn across the threshold into that forbidden room. I found myself in utter darkness and a piercing shriek must have echoed throughout the whole house, for in an instant my father was rushing up the stairs. I was really there in the room because I had walked in my sleep. But that defeat or dividing of the will proved in itself a victory: the shock broke the spell and I was no longer summoned at night by the man called Shakespeare. . . .

Once a month, on Sunday, a bottle of stout appeared on the table when the cloth had been laid for the midday meal. Wrapping a napkin carefully around the nape, my mother drew the cork. Always I watched the small rite with interest, for I knew, then, that Grandfather Browne was coming. But the solitary black bottle with the tawny label which had a harp on it, seemed to me in some obscure way a sign of evil. There was a mystery about my grandfather and I knew that he was in disgrace. This was all the more surprising because he was so venerable in appearance, having a long white beard, small, pale, blue eyes, a lofty brow and bald top. He spoke in a gentle way, and seemed to be in awe of my mother. Often my sister Kathleen has told me that when she was smaller than I was at the time, he used to take her on his knee and make her promise that she would never become a nun. Despite his gentle wickedness, I gazed up at him with respect. Long ago he used to meet with other Fenian conspirators in the loft of a grain-store in Thomas Street where Lord Edward Fitzgerald had been arrested by the cruel Major Sirr at the beginning of the century. Beyond that, was a further past of his and I was well aware of it, for in our narrow hall there was a portrait of him in a heavy gilded frame as a lad beside his pony. On the opposite wall was another of my great-grandmother, Ellen Dardis of Meath. These old oil paintings, together with the pedestal on which was a bust of Napoleon bought by my mother at one of the auctions to which she hastened so often, gave grandeur to the gloomy hall, not to speak of the pheasant on the ledge of the fanlight. But this grandeur was not much compared with the display in the parlour, with its large cabinet, painted fire-screen, and the piano on which my eldest sister played, long before I was taught the violin. Here, too, was a glass chandelier, from which I was given a few broken prisms that concealed triangular sevenfold glories. On Sunday evenings, when the fire was glowing in the parlour, and the incandescent mantles were lit, the chandelier was a-dazzle. I owe to it my first moment of identity, for when I was held up to it as an infant, I twinkled into consciousness of a self.

The disgrace in which my grandfather lived must have had an influence upon me, for in secret I knew that I was deserving of the same treatment. It was comforting to find that so venerable a man could be as wicked as I was for somehow that seemed to disprove the stern morality of our family life. Truth to tell, I was guilty of all the little acts of curiosity about myself and others which have been set down by Freud and are denied with such vehemence by those who insist on the perfect innocence of childhood. Had I known that we cannot sin until the age of seven, which theologians hold to be the age of reason and consent, I might have been spared much anxiety and have rejoiced in my desire for knowledge. My mother was not, indeed, a religious fanatic or a ceaseless church-goer, indeed she was obeying an old Dublin custom when she refused to invite especially any clergyman to the house. But she had that stern Victorian sense of duty which spread to our country in the second half of the last century. So rare, so refined was this sense of morality which my sisters and I drew from her example, that, in comparison with it, the religion of the churches we attended seemed gross. In consequence it was at Mass that I got my earliest intimations of immorality, for the language of religion belonged to franker centuries. It was mainly through some of the scriptural texts which the priest read out in the short sermon on Sunday that I became conscious of the restraint in our own home life. I remember clearly my feelings of horror – as if I had some hereditary knowledge of forbidden things – when I heard for the first time *Matthew* 9.20. Because of this moral delicacy, even our family prayers became an ordeal which grew worse with every year. We said the Rosary each evening and when my Mother gave out the first half of the *Hail Mary* to which we said the response, her voice always changed as she came to the last words, 'And blessed is the fruit of thy Womb, Jesus.' The pace quickened and she ran them together. When, in turn, we said them, we imitated her rapid sing-song. The sentence was completely incomprehensible to me, but I suspected that it was improper, although it had been first spoken by the Angel Gabriel.

Strangely enough I enjoyed another experience which is usually reserved for little Protestants. Before I could spell out my letters I used to turn the heavy pages of our family Bible and, needless to say, it was the Douai version. I suspect that the illustrations in it must have been by Gustave Doré, so copious were they. Many of those I enjoyed were horrible depictions of battles, flights, torture and execution. I can still see that huge captive in one of them, tied down to a trestle, his limbs being chopped off with blades. But there was a full page plate to which I constantly turned, peepingly, for it was always there waiting for my shocked glance. It displayed a group of unclad fathers and mothers with their children clinging to rock or branch as the waters of the Flood rose towards them. Turning from it, I sought the pictures of fire descending from Heaven on false altars and the ground opening to swallow the wicked. I was dealing with something which was quite near. For, one Sunday morning after Mass, my sisters and I went down to the railings of Rutland Square to see the charred remains of the vast marquee which

193

had been destroyed the night before by a stroke of lightning. Within it had been the Swiss Village, as it was called, this being a panoramic model of the Alps and their valleys. We knew that God sent fire from Heaven because the Exhibition had been open on the previous Sunday.

From TWICE ROUND THE BLACK CHURCH

Austin Clarke (1896–1974), poet, novelist and dramatist, was born in Dublin. He worked in England 1929–37. He then lived at Templeogue, Co. Dublin, founding with Rióbeard O'Farachain the Dublin Verse-Speaking Society in 1940 and the Lyric Theatre Company in 1944. His *Collected Poems* were published in 1974.

The Hill of Healing

At half-past eight in the morning, washed and dressed, with a thick handkerchief over his eyes, Johnny, helped by his mother, ate sparingly of his bread and tea, for he was soon to be given over to a power that could do many things to hurt and frighten him, and force him to suffer a fuller measure of pain.

He went down the street, holding his mother's hand, as slowly as he could, so that what was going to come to pass might not come too quickly. Opposite the end of the street, he heard a tram stop, and felt his mother lifting him inside and helping him on to a seat, and saying, if he was good and gave the doctor no trouble, she'd buy him a sponge cake, and they'd take the tram home again. The tram, pulled by patient, muscle-wrenched horses, jingled along, stopping now and again to take passengers on and let passengers off, each pull, to get the tram restarted, giving the horses a terrible strain. The conductor came along, with his money-bag and gleaming silver punch, and gathered the fares, tuppence for his mother and a half fare of a penny for him. He heard the punch ring with a clear shrillness as the conductor holed the tickets which were given to Johnny by his mother to hold, a red one for her, she said, and a yellow one for him; an' maybe you'll be able to look at them when we're comin' back, for the doctors may do you so much good that you may be able to fling the bandage off when we leave the hospital.

They got out at Westland Row, and his mother led him down Lincoln Place till they came to the hospital, a timid shabby-looking place, having a concrete path, with a few beds dotted with geraniums, before the entrance which wasn't any bigger than the two windows that would form the front of a grocer's shop. Over the big shop-like windows, in big letters, were the words, St Mark's Ophthalmic Hospital for Diseases of the Eye and Ear. Going inside, they found themselves in a long narrow hall, divided in two by a barrier of polished pine. At the upper end were two doors, one to let the patients in to the doctors, and the other to let them out when the doctors had finished with them for the time being. The hall was furnished with long, highly polished, golden-coloured pitch-pine benches on which a number of men, women, and children were sitting, slowly moving up to the door leading to the room where the doctors were. Near the entrance was a huge stove, and near this stove was a table on which, like an offering on an altar, was a big book enshrining the details of the patients' names, homes, and occupations. At this table sat a big, heavy, stout man of sixty-five with a white beard, a short bulgy neck, an incessant cough, a huge head, the skull of which was bald and hard and pink and polished like the pine benches. He was called Francis.

Johnny's mother gave the details asked for – his age, where he lived, and that he suffered from a disease of the eyes; and when Francis was told that the boy's father was dead, he shoved the word orphan into the space required to denote the father's occupation. The sixpence was handed over, and they were given a ticket of admission which would also be used by the doctor to write down the prescribed remedies to be applied to the diseased eyes. These were made up and handed out to the patients at the dispensary, a little closed-in booth-like space with a sliding panel, stuck in a corner of the hall. They got, too, a large sheet fixed in a cardboard protector, having on it diagrams of the eye, so that the doctor could record the origin, nature, and progress of the ailment, to be filed and retained by the hospital for future reference. They sat down on the bench among the patients, and waited for their turn. The people were being admitted in batches of five or six at a time, the rest moving up nearer as the others went in. As they waited and moved up and waited, his mother read what was written on the ticket:

St Mark's Ophthalmic Hospital for Accidents
and Diseases of the Eye and Ear

———————

Out-patients attending this Institution, under the care of
MR STORY
are to attend on
Mondays, Wednesdays, and Fridays
before ten o'clock
Each person (not a pauper) will pay sixpence for a ticket
which will last for one month from date of issue. This
Ticket must be kept clean, and presented open at each
visit, and preserved when the attendance ceases.

196

Johnny heard the people round him talking of their complaints, their pain, and their hopes of improvement.

–I have to go months yet, he heard a voice say, before there'll be any improvement. Steel chips in a foundry flew into me eye, an' they had to get them out with a magnet. They made me jump when they were doin' it, I can tell you.

–He had to cut the sthring, said a voice a little nearer, to separate the bad blind eye from the good one, an' now he's breakin' his arse to cut the blind one out altogether, sayin' that it's no use havin' a dead eye in your head; but I have me own opinion about that, for the dead one isn't so disfigurin', if you don't examine it too closely, so it 'tisn't.

–It's wonderful, murmured another voice, what a lot of things a man can do without, accordin' to the doctors.

–Some o' the buggers would give up the spendin' of the first night with a lovely woman he was after marryin' for a half-hour's hackin' at a man, said the first voice.

–The first real touch o' spring is comin' into the air at last, said a soft voice, a little lower down; in the people's park yesterday the main beds were a mass o' yellow daffodils. The whole time I was gettin' a mug o' tea an' a chunk o' bread down me, I was lookin' at them.

–Geraniums, red geraniums for me, said an answering voice, every time, every time.

–I don't know, I don't rightly know, answered the soft voice; to me, red geraniums or geraniums of any other colour seem to have a stand-offish look, always, while daffodils seem to welcome you to come in and walk about in the midst of them.

There was a moment's silence, then Johnny heard the second voice saying, maybe you're right, but I still hold to the red geraniums.

–See that man sittin' opposite, said a woman to his mother, have a glance at his ticket, and you'll see it's printed in red – don't look over too sudden – see?

–Yes, he heard his mother say, I see it's printed in red, while ours is printed in black. Why is that, now?

–Because he's a pauper, and doesn't, as we do, pay for his treatment.

Johnny felt a glow of pride. He wasn't a pauper, and he held the card of admission out so that all could see it was printed in black.

Suddenly they found themselves in the doctor's room, and a nurse made them sit down on a special bench to wait for Mr Story. It was a room full of a frightening light, for the whole north wall was a window from side to side, and from floor to ceiling. There was a ceaseless sound of instruments being taken from trays and being put back again. Tinkle, tinkle, tinkle, they went, and cold sweat formed on Johnny's brow. All round the wall terrible pictures of diseases of the eye and ear were hanging. A nurse, in a blue calico dress, with narrow white stripes, was hurrying here and there, attending to the doctors; and everywhere there was a feeling of quiet, broken by a man's moan, or by a child's cry, that made Johnny tense his body with resentment and resistance.

At last, Mr Story, a tall thin man, with a sharp face and an elegantly pointed reddish beard, came over to them, and said shortly, bring the boy over to the window. Johnny was led over to the window, and the bandage taken from his eyes: the light, the light, the cursed, blasted, blinding light! He was seated on a chair; he was fixed between the doctor's legs; his head was bent back as far as a head can go; he could feel the doctor's fingers pressing into his cheek just below his eyes: the light, the light, the cursed, blasted, blinding light!

Open your eyes, said Story, and look out of the window; go on, open your eyes, like a good little boy.

–Open your eyes for the doctor, Johnny, said his mother.

–Open your eyes, said Story, sharply, open your eyes, at once, sir.

But the cursed, blasted, blinding light flooded pain in through the lids, and he kept them tightly closed. His mother nervously shook his arm.

–Open your eyes, you young rascal, she said.

But he sat, stiff, firm, and silent, and kept them closed.

–Story beckoned to two students. One of them held his head from behind the chair, the other held his arms, but still, firm, and silent, he kept them closed. His obstinacy forced them into fierceness; they took him out of the chair, while his mother, embarrassed, threatened him with all sorts of violence when she got him home. They stretched him, on his back, froglike, on the floor, students holding his legs, nurses holding his arms, while Story, kneeling beside him, pressed his fingers under his eyes firmly and gently, till with an exasperated yell, Johnny was forced to open them, and Story, from a tiny glass container, instantly injected into his eyes a tiny stream of what looked like cold water, which spread like a cooling balm over the burning ulcerated surface of his eye alls.

Silently, then, he submitted to a fuller examination in a pitch-dark room, filled with little cubicles, in each of which a gas-jet flared; and from a mirror-like instrument strapped on the doctor's head, Story searched his inner eye for a fuller indication of the disease that took from his life the sense of sight in agony and sweat. After two hours of examination and treatment, Story returned to his desk, and beckoned to

Johnny's mother to come over to him. She came, slowly and anxiously, and listened to what the doctor had to say.

–The boy will not be blind, he said, writing rapidly on the case-sheet, but getting him well's going to be a long job. Bathe the eyes regularly in water as hot as he can bear it, afterwards with a lotion they will give you at the dispensary. Most important of all, some of the ointment, as much as will fit on the top of your finger, is to be inserted underneath the lids – not on, mind you, but underneath the lids – every night and every morning; and the boy will have to wear a bandage for a long time. He is to be given nourishing food, and he is to take a teaspoonful of Parrish's Food, after each meal.

–Can he go to school, doctor? asked the mother.

–No, no school, he said snappily. His eyes must be given absolute rest. No school for a long, long time.

–If he doesn't go to school, sir, he'll grow up to be a dunce.

–Better to be a dunce than to be a blind man, said the doctor. The boy must be brought here on each Monday, Wednesday, and Friday till an improvement removes the necessity for attendance oftener than once a week. Get these remedies at the dispensary, he added, giving her the prescription, do all that I've told you, be patient, and don't let the boy go to school; and Mr Story, with his elegant white hands, his red pointed beard and his morning coat, hurried away, followed by a flock of students, to attend to another patient.

–Me eyes must be pretty bad, said Johnny to his mother, as she was being fitted out with ointment, lotion, syrup, and bandage, at the dispensary, when he won't let me go to school.

Not to have to go to school – that was a thought full of a sweet savour. No schoolmaster, no lessons, no wear and tear of the mind with reading, writing, and arithmetic. He was saved from being one of the little slaves of the slate and satchel.

–It won't be nice, he murmured to his mother, if, when I grow up, I amn't able to read and write, will it ma?

–No, said she, it would be terrible; but, please God, you'll soon be well enough to go, for it might easily be as well to be blind as not to be able to read or write.

Then a nurse heavily bandaged his eyes, and his mother led him forth from the hospital, having finished his first day with an Institution that was to know him so well in the future that the doors nearly opened of their own accord when they saw him coming.

From I KNOCK AT THE DOOR

Sean O'Casey (1884–1964), dramatist, was born in Dublin, the youngest of thirteen children of an impoverished Protestant family. He started work as a labourer, but achieved fame as a writer with *Juno and the Paycock*, first performed at the Abbey Theatre. *I Knock at the Door* is the first of six autobiographical works.

The New Suit

Leaving the grandmother at home to look after the house, the Dillon family set forth to shear the sheep. The two oldest children, Mary and Thomas, walked with their parents. Mary was eighteen and Thomas was sixteen, so they had already assumed the dignified manner of grown-up people to whom such an event was no longer an exciting adventure. In fact, Mary was whispering about a coming wedding in a neighbouring village as she walked with her mother, while Thomas brought up the rear with his father and talked in a loud voice about the condition of the crops with the pompous arrogance of adolescence.

The other four children, however, bolted from the yard and ran at full speed until they entered the narrow lane that led to the uplands east of the village. Three of them were girls, all wearing white pinafores and with coloured ribbons tied to the ends of their plaited hair. They chattered and sang little snatches of song in chorus as they hopped along the smooth stones of the lane on their bare feet.

The youngest child was a boy called Jimmy, now in his seventh year. He ran far in front of all the others, pausing once in a while to look back and urge the laggards to make more haste. His round face looked so solemn that it was hard to say whether he felt happy or miserable. The fact was that he had been promised a new suit from this year's wool. The promise had been made as early as last Christmas and it had been repeated several times since then by both his father and mother on his ardent insistence. Yet he still could not quite believe that he would really get the suit, and the torture of waiting was almost equal to the ecstatic pleasure of anticipation.

Hitherto he had received his clothes in fragments. One year he would get a pair of trousers and the next year he would get a jacket. So he never had the pleasure of wearing a full suit, with all the garments of the same age. The trousers would be patched by the time he got a new jacket. Then, again, the jacket would be faded and threadbare before he got a new pair of trousers. The thought of wearing a whole new suit for the first time in his life was too good to be true, in spite of all the promises. For that reason, he was determined to keep a close eye on the wool, from the moment it was cut from the sheep's back until it was cloth in the hands of the tailor.

The sheep were in a long, narrow glen, which had a tall fence all around it. They stood in a row beneath the fence when Jimmy arrived. Although the morning was not far advanced, the sun was already hot and the animals were seeking shelter from it. They panted with exhaustion as they pressed close to the fence with their heads lowered.

'Chown, chown,' Jimmy called to them. 'You'll soon be running around in your naked pelts.'

The sheep raised their heads eagerly and looked at the boy.

'Maa,' they said expectantly.

Then they all gathered together in a group and stared at him furtively, fearing that he was accompanied by his dog, which loved to worry them. Six of them were large and white, wearing such a heavy coat of wool that their backs were quite flat. The other five were little mountain sheep with dark wool that grew short and curly. There were five lambs of that year's increase with the flock. Three of the lambs were already half-grown and they had their tails cut. They had been held over from the sale for breeding. The other two lambs were very young. They kept trying to suckle their mother.

Jimmy and his three little sisters had the sheep all herded into a corner when the others arrived. Then four of the white sheep were thrown on their backs and the shearing began. Jimmy held down the head of the animal his mother was shearing. At first the sheep kept making attempts to rise when she felt the shears against her pelt.

'You'd think she doesn't want to lose her wool,' Jimmy said, 'the way she keeps moving around.'

'She's afraid,' his mother said, 'That's why she keeps trying to get up.'

'Does she think we're going to kill her?' Jimmy said.

'Maybe she does,' said his mother.

'But you told me a sheep is a blessed animal,' Jimmy said. 'You said that God gave her wool so that we could have new clothes.'

'That's true,' his mother said. 'She is a blessed animal, not like a wicked goat that has no wool and is a thief into the bargain.'

'Then why would she be afraid we're going to kill her?' Jimmy said. 'God must have told her about her wool and why she has it, if she is blessed.'

'You hold her head and stop talking,' his mother said. 'Otherwise I might cut her with the shears.'

'You mustn't cut her, Mother,' Jimmy said. 'It would be a sin to cut a blessed animal. It might put bad luck on my new suit.'

'All right, then,' the mother said. 'You hold her and I won't cut her.'

The sheep lay quite still when all the wool had been cut from around her neck and shoulders. Now the shears were cutting deep swaths in the thick wool along her back. The thin hairs, packed closely together, were as delicate as silk near the roots. They were moist with oil and they shone brightly in the sunlight.

'Did God tell people how to make clothes of sheep's wool?' Jimmy said.

'He did,' said the mother.

'Who did He tell about it?' said Jimmy.

'He told a saint,' said the mother.

'Did He tell him everything all at once?' said Jimmy. 'How to shear and spin and weave and be a tailor, too?'

'He did,' said the mother.

'What was the saint's name?' said Jimmy.

'I don't know,' said the mother.

'That's a pity,' Jimmy said. 'I'd like to say a prayer to him and ask him to keep Neddy the tailor from drinking when he is making my new suit. But I can't say a prayer to him if I don't know his name. It's queer, though, that you wouldn't know the name of a great saint like that. He should be the most famous of all saints, if he taught the people how to make clothes out of wool. Only for him the people would die of cold in winter.'

'If you're a good boy,' his mother said, 'until Neddy the tailor comes to make your suit, then God will keep Neddy sober. So he won't make a botch, same as he does with clothes when he is drinking. Otherwise he'll get drunk and your suit will be so terrible that you'll be ashamed to wear it. You mustn't ask me any more questions about this saint and that saint. You must be a good boy and not ask foolish questions.'

'Oh! I will, Mother,' Jimmy said, 'I'll do everything you tell me, and I don't care who the saint was.'

The shearing continued until all the sheep were stripped of their wool. According as each sheep was released, she shook herself and began to graze with great energy, pausing now and again to murmur with satisfaction at her relief. The mother of the youngest lambs, however, had great difficulty in getting her offspring to recognize her nakedness. They

203

were startled when they saw her approach, stripped of her wool. So they ran away from her and paid no heed to her frantic bleating. Finally, they had to be caught and put to her udder. Then they recognized her and suckled.

The wool was all gathered up, put into bags, and brought home. Then the womenfolk took it in hand, to prepare it for the weaver. Jimmy did his best to help with every operation. When it was washed and spread out on a field to bleach, he felt very important because he was allowed to stand guard over it all day. Then it was teased and carded into rolls for spinning. He also helped with the spinning. As the rolls of thread came off the spindle, he held them while his sister Mary wound them on to a ball. The white thread was made into one ball and the grey thread into another. When all the wool was spun, the ball of white thread was of enormous size.

Jimmy accompanied his mother to the weaver's house with the thread. It was in another village nearly three miles distant. She put on her best clothes for the occasion and Jimmy felt terribly ashamed of his patched trousers as he trotted along beside her. Yet he would not stay at home on any account, for fear something dreadful might happen to the precious thread in his absence. Furthermore, he wanted to ask the weaver the name of that famous saint to whom God had given the secret of cloth making. Then he could ask the saint in prayer every night to keep Neddy the tailor sober.

When he arrived at the weaver's house, however, he lost courage. He stood within the kitchen door and gaped in silent wonder at the loom. It was placed in a sunken room that had no partition on the side facing the kitchen, so that he could see the whole process of weaving from where he stood. The intricate movements of the shuttles and the miraculous way the thread was changed into cloth convinced the little boy that this was a mystery similar to what happened on the altar during Mass. It pertained to God and it was just as well not to pry into it for fear of making God angry. Even so, the mysterious process acted on him as a magnet. Little by little, he crept along the wall of the kitchen until he was close to the weaver.

'Well, young man,' said the weaver, 'do you want to learn how cloth is made?'

'Come over here, Jimmy,' said his mother, who was seated by the fireplace. 'Don't interfere with the work.'

'He's not doing any harm,' the weaver said. 'Let him stay where he is.'

The weaver was a small man, with black hair and very sallow skin.

He had such merry eyes that Jimmy was not the least afraid of him. So the child suddenly got courage and determined to seize the opportunity.

'Do you know the name of the saint?' he said to the weaver.

'Pay no attention to him,' the mother said, addressing the weaver apologetically. 'He asks such strange questions.'

The weaver bent close to the little boy and said: 'What saint is that, comrade?'

'The saint that told people how to make clothes out of wool,' said Jimmy.

'Oh, I see,' said the weaver, looking very solemn all of a sudden. 'Well. Now that's a long story, but I'll tell you about it. It's a sad story, as well as being a long one. For the truth is that we don't know the name of the saint that taught the people how to make clothes out of wool, no more than we know the name of the saint that taught people how to plough, or to make houses.'

'Oh, that's a great pity," said Jimmy despondently. 'Does nobody know, not even the priest?'

'No,' said the weaver solemnly. 'Not even the priest. Everybody has forgotten the names of these great saints. That's because people were pagans in the past and there were only a few good people among them. The good people were the saints. All the others were sinful and contrary. They only remembered the names of people that were wicked like themselves, kings and tyrants and landlords and generals that made war, usurers that robbed the poor and notorious criminals of every kind. And not only did they forget the names of the saints that were their benefactors, but they even persecuted them and sometimes put them to death.'

'That's terrible,' Jimmy said. 'I thought surely you'd know the name of the saint that told people how to make cloth out of wool. I have a reason for wanting to know.'

'Will you be quiet now?' Jimmy's mother said. 'You have said enough.'

She took Jimmy away before he could ask the weaver any more questions. The little boy wept that night in bed, terrified by the weaver's melancholy description of humanity and convinced that some disaster would happen at the last moment to ruin his chance of getting a new suit.

Then again his hopes rose to a new height when the finished cloth came from the weaver. The thickening-trough was brought into the kitchen. His mother and his sister Mary sat at the ends of the long wooden trough in their bare feet. The cloth was laid in the centre of the trough, a few yards at a time. Sour water was poured on it, to soften it for the thickening. Then the women kicked at it rhythmically, until it had reached the required thickness.

The great moment had at last arrived. The cloth was ready for the tailor. Jimmy was awake at dawn on the morning his brother Thomas was going in the cart to fetch that important personage. The little boy was in such an excited state that his mother had great difficulty in getting him to eat his breakfast. After his brother had left, his agitation increased. His mother could not move a yard around the house without having him at her apron strings. Finally, she took him to task.

'What ails you now?' she said. 'Are you still afraid you won't get your suit?'

'No, Mother,' Jimmy said. 'I'm afraid that Neddy has been drinking last night and that he'll make a botch of it. I couldn't find out the name of the saint, so I couldn't pray and ask him to keep Neddy from drinking.'

'Never mind,' said his mother. 'We'll soon know whether he has been drinking last night or not. We'll know as soon as he puts foot in the house.'

'How will we know?' said Jimmy.

'That's easy,' said his mother. 'As soon as he comes into the house I'm going to offer him a cup of tea. If he refuses the tea and asks for a drink of sour milk instead of it, he has been drinking. But if he drinks the tea and if sweat begins to pour from his face after he drinks it, then he has been sober last night and he'll make good clothes.'

When at last the heavy cart came rumbling up the road towards the village, Jimmy ran down to the yard gate to meet it. There was the tailor sitting on the bottom of the cart, with his legs curled up under him and his head bent in a gloomy attitude. The boy completely lost all hope. The tailor's posture convinced him that the man had been exceptionally wicked on the previous evening. Then the cart halted in the yard. Thomas jumped down and took the tailor's gear into the house. The tailor himself, after looking about him for almost a minute in gloomy silence, also descended and limped indoors.

He was a very thin man, with a club foot and an enormous Adam's apple. His face was deadly pale and he had heavy grey eyebrows that gave his blue eyes a fierce expression. He suffered from asthma and he kept drawing in deep breaths with a hissing sound. Every time he took a deep breath, his Adam's apple rose up as large as a small potato in his throat, paused and then retreated.

206

'A hundred thousand welcomes to you, tailor,' said Jimmy's mother. 'Sit down and have a cup of tea.'

Jimmy put his forefinger between his front teeth and waited for the tailor's reply.

'Thank you, ma'am,' said the tailor. 'I'll have a cup of tea if it's not too much trouble.'

'Oh, it's no trouble at all,' Jimmy said, unable to keep silent owing to the happiness that suddenly overwhelmed him. 'We have it all ready to see would you drink it. We were afraid you would rather have sour milk.'

The mother picked up the tongs from the fireplace and threatened Jimmy with it. The boy blushed to the roots of his hair and retired into a corner, horrified by his mistake. The tailor, however, looked at the boy seriously for a few moments and then burst out laughing.

'Tare an' ouns,' he said after he had laughed his fill. 'I'll make the best suit I ever made in my life, just because you made me laugh. Any boy that makes me laugh deserves the best suit that was ever made. A good laugh is worth a good suit any day. Get ready now till I measure you.'

So Jimmy became happy again. The tailor's gear was laid out on a big table and when the tailor had drunk his tea Jimmy was measured. Then the tailor set to work with furious energy, pausing now and again to burst out into a peal of hearty laughter.

'Tare an' ouns,' he repeated after each laugh. 'That deserves a good suit if anything ever did.'

He kept his promise, too, for the little suit fitted perfectly and on the following Sunday Jimmy was the envy of all the other village boys as he went to church.

———◆◆———

Liam O'Flaherty (1897–1984), novelist and short story writer, was born in the Aran Islands. After serving at the front in World War I, he led a group of dockers, seized the Rotunda in Dublin, and held it for a few days in 1921, and was an active Republican in the Civil War.

JOYCE CARY

Clouds Sailing

There is no more beautiful view in the world than that great lough, seventy square miles of salt water, from the mountains of Annish. We had heard my father call it beautiful, and so we enjoyed it with our minds as well as our feelings; keenly with both together. Wherever we went in Annish we were among the mountains and saw the lough or the ocean; often, from some high place, the whole Annish peninsula, between the two great loughs; and the Atlantic, high up in the sky, seeming like a mountain of water higher than the tallest of land. So that my memories are full of enormous skies, as bright as water, in which clouds sailed bigger than any others; fleets of monsters moving in one vast school up from the horizon and over my head, a million miles up, as it seemed to me, and then down again over the far-off mountains of Derry. They seemed to follow a curving surface of air concentric with the curve of the Atlantic which I could see bending down on either hand, a bow, which, even as a child of three or four, I knew to be the actual shape of the earth. Some grown-up, perhaps my father, had printed that upon my imagination, so that even while I was playing some childish game in the heather, red Indians or Eskimos, if I caught sight of the ocean with the tail of my eye, I would feel suddenly the roundness and independence of the world beneath me. I would feel it like a ship under my feet moving through air just like a larger stiffer cloud, and this gave me an extraordinary exhilaration. . . .

We travelled through this enormous and magnificent scene in tranquil happiness. We were tired from running about in the heather and already growing hungry we felt the nearness of supper, and bed, with the calm faith which belongs only to children and saints devoted to the love of God and sure of the delights of communing with him. In that faith, that certainty of coming joys, we existed in a contentment so profound that it was like a lazy kind of drunkenness. I can't count how many times I enjoyed that sense, riding in a sidecar whose swaying motion would have put me to sleep if I had not been obliged to hold on; so that while my body and head and legs were all swinging together in a half dream, my hand tightly clutched some other child's body; and the memory of bathing, shouting, tea, the blue smoke of picnic fires, was mixed with the dark evening clouds shaped like flying geese, the tall water stretching up to the top of the world, the mountains sinking into darkness like whales into the ocean and over all a sky so deep that the stars, faint green sparks, seemed lost in it and the very sense of it made the heart light and proud, like a bird.

From A HOUSE OF CHILDREN

Joyce Cary (1888–1957), artist and novelist, was born in Londonderry. Out of his political and military service in West Africa 1913–20, came four novels, including *Mr Johnson*; three about art followed, including *The Horse's Mouth*. Later, he wrote a political trilogy, starting with *Prisoner of Grace*. A further study of childhood is *Charley is My Darling*.

Tinkers

I had seen that tilt cart before! And the long, dark man who lounged on the seat, puffing a blackened clay pipe and staring at us with glittering mocking eyes – I had seen him too.

Dinny and I, on a March Monday morning, instead of going downhill to the convent school, had climbed and climbed until we were tired. We sat on the edge of the Fair Green and ate the bread and butter we should have kept until playtime. We didn't know what to do. It was grand to be sitting on the grass when the other children were chanting 'The cat sat on the mat,' or 'One and one make two; two and two make four.' But the wind was piercing and dust whirled along the road in dancing pyramids turned upside down. Our faces were dirty and our mouths dry. And what would happen when we went back home? It was the first time we had mitched. I watched Dinny's fat, cheerful face grow serious. Suddenly he dug his fists into his eyes and roared. I roared too. I longed for the high-backed benches in the classroom, the counting-frame with its coloured beads, the monstrous blackboard and Sister Alphonse, her robes smeared with chalk, her big white hands beating time, singing louder than all the children together.

Another sound rose above our weeping – hard, unkind laughter. I looked up at a tall, dark man standing in the roadway. His clothes were tattered and a yellow handkerchief was twisted about his head. He stood with his hands on his hips, swinging backwards and forwards, showing his sharp teeth in a mocking grin. Behind the man was a battered cart, drawn by a bony white horse. The cart had a torn, dirty-white cover and a row of babies' faces peered at us from the back. A young woman with an armful of sticks leaned against the shaft and an old woman, hidden in a black shawl, held her hand over her eyes as she looked at us. Other tinkers were hurrying along the road, each one loaded. I was so terrified I shut my eyes.

'Two little mitchers,' chuckled the man with the yellow handkerchief.

'An' I'm wonderin' what the dacent, very respectable people of Cork will do when they catch 'em.'

Dinny clutched my hand and we both howled louder.

'I suppose yez set out to jine the tinkers,' went on the dark man. 'Sure we've more childer than we know what to do wid. Ye can't sell 'em at a fair. Ye can't ate 'em for yer dinner. Still an' all, I'm terrible soft-hearted an' we'll squeeze in two more. Jump in there under the sate an', when the polis come sarchin', don't let the ghost of a sound out of yez.'

I opened my eyes to see was he pretending. But he stood there frowning and all his tribe looked so serious.

Dinny jumped up, pulling me with him. Away we ran. The tinkers' laughter followed us. I thought I could hear the dark man's feet pounding the road. Dinny still held my hand. He could run much faster, but he kept beside me. You could always trust Dinny. When we dared look back the tinkers had drawn their cart against a clump of bushes and the white horse was grazing. A fire of sticks blazed and not one of the tattered group bothered to gaze in our direction.

We didn't venture near the school. We went in to Mrs Foley and told our adventure. She was hanging wet clothes on the line at the back of her tumbledown little house. But she sat on her upturned bucket and listened with great sympathy.

'Ye poor scraps. Ye must have been demented. Don't I know 'tis great fun goin' mitchin'. But, mark me words – school's the safe place. The tinkers'll never come next or nigh ye while yez are in the school wid Sister Alphonse!'

'We weren't axactly mitchin',' explained Dinny.

'Ah, well, yez're only young once,' sighed Mrs Foley. 'Come in till I blow up the fire an' heat a sup of tay. 'Twill comfort yez.'

We drank the hot stewed tea. She found us two clay pipes and we blew soap bubbles with her washing water. When school time was over I went home across the road. Mrs Foley never told on us and Dinny and I kept our mitching a secret. But I dreamed night after night that the terrible tinker had put me into his cart with the tins and the babies. And here he was, sitting up in his chair, smoking steadily, his followers straggling over the roadway, leaving no room for our donkey to pass.

Peadar Keeley whistled and tried to draw Moddy to the side. But Moddy liked the centre of the road and kept on until her nose butted the white horse's. Mrs Hennessy sat up straight and folded her arms. She gazed at the dark tinker so calmly that he took his pipe from his mouth and held up his hand in greeting. Then he saw me. He flung back his head and laughed.

'Mitchin' again!' he cried. ' 'Pon me word, ye're a little strap!'

'I'm not mitching!' I declared, very brave now I had grown-up friends to protect me. 'I'm going visiting with Mrs Hennessy.'

The tinker stared at the storyteller. He stood up in the cart and bowed.

'The road's yours, ma'am,' he said grandly. 'I'd no notion 'twas yerself, Mrs Hennessy.'

With a tug of the reins he swung the white horse so that the restless, crowding tinkers had to scatter.

'Thank ye kindly, sir,' said Mrs Hennessy.

Moddy stuck one ear forward and trotted on, looking as pleased and proud as a donkey can look, while the tinkers made way for us.

'If that don't bate all!' exclaimed Peadar Keeley. 'Don't tell me! Didn't I alwys say 'tis better to have a gift than a crock of gold? If I'd only been a storyteller, or mebbe a fiddler instead of a turf carrier!'

Half asleep, leaning against Mrs Hennessy; warm, yet feeling the sweet night air, I saw the stone walls black against the white road. The bushes were black too, and seemed to leap and clutch as we went by. I had never seen such strange bushes, but I had never been out so late before.

'I'm not a bit afraid,' I thought proudly.

Indeed I had no reason to be afraid, with Mrs Hennessy holding me close and Peadar and Moddy just ahead, their little shadows trotting along with them. Peadar was still talking when I fell asleep. I slept while we passed through Macroom and crossed the river by the little stone bridge.

From A Storyteller's Childhood

———◆◇◆———

Patricia Lynch (1898–1972), author of children's novels (including *The Turf Cutter's Donkey*), was born in Cork, though the family moved to England after her father's death. She was sent to Ireland in 1916 by Sylvia Pankhurst to write about the Rising. From her marriage in 1920, she lived in Dublin.

KATE O'BRIEN

The French Test

The French test for the Emulation had by tradition to be severe, and Mother Felicita honourably set Anna a laborious one. She sat her in front of some sheets of foolscap and told her to write from memory and in full each of the four regular verb conjugations: *donner*, *finir*, *recevoir*, and *vendre*, the principal parts of each and, in order, the tenses derived from each principal part. She allotted her two hours for the task.

It was a heavy physical labour, but Anna knew how to conjugate regular verbs, and she set to work resolutely. At the end of two hours, a little tired from the sustained struggle to be tidy and systematic, and believing she had made no really bad mistake, she gave her foolscap sheets to Mother Felicita.

This was at midday. The results of the French tests would be announced during *goûter*, and those who had accomplished 70 per cent would spend the evening dreaming a little hysterically of the next day's Emulation. Those who had failed – there were always some – would withdraw to cry in the lavatory, or on the landing by the Foundress's bust, and their friends would put little holy pictures in their desks with 'Cheer up' or *'Priez pour moi'* written on the backs.

Mother Mary Andrew did not customarily take *goûter* with the school. For that meal, in the interests of French conversation, Mère Marie-Claire, a lively tough nun not long out of Sainte Fontaine, sat in authority at Foundress's table. And as she taught all the senior French, it was fitting that she should strike the gong half-way through *goûter* and read the French test results.

There were some gasps of relief; there were some sad casualties – Cecilia Hooley being meanly served, everyone felt, with sixty-eight marks. But last on the list, sole representative of Second Preparatory, Anna Murphy sailed in safely with seventy-five. She was still the school baby, and the school cheered, and Mère Marie-Claire smiled down at

213

her and said: '*Mes félicitations, Anna; que ça continue, ma petite.*' So Anna felt happy and spent a happy evening.

That night she said her prayers well; she tried to be polite at supper, kept her elbows in and attended to her neighbour. At night recreation the others wanted to play 'Puss-in-the-corner', so she did not ask for '*Meunier, tu dors*'. In the dormitory she brushed her teeth with care, although she was very sleepy. She did not break silence once in the dressing-room, and as she went back between the rows of stiff white damasked curtains to her own cubicle, felt as peaceful as if she were in bed. Where the pools are bright and deep, she said to herself, where the grey trout lies asleep, up the river and o'er the lea ... but when she passed Our Lady's alcove she did not forget the convention of pausing to say a goodnight 'Hail Mary'. Monica Honan, a Child of Mary, was doing so at the same time, and Anna was careful to imitate her attitude before the statue.

As she stood there imagining herself into the importance of Monica Honan, as she stood there in her red dressing-gown and slippers, with her sponge-basket in her hands and her straight hair in a plait, Mother Mary Andrew came to the alcove and tapped her shoulder.

'I wish to speak to you, Anna.'

Anna was too sleepy to be surprised.

'Yes, Mother Mary Andrew.'

The nun sat down at a little table near the alcove where, under a dimmed light, she was accustomed to sit on guard, correcting exercises or reading her Office, until silence and sleep filled the dormitory. Quiet was already descending on the cubicles, and only the lowered alcove light burnt in the vast, shadowed room, so Mother Mary Andrew spoke softly.

'There has been a mistake about your French test, Anna, and you will *not* be in the Emulation tomorrow.'

Anna stared at her. What had been said drifted slowly into her sleepy brain.

'A mistake?'

'Yes. A very foolish mistake – of your own making.' Mother Mary Andrew opened the drawer of the table and produced the foolscap sheets of Anna's French conjugations. She laid them down and the child saw on the front page, in Mother Felicita's marking, a big blue-pencil 75/100 V.G. – but crossed through now by a red pencil, and replaced by a big red O. She could only stare at first. She felt very frightened.

'You – you've put a nought,' she said at last.

'Yes, Anna – because that is what it merits.'

'All my verbs? Oh, why did you? They're not all wrong! They couldn't be?'

'Certainly they're not all wrong. But in one conjugation you made a mistake so silly as to show that you have no understanding of what you are doing, and so cannot receive marks like an intelligent schoolgirl.'

'But – I got seventy-five. Mother Felicita gave me –'

'Mother Felicita is very kind to you, far too kind – and she evidently thinks that your getting the other conjugations right excuses the absurdity of your conjugating of *finir*. However, I disagree with her, and have told her that you are clearly too young for examinations, and for Emulation holidays!'

'But *finir* – I – I know it! *Finir, finissant, fini, je finis, je finis.* Oh, what did I do? What did I do?'

Anna wailed this question. There were uneasy stirrings in cubicles near by. Some listening girls had been tortured by Mother Mary Andrew in their time, and felt frightened now for the child they could not help.

'Be quiet, you insolent little girl! Look and see for yourself what you did.'

Anna looked. She had written the present participle of *finir* as *finant*. The error had been logically carried through the subsidiary parts of the verb which derived from the present participle, so that she had written *Je finais, que je fine,* and *que je fine.* Beside the initial mistake Mother Felicita had put a gentle blue cross of protest, and had written 'Anna! Anna!' in the margin. And her pencil streaked through the derivative errors.

But all this blue reasonableness had now been slashed with red.

Anna was completely bewildered. She saw the foolishness of her mistake, which really was only foolishness, because she knew quite well about *finissant* and *que je finisse.* But Mother Felicita had taken away twenty-five marks for it – and there were no other mistakes. She was sorry to have been so silly as to write *finant*, but she could not understand why she might have *no* marks, and no Emulation.

'I only made that one mistake,' she said shakily. 'That's why I got seventy-five.'

'You dare to call it *one* mistake?'

'It is only one mistake. How silly.' Anna's courage flowed back for a second. 'Because you see, when I put *finant* I had to put the others. It would have been sillier even if I didn't. Oh, don't you see?'

'How dare you try to instruct me, miss?'

'Oh, I'm sorry, Mother Mary Andrew! Please, please let me have my marks! Oh, it was only that one word! It isn't fair! Mother Felicita –'

She was crying wildly, her head down on the foolscap sheets. She knew that she was in the grip of omnipotence, that there was no Emulation, and that she only wanted to be at home, with Charlie.

There were twistings, mutterings, behind some curtains.

Mother Mary Andrew took Anna's shoulder in her enormous hand and shook her.

'Be quiet, you impertinent child! Everything you say proves that you are only a baby and unfit for an Emulation holiday – even if this paper did not show it conclusively!'

The words were hissed in a half-whisper. Anna wailed out loud in reply:

'Go away, go away! I'm going home! I'm going to run away! If my Daddy were here – oh, Daddy! – oh, oh!'

Mother Mary Andrew shook her again and hissed at her to be quiet. Then she half dragged, half carried her to her cubicle and pushed her inside.

'Get yourself to bed at once, miss – I'll wait here until I know you're undressed and in bed. And don't forget an Act of Contrition, if you please!'

She began to pace up and down the aisle outside the cubicles, uttering hisses for silence to the uneasy occupants.

Anna sank in a heap in her dark cubicle, on the strip of carpet. She did not cry out loud any more, but she was choking and shaking with tears. She had never before been the victim of an injustice which she could see; she had never been shaken and dragged, and arbitrarily refused a pleasure she had won and been promised. She had never been flung into a dark place, crying, and left to find her nightdress in the dark, and go to bed crying.

Molly Redmond was in the next cubicle. She ran her hand down under the stiff white curtain, and groped on the floor for Anna. When she found her shoulder she thrust her head under the curtain too, risking its starchy rattle. She dared not speak, but she stretched more than half-way out of her bed and caressed the sobbing child, but Anna did not seem to feel her, and just shivered and choked where she lay. In terror Molly slipped her whole self under the curtain and bending over Anna picked her up and seated her on the bed. She found her nightdress under the pillow, and keeping an arm around her, kissing the hot, wet face, but silent as death, she undressed her. As she pulled the nightdress over

216

Anna's head, Mother Mary Andrew entered the cubicle and gripped her by the shoulders.

'How dare you leave your bed and enter another. Insubordination *and* immodesty! I suppose you know that I could give you a mark for conduct now, or have you expelled! Let go of that nightdress and return to your bed at once!'

She dragged Molly away from Anna with violence.

'She was lying on the floor – she couldn't undress herself.'

'No excuses, Molly Redmond! For an action like this there *are* none.'

'Oh, she's only a baby – and she *deserves* the Emulation –'

'So you've been listening to what wasn't your concern! I might have known – coming from your sort of home. There are some things which unfortunately no education can eliminate.'

Mother Mary Andrew pushed the girl out of the cubicle and round into her own. Molly fought under the terrible grip of her hand.

'How dare you say that about my home? How dare you insult me in this way?' she sobbed.

Mother Mary Andrew flung her into the cubicle and stood on guard outside the curtain until she thought her two victims were asleep. Then she withdrew to her own sleeping place, afar in the shadow of the inner dormitory.

Then Molly slipped back again under the curtain. Anna was huddled in a twitching, choking heap on the quilt – her nightdress only half on, as she had been left. Molly got her second arm into it, and buttoned her up. She put her day-clothes on the chair and picked the little girl up to settle her in bed.

Anna's arm went round her then, and she awoke and gave a wail which Molly hushed against her shoulder. But the shaking of the small body distressed her very much. She was twelve years old, and the sobbing burden in her arms made her feel grown up and brave and tender.

'I want to go home. I want Charlie,' Anna was saying.

Molly got into her bed with her and rocked her to sleep in her arms.

From The Land of Spices

———•◦•———

Kate O'Brien (1897–1974), novelist, dramatist and journalist, was born in Limerick. She was a governess in Spain, then lived in England for twenty years, and returned to Ireland before settling in Kent. She won the Hawthornden and James Tait Black Prizes.

Concentration Camp

Grief in childhood is complicated with many other miseries. I was taken into the bedroom where my mother lay dead; as they said, 'to see her', in reality, as I at once knew, 'to see it'. There was nothing that a grown-up would call disfigurement – except for that total disfigurement which is death itself. Grief was overwhelmed in terror. To this day I do not know what they mean when they call dead bodies beautiful. The ugliest man alive is an angel of beauty compared with the loveliest of the dead. Against all the subsequent paraphernalia of coffin, flowers, hearse, and funeral I reacted with horror. I even lectured one of my aunts on the absurdity of mourning clothes in a style which would have seemed to most adults both heartless and precocious; but this was our dear Aunt Annie, my maternal uncle's Canadian wife, a woman almost as sensible and sunny as my mother herself. To my hatred for what I already felt to be all the fuss and flummery of the funeral I may perhaps trace something in me which I now recognize as a defect but which I have never fully overcome – a distaste for all that is public, all that belongs to the collective; a boorish inaptitude for formality.

My mother's death was the occasion of what some (but not I) might regard as my first religious experience. When her case was pronounced hopeless I remembered what I had been taught; that prayers offered in faith would be granted. I accordingly set myself to produce by will-power a firm belief that my prayers for her recovery would be successful; and, as I thought, I achieved it. When nevertheless she died I shifted my ground and worked myself into a belief that there was to be a miracle. The interesting thing is that my disappointment produced no results beyond itself. The thing hadn't worked, but I was used to things not working, and I thought no more about it. I think the truth is that the belief into which I had hypnotized myself was itself too irreligious for its failure to cause any religious revolution. I had approached God, or my idea of God, without love, without awe, even without fear. He was, in

218

my mental picture of this miracle, to appear neither as Saviour nor as Judge, but merely as a magician; and when He had done what was required of Him I supposed He would simply – well, go away. It never crossed my mind that the tremendous contact which I solicited should have any consequences beyond restoring the *status quo*. I imagine that a 'faith' of this kind is often generated in children and that its disappointment is of no religious importance; just as the things believed in, if they could happen and be only as the child pictures them, would be of no religious importance either.

With my mother's death all settled happiness, all that was tranquil and reliable, disappeared from my life. There was to be much fun, many pleasures, many stabs of Joy; but no more of the old security. It was sea and islands now; the great continent had sunk like Atlantis.

Clop-clop-clop-clop ... we are in a four-wheeler rattling over the uneven squaresets of the Belfast streets through the damp twilight of a September evening, 1908; my father, my brother, and I. I am going to school for the first time. We are in low spirits. My brother, who has most reason to be so, for he alone knows what we are going to, shows his feelings least. He is already a veteran. I perhaps am buoyed up by a little excitement, but very little. The most important fact at the moment is the horrible clothes I have been made to put on. Only this morning – only two hours ago – I was running wild in shorts and blazer and sandshoes. Now I am choking and sweating, itching too, in thick dark stuff, throttled by an Eton collar, my feet already aching with unaccustomed boots. I am wearing knickerbockers that button at the knee. Every night for some forty weeks of every year and for many a year I am to see the red, smarting imprint of those buttons in my flesh when I undress. Worst of all is the bowler-hat, apparently made of iron, which grasps my head. I have read of boys in the same predicament who welcomed such things as signs of growing up; I had no such feeling. Nothing in my experience had ever suggested to me that it was nicer to be a schoolboy than a child or nicer to be a man than a schoolboy. My brother never talked much about school in the holidays. My father, whom I implicitly believed, represented adult life as one of incessant drudgery under the continual threat of financial ruin. In this he did not mean to deceive us. Such was his temperament that when he exclaimed, as he frequently did, 'There'll soon be nothing for it but the workhouse,' he momentarily believed, or at least felt, what he said. I took it all literally and had the gloomiest anticipation of adult life. In the meantime, the putting on of the school clothes was, I well knew, the assumption of a prison uniform.

We reach the quay and go on board the old 'Fleetwood boat'; after some miserable strolling about the deck my father bids us good-bye. He is deeply moved; I, alas, am mainly embarrassed and self-conscious. When he has gone ashore we almost, by comparison, cheer up. My brother begins to show me over the ship and tell me about all the other shipping in sight. He is an experienced traveller and a complete man of the world. A certain agreeable excitement steals over me. I like the reflected port and starboard lights on the oily water, the rattle of winches, the warm smell from the engine-room skylight. We cast off. The black space widens between us and the quay; I feel the throb of screws underneath me. Soon we are dropping down the Lough and there is a taste of salt on one's lips, and that cluster of lights astern, receding from us, is everything I have known. Later, when we have gone to our bunks, it begins to blow. It is a rough night and my brother is sea-sick. I absurdly envy him this accomplishment. He is behaving as experienced travellers should. By great efforts I succeed in vomiting; but it is a poor affair – I was, and am, an obstinately good sailor.

No Englishman will be able to understand my first impressions of England. When we disembarked, I suppose at about six next morning (but it seemed to be midnight), I found myself in a world to which I reacted with immediate hatred. The flats of Lancashire in the early morning are in reality a dismal sight; to me they were like the banks of the Styx. The strange English accents with which I was surrounded seemed like the voices of demons. But what was worst was the English landscape from Fleetwood to Euston. Even to my adult eye that main line still appears to run through the dullest and most unfriendly strip in the island. But to a child who had always lived near the sea and in sight of high ridges it appeared as I suppose Russia might appear to an English boy. The flatness! The interminableness! The miles and miles of featureless land, shutting one in from the sea, imprisoning, suffocating! Everything was wrong; wooden fences instead of stone walls and hedges, red brick farmhouses instead of white cottages, the fields too big, haystacks the wrong shape. Well does the *Kalevala* say that in the stranger's house the floor is full of knots. I have made up the quarrel since; but at that moment I conceived a hatred for England which took many years to heal.

Our destination was the little town of – let us call it Belsen – in Hertfordshire. 'Green Hertfordshire', Lamb calls it; but it was not green to a boy bred in County Down. It was flat Hertfordshire, flinty Hertfordshire, Hertfordshire of the yellow soil. There is the same difference between the climate of Ireland and of England as between that of England and the Continent. There was far more weather at Belsen than I had ever met before; there I first knew bitter frost and stinging fog, sweltering heat and thunderstorms on the great scale. There, through the curtainless dormitory windows, I first came to know the ghastly beauty of the full moon.

The school, as I first knew it, consisted of some eight or nine boarders and about as many day-boys. Organized games, except for endless rounders in the flinty playground, had long been moribund and were finally abandoned not very long after my arrival. There was no bathing except one's weekly bath in the bathroom. I was already doing Latin exercises (as taught by my mother) when I went there in 1908, and I was still doing Latin exercises when I left there in 1910; I had never got in sight of a Roman author. The only stimulating element in the teaching consisted of a few well-used canes which hung on the green iron chimney-piece of the single schoolroom. The teaching staff consisted of the headmaster and proprietor (we called him Oldie), his grown-up son (Wee Wee), and an usher. The ushers succeeded one another with great rapidity; one lasted for less than a week. Another was dismissed in the presence of the boys, with a rider from Oldie to the effect that if he were not in Holy Orders he would kick him downstairs. This curious scene took place in the dormitory, though I cannot remember why. All these ushers (except the one who stayed less than a week) were obviously as much in awe of Oldie as we. But there came a time when there were no more ushers, and Oldie's youngest daughter taught the junior pupils. By that time there were only five boarders, and Oldie finally gave up his school and sought a cure of souls. I was one of the last survivors, and left the ship only when she went down under us.

Oldie lived in a solitude of power, like a sea-captain in the days of sail. No man or woman in that house spoke to him as an equal. No one except Wee Wee initiated conversation with him at all. At meal times we boys had a glimpse of his family life. His son sat on his right hand; they two had separate food. His wife and three grown-up daughters (silent), the usher (silent), and the boys (silent) munched their inferior messes. His wife, though I think she never addressed Oldie, was allowed to make something of a reply to him; the girls – three tragic figures, dressed summer and winter in the same shabby black – never went beyond an almost whispered 'Yes, Papa', or 'No, Papa', on the rare occasions when they were addressed. Few visitors entered the house. Beer, which Oldie

221

and Wee Wee drank regularly at dinner, was offered to the usher but he was expected to refuse; the one who accepted got his pint, but was taught his place by being asked a few moments later in a voice of thunderous iron, 'Perhaps you would like a little *more* beer, Mr N.?' Mr N., a man of spirit, replied casually, 'Well, thank you, Mr C., I think I would.' He was the one who did not stay till the end of his first week; and the rest of that day was a black one for us boys.

I myself was rather a pet or mascot of Oldie's – a position which I swear I never sought and of which the advantages were purely negative. Even my brother was not one of his favourite victims. For he had his favourite victims, boys who could do nothing right. I have known Oldie enter the schoolroom after breakfast, cast his eyes round, and remark, 'Oh, there you are, Rees, you horrid boy. If I'm not too tired I shall give you a good drubbing this afternoon.' He was not angry, nor was he joking. He was a big, bearded man with full lips like an Assyrian king on a monument, immensely strong, physically dirty. Everyone talks of sadism nowadays but I question whether his cruelty had any erotic element in it. I half divined then, and seem to see clearly now, what all his whipping-boys had in common. They were the boys who fell below a certain social status, the boys with vulgar accents. Poor P. – dear, honest, hard-working, friendly, healthily pious P. – was flogged incessantly, I now think, for one offence only; he was the son of a dentist. I have seen Oldie make that child bend down at one end of the schoolroom and then take a run of the room's length at each stroke; but P. was the trained sufferer of countless thrashings and no sound escaped him until, towards the end of the torture, there came a noise quite unlike a human utterance. That peculiar croaking or rattling cry, that, and the grey faces of all the other boys, and their deathlike stillness, are among the memories I could willingly dispense with.*

The curious thing is that despite all this cruelty we did surprisingly little work. This may have been partly because the cruelty was irrational and unpredictable; but it was partly because of the curious methods employed. Except at geometry (which he really liked) it might be said that Oldie did not teach at all. He called his class up and asked questions. When the replies were unsatisfactory he said in a low, calm voice, 'Bring me my cane. I see I shall need it.' If a boy became confused Oldie flogged the desk, shouting in a crescendo, 'Think – Think – THINK!!' Then, as the prelude to execution, he muttered, 'Come out, come out,

* This punishment was for a mistake in a geometrical proof.

come out.' When really angry he proceeded to antics; worming for wax in his ear with his little finger and babbling, 'Aye, aye, aye, aye ...' I have seen him leap up and dance round and round like a performing bear. Meanwhile, almost in whispers, Wee Wee or the usher, or (later) Oldie's youngest daughter, was questioning us juniors at another desk. 'Lessons' of this sort did not take very long; what was to be done with the boys for the rest of the time? Oldie had decided that they could, with least trouble to himself, be made to do arithmetic. Accordingly, when you entered school at nine o'clock you took your slate and began doing sums. Presently you were called up to 'say a lesson'. When that was finished you went back to your place and did more sums – and so for ever. All the other arts and sciences thus appeared as islands (mostly rocky and dangerous islands)

> *Which like to rich and various gems inlaid*
> *The unadorned bosom of the deep*

– the deep being a shoreless ocean of arithmetic. At the end of the morning you had to say how many sums you had done; and it was not quite safe to lie. But supervision was slack and very little assistance was given. My brother – I have told you that he was already a man of the world – soon found the proper solution. He announced every morning with perfect truth that he had done five sums; he did not add that they were the same five every day. It would be interesting to know how many thousand times he did them.

From SURPRISED BY JOY

———◦◦———

C. S. Lewis (1898–1963), academic, popular theologian and novelist, was born in Belfast. He was a Fellow of Magdalen College, Oxford, and then from 1954 Professor of Medieval and Renaissance English at Cambridge. His works include *The Allegory of Love, The Screwtape Letters* and, for children, the 'Narnia' series of adventures which begins with *The Lion, the Witch and the Wardrobe*.

T. R. HENN

The Funeral

On November the tenth 1915, my Father died. He had been ill for many months; how ill I, with a boy's carelessness, did not notice. He had spent some weeks in the summer in a nursing home at Limerick, and then, I imagine, realizing how hopeless his condition was, returned to die at Paradise, in the room overlooking the Italian garden. I should have been forewarned; for on the morning of my return to school for the September term, he called me to his room, with the dog-cart waiting at the door, made me kneel down and blessed me. No doubt it was a ritual handed on to him. I can remember little of what he said except: 'You are coming into the world. I am going out.' Yet it made a double impression, for in the middle my Mother burst into the room, impatient at the delay, saying that I would surely miss the train at the station, twelve miles off. Angrily he told her to go and leave us alone. We caught the train, and I went to school as usual.

On the morning of the tenth I woke up with excitement, anticipating letters and parcels for my birthday. These would be handed out in the eleven o'clock break. At about nine the headmaster sent for me and took me to walk round the paths of the big square walled garden. No doubt he was kind in breaking the news; but he kept on repeating (that is all I can remember of the interview) that though I was going home that day, I must be sure to return as soon as possible and make up the time I had lost, since I was sitting for a scholarship at the end of term.

The train left some hours later. It was bitterly cold with intermittent snow. I was sent to the matron's room to wait, and played idly with something, perhaps a jigsaw puzzle. It came with a curious shock, for I seemed wholly numb, when after a long silence the matron looked at me and said: 'Oh, Henn, I *am* sorry for you.' I got on the train, which crawled wearily through the starved November countryside. At a desolate junction, I remember looking longingly at some dish or other in a glass-case in the waiting-room – sardines on toast – which I could not buy, for I had been given only my train-fare and nothing over. Finally, in the late evening I arrived at Ennis, the country town, where I was met by friends and put up for the night. The next morning I was driven out to Paradise. In the hall the impression was of an intense quiet blackness: my Mother and my sisters in the heavy veiled mourning of the time, all speaking with hushed voices, and faces that seemed unnaturally white. Two events stand out. My Mother asked me if I wished to see my Father before he was put into his coffin. I hesitated, and finally said that I did not. In after years this seemed something of a betrayal. I rationalized it by trying to convince myself that I wished to remember him as he had been that summer, in the low room looking out on the small Italian garden and the woods: I used to sit by his bedside after my return from the River, and go over with him the day's events, pool by pool and cast by cast.

The funeral was not for two days; my Mother decided wisely that there was little point in my hanging about the desolate hushed house, and suggested that I should take my gun and go out. I had never before seen the woods in autumn; they were lying leaf-meal, wet and cold, and I wandered round them with one of the boys. I cannot remember that I shot anything, and I think the people on the estate were rather scandalized.

The day of the funeral there was a high gale with sleet and snow; the great woods that screened the house from the south-west were in trouble, and a number of trees were blown down. It was a custom with us that the womenfolk should not go to the grave-side; my Father had thought it too great an emotional strain. The first part of the service was held in the hall, with its big glass door looking out over the Shannon: a faint light coming through the Victorian Gothic stained-glass windows at the sides, that carried various family coats-of-arms. There was an immense polished chest, holding tennis-gear and the like. On the walls hung curved cavalry swords in their leather-and-brass scabbards. I remember that I was taught to kiss weapon-steel if I ever had occasion to unsheathe it. (These swords were later taken by the IRA on one of their many raids.) The coffin stood on two stools, whose supports were negro boys carved in ebony. After the preliminary service it was carried on the shoulders of men, a great body of the tenantry following, half a mile across the fields, to the tiny burial-ground on the hill. The scene was impressed vividly on me, for this was the first funeral I had seen: the hill-top looking out over the estuary, with its screen of small storm-bent larches and firs, and clumps of rhododendrons below; the mass of brown-red shale and earth by the grave-side; the white surplice of the Canon; the driven sleety snow. The coffin was lowered slowly and clumsily on ropes, into some inches of snow and water; the three handfuls of earth sounded muffled upon its lid, even as Browne set them out in the fifth chapter of *Urne Buriall*:

Now since these dead bones ...

Many years afterwards the emotion returned in verse:

Why should the dead go down into water, and the snowflakes
Melt on the coffin lid?
O but the empty house, and the rusting gun
And all that wisdom gone when I needed it so.

I went back to school, to return again for the Christmas holidays. It was then that the first numbness of loss, that is like the blow of a bullet, came back painfully into life. Part of the house was shut up; my Mother and I lived mainly in the library, which was small and relatively draught-proof. We still had two maids, but the whole establishment had contracted and changed. There occurred one of those small ridiculous incidents that loom so large and so bitterly in life. In the smoking-room which looked on to the inner courtyard and served as a study, gun-room and office, where the country-people came with their disputes and troubles, my Father had a large black desk. Many associations were clustered about it; it had been one of my earliest memories of Sligo. In it my Father had kept on one side his fishing-tackle, reels, fly-tying material; on the other, his diaries and miscellaneous papers. My Mother had taken the desk, tumbled the contents into a vast heap, and put them in a disused room. I was resentful and very angry, not quite knowing why. Some *mana* had passed, and the gulf widened between my Mother and myself.

From FIVE ARCHES

———•◦•———

T. R. Henn (1901–74), academic and writer, was born in Sligo. During World War II he became a brigadier. He was President of St Catherine's College, Cambridge 1951–61.

L. A. G. STRONG

The Tram Ride

The tram was one of the big new ones, with a covered top. They climbed up, and took seats near the front. Nicky preferred the other kind, because he could watch the trailer skimming along on the wire overhead, and hear its song; but the back door of the tram was open, and he soon realized that he could hear the trailer, even if he couldn't see it.

The top of the tram was crowded. Big men smoking pipes sat around; he could not see properly in front of him. Soon they started, the tram nosing its way suspiciously along in all the traffic, crawling up past the Bank, past Trinity, along the Green, and then, with a sound of pleasure, beginning to go faster along the clearer roads towards Merrion Square. The narrow sides of the streets fell away, the tall gloomy houses were succeeded by smaller, kindlier houses; they were in suburban roads, gentler, friendlier roads, with trees, and already, though they were headed away from the sunset, the skies were lighter, the air came fresher, and the song of the trailer grew to the steady rising and falling buzz that Nicky loved so well. Wider and wider the roads became, lighter the skies, and faster the tram sped homeward. The big men sitting around them had to raise their voices to be heard. Nicky looked at them, watching the play of their faces, as they uttered words he could not hear; watching them puff at their great pipes, or knock them out against the leg of the seat; bewildered by the bawling of their voices. Then the houses fell right away, and they were out on the open road by Merrion, rushing along by the wide stretch of the sands and the Bay. Evening was coming on; the arm of Howth lay far-flung and dim; the sands stretched away, limitless, glimmering; one could not discern where they met the sea. On them here and there, far out, stooped the tiny black figures of the cockle gatherers. The tram stopped for a moment, and a new noise roused Nicky. He looked and saw, quite close to the road, the railway, with a train rushing along towards them, its engine straddling widely, the clank of its mechanism echoing off the low brown wall between it and the sands. Then the tram started off again, drowning the train's sound, till he could hear only a soft woolly puffing as it rushed past. The wall looked extraordinarily clear and close, because there was nothing definite beyond it, only the soft shimmer of the sands. A couple of boys were walking along the top of it, balancing, their arms outstretched delicately against the frail evening air.

The tram gathered speed, and the song of the trailer rose in ecstasy. Nicky's head began to nod. He was sleepy. The song of the trailer rose and fell, rose and fell; the skies kept opening and shutting, opening and shutting, with a roaring of alternate light and darkness: and every now and then something bumped him into a fresh awareness of his surroundings.

It was darker. They had passed Booterstown; they were among trees. The voices of two men talking came to him with a sudden unnatural loudness.

'Yes,' said one. 'I hope to go and see him to-morra. But sure, to-morra where might I be? I might be in Rathdrum, the same as I was tellin' ye. I might be in Dublin, I might be in Foxrock, or in Malahide – '

'Or in God's pocket,' put in the second voice.

There was a silence, in which the first speaker, a big, red-faced man, stared at his companion.

'Faith,' he said at last. 'Ye must be a very religious man.'

'Oh,' said the other, well content with the impression he had produced, 'I wouldn't tell ye that for certain, now.'

Then Nicky, after one blink at the main street of Blackrock, fell asleep in good earnest, and knew no more till his mother was shaking him and telling him they were just coming to Sandycove station.

'We're getting down a stop sooner,' she explained 'because Daddy wants to get some tobacco.'

It was cold out of the tram. A wind was blowing. Nicky's legs were stiff. He walked along reluctantly, holding fast to his mother's hand. Their father strode on ahead to the tobacco shop, Jack trotting beside him. Nicky blinked, and tagged along, enduring, till they should reach home.

Their father had not come out of the shop by the time they reached it, so they stood, looking in at the window. George, who after his own manner had been walking by himself just behind them, on the edge of the pavement, was for the moment forgotten. A breeze stirred along the street, raising a newspaper, which careered grotesquely along till it hit a wall. Laura snuggled her chin down into her collar, and shivered.

The door swung open, and Nicky's father stood beside them.

'You needn't have waited,' he said, half apologetically. 'I'm sorry to have – Merciful God! Look at that child!'

He pointed. Laura stood frozen with horror. A tram was rushing down the short hill, full speed round the curve. Almost in the path of it, close beside the lines, stood George. They saw him look coolly at it, stretch out his hand, as if calculating his distance, then shift his feet a little nearer. Suddenly the street was full of shouting. White faced, the tram-driver shoved on his brakes. With a hideous grind, that sharpened to a shriek of anguished metal, the tram slid to a halt, sparks flying viciously from beneath its wheels. Recovering himself with an oath, Nicky's father ran forward: but other hands were there before him, and George was dragged off to the pavement and to safety.

He stared at them all with a calm and dreamy amazement.

'But it's quite all right,' he kept repeating. 'I only wanted to touch it as it went past.'

From SEA WALL

L. A. G. Strong (1898–1958), poet, novelist and broadcaster, was born in Plymouth of Irish parents, and spent many holidays in Ireland as a child.

Bowen's Court

I remember our Sunday tramrides out to Mount Temple from Herbert Place. Those first winters, we spent many Sundays there. The terraced lawns, the big double drawing-room and the enchanting persiflage of the uncles and aunts on me very early worked their spell: I remember my grandmother's decisive manner and animated face. On weekdays I wore a Robert-like, buttoned-up reefer coat, and was gratified by strangers calling me 'Sonny', but on Sundays my sex proclaimed itself by the wearing of a white fuzzy muff, slung round my neck on a cord, a white coat and a white saucer-shaped hat with an ostrich feather peeping over the brim. With my grandmother's death Mount Temple came to an end: the house was sold and the Colleys scattered. My mother's brothers and sisters, for different reasons, gravitated to England or even further abroad. Only Aunt Maud, at that time occupied with the conversion of Jews in Dublin, and other interests, remained for some time in lodgings at the other side (from us) of the canal. And my mother's eldest and much-loved brother George settled in bachelor lodgings in Herbert Place, two or three doors away from No. 15. He had been left deaf by an illness when he was very young, but he lip-read and, quite apart from the lips, read character and sized up a situation with almost disconcering exactitude. His great interest was motor cars; he kept the earliest kind, and I remember going for dreamlike drives with him. He came placidly in and out of No. 15, and he was to support my mother through the worst of her years.

As a mother my mother was far from vague; she had many ideas, but none of them foolish ones. She arranged for me to drink a good deal of milk, because she believed that children who drank tea early grew up rather runty, or like jockeys; she made me wear gloves, because Bowens got freckled hands; she did not let me learn to read till I was seven, because she perceived that Bowens overworked their brains. It was her great wish (survival, perhaps, of the expectations she had formed of

Robert) that I should not be muffish. Though horses bored and alarmed her, and bored Henry, she insisted that I should learn to ride – on a sofa-broad white Iceland pony called Softnose – not long after I was able to stand, and, mortified by her own late start in dancing, she sent me to dancing-class at about that time. Determined that I should be with literate people, she dismissed my nurse for a governess when I was four years old. My first governess was not a great success: she was not very literate, looked like a Manet and found Bowen's Court *triste*. My mother insisted that I must not be shy; she considered shyness common and, still worse, dull; she detested children who 'burrowed' when they were introduced. To counteract effects of my being an only child she plunged me into the middle of young society. In Dublin, in County Cork I was seldom alone – or if I were I do not remember it. Her quest of ordinariness for me was quite successful: I was neither interesting nor dreamy, nor, except in the use of long words, original. She gave me – most important of all as a start in life – the radiant, confident feeling of being loved. But her behaviour with me was never fatuous; she tried very hard to be critical. She explained to me, with a belyingly hopeful look, that I would never be pretty, but that she hoped I would grow up to have a nice character.

In Dublin there were, of course, plenty of children, and in County Cork I was as social as Henry III. Most of the houses known in Henry III's day, and others new since his day, had put out children, and where there were no children we were kindly received. There were a great many parties. At Bowen's Court one used to jump on the steps with excitement as a vibration throughout the silent country developed into a rumble of carriage-wheels – the little So-and-Sos coming to tea. The governesses made friends, exchanged novels and taught each other to plait crêpe paper hats. They kept dry jerseys and changes of knickers for when each other's charges fell into the stream or river near which each big house was unerringly placed, and beside which we always wanted to play. And on summer Sunday mornings at Farahy church we had, in those days of King Edward, quite a parade – the little Olivers from Rockmills, the little Gateses from the other side of Kildorrery, myself and the little Johnsons from Lisnagorneen. The sun winked in through the trees and the south windows on to pewfuls of little girls in white muslin dresses and starched white muslin hats, and of little boys in sailor suits. Parents, grandmothers (there was 'old Mrs Oliver'), visitors, governesses, Protestant farmers and, packed at the back, the Protestant servants of all households, composed the rest of the congregation; the organ was played either by Mrs Oliver or by Mrs Gates, and we all sang loud, confident Protestant hymns. The rector loved all insects, and was said to encourage the ingress of wasps to church; he had a sharp sense of the sins of society, and sometimes he used to denounce us from the pulpit. The Olivers – I think in surviving protest against the shutting-down of their Rockmills church, of which nothing but spire and weatherfish now remained – always used to come in a little late, clattering booted over the grating in the aisle. After church we all trooped down to the Farahy gate, to watch the horses being unhitched from the gateposts and backed into the shafts of the wagonettes and the traps. . . .

Like every one else's, my early summers were fine. My mother had a white India-muslin dress, on which the silk embroidery turned to parchment-yellow: from the hem a green rim never quite laundered out – the dress was always trailing over the grass. We used to have tea where my grandmother had had tea, in the spongy, shady corner of the big tennis lawn. She tried to drive the phaeton, but she did not drive well and my father thought the enterprise a mistake. I remember standing with her, in the sunset, at the end of one of the Bowen's Court fields: at the other end stood a horse, quietly eating, so she took my hand and said in her most controlled voice: 'We won't be frightened, will we?'

At three I was taken to England to visit my Fiennes first cousins, and when I was six they visited Bowen's Court. When I was five a little girl called Gerry, whose parents were in India, came to live with us for a year – she was very pretty indeed, with brown eyes and a cleft chin, and she was mad on horses. At Bowen's Court, she and I slept in the four-windowed bedroom over the drawing-room that had been my nursery from the first. On one pane of a window my name is written, with the diamond in my mother's big ring.

It was in the year Gerry was with us that the shadow I did not notice began to form. My mother had been right in her intuition that all Bowens, and Henry VI in particular, overtaxed their brains. Henry had left the Bar for the Land Commission: he became an examiner of titles in one of the most technical branches of the Court. The rhythm of his intellectual life changed, and became too much accelerated: under the attraction and excitement of his special subject, and under new conditions that did not suit him (the solitude and high pressure of an office after the chatty amenities of the Law Library) he consistently worked too hard, till, day and night, his work was never out of his mind. At the same time, he was prey to a private worry: owing to some misjudgement or inattention he had lost some of his capital – a sum that, in view of

232

what were his father's finances, appears really pathetically small. Self-reproach, and a fear that my mother and I might suffer, pressed further upon his desperate tiredness. He was in the grip of a sort of prolonged, relentless *coup de trois heures*: he began to see the past as a burning pattern not of his own injuries but of his own mistakes. His childish isolation from the rest of the Bowens, the Calvinism of nursery teaching, his mother's death and its reason, his struggles against his father, followed by Robert's darkness of mind and death, the anxieties with which, as the young Boss, he had attempted to rule his younger brothers and sisters – pain from the past, sense of losing grip on the present and dread of the future all rushed in on him now. The illness that stole six years of Henry VI's life from him was called anaemia of the brain.

Much of the physical weakness was to be traced back to early days. I have described the cheerlessness of *that* Bowen's Court nursery: Robert's heir, like all the rest of his children, had been under-nourished. On top of this, he had overdrawn on himself by growing tall so quickly, thinking so hard – no attempt had been made to slack Henry down. When he had been promoted to Robert's dinner table, when he was at school, at college, it must have been always the same – he bolted his food absently, and he had not the temperament that makes for a good digestion. And on uncertain digestion followed uncertain sleep. As one instinctively seeks health he had always sought merriness, gentleness, simple things, but the apparent placidity of his own nature was decep- tive. For marriage he had chosen a beautiful companion, some one who in his keeping had acquired a calm she did not by nature have – but not a capable soul who would mother him. He had been exposed, through no wish of Florence's, to more than the usual discomforts of a young *ménage*: as had already appeared at Mount Temple, she was not a born housekeeper. Henry had said once that he liked chops, so chops, in all stages of over and undercooking, appeared with affectionate regularity. In the first years of their marriage they had had some shocking cooks. There did finally come to them as a cook a Kerry girl, Margaret, who was an angel: through one of the worst phases of Henry's illness she was one of the few friends to whom he would listen, but her wise care and good cooking came too late. Henry, as a man in his early forties, needed much he did not get and did not consciously want. He was in no position to overwork, as he overworked from his start with the Land Commission.

My father and mother were accustomed to be together in long phases of happy absence of mind, punctuated by impetuous moments when they communicated to one another their thoughts. When she came down to earth, she could be very perceptive, but she was not observant in the ordinary way. I believe that for months, at the outset of his illness, she only found him more absent-minded than usual. She would have feared to hurt him by commenting on his increasing sombreness, or on the irritability to the point of violence that was so very unlike him. If his estrangement from her, that she could not understand, hurt her, it hurt too much for her to speak of it. For a long time she, who as a girl had been so stormy, went on flying her flag of serenity: she may have told herself that she was imagining things. The world saw what was the matter before she did. The dignity or detachment that lay behind her intimacies with people made it hard for friends to speak bluntly to her. Her mother was dead, her brothers and sisters, with the exception of George, scattered, and she was more alone than she really knew. But I think it must have been from something *somebody* said that she first realized the truth about Henry's state.

From her and me, from the safeness of Herbert Place with its canal reflections and friendly hum of the sawmill, from Bowen's Court and its people and the guests on the steps he was being drawn away. He saw these things in the distance and through black glass, till to see them became the most terrible thing of all. He wanted to be with me, because I was a child and his child. And with strangers he remained most like himself, because his habit of courtesy was stronger than any illness. He was at ease with my Uncle George, who used to come and take him for long walks, round the Dublin roads or along Sandymount strand.

From Bowen's Court

———•○•———

Elizabeth Bowen (1899–1973), novelist and short story writer, was born in Dublin. She lived most of her life in England, but on her father's death in 1928 she inherited the family estate, Bowen's Court, in Co. Cork. Her novels include *The Last September*, *The Heat of the Day* and *Eva Trout*.

SEAN O'FAOLAIN

Into the Attics

To the outsider observing us three brothers we must have seemed to lead a wretchedly dull life, we were so severely disciplined. Our daily routine was adamant. We rose at eight, except during Lent, when my mother would awaken us at half-past six for seven o'clock Mass, often having to tear the bedclothes aside before she could rouse us from our drug of sleep. At such moments you must see the three of us strewn in one big featherbed like three white-robed puppets, a bed so big that it almost filled our attic bedroom at the tip-top of the house.

I must pause at the mention of these attics. They were garrets that had originally been intended as boxrooms. Their ceilings sloped to the floor like tents, and they were lighted and ventilated only by skylights which were raised by means of notched bars. When it rained heavily we could not open the sloping windows more than an inch, and in the hottest weather they could not be opened higher than the length of the brief bar. The result was that in the summer the garrets were too hot and in the winter too cold: there was, of course, no way of heating them. Nevertheless, when we moved into this house – I am now talking of Number 5 Half Moon Street, to which we went after a few years in Number 16, our first house over the quayside pub, sideways to the stage door – my mother saw at once that if we used the garrets as sleeping quarters she would have more bedrooms for her lodgers; so she occupied one garret, my father another, we three children slept in a third, and the servant girl, or slavey, had the fourth. Since my mother used the large space outside these four partitioned-off garrets as a drying room, we often made our way to bed between damp curtains of shirts, sheets and tablecloths. That we slept in attics was therefore not so much a measure of our poverty as of our parsimony, and another token of the thrifty principle that dominated all our lives – my father's and mother's constant anxiety to make enough money to give their three children a good education. Here I am not trying to suggest that we were not really poor:

a father of three children earning one pound sterling per week was a poor man even by pre-1914 values. I am saying that we, that is my father and mother, were of that class of poor folk who refuse to accept their poverty and all the natural and easy compensations of poverty. One may be happy though poor; to be poor, frugal, parsimonious and ambitious is quite another matter. It leads to a dull and disciplined degradation of life. This dragging us out of our warm cocoon of sleep at half-past six of a cold morning was part of it.

As we three sleep-heavy children stirred or turned in the unwelcome cold my mother would cry heartily to us: 'Up! Up! I come, said the Lord, like a thief in the night seeking whom I may DEVOUR! Rise from your slumbers! Woe to the weak and lukewarm of heart – I spit them out of my mouth. Up! Up! Come to me all ye that labour and are burthened and I will refresh ye. Think of the poor souls suffering in Purgatory at this minute, waiting for your prayers. Think of poor Ned Keating who used to let ye in free to the Opera House and died only last month. Is this your return to him? There he is down there burning like hot coal! Up! Up with ye! Say but the word and my soul shall be healed. A fine bright cold hardy morning, with the crow putting out his tongue and ye still in bed!'

At that raw spring hour, mid-February or early March, the sky would be as beautifully cold as a mackerel, bluish-white at its base, everywhere else a dark bruise-blue except where gas lamps in the streets let in a pale green-whitish-yellow, and to my memory it seems as if always there had just been a soft fall of rain. The slavey would still be snoring in her attic, the kitchen fire black, the streets empty and silent, damp and cold, the church suddenly glaringly bright, but also cold, and I fear my prayers were mostly damp and cold too. There was always for me an exciting, strange beauty in those dark and empty streets in contrast with the suddenly bright church. Afterwards they were less interesting. The sky had lightened, the lamps were extinguished, a few other people were abroad, a milkman, the first tram, early workers. I felt less special.

After breakfast we went off to school, the three of us together, walking there in all weathers, since pennies for trams were as scarce as pennies for pocket money. Not that we ever had any such thing as pocket money, barring a halfpenny now and again to buy sweets, shared between us with meticulous justice, so that if an odd sweet were left over we drew lots for it. From school we returned at three o'clock directly, strictly forbidden to loiter on the way, and, above all, forbidden to consort with 'barefooted little boys', 'corner boys', or 'blackguards'. This meant that we never met or played with our fellows out of school.

236

Indeed, throughout my entire childhood, I did not have a single friend. After dinner, eaten in the kitchen, our sole living room since every other room was given up to the *artistes*, we were sent off, again in a bunch, for the usual walk up Wellington Road and down Saint Luke's, dropping in along the way to some church to say the Stations of the Cross. On our return from this daily walk we would sit at the long kitchen table to do our homework until suppertime, and after supper we would study again unless it was our night for the Confraternity or one of those divine nights when we had a free ticket for the play at the Opera House. And so to bed, up the long stairs, carrying a candle in a candlestick, first on the carpeted stretch, then on the lino stretch, and lastly on the bare boards with the nails shining like silver, into the attics.

From Vive Moi!

Sean O'Faolain (1900–   ), short story writer, was born John Whelan, in Cork. He served with the IRA in the Civil War, and taught in the USA and England before returning to Ireland, where he edited the *Bell*. His *Collected Stories* were published in 1981.

At the Altar

The convent door, opening slightly, made a crack in the morning darkness and from the harshness of the street Martin slipped into the soft obscurity of the hall. As he went up the polished stairs towards the Oratory, the black-and-white figures rustled on their aloof coming and going.

In the little vestry, warm with the incense of many years, he put on his silver-buckled slippers, regretting that his gorgeous red soutane could be worn only for a bishop, but glad that his black one, with its long folds, was so dignified and gracefully made. Having carefully put on the second-best surplice with the deep crochet work at sleeve and hem, he walked up and down the room to make the well-cut soutane curvet about his ankles.

With quiet superiority he allowed the vestry nun to make the preliminary preparations, but he himself lit the candles on the altar, and cast an appraising eye on the nun's arrangement of the Missal, of the wine and water cruets. He moved the cruets about half an inch from where the nun had placed them, just to show that the final responsibility was his. However holy she might be, however important among nuns, she was below Martin Matthew Reilly this morning. No woman, no nun, no female saint, could do what he was about to do – serve at Mass. No woman could serve the wine, pour water on the priest's fingers crossed on the chalice, nor could she, bending on one knee and holding the Missal itself, feel the priest's chasuble brush the face and hear his blessing pass overhead to the kneeling church. The priest said Mass, repeating in a bloodless manner the bloody sacrifice of Calvary. Beyond the priest was the Bishop, beyond the Bishop, the Cardinals and the Pope, and behind the Pope were Peter and the Apostles, grouped around God. And next to the priest came Martin Matthew Reilly.

When Father Riordan came he gave no greeting other than a courteous bow, and this, too, pleased Martin. Until Mass had been said, and

Communion administered, it was unseemly to grin and stutter greetings, as little Father Flaherty did; not downright bad, as eating after midnight would have been, but very objectionable, in Martin's opinion. Whereas a bow, a courteous bow, was just right. And he loved to give a deep, slow bow in reply. That was one of Father Riordan's many charms for him. With Father Riordan, he could try those handsome gestures which he saw done by people in plays, by his pretty Aunt Mary, by Niave's small, thin mother. Ah, how nicely girls moved always. Even when tumbling they always managed to come down in a graceful position. Even stolid Muriel Norburton had not been ungraceful in her reverse turn-overs; and when Gertrude had shaken her leg at him it probably had been shocking, but it had also been very gracefully done.

But, great heavens, what was he doing! Thinking about girls at such a moment, about girls showing the whole of their legs and glimpses of their underclothes! And Protestant girls! Good God, had he gone and committed a sin, just as he was about to serve Mass? And the Celestines' special dawn Mass!

Was it a sin? He removed a twist from Father Riordan's stole. Was it a bad thought? He smoothed the end of Father Riordan's chasuble. Some of the horror retreated from around his heart. It was not, he felt sure, a bad thought at other times. But could it be a bad thought just before serving Mass? Could it? He picked up Father Riordan's biretta. Then relief came to him. Why, even – 'and remember only *even*', he told himself – even if it were a bad thought, he had not yielded to it. And the sin could only lie in 'giving way to bad thoughts'! Therefore, if it had been the devil – and he did not admit the point – who had sent the thought, the result had been a victory for goodness, so the position was actually better than if he had never had the thought at all! In happiness, he bowed gently to Father Riordan to indicate that all was now ready and, going to the door of the vestry, he rang the little bell.

As with bowed heads and fingers correctly joined before his face he preceded Father Riordan to the Oratory, he prepared himself to give this Mass a perfect service. Not once would he sink on to his heels or droop his back. Not once would he fiddle with the bell, nor scratch his knees, no matter how weary they became. Thank goodness Father Riordan would not rush up the altar steps and come rushing down again, rubbing his neck like little Father Flaherty, dropping things and saying 'Oh, dear me!' Father Riordan would move and speak with care and dignity. On the other hand, he would not take all the morning at it, like poor old Father Ryan, crawling about all over the place, and making one wonder if he might not at any moment make some dreadful mistake. No, Father Riordan was the perfect priest. Perfect. And he had said, 'The perfect beauty of the Catholic Faith itself!'

'*Introibo ad altare Dei*,' prayed Father Riordan at the foot of the altar steps, 'I will go unto the altar of God.'

And Martin answered boldly, '*Ad Deum qui laetificat juventutem meam* – to God Who rejoiceth my youth.' And under the influence of the place, the hour, the resolve to give perfect service to this Mass, he said to himself, 'Yes, I will go unto the altar of God Who rejoices my youth and Who made the perfect beauty of the Catholic Faith itself.'

The words seemed to him to declare an extraordinary revelation, which so filled him with awe and delight that, when he knelt on the steps after Father Riordan had gone to the Epistle side, he smiled at the priest's back, at the vases of Christmas roses, smiled straight at the door of the Tabernacle itself.

This rather excited joy lasted until, while standing behind Father Riordan, waiting to carry the Missal to the Gospel side, he remembered his promise to pray for Mr Burns. While he prayed earnestly that Mr Burns would soon come back to God and the Church, the excitement flowed into a sweet contentment.

Carefully following each sequence of the ordered service, timing his slow walk to bring him at just the correct moment to just the correct part of the altar, gratefully making each bow and movement respond to Father Riordan's care and dignity, he felt that nothing could excel this quiet Mass, with the nuns' voices behind him, rising now and again in the Gloria or the Credo. The Gregorian Chant had now in his ears a sweetness which it lacked when it thundered from the throats of hundreds of ecclesiastics in the magnificence of the Bishop's High Mass. Feeling so strongly this morning a mood which he had always loved, loving Father Riordan all the more because his presence accorded so well with that mood, he moved and served in a kind of rapture. When the Consecration came and, prostrate along the steps with the bell ready beside his hand, he looked up at the Host held above Father Riordan's head, it was from a heart full of happiness and adoration that he murmured, 'My Lord and my God.'

He knelt before Father Riordan for Communion and when he received the wafer on his tongue he thought that this was the best Communion he had ever made, that never again would it be necessary to go to Confession before Communion because he would never again have any sins to blot out his state of grace.

With the wafer melting behind closed lips, he held the great silver candlestick beside the ciborium flashing in Father Riordan's hands as the priest moved with the Sacrament from nun to nun kneeling along the step which separated their pews from the Sanctuary. The nuns' pale hands passed the napkin from chin to chin; the upturned faces, thin, broad, plump, might have been the faces in the Dublin waxworks, so cold were they in the light of the candle, so fixed in devotion. One after another, the white faces in line toppled over, as nun after nun bent her head.

Back at the altar, he found the last movements of the Mass coming all too soon. '*Ite, missa est*,' Father Riordan looked down at him; and '*Deo Gratias*,' answered Martin, wondering how he and other boys had ever thought it funny to say 'Thanks be to God' because Mass was nearly over.

The Last Gospel having been said, he waited eagerly for the *De Profundis* because he always liked to remember that only in Ireland of all the countries in the world was the *De Profundis* said after Mass and that its purpose was to pray for the souls of all those Irish people whose records had been lost in the Penal Days. Nothing could have pleased him more than to close this Mass with prayers for those far-off countrymen of his who had suffered for God and Ireland under England's laws.

For the last time he raised the hem of the chasuble from Father Riordan's heels as the priest went up the altar steps; for the last time he bowed to Father Riordan's descent. For the last time, with a swinging of his soutane, he measured his pace before Father Riordan coming away from the altar of God.

Back in the vestry, Father Riordan and he shook hands. 'A Happy Christmas to us!'

From THY TEARS MIGHT CEASE

———•◦•———

Michael Farrell (1899–1962), sometime medical student, journalist and, finally, successful businessman, was born in Carlow. He began work on this, his only novel, in the early 1930s and worked at it until his death, unable to let it be published. It was posthumously edited for publication by Monk Gibbon.

The Homeland

In April 1916 a handful of Irishmen took over the city of Dublin and were finally surrounded and overwhelmed by British troops with artillery. The daily papers showed Dublin as they showed Belgian cities destroyed by the Germans, as smoking ruins inhabited by men with rifles and machine guns. At first my only reaction was horror that Irishmen could commit such a crime against England. I was sure that phase had ended with the Boer War in which Father had fought, because one of his favourite songs said so:

> *You used to call us traitors because*
> *of agitators,*
> *But you can't call us traitors now.*

But the English were calling us traitors again, and they seemed to be right. It was a difficult situation for a boy of twelve with no spiritual homeland but that of the English public schools, and no real friends but those imaginary friends he knew there. I had defended their code of honour with nothing to support me but faith, and now, even if the miracle happened and Big Tim Fahy returned from Chicago with bags of money and sent me to school in England, I should be looked on with distrust – almost, God help me, as if I were a German who said *Donner und Blitzen*, which was what all Germans said.

The English shot the first batch of Irish leaders, and this was a worse shock, for the newspapers said – the pro-British ones with a sneer – that several of them had been poets, and I was in favour of poets. One of them, Patrick Pearse, on the night before his execution had written some poems, one of them to his mother – which showed him a man of nice feeling – and another, which contained lines I still remember:

> *The beauty of this world hath made me sad –*
> *This beauty that will pass.*

Sometimes my heart hath shaken with great joy
To see a leaping squirrel in a tree,
Or a red ladybird upon a stalk ...

What made it worse was that most of his poetry had been written in Irish, the language I had abandoned in favour of Flemish. And Corkery, who had introduced me to Irish, I had not seen for years. But I still had an old primer that had been thrown into a corner, and I started trying to re-learn all that I had forgotten. A revolution had begun in Ireland, but it was nothing to the revolution that had begun in me. It is only in the imagination that the great tragedies take place, and I had only my imagination to live in. I enjoyed English school stories as much as ever, but already I was developing a bad conscience about them. The heroes of those stories, the Invisible Presences, I knew, must look on me as a traitor. They reminded me of how they had taken me in and made me one of themselves, and I had to reply that if I was different, it was because of what they and theirs had done to make me so. For months I read almost nothing but Irish history and the result was horrifying. I wrote my first essay, which listed all the atrocities I could discover that had been committed by the English in the previous hundred years or so, but it had no more effect than the deceived husband's listing of his wife's infidelities has on his need of her. My heart still cried out for the Invisible Presences.

In the early mornings Mother and I went into town to the Franciscan or Augustinian church where Mass was said for the dead rebels, and on the way back we bought picture postcards of them. One afternoon when we were walking in the country we met Corkery, and I asked him how I could take up Irish again. After that I went on Saturday afternoons to the children's class at the Gaelic League hall in Queen Street. The Irish we spoke was of less importance to me than the folk songs we learned, and these than the kilt that one of the boys wore. I felt my own position keenly. Not only was I suspect to the Invisible Presences; with a father and uncle in the British Army I was suspect to loyal children as well. But no one could suspect the loyalty of a boy who wore a kilt, and I persecuted my mother till she made one for me. She did not find it easy, as kilts were not worn in her young days.

Somewhere or other I had picked up Eleanor Hull's *Cuchulain*, a re-telling of the Ulster sagas for children, and that became a new ideal. Nobody in any English school story I had read had done things as remarkable as that child had done by the age of seven. But for me, even

243

his deeds were small compared with what he said when he actually was seven and some druid prophesied a short life for him. 'Little I care though I were to live but a day and a night if only my fame and adventures lived after me.' No one had ever better expressed my own view of life.

Having exhausted most of the books in the children's department of the library, I had discovered the adult one, and, by using a ticket I had got for Mother, I could borrow a school story from upstairs and a book on history downstairs. It took real courage to face the adult library of those days. There was a card catalogue and a long counter surmounted by a primitive device known as an Indicator – a huge glass case where all the book numbers were shown in blue (which meant they were available) or red (which meant they were not). If you were a scholarly person and could deduce from the author and title whether a book was readable or not, it didn't matter perhaps, but if, like me, you knew nothing about books, you might often walk back the two miles home in rage and disgust with something you couldn't even read. Education was very hard.

One of the grown-up books I borrowed was O'Curry's *Manuscript Materials*, which contained a lot about Cu Chulainn. No more than O'Curry himself was I put off by the fact that this was in a form of Irish I didn't know, ranging from the eighth to the twelfth century (I never allowed myself to be deflected by details); and, casting myself in the part of a medieval scribe, I copied it out with coloured initials imitated from the *Book of Kells*.

But though I knew as little about the hero of a modern English public-school story as I did about the hero of a primitive saga, imitating the one turned out to be child's play compared with imitating the other, and I nearly ruptured myself trying to perform the least of the feats Cu Chulainn had performed when he was barely half my age. It seemed I had wasted my time practising with a bow, for the Irish had no use for it, and I had to begin all over again with a slingshot; but though I practised hard, I never came within measurable distance of killing someone in a crowd half a mile away. It was difficult enough to hit a gate post at twenty yards, and even then my heart was in my mouth for fear I should break a window and have the police after me.

Most of my endeavours were wasted on a single episode in Cu Chulainn's infancy. He left home when he was little more than a toddler, hurling his toy spear before him, pucking his hurling ball after that, throwing his hurling stick after the ball, and then catching all three before they alighted. No one who has not tried that simple feat can imagine how difficult it is. There was more sense in the story of how he killed the great watch-dog by throwing the hurling ball down its gullet and then beating it over the head with his hurley, and I practised that, too, beginning with very small dogs; but, knowing my character much better than I did, they decided I only wanted to play with them, and ran away with the ball. When they finally let me catch up on them and grinned at me with the ball between their teeth, I could no more hit them with the hurley than I could do anything else that Cu Chulainn had done. I was crazy about dogs and cats. I saw clearly that the Irish race had gone to hell since saga times, and that this was what had enabled the English to do what they liked with us.

Queer treasures I clutched to my chest, coming over Parnell Bridge in the evening on my way from the Public Library. Once it was a collection of Irish folk music, and I proudly copied the O'Donovan clan march in staff notation, hoping to find someone who would sing it to me. Father had earlier discovered the O'Donovan coat of arms, and I had discovered that there was a village called Castle Donovan in West Cork. The family was obviously something. Sometimes I took out in Mother's name an art book or a novel by Canon Sheehan, who was parish priest of a County Cork town, and had a most unclerical passion for novel writing. He had been greatly praised by a Russian writer called Tolstoy, and later I learned that his clerical enemies had sent one of his novels to Rome in the hope of having it condemned for heresy, but the Papal authorities, mistaking the purpose of the submission, gave Sheehan a D.D. instead. He shared with the authors of the boys' weeklies a weakness for foreign languages, and printed lengthy extracts from Goethe in the original, and ever since I have been torn between two attitudes to this practice. With one half of my mind I regard it as detestable snobbery, but with the other I think it the only sensible way of influencing young people like myself. If the original monkey had not despised monkeys he would never have invented clothes, and I should not have bothered to learn Goethe's *Symbolen* by heart. Never having anyone to teach me, I learned only by pretending to know. I played at reading foreign languages and tenth-century Irish, at being a priest and saying Mass, at singing from staff notation and copying out pieces of music when I didn't know one note from another, at being a painter and a theatrical producer. It is not a form of education I would recommend to anyone, nor should I ever get a degree in French, German, Latin, music, or even Middle Irish, but I still catch myself out at it, playing at

245

scholarship and correcting the experts, and sometimes a little streak of lunatic vanity that runs through it all suggests that I may be right and everybody else wrong.

From An Only Child

———•◦•———

Frank O'Connor (1903–66), short story writer and critic, was born Michael O'Donovan, in Cork. He was imprisoned at the time of the Civil War for his Republican activities. He lectured in the USA during the 1950s, returning to Ireland in 1960.

MAURICE O'SULLIVAN

The First Return

In half an hour he came back. We were ready waiting, and I longing for the road in order to see the country, for I had no knowledge of it, and so my father was giving me the name of every place. Before long I could see the sea, ever and ever, till we came to Slea Head.

'Now, Maurice, see your native place!' said my father, stretching out his hand north-west to a small island which had been torn out from the mainland. I could not speak; a lump came in my throat when I saw the Island.

'But how can the horse get in there?' said I at last.

'We will go in with a curragh,' said my father.

'What sort of a thing is a curragh?' said I.

I stopped questioning, and went on thinking and looking out. I saw little white houses huddled together in the middle of the Island, a great wild hill straight to the west with no more houses to be seen, only a tower on the peak of the hill and the hillside white with sheep. I did not like the look of it. I think, said I to myself, it is not a good place. While those thoughts were passing through my mind, the car stopped, the people got out and my father lifted me down.

'Where are we going now?' said I.

It was a week-day, and, as soon as we reached the top of the cliff, the King of the Island came up with his post-bag on his back. He spoke to my father, but not a word could I understand. There were many others round the place and they all with their own talk. I don't know in the world, said I in my own mind, will the day ever come when I will be able to understand them.

The King turned to me: 'Musha, how are you?' said he, stretching out his hand.

I looked at him – a fine, courteous, mannerly, well-favoured man.

'Thank you very much,' said I (in English).

'The devil,' said he. 'I think you have no understanding of the Irish?'

247

'I have not,' said I.

But he himself had the two languages, fluent and vigorous. 'How does it please you to be going into the Island?' he asked me.

'I don't know,' said I. 'It does not look too nice altogether.'

'Upon my word, Shaun,' said the King, turning to my father, 'it is time for us to be starting in.' And he began to move down.

I was watching the white crests on the sea below. A good gale of wind was blowing from the south-west. We moved down through a great cliff, a rough, narrow little path before us. When I came in sight of the quay, what did I see but twenty black beetles twice as big as a cow!

'Oh, dad,' said I, 'are those beetles dangerous?'

The King gave a big, hearty laugh which took an echo out of the cliff, for he was a fine strong man with a voice without any hoarseness.

'Indeed, my boy,' said he, 'it is no bad guess you made, and you are not the first that gave them that name.'

When we got down to the quay, I looked up at the height of the cliff above me, yellow vetchling growing here and there, a terrible noise from the waves breaking below. I saw a big black bird up in the middle of the cliff where it had made its nest. Oh Lord, said I to myself, how do you keep your senses up there at all!

Then I turned my eyes towards the slip and what did I see but one of the big black beetles walking out towards me. My heart leapt. I caught hold of my aunt's shawl, crying, 'Oh, the beetle!'

'Have no fear,' said she, 'that is a curragh they are carrying down on their backs.' And she snatched another kiss from me. I thought of telling her that it was a nasty habit of women, but I held my tongue.

The curragh was now afloat, like a cork on the water, as light as an egg-shell. In went my uncle, and the way he set her rocking I thought every moment she would overturn. In went the King, and, faith, I was sure she would go down with the weight that was in the man. I was the last to be put in. The King was seated at his ease on the thwart, his pipe lit. My aunts were in the stern, I at their feet sitting on a tin of sweets.

'Now,' said the King, 'let us move her out in the name of God.'

Soon the curragh was mounting the waves, then down again on the other side, sending bright jets of foam into the air every time she struck the water. I liked it well until we were in Mid-Bay. Then I began to feel my guts going in and out of each other, and as the curragh rose and fell I became seven times worse. I cried out.

'Have no fear,' said my father.

'Oh, it isn't fear, but something is coming over me which isn't right.'

'Lift up your head, my boy,' said the King, 'and take a whiff of the wind.'

I did so, but it was no help. Before long a streak of pain ran across my chest. I wanted to throw up. I tried, but I could not.

'Heave it up,' said the King, 'and nothing more will avail you.'

Seven attempts I made, but with no success.

'Put your hand back in your throat,' said my father, 'as far back as it will go, and then you will have it.'

I did as he said, but I did not like it.

'Have no fear,' said my father.

'But isn't it the way I am worst when I put my hand back in my mouth?'

'Don't mind that, but leave it well back until the burden comes up.'

I tried again and again. Every time I pushed my hand back the desire to retch would run through my body. I kept my hand back patiently, ever and ever, till at last I felt my belly beating against the small of my back. Then up came the burden and I threw it out.

My uncle was on the thwart in the bows rowing hard. He looked at me and gave out a great rush of talk. But, alas, I no more knew what he was saying than the oar in his hand.

We were only a quarter of a mile from land now, with a fine view of the Island before us. The wind had dropped. There was not a breath in the sky, a dead calm on the sea, a wisp of smoke rising up straight from every chimney on the Island; the sun as yellow as gold shining over the Pass of the Hill-slope from the west; a curragh towards us from the north, and another from the south; an echo in the coves from the barking of the dogs, and, when that ceased, the corncrake crying 'Droach, droach, droach'. The beauty of the place filled my heart with delight. Soon I saw people running down by every path – two, three, four. At last it was beyond me to count them. They were coming like ants, some of them running, others walking slowly, till they were all together in a crowd above the quay.

We went in through a narrow creek no wider than the curragh. My eyes opened wide as I looked at the pool within. Not an inch of the slip but was covered with children and grown men. You would think it was greed was on them to tear the curragh asunder, and they chattering and clamouring like a flock of geese a dog would send scattering.

The curragh stretched up alongside the slip. I got out. The crowd closed round, all but the children who gathered round myself, every one of them staring at me, some with a finger in their mouths, others coming up behind me. A shame-faced feeling came over me with the way they were peering at me. When I looked at them they would smile and hide their faces one behind another.

'Be off!' said the King to the children who were in his way. They scattered in fear. And now the men had the curragh on their backs and were putting her on the stays. I was standing on the top of the slip, a little afraid, for before me was a stout little lad as plump as a young pig. He kept staring at me out of his big blue eyes, his nose dripping, his finger in his mouth and he chewing it. He looked at my head and then at my feet. Then he moved round to examine me behind. I could feel his warm breath on the back of my neck. I put my hand in my pocket and gave him some sweets so that he would take his close face away from me, upon which he ran off to the others. But when they saw the sweets they all came round again pressing in upon me.

At that moment down the path came an old man. He looked at me smiling. Coming up, he embraced and kissed me and began to talk to me in fine English.

'Who are you?' said I.

'Och, isn't it a strange thing that you would not know your own grandfather?' said he, with a laugh. 'Come up with me now,' said he, taking me by the hand. But, oh Lord, it was a good half-hour before we reached the house on account of all the old women who came out to welcome me. 'The devil take you,' said an old man who was standing near, 'don't choke the child!'

The house put great wonder on me. I had never seen the like of it before. It was small and narrow, with a felt roof, the walls outside and in bright with lime, a fine glowing fire sending warmth into every corner, and four súgán chairs around the hearth. I sat down on one of them. A dog was lying in the cinders. When I patted him with my hand he leapt up with a growl, drew his tail between his legs, and slunk away into the corner.

I had two sisters and two brothers in the house, so I did not feel lonesome. When everything was ready we sat in to the table. And a fine, wholesome table it was for good, broken potatoes and two big plates of yellow bream – the custom of the Island at the fall of night.

From TWENTY YEARS A'GROWING (tr. by Moya Llewelyn Davies and George Thomson)

————•◦•————

Maurice O'Sullivan (1904–50), author, was born on the Great Blasket Island. He was a member of the Civic Guard 1927–33. He was drowned while bathing at Connemara.

'A Gay Little Bit'

The boy whom I loved for the last three years I was at St Wulfric's was called Tony Watson. He was small, brown, wiry, good at games, untidy and silent, with a low brow, green eyes, and a fringe of rough short hair. I describe him because he is a type that has recurred through my life and which gets me into trouble. It is that faunlike, extrovert creature with a streak of madness and cruelty, not clever, but narcissistic and quick to adapt itself to clever people. In appearance it is between colours with a small mouth, slanting eyes, and lemon-yellow skin.

By the time I was twelve all four types to which I am susceptible had appeared. I do not know whether it is glands, numerology, the stars or mere environment which dispose one to these fierce sympathies, inherited as if from another life, but by now I recognize my kindred forms with some familiarity: the Faun, the Redhead, the Extreme Blonde, and the Dark Friend.

The Fauns well know their fatal power which a series of conquests have made obvious and they derive a pleasure that I mistake for reciprocation, from the spectacle of its workings. Age is often unkind to these charmers and the world is apt to turn against them. With the other types my relations are happier. I supply them with vitality and intensive cultivation, they provide me with affection, balance, loyalty, good taste. The Extreme Blondes are quiet, intelligent, humorous, receptive; they have an impressive reserve against which I roll, like the Atlantic Ocean on the Cornish cliffs, confident that they will be able to withstand me. The Dark Friends are the most sympathetic; they have brown eyes and oval faces; they like my jokes and look after me when I am ill, but it is one of the hardships of romantic love that rarely is it bestowed on people like ourselves and the Dark Friends end by being Consolers. The Redheads have some of the quieting effect of the Extreme Blondes but they may suddenly become as deleterious as the Faun. They are a special type, not the dreamy, brown-eyed, long-faced auburn, nor the aggressive albino, but the gay, thin, dashing green-eyed variety.

Being an only child I romanticized sisterhood, I wanted an Electra and longed for a relationship with sister types of the same age. I liked health and equality in women, an implicit friendship. I desired the same for my imaginary brothers. The Dark Friends and the Extreme Blondes supplied this, the Redheads added an excitement which raised it to perfection. And then the exotic Faun would reappear and all peace of mind would vanish. As with other only children my desire for a brother or a sister was so strong that I came to see existence in terms of the couple; in whatever group I found myself I would inevitably end by sharing my life with one other, driven by an inner selection through a course of trial and error till after forming one of a group of four or five and then of a trio, I achieved my destiny as one half of a pair.

I christened this search for the *'dimidium animae meae'* the Pair System, and I was fascinated, when later I read the Symposium of Plato, to come across his theory that human beings had once been double and were for ever seeking the counterpart from whom they had been so rudely forced. We were all one half of a Siamese Twin.

> *The brothered one, the not alone*
> *The brothered and the hated.*

But it is a romantic theory and it is part of the romantic's misfortune that in the search for his affinity he is not guided by a community of interests but by those intimations which are the appeal of a mouth or an eye, an appeal which is not even private, so that the spectacle is presented of half a dozen Platonic half-men trying to unite with the same indifferent alter ego. Love at first sight – and the first sight is the supreme consummation for romantics – is an intuition bred by habit of the person who can do us harm.

Yet Tony Watson let me down lightly. He was a wild little boy with plenty of character but not of the right kind. He taught me to smoke (which I hated); to rag in the corridors at night, fighting among the coats hanging from their pegs, and to take part on the downs in gang warfare, which I adored. He moved in a fast set of hard-smoking and hard-swearing cronies from whom he protected me. Our unlikeness made us over-polite. He accepted my devotion, even to a poem beginning, 'Watson, the silent, Watson, the dauntless' and showed me, in return, an extraordinary drawing, a Parthenon Frieze on sheets of paper stuck together that unfolded like a concertina, to reveal a long procession of soldiers – cavalry, infantry, artillery, wounded and dying, doctors, nurses, ghurkas, staff-officers, and engineers on their way to the war.

For most of us the war was skin-deep. The *Titanic* had gone down, the passengers all singing, 'Nearer my God to Thee' – that was terrible – and now the war: pins stuck in maps, the Kaiser dying of cancer of the throat, Kitchener drowned, ration cards, Business as Usual, a day when we were told of the Battle of Jutland and another when we heard that a terrible thing had happened, a revolution in Russia with a monster called Kerensky now in power. None of us, except perhaps Orwell, believed that England could lose the war or that we would grow up to fight in it, nor were we old enough to understand the peril of our elder cousins or the tragedy when – like Uncle Granville's only son – they were killed on the first day of the Gallipoli slaughter. And meanwhile Watson's exact and bloodthirsty pageant grew fuller, a page at a time, till it stretched, by 1917, the whole length of the schoolroom.

Tony shared my love of animals and drew for me pictures of foxes in lonely postures barking to the moon. I had several excruciating moments with him. Once we vowed blood-brotherhood in the Albanian fashion. Tony cut a cross on each left hand and we held the bleeding scratches together. Another time, left in the bathroom alone, he came up to me, wrapped in his bath towel, and pursed his lips for a kiss. My spinster modesty made me flinch. He turned away and never did it again while for weeks I lay awake angry and miserable. He slept in a dormitory called the Red Room; I was in a two-bedded one across the passage with the Dark Friend, his cousin, Frankie Wright. Tony would come over in the morning after a night of pillow fighting, gang reprisals, and smoking on the roof, and get into my bed where my innocence hung round my neck like an albatross. Then the eight o'clock bell would ring and we would troop down to the ghastly plunge-bath. There was a smell of gooseflesh and slimy water. One by one, under the cold eye of Sambo and to the accompaniment of such comments as 'Go on Marsden, you stink like a polecat', we dived or jumped in until it was the turn of the group of water-funks who shrank down the steps, groaning wer-wer-wer, while the sergeant-major waited to haul them out from the stagnant depths by a rope attached to a pole. When the last had been towed it was time to dress and go on the asphalt for 'gym'.

Year by year, the air, the discipline, the teaching, the association with other boys and the driving will of Flip took effect on me. I grew strong and healthy and appeared to be normal for I became a good mixer, a gay little bit who was quick to spot whom to make up to in a group and how to do it. I knew how far to go in teasing and responding to teasing and

253

became famous for my 'repartee'. I had a theory that there was one repartee effective for every situation and spent weeks in elaborating it. At that time the magic phrase seemed, 'Dear me, how very uninteresting!' If I had to choose one now it would be, 'This is a very bad moment for both of us.' I kept a Funny Book which contained satirical poems and character sketches. I became good at history, that is to say I learnt dates easily, knew which battle was fought in the snow and who was 'the little gentleman in black velvet'. I read Dickens, Thackeray, Carlyle, and Scott and got marks for them, and for pleasure John Buchan. It was time for me to go up for a scholarship. I had crammed Watson energetically for the common entrance, which he just managed to pass, and when I saw him again in the holidays he was a dapper public schoolboy with his hair brushed back, a felt hat and a cane, and we had nothing to say to each other.

My first attempt at scholarship was at Wellington with Orwell. I hated every moment: the blue-suited prefects bustling about the dismal brick and slate, the Wellingtonias and rhododendrons, infertile flora of the Bagshot sand. It was winter and an old four-wheeler bore me from the examinations to my great-aunts with whom I was staying. The musical groaning of the wheels and springs in the winter stillness had a profound effect and I felt like Childe Roland, mystical and Celtic. Pines and heather, the whortle-bearing ridges, seemed to have a message for me, to be the background for some great event as I trundled over them after the afternoon paper. Orwell got a scholarship which he did not take. I failed but the experience was considered good practice.

A year later I went up for Eton, which was very different. Sambo took charge of us; he knew many people there and we had tea with old Wulfrician boys and masters. I had a moment on Windsor Bridge; it was summer, and, after the coast, the greenness of the lush Thames Valley was enervating and oppressive; everything seemed splendid and decadent, the huge stale elms, the boys in their many-coloured caps and blazers, the top hats, the strawberries and cream, the smell of wistaria. I looked over the bridge as a boy in an outrigger came gliding past, like a waterboatman. Two Etonians were standing on the bridge and I heard one remark, 'Really that man Wilkinson's not at all a bad oar.' The foppish drawl, the two boys with their hats on the back of their heads, the graceful sculler underneath, seemed the incarnation of elegance and maturity.

There was no doubt that this was the place for me, for all of it was, from the St Wulfric's point of view, utterly and absorbingly evil. I got in twelfth on History and English as Orwell, after Wellington, had done the year before. In case there was no vacancy I went up for one more scholarship, this time at Charterhouse where we did the examination in a cellar during an air raid.

From A GEORGIAN BOYHOOD

———◆◇◆———

Cyril Connolly (1903–74). essayist, journalist and critic, was born in Coventry of an English father and an Irish mother. He was founder-editor of *Horizon*.

Nursery Perils

When we were children the food in the nursery was quite poisonously disgusting. None of the fruit juice and vitamins of today for us – oranges only at Christmastime and porridge every morning, variable porridge slung together by the kitchen maid, followed by white bread and butter and Golden Syrup. Boiled eggs were for Sundays and sausages for birthdays. I don't think Mummie gave us a thought – she left the ordering of nursery meals to the cook, who sent up whatever came easiest, mostly rabbit stews and custard puddings riddled with holes. No wonder the nannies left in quick succession.

Why do I hate the word 'crusted'? Because I feel with my lips the boiled milk, crusted since the night before, round the rim of the mug out of which I must finish my breakfast milk. . . . I am again in the darkness of the nursery, the curtains drawn against the winter morning outside. Nannie is dragging on her corsets under her great nightdress. Baby Hubert is walking up and down his cot in a dirty nightdress. The nursery maid is pouring paraffin on a sulky nursery fire. I fix my eyes on the strip of morning light where wooden rings join curtains to curtain pole and think about my bantams. . . . Even then I knew how to ignore things. I knew how to behave.

I don't blame Mummie for all this. She simply did not want to know what was going on in the nursery. She had had us and she longed to forget the horror of it once and for all. She engaged nannie after nannie with excellent references, and if they could not be trusted to look after us, she was even less able to compete. She didn't really like children; she didn't like dogs either, and she had no enjoyment of food, for she ate almost nothing.

She was sincerely shocked and appalled on the day when the house-maid came to tell her that our final nannie was lying on her bed in a drunken stupor with my brother Hubert beside her in another drunken stupor, while I was lighting a fire in the day nursery with the help of a tin of paraffin. The nannie was sacked, but given quite a good reference with no mention of her drinking; that would have been too unkind and unnecessary, since she promised to reform. Her next charge (only a Dublin baby) almost died of drink, and its mother wrote a very common, hysterical letter, which Mummie naturally put in the fire and forgot about. Exhausted, bored, and disgusted by nannies, she engaged a governess who would begin my education and at the same time keep an eye on the nursery maid who was to be in charge of Hubert's more menial four-year-old necessities.

From GOOD BEHAVIOUR

Molly Keane (1905–) née Skrine, novelist and dramatist under the name of M. J. Farrell as well as her own, the daughter of an Anglo-Irish squire and the poet Moira O'Neill, grew up in Co. Wexford.

A Bear Called Bouncer

Christmas and Easter were the high spots of our year, as Sunday was of our week. Christmas Day was waking in the dark, an excitement intolerably protracted, for my father's duties were so heavy in the morning that we did not open our presents till after the midday meal. On my sixth or seventh Christmas there was a whole trunkful of them for me. Yet there never seemed quite enough. All through my childhood I longed passionately for a pedal motorcar and importunately hinted at my need for it; but no pedal motorcar arrived. One year, after Knos had taken me for her Christmas shopping to a store in Westbourne Grove, she unpacked a parcel containing a dozen or so penny toys – garish little metal toys, shining like the baubles on a Christmas tree (for some reason we never had a Christmas tree in our house, but I had seen them at children's parties). I assumed that these toys were all for me, and my spirits were dreadfully dashed when I saw Knos wrap each of them up in a separate parcel, and she told me she was sending them to her nephews and nieces in Ireland. I received many noble presents; but I remained faithful to a battered teddy-bear called Bouncer, who was like a brother to me: one Christmas, when I had been given an altogether superior woolly animal, I felt an upsurge of compunction, compassion, and fiinging away the superior animal, rushed off to assure Bouncer of my fidelity and unswerving love.

It is an odd thing, this awakening of the emotion of pity in children, who are so egotistical, so remorselessly exacting and on the make. I remember, while I was still a child, seeing a beggar in Craven Terrace, and being suddenly flooded with a pity that drowned every other feeling and, even though I gave him my twopence pocket-money, kept me worrying about him for days afterwards.

Easters at Lancaster Gate stand out in higher colour than Christ-mases – the colours of daffodils on the Praed Street barrows, of grand houses repainted white, of ribbons round Easter eggs, and the delicate markings of imitation birds' eggs made from sugar and snugly nested in white cotton-wool. Easter was the end of Lent, which we took seriously in our household as a period of self-denial: the lugubrious Passiontide hymns, bathed in gloom and redeeming blood, changed overnight into trumpeting alleluiahs: and with any luck the weather was now warm enough for me to go out and play on the balcony.

The balcony was my watch-tower and favourite playground. From it I commanded the cross-roads, a bun-shop at the corner, a cab-rank, a pillar-box over which I had been sick during my first outing after whooping cough, drays coming down from Paddington Station, cabs driving up towards it with men running behind them in the hope of a tip for opening the door and helping with the luggage, the errand-boys whistling on their bicycles, the muffin men, the barrel organs and German bands.

One day, playing on this balcony, I heard a great hullabaloo of men shouting, hooves and wheels thundering. A dray horse had bolted. I saw the driver try to turn it right at the crossroads: the dray, yawing behind the huge horse, knocked sideways a cab on the rank, and the horse, falling, slithered to a stop in a tangle of harness and broken shafts. It had all occurred too fast for me to be frightened. I watched the accident without any emotion, curiously: yet there is in my mind no picture of what happened next. Was the driver injured? the horse shot? A little later, Knos took me out for a walk. Where the horse had fallen there was a pool of blood, which had dyed the sawdust thrown over it, and in the gutter something lay wrapped round with bloodstained sacking: this, I was convinced, must be one of the horse's hooves and fetlocks, torn off in the accident. A bit further up towards Paddington Station, the road was littered for yards with glass and the tiny coloured sweets called 'hundreds of thousands'. When they had seen the runaway approaching, some men had rushed into a sweet-shop, snatched up these bottles of sweets, and hurled them at the horse – a more ineffective method of stopping a runaway horse, and a more bizarre instance of group hysteria, can hardly be imagined. For years after this I had heroic phantasies of throwing myself at the head of a bolting horse, stopping it, calming it down, dusting my hands in an insouciant manner, and walking away without giving my name.

The parapet which walled our balcony on three sides was a broad one, and the top of it provided a magnificent road for my toy motor-cars. Lines of wooden bricks made the pavements on either side; and for hours, weeks, years I steered my motors along, turning, backing, threading the traffic, drawing up neatly at the pavement, in a coma of concentration. It was the game I never tired of; and my passion for driving cars, which has lasted for nearly forty years since I learnt on my father's second-hand Calcott in 1920, was no doubt sown in me thus. The balcony is associated with Easter, not only because my motoring season started about then, but because one Easter Day I was given an extraordinary motor vehicle made of plaited straw and containing a large chocolate egg – a vehicle that affronted my sense of verisimilitude, yet charmed me by its eccentricity.

Sometimes a carriage or an electric brougham would draw up in the narrow street outside our front door, and one of my father's lady parishioners would take me out for a drive in the Park or to accompany her on her shopping. The faces of these gentlewomen are all lost to me, but a faint, diffused impression of luxury lingers in my mind: the touch of furs, silk, a bearskin carriage rug: smells of violets and warm leather: a silver box containing wafer-thin gelatine sweets which one lady always offered me, and the delicious short-cake biscuits of another: the shopkeepers hurrying out of shops and bowing beside the carriage to take their orders. These ladies always seemed to me pretty old. I was the kind of small boy, I have to confess, who is nice to old ladies: it is commonly supposed a disreputable trait, whose owners will later go to the bad, become milksops or confidence men, blackmailers or murderers. However, there it is, they liked me and so I liked them; and I enjoyed visiting their houses, that seemed treasure caves after ours, mysterious and glowing, the blinds drawn against the sunlight, the butlers and starched maid-servants, the aquarium in a window recess, the solitaire boards and bowls of pot-pourri, and the inexhaustible store of knick-knacks taken out from glass cases for me to look at.

When I was alone with these ladies, I chattered away; but, if my father or Knos were there, I often fell silent, for I liked being in the limelight – a normal enough characteristic with spirited children, only children especially, but one which can continue into later life and become a handicap. It took me, at any rate, many years to grow out of it. Even in my thirties and forties I sometimes came away from parties, my mind overcast by a sort of unfocused depression, disappointment, moroseness, which self-examination showed to be a cloak for the sense of social failure, for a chagrin at not being the centre of the picture, that during the party I had refused to admit. A child's excessive need for the limelight is said by some psychologists to stem from a basic insecurity. It may have been so with me, for there is no knowing how deeply I was unsettled by my mother's death: all I can say now is that, if such basic insecurity did exist within me, there was a strong, cushioning layer of security between it and my consciousness, so that the occasions were infrequent when I felt anxious, deserted, or unsustained.

Until I went to school, though I enjoyed the company of other children, I had few opportunities for doing so. I got on best with one or two companions at a time: children's parties, which were more formal and pretentious than they commonly are today, and where every child but myself seemed to know most of the others, were ordeals that I anticipated with dread and entered with anxiety and bewilderment. Even now, much as I love small parties, at large ones – and particularly that graceless, deafening, suffocating inferno, the cocktail party – I develop acute symptoms of claustrophobia and disorientation. The party games I dreaded were those in which I could be, and so often was, humiliated, counted out, shown up: but I soon lost my shyness and thoroughly enjoyed myself if the game involved a lot of physical movement – Musical Chairs, General Post, or those glorious wooden switchbacks along which one careered up and down across the length of a room.

On the strength of this, I should have enjoyed dancing. But I had never been taught to dance, and a traumatic experience ended my dancing days for ever at the age of seven. One of my father's parishioners, who was Lord Mayor of London, invited us to a Children's Ball at the Mansion House. It was a fancy-dress ball, and I went in my smart white sailor suit with long trousers. I hopped about cheerfully enough for an hour or two, and ate freely of the Mayoral refreshments. But then came the climax of the evening. The children, and there seemed to be thousands of them, were marshalled two by two for a procession past the Lord Mayor's throne. Unluckily, I was put almost at the head of this procession, so that by the time its tail had got through the main hall where the grown-ups were watching, its vanguard was a great distance away. I found myself, amid a horde of children, in a large, glittering room, lost. There was no-one I could ask, or at least dared ask, the way back. The experience of being lost in a crowd is, for a child, a truly formidable one. Hemmed in on all sides, yet utterly alone, I panicked, pushing my way through the children, stumbling from room to room, some crowded, some empty, but despairingly certain that I should never find the right one. Though it was only a few minutes before my father found me, the nightmare seemed endless.

It is likely that the loss of my mother created a lesion in my mind,

261

producing those gushes of panic, as at the Mansion House or in bed at night, when I felt lost, deserted, trapped in an aloneness from which I could not break out – a sort of transparent prison, like the empty jam-jar to the wasp. But these occasions were rare: it was seldom that my solitude made me aware of itself by thus turning upon me. Indeed, my most poignantly happy memory of the early years at Lancaster Gate is that of lying awake, alone in my bedroom, and hearing the whistles of locomotives from Paddington Station or the music of a German band in the dark streets below my window. Both were melancholy sounds, but the melancholy was a delicious one, remote, soothing, and the sounds came to me like intimations of some cosmic sadness from which, though I half recognized it, I was myself still blissfully immune.

The German bands, playing waltzes or popular airs with an unvaried dolefulness, are linked in my mind with night, lamplight shining on wet streets empty save for an occasional hansom cab, and my own warm bed. I was ravished most of all by the cornet when it played alone, its harsh and plangent tone the very voice of romantic longing: thirty years later these images, and the tunes which evoked them, gathered into a poem, 'Cornet Solo':

> Strange how those yearning airs could sweeten
> And still enlighten
> The hours when solitude gave me her breast.

So too with the railway noises from Paddington and Royal Oak – the rhythmic puffings, the syncopated percussion of trucks in the shunting yard, and above all, the engines' whistling – a disembodied cry that seemed to come out of the whole night around me and tempt my heart away into incalculable distances. Some of the engines that whistled were shunting, others arriving at the terminus; but for me, though I never formulated it thus in my mind, the sound was always a sound of departure, an intimation of passing away, transience, regret. This sound, too, has emerged in a poem, 'Last Words', where I ask which of my selves is to sum up my life for me at the end:

> —The child, who in London's infinite, intimate darkness
> Out of time's reach,
> Heard nightly an engine whistle, remote and pure
> As a call from the edge
> Of nothing, and soon in the music of departure
> Had perfect pitch?

From THE BURIED DAY

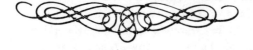

Cecil Day Lewis (1904–72), poet and novelist, was born in Ballintubber, the son of a Church of Ireland clergyman. The family moved to England in 1905, and after the death of his mother he was looked after by her sister. He was Professor of Poetry at Oxford 1951–6. His *Collected Poems* were published in 1954. He wrote many detective novels as Nicholas Blake.

Elizabeth

Elizabeth, frigidly stretched,
On a spring day surprised us
With her starched dignity and the quietness
Of her hands clasping a black cross.

With book and candle and holy-water dish
She received us in the room with the blind down.
Her eyes were peculiarly closed and we knelt shyly
Noticing the blot of her hair on the white pillow.

We met that evening by the crumbling wall
In the field behind the house where I lived
And talked it over but could find no reason
Why she had left us whom she had liked so much.

Death, yes, we understood: something to do
With age and decay, decrepit bodies.
But here was this vigorous one, aloof and prim,
Who would not answer our furtive whispers.

Next morning, hearing the priest call her name,
I fled outside, being full of certainty,
And cried my seven years against the church's stone wall.
For eighteen years I did not speak her name.

Until this autumn day when, in a gale,
A sapling fell outside my window, its branches
Rebelliously blotting the lawn's green. Suddenly, I thought
Of Elizabeth, frigidly stretched.

Valentin Iremonger (1918–), diplomat, poet and dramatist, was born in Dublin. He has been Irish Ambassador to Sweden, Norway and Finland; India; Luxembourg; and Portugal.

... And My Mother's Face

... And my mother's face I see it from below it's like nothing
I ever saw

we are on a veranda smothered in verbena the scented sun
dapples the red tiles yes I assure you

the huge head hatted with birds and flowers is bowed down
over my curls the eyes burn with severe love I offer her mine
pale upcast to the sky whence cometh our help and which I
know perhaps even then with time shall pass away

in a word bolt upright on a cushion on my knees whelmed in a
nightshirt I pray according to her instructions that's not all she
closes her eyes and drones a snatch of the so-called Apostles'
Creed I steal a look at her lips

she stops her eyes burn down on me again I cast up mine in
haste and repeat awry

the air thrills with the hum of insects

that's all it goes out like a lamp blown out

From How It Is

———◦◦———

Samuel Beckett (1906–   ), novelist and dramatist, was born in
Foxrock, Dublin, but since the early 1930s has lived in France,
writing mainly in French. The best-known of his controversial
plays is *Waiting for Godot*. He was awarded the Nobel Prize for
Literature in 1969. His *Collected Poems* were published in 1977.

Carrickfergus

I was born in Belfast between the mountain and the gantries
  To the hooting of lost sirens and the clang of trams:
Thence to Smoky Carrick in County Antrim
  Where the bottle-neck harbour collects the mud which jams

The little boats beneath the Norman castle,
  The pier shining with lumps of crystal salt;
The Scotch Quarter was a line of residential houses
  But the Irish Quarter was a slum for the blind and halt.

The brook ran yellow from the factory stinking of chlorine,
  The yarn-mill called its funeral cry at noon;
Our lights looked over the lough to the lights of Bangor
  Under the peacock aura of a drowning moon.

The Norman walled this town against the country
  To stop his ears to the yelping of his slave
And built a church in the form of a cross but denoting
  The list of Christ on the cross in the angle of the nave.

I was the rector's son, born to the anglican order,
  Banned for ever from the candles of the Irish poor;
The Chichesters knelt in marble at the end of a transept
  With ruffs about their necks, their portion sure.

The war came and a huge camp of soldiers
  Grew from the ground in sight of our house with long
Dummies hanging from gibbets for bayonet practice
  And the sentry's challenge echoing all day long;

A Yorkshire terrier ran in and out by the gate-lodge
  Barred to civilians, yapping as if taking affront:
Marching at ease and singing, 'Who Killed Cock Robin?'
  The troops went out by the lodge and off to the Front.

The steamer was camouflaged that took me to England –
  Sweat and khaki in the Carlisle train;
I thought that the war would last for ever and sugar
  Be always rationed and that never again

Would the weekly papers not have photos of sandbags
  And my governess not make bandages from moss
And people not have maps above the fireplace
  With flags on pins moving across and across –

Across the hawthorn hedge the noise of bugles,
  Flares across the night,
Somewhere on the lough was a prison ship for Germans,
  A cage across their sight.

I went to school in Dorset, the world of parents
  Contracted into a puppet world of sons
Far from the mill girls, the smell of porter, the salt-mines
  And the soldiers with their guns.

———•◦•———

Louis MacNeice (1907–63), poet, was born in Belfast, the son of the
future Bishop of Down, Connor and Dromore. He joined the BBC
as a features writer and producer in 1941, having previously
lectured in classics at Birmingham University and in Greek at
Bedford College, London University.

The Pink Bib

I was sent to school at four. I didn't want to go, for I had heard stories of Miss Cassidy, the principal teacher, and the assistant, Miss Moore. Once I had caught a glimpse of Miss Cassidy walking to her school, and I didn't ever want to see her again. She had a bundle of yellow canes, with crooks on them, under her arm, and she looked like a girl that could use them for all they were worth. She was a big woman with a heavy, coarse face, and across her round, massive shoulders she wore a small red shawl. In winter she wore heavy hob-nailed boots of my father's making. She liked my father because he wouldn't object, no matter how hard she used the cane on any of his children. She didn't like our neighbour, John Gorman. 'Gorman,' she said, 'beats his children with a straw.' Miss Cassidy was around fourteen stone in weight and above five feet in height. The assistant mistress, Miss Moore, was thin and wiry. I heard enough about her to make me want to go to America.

'Miss Moore,' George Maguire said once, 'she could cut cowld iron with her tongue.' George was my friend; he put nicknames on the teachers and advised me not to go to school. He called Miss Cassidy 'Sally' and Miss Moore 'Cutty'.

'Sally and Cutty will rise welts on ye, Paddy,' he told me. 'The schoolin' is no good for anybody that has to make a livin' at worm-cuttin'.'

I liked George very much for these words as well as for the fairy tales he told me. I have good reason to remember the first day I went to school. I am always good at creating a first impression, and afterwards going flat.

One of my sisters dragged me into the school. I was wearing the pink bib. I was put sitting on a seat near the door till such time as Miss Cassidy could come to me. A little girl beside me spilled ink over my hands. When Miss Cassidy came and saw my hands she went into the tantrums.

'Go outside at once and wash your filthy hands,' she commanded.

There was a pail of water outside the door which I knew nothing of. What I had was a vague notion of water being under a railway bridge somewhere. I found the bridge but not the water, so I sat down in a cranny among slaty stones and spat on my fingers. When I didn't return to the school and couldn't be found outside it, there was a great commotion. My sister Mary was hurried home after me.

'Of course he went home, the little rat!' Miss Cassidy said.

The assistant mistress agreed with her. I wasn't at home, and my mother and father were nearly frantic as they made for the school.

In the meantime all the boys and girls had been turned into sleuth-hounds. I was discovered at the end of a half-hour by two big boys. I heard them prancing down the railway slope on the farther side of the bridge. I peeped around the corner and withdrew my nose quickly again. I thought I saw one of the boys look under a whin bush.

'Where in the name of Moses did the cobbler's gossoon go?' one asked the other.

'The fairies must have taken him,' said the other.

'What will the Kavanagh say?'

I put my nose round the corner again but didn't withdraw it in time. They eyed me.

'Did you spot anything?' the tallest boy queried.

'The little bastard,' the other fellow replied. 'Trying to play hide and seek.'

They were very proud of their capture. As they led me down towards the school gate I saw my mother facing up to Miss Cassidy. Miss Cassidy was shivering in her shoes, and my mother wasn't using very lady-like language.

'They'll tear the livers out of each other,' one of my warders said.

'It'll be worth watching this,' said the other. There was no fight after all. My discovery settled the whole thing. Miss Cassidy wept and my parents didn't try to stop her, I think. Miss Cassidy was past her prime when I went to school; she had taught some of the fathers and mothers of my companions. ...

When I had discarded the pink bib and had been let into the secrets of trousers and their buttons I soon showed what I could do in the business of clothes distinction. My mother was a careful and thrifty woman and she kept the holes patched, patch on top of patch of every shade and pattern, till I had a coat as many-coloured as Joseph. There travelled a beggar around our place in those days whose wearables rivalled mine in their improvized melodies. Myles Courtney was the beggar's name. Miss Cassidy thought it would be a good joke to call me Myles Courtney. My father heard of it; he wasn't just pleased. To put a nickname on a person in Ireland was ever the most terrible weapon in use. The old poets did it and the names never came unstuck for seven generations.

My father accosted Miss Cassidy on her way to school. She went down on her two knees in the gutter and cried for mercy, which was forthcoming. The name wasn't well gummed on the back and I lost it.

From THE GREEN FOOL

Patrick Kavanagh (1905–67), novelist, poet and critic, was born in Iniskeen, Co. Monaghan, and grew up on a small farm before becoming a journalist. His *Collected Poems* were published in 1964, and *Collected Pruse* in 1967.

PATRICK SHEA

Sounds of Thunder

Our first school was St Clare's Convent which was near the barrack. At
the age of seven the boys had to leave it and enrol in the national school.
From the fields behind the convent we could see the all-male establishment in which our educational future lay. We saw an open door high in a
grey gable and from the darkness beyond we could hear the angry roars
of the Principal, a sound that carried a chilling threat across the
meadows as the time for the change approached.

Deerpark National School for boys was in the upper floor of a very
old, two-storeyed stone building, the ground floor of which had long
since been abandoned as habitable accommodation and become the
resting place of an accumulation of domestic jetsam through which tall,
rank weeds reached out towards the gaping holes where windows had
once been. Entrance to the school was by way of an iron-balustraded,
stone staircase to a door up in the gable which opened into one large
rectangular room. That room was the school; there six classes, a total of
perhaps eighty or ninety boys, were under the care of three men
teachers.

Along one side of the room, set at right angles to the wall, were long
desks bearing the inkstains and the scraped initials of many generations.
Here sat half of the boys, whilst the others stood in three semi-circular
classes, one at each end of the room and one around the open turf fire
which was midway along one of the longer walls. Each teacher had two
classes; one sitting doing written work and one standing 'being taught'.

In Deerpark National School silence, even for one moment, was
unknown. All through the day the teachers explained, ranted, interro-
gated, swung their canes; boys shouted out answers, read set pieces or
recited prayers. Every half hour the sitting and the standing classes
exchanged places with a shuffle and a clatter that made the floor quiver.
In winter the heat was fairly shared, each class having one period each
day around the fire (which was only just and fair since periodically the

pupils were required to bring tuppence each for the purchase of a load of turf). The wall decorations consisted of a tonic-solfa chart, two maps of Ireland, on one of which the place names were in Irish, and a chart giving the Ten Commandments and endorsed with the approval of the Commissioners of National Education. At the back of the school building, through a wasteland of nettles, a muddy path led to the malodorous 'toilets', the creation of some long-forgotten handyman whose skills did not include plumbing.

Even by the Spartan standards of sixty years ago, this must have been one of the worst-provided schools in Ireland. Yet the three teachers who spent their days trying to cultivate the seeds of knowledge in such an umpromising garden managed, in their different ways, to achieve the seemingly impossible, for Deerpark School had a reputation for scholarship that ridiculed its appearance.

The junior teacher was a small, bespectacled, fretful man with receding, fuzzy hair and a neglected, underslept appearance. He was a visionary and his vision was a free Ireland cleansed of everything that had come from England, including its language. From him we heard that taxes raised in Ireland kept the English in sinful luxury, that in a free, independent Ireland there would be little or no need for taxation. I have a particular reason for remembering him. He it was who, shortly after I had started at Deerpark School, took me out in front of the class to belabour me until his yellow cane had stung half of my body into throbbing agony, sending me home crying bitter tears, humiliated and angry and full of despair. That evening Father sat down with me and, patiently taking me through my schoolbooks, persuaded me that the tasks which I was being set were not beyond my capabilities. For the rest of my time in that man's class I never got a sum wrong or gave an incorrect answer or failed in any test he set me and as the months passed my response to his signs of growing respect was unsmiling, silent and wholly satisfying enmity. My inspiration was not the pursuit of knowledge; I was punishing my torturer with weapons against which he had no defence. Such excellence was not to be the pattern of my later studies but when I went on from him to higher things I was a grim, triumphant eight-year-old.

The other assistant was a tall, pale, very thin, monosyllabic hurley player who conveyed his message with an economy of words and threatening solemnity. He never smiled, he taught well and he used his cane with chilling accuracy; he well knew that a sharp stroke delivered on the end finger joints sent a shudder of pain right to his victim's toes.

273

For lesser misdemeanours the offender might find himself virtually suspended from a tuft of his short neck hairs clamped between the teacher's thumb and forefinger. He took singing; two classes combined for one hour once a week during which we fairly belted out 'The Minstrel Boy', 'Let Erin Remember', 'A Nation Once Again' and, out of respect for the Principal's native county, 'The Bells of Shandon'. He also presided over the weekly science lesson at which, after a lunchtime of preparation and with the aid of equipment consisting of a basin, a few test tubes, a tiny spirit heater, some pieces of glass tubing and a zinc bucket with water drawn from the roadside pump, he demonstrated by experiment such mysterious phenomena as atmospheric pressure, the distillation of water and the working of the thermometer. It was an hour of magical interest.

The terror and the inspiration of that crowded room was the Principal, a stocky, pugnacious Corkman with a bushy black moustache, short curly hair sitting on a rectangular forehead, lively brown eyes peering from beneath thick black eyebrows, the body of an oriental wrestler and the supple knees and light step of an athlete. He dressed in a navy blue serge suit that shone when he moved. From the watchchain that stretched across his wide waistcoat two silver medals hung; it was said that they were trophies of the boxing ring and that could well have been true. He had a ferocious temper, a liberal mind, the talents of a circus clown and a vast knowledge of greyhound coursing, horse-racing and boxing. His place in the room was beside the door where he sat in a wooden armchair behind a deal table with his 'Standing' class gathered around him. On the wall behind him hung a large rectangular display card with, on one side, in heavy black letters, the words 'SECULAR INSTRUCTION' and on the other 'RELIGIOUS INSTRUCTION'. The finger-worn stains on the bottom corners of the card bore witness to his punctiliousness in ensuring that, as required by the rules of the Commissioners of National Education, the exposed side truly conveyed what was going on in the school.

The Master (as the Principal was known to the townspeople) lived on the Leinster side of the town and every morning he walked to school reading his *Irish Independent*. Pupils dallying along the way knew that they must be in school before him; on his morning journey, every time he came into a street he must have seen a scurrying of small boys disappearing around the corner at the other end. If a mother had a son whose objection to education had reached the point of rebellion, the rebel was pushed on to the footpath ahead of the oncoming walker and his day was

274

made. On most mornings the Master arrived at the school with two or three unwilling scholars trotting fearfully in front of him.

If it was learned that a pupil was 'mitching' he was sought and invariably found in Kelly's Wood which was beside the school. The Master would bring out a dozen of the bigger boys and deploy them at strategic points around the wood. At a word of command the search would begin and when the maverick had been run to earth the search party would be gathered around him for the march back to school, the Master leading, carrying the school broom over his shoulder and the whole company singing 'The Minstrel Boy to the Wood Has Gone'. The fate of mitchers, none of whom, it seemed, ever escaped detection, planted in my mind at that early age the belief that life is hard for those who don't conform.

For those in the Master's class the most dreaded time of the day was the first period in the morning when he called for the results of the previous night's homework. The boys stood in a semi-circle around his table and when the moment came to exhibit the harvest of their toil, copy books had to be held up, face high, pages outward, for scrutiny by the Master. He would begin at the top of the class and walk slowly from boy to boy, hands clasped behind his back, cane switching against his trouser-leg, commenting pungently on what he beheld. If the results were below his expectations the exposed knuckles of the exhibitor might get a sharp rap of the cane or the Master might bring his large hand down on the book, sending it crashing into the face behind it. If the symbols on the page before him were disfigured by blots or clumsily executed alterations he might bring his arm swinging up from his side and with the back of his hand send the copy-book flying to the ceiling with a roar of, 'Take it away before I vomit.' The Master's inspection began at the end of the class at which the best pupils stood (continuous competition for privileged places being a feature of every class) and as he moved purposefully along in descending order of merit his judgements grew louder and more violent, he called upon the Almighty to bear witness to his unproductive labours and the veins stood out on his strong forehead as the whole performance ended in a riotous tirade of anger and abuse and self-pity. Countless must have been the heartbeats I missed when, having listened in terror to the approaching storm, I saw below the bottom of my open book that the shiny, black boots had stopped opposite me and I knew that my uncertain efforts were under the scrutiny of those black, angry eyes.

The Master was the most respected man in the town, feared alike by his pupils and their parents. His appearance in the noisiest street brought immediate silence. Most of his pupils came from very poor homes and he was determined to make something of them whether or not they liked it. Those who had no ideas about how they would one day earn a living were told what their careers would be and if the normal curriculum did not cater for their particular needs, he organized tuition in whatever subjects were necessary for entry to their chosen occupations. He knew what was good for them and even if it meant teaching by terror, they got it.

But life in Deerpark National School was not all violence and anger. The Master was a superb entertainer. In the midst of the most passionate outburst his anger could suddenly subside and the face of the clown appear. His stories were the best we had ever heard, he could mimic complaining parents, the other teachers, the school inspector, even the Parish Priest. If he encountered a travelling musician or a juggler or a man with performing animals he would engage him to entertain us. We would bring a penny each for the visiting artiste and for a whole afternoon the desks would be pushed to the end of the room and we would be treated to professional entertainment which the Master presided over like a proud ringmaster. If he got tired teaching he would gather us close around the table and tell us about great boxers and horses and running dogs. We shared his admiration for Jack Dempsey and Georges Carpentier and we heard from him about the short-tailed greyhound that won the Waterloo Cup. He was a comedian and a scholar and a holy terror and he was the best teacher I have ever known.

From VOICES AND THE SOUND OF DRUMS

———•o•———

Patrick Shea (1908–86), civil servant and dramatist, was Permanent Secretary, Northern Ireland Ministry of Education 1969–73, and Chairman, Enterprise Ulster 1973–9.

They're All Called Jams O'Donnell

I was seven years old when I was sent to school. I was tough, small and
thin, wearing grey-wool breeches but otherwise unclothed above and
below. Many other children besides me were going to school that
morning with the stain of the ashes still on the breeches of many of them.
Some of them were crawling along the road, unable to walk. Many were
from Dingle, some from Gweedore, another group floated in from Aran.
All of us were strong and hearty on our first school day. A sod of turf was
under the armpit of each one of us. Hearty and strong were we!

The master was named Osborne O'Loonassa. He was dark, spare and
tall and unhealthy with a sharp, sour look on his face where the bones
were protruding through the yellow skin. A ferocity of anger stood on his
forehead as permanent as his hair and he cared not a whit for anyone.

We all gathered into the schoolhouse, a small unlovely hut where the
rain ran down the walls and everything was soft and damp. We all sat on
benches, without a word or a sound for fear of the master. He cast his
venomous eyes over the room and they alighted on me where they
stopped. By jove! I did not find his look pleasant while these two eyes
were sifting me. After a while he directed a long yellow finger at me and
said:

–Phwat is yer nam?

I did not understand what he said nor any other type of speech which
is practised in foreign parts because I had only Gaelic as a mode of
expression and as a protection against the difficulties of life. I could only
stare at him, dumb with fear. I then saw a great fit of rage come over him
and gradually increase exactly like a rain-cloud. I looked around timidly
at the other boys. I heard a whisper at my back:

–Your name he wants!

My heart leaped with joy at this assistance and I was grateful to him
who prompted me. I looked politely at the master and replied to him:

–Bonaparte, son of Michelangelo, son of Peter, son of Owen, son of Thomas's Sarah, grand-daughter of John's Mary, grand-daughter of James, son of Dermot . . .

Before I had uttered or half-uttered my name, a rabid bark issued from the master and he beckoned to me with his finger. By the time I had reached him, he had an oar in his grasp. Anger had come over him in a flood-tide at this stage and he had a businesslike grip of the oar in his two hands. He drew it over his shoulder and brought it down hard upon me with a swish of air, dealing me a destructive blow on the skull. I fainted from that blow but before I became totally unconscious I heard him scream:

–Yer nam, said he, is Jams O'Donnell!

Jams O'Donnell? These two words were singing in my ears when feeling returned to me. I found that I was lying on my side on the floor, my breeches, hair and all my person saturated with the streams of blood which flowed from the split caused by the oar in my skull. When my eyes were in operation again, there was another youngster on his feet being asked his name. It was apparent that this child lacked shrewdness completely and had not drawn good beneficial lessons for himself from the beating which I had received because he replied to the master, giving his common name as I had. The master again brandished the oar which was in his grasp and did not cease until he was shedding blood plentifully, the youngster being left unconscious and stretched out on the floor, a bloodied bundle. And during the beating the master screamed once more:

–Yer nam is Jams O'Donnell!

He continued in this manner until every creature in the school had been struck down by him and all had been named *Jams O'Donnell*. No young skull in the countryside that day remained unsplit. Of course, there were many unable to walk by the afternoon and were transported home by relatives. It was a pitiable thing for those who had to swim back to Aran that evening and were without a bite of food or a sup of milk since morning.

When I myself reached home, my mother was there boiling potatoes for the pigs and I asked her for a couple for lunch. I received them and ate them with only a little pinch of salt. The bad situation in the school was bothering me all this time and I decided to question my mother.

–Woman, said I, I've heard that every fellow in this place is called *Jams O'Donnell*. If that's the way it is, it's a wonderful world we have and isn't O'Donnell the wonderful man and the number of children he has?

–'Tis true for you, said she.

–If 'tis true itself, said I, I've no understanding of that same truth.

–If that's the way, said she, don't you understand that it's Gaels that live in this side of the country and that they can't escape from fate? It was always said and written that every Gaelic youngster is hit on his first school day because he doesn't understand English and the foreign form of his name and that no one has any respect for him because he's Gaelic to the marrow. There's no other business going on in school that day but punishment and revenge and the same fooling about *Jams O'Donnell*. Alas! I don't think that there'll ever be any good settlement for the Gaels but only hardship for them always. The Old-Grey-Fellow was also hit one day of his life and called *Jams O'Donnell* as well.

–Woman, said I, what you say is amazing and I don't think I'll ever go back to that school but it's now the end of my learning!

–You're shrewd, said she, in your early youth.

From THE POOR MOUTH

Flann O'Brien was one of the pen-names of Brian O'Nolan (1911–66), novelist, dramatist and journalist, who was born in Strabane, Co. Tyrone. Until his retirement in 1953, he was a civil servant.

Prep School

My father was an educated man. He'd won literary prizes at Charter-house. He'd become a barrister. His knowledge and appreciation of English literature was as wide as anyone's I've ever known. But not the faintest shadow of it had rubbed off on to me.

Presumably he'd tried to stimulate my mind into the enjoyment and therefore the benefits of the formal education that had cost him so much money down the years. He always had a marked family pride. Once, he described us as being 'slightly upper-middle class'.

Surely he should have worked harder on me?

Though the gap is supposed to be narrowing, education or the lack of it discriminates as sternly between the classes as first and third railway tickets, and the Lord always had an instinctive tendency towards travelling first.

I'd have thought that an educated son would have been almost essential to his *amour propre*. But perhaps the imposition of the discip-line that this involved would have been repugnant to his reserved and diffident nature – diffident, at least, where personal relationships were concerned.

In the matter of my education my mother could have been of little help to him.

The only formal teaching she'd ever received had been in learning to draw at the Dublin School of Art, and later on at the Slade. To this day she counts on her fingers, and her spelling is an extraordinary scramble of phonetic sounds or, at any rate, of sounds that she believes to be phonetic.

And, finally and always, she's believed that there is no point in pushing people, particularly children. For them she's always been certain that 'it will all come right in the end'.

The Lord, at least, pushed me into Crawley's Preparatory School, St

Stephen's Green, in Dublin. He'd gone there himself, and was proud of his academic record, but the only memory I retain of Crawley's is a dark cellar and terror so dreadful that the only way I could contain it was by trying to stand outside myself, telling myself that it must come to an end, that sooner or later I would be safe on the top deck of the No. 15 tram, going home. Crawley's was a day-school, or I might not have survived it.

The trouble was two enormous brothers. To me they looked like fully grown men. One had flaming red hair, and a temper that became more and more demoniac the longer he persecuted me. The other was dark and sinister, and invented new tortures for his brother to carry out.

These ceremonies – they had the feeling of ceremonies in their set form and fixed denouement – were conducted in the cloakroom, a cellar in this old Georgian house, and they terminated in my head being shoved into a revolting lavatory bowl by the red-haired brother, while the dark one pulled the chain.

I'd imagine they picked on me because I was very tall and very thin, and my stammer made me almost completely inarticulate.

But those possessed and dreadful brothers did one thing for me. They gave me a life-long conviction that anger and violence are an actual waste of time. I remember I had to walk half a mile every morning from our house to the tram terminus in Terenure, and then sit in the tram for another half hour, with the brothers and the lavatory bowl getting nearer every minute, and the only thing I really objected to, in an utterly numb and miserable way, was this waste of time.

I could have been doing anything else, but here I had to sit on top of the tram as it lurched and howled down the long drabness of Rathmines Road, waiting for the moment to come when I walked into the cellar to hang up my coat, and to provoke the brothers to their inexplicable furies – furies that no appeal to reason could disperse.

It was a comfort, on top of the tram, to look forward to my approaching misery as a waste of time – a period of hours in which no nice or funny or interesting thing would happen, a time of limbo, of non-life.

Years later, at a party in London, a jolly psychiatrist in an eccentric but exceedingly smart suit, heard me telling someone that I regarded anger as a waste of time.

'But what would you prefer to do with this time which is wasted, as you say, upon anger?' he wanted to know.

'Live it,' I said, to my own satisfaction but not, as it turned out, to his. He thought it stemmed from a subconscious refusal to accept reality, but then he hadn't known the demon brothers and, at his prices, I wasn't prepared to lay their record before him.

Neither was I prepared to tell my mother, nor anyone else, about them. It seemed to me that the three of us had a secret so shameful that we could only keep it to ourselves. I don't remember any other boys being involved, or even being in the cellar, while we were conducting our rites, but I suppose many of them must have known what was going on.

And my mother must have guessed, because one afternoon she called for me at the school apparently by accident, saying she'd been shopping. I was outside on the pavement, when she arrived, with a number of boys of my own class. When we got home she said to the Lord, 'We'll have to find Paddy another school. He's getting much too tall for Crawley's. When I saw him this afternoon he looked like a tree surrounded by a lot of little dogs.'

From My Life and Easy Times

Patrick Campbell, Baron Glenavy (1913–80), journalist, broadcaster and television personality, was born in Dublin. He contributed humorous columns to many journals and newspapers.

BRIDGET BOLAND

Gallic Diversions

When it rained, which (surely more often than I remember?) it sometimes did even in Wissant, we younger ones played in the *buanderie*, which we called the *bu*, the wash-house built away from the house in an angle of the garden wall, with a huge boiler and copper used particularly for the annual *grande lessive*, when Charlotte-from-over-the-way came to help Mme Noël, and every stitch of linen in the house was washed and spread out to bleach on the sand dunes. Here, on the huge white-scrubbed table in the middle, used for the ironing, we would play cards, notably *bouchon*. This was an improved version of Snap, taught us by some of the 'villa children': a cork from a wine bottle stood in the middle of the table, and, when two cards of the same value were turned up, instead of crying 'Snap!' every grabbed for it. Finger-nails were examined before this game was played, and anyone whose nails were adjudged too long was sent to cut them. My mother, as Eily once remarked, was 'awfully good at rain', and knew a lot of games for bad weather, most of them taught her by kindly ladies who had taken pity on the little girl sitting alone in the corners of hotel lounges in her childhood. The best of these were infinite varieties of paper folding and cutting, including origami and one now marketed as 'Tangrams'. We drew and cut out paper dolls, and made and painted complete wardrobes to dress them in (with little folding flaps of paper over the shoulders and round the waists). When we got bored with contemporary dresses for them she showed us how to turn them into knights in armour and their ladies, Robin Hood characters, kings and queens and courtiers of different periods. We made paper houses, and once, carried away after a visit to St Omer not far away, we built a whole cathedral propped up inside with books, complete with flying buttresses and stained-glass windows made of toffee papers. Then she would give prizes for designing jackets for our favourite books, and for illustrating the stories. The

fact that none of us except Anne were much good added to the entertainment.

There was very little excitement in the village. The only transport,
apart from the fish lorries that came every morning to take the catch of
the half-dozen boats to Boulogne or Calais for Paris, was George's bus,
that went twice a week to Calais. George was an Englishman who, as a
soldier in the 1914–18 War, married a local girl. He was reputed to have
poured paraffin over his mother-in-law, who owned the grocer's shop,
and set fire to her, but with no lasting results. The engine of his bus had
been originally, everyone said, that of the German submarine whose
wreck could still be seen at low tide. My brother, who examined it with
interest, confirmed the probability of this. Occasionally a special bus
would stop in the village while taking English tourists for a trip along
the coast road, they having landed at one port in the morning and
intending to return home from the other that night. We always hid, or
someone in the village would be sure to pounce on us for explanations of
what the poor creatures wanted. It was in fact always tea, and we knew
from experience that they wouldn't like what they would be offered at
the hotel – and there was nowhere else. We were sorry for them, for it
was a very dull road, and my mother, having her own strong views on
tea, every year brought over an immense packet of Lipton's as a gift to
the hotel for their benefit, and had explained about thin bread and
butter, and about jam being different from *compôte de fruit*; but we
were bitterly ashamed of them, and stressed heavily that we were Irish
and quite different. This, the village assured us politely, saw itself, but
we could at least speak their language and find out why they were so
cross. They behaved abominably. In the Twenties the exchange was
heavily in the pound's favour, and in Calais, we had often heard, they
used to throw their small change over the ship's side onto the quays
before they left for the natives to scramble for; when one bus load, who
were at least good tempered, did this in the village as they were leaving,
a group of fisherboys, lounging on the bridge, picked the coins up and
flung them back into their faces at close range. One group flung the
beautiful crusty slices of bread on the hotel floor and ground it in with
their heels to express their disgust, and they would often fish out the tea
bags that preceded my mother's gifts of Lipton's and fling them out of
the window in their rage. Another scene of violence occurred one
Sunday outside the church, where a bus load were appalled to see all the

little girls who were going down to the beach after High Mass pulling their dresses off over their heads as they came down the steps and revealing the bathing dresses they wore underneath and tossing them, with their Sunday hats, to waiting relatives, while the little boys wriggled out of their shirts and trousers. The English rushed forward and boxed the ears of any they could catch, while my mother tried to explain to their indignant parents about the Non-conformist Conscience, failing until she hit on the idea of saying that they didn't approve of wine either, which so paralysed the natives with amazement that the bus load got away fairly intact. But Wissant certainly made no contribution to the *entente cordiale*.

Peculiarly disliked at one period by the natives was the *Continental Daily Mail*, an edition of the paper printed, I imagine, in Paris. It used to fly a plane up and down along the coast spoiling the heavens with hideous sky-writing advertisements; but one year the paper delighted my heart. They ran a competition at all the resorts along the northern coast for the best sandcastles made by children. As our Mayor had written a particularly virulent objection to the sky-writing they included Wissant as a 'resort' as a gesture of goodwill, though the handful of visitors it could house and its lack of any amenities for their entertainment scarcely merited the honour. I considered myself a dab at the art, and I needed the money: I wanted a particularly splendid kite to be had at the village general store. No humdrum castle for me; I decided to overpower the judges with a magnificently sculptured tomb, with the figures of a crusader and his lady lying atop with their little dog at their feet. The village was shocked to the core: hovering on the sand dunes above the beach so as not to seem to give support to the hated *Daily Mail*, they could not see the finer points of my work, it seemed to them to represent a man and woman in bed together (with the hump of a stone hot-water bottle at their feet), absolutely not a suitable subject for a little girl to choose. As a matter of fact I had to explain what it did represent to the judges, but I won the prize. As I crossed the bridge over the millstream to the shop I tore off as usual a leaf from the tall bullrushes that overtopped it for the delicious feeling of tearing its crispness, and, my mind aloft with the coveted kite I was on my way to buy, I shredded the precious note in my hand as well. Even the pangs of unrequited love in later years were not more bitter than my grief when I saw what I had done. Although my father, still laughing over the village's reaction to my masterpiece, which had been reported to him at the tennis courts, made good the loss, and it proved the best kite ever seen on the beach, it still hurts me to think of that lost note.

From AT MYMOTHER'S KNEE

Bridget Boland (1913–   ), novelist, dramatist and screenwriter, spent her earliest years in London and in South Kerry, which her father represented in the House of Commons.

The Castle

We used to visit our relatives in the castle at Carrigrohane about once a month during the summer. Whenever we left Tivoli to undertake the journey I was in a simmering state of excitement. The expedition entailed a tram ride into Cork city and then on by railway to Carrigrohane.

This train was called the Muskerry Railway, a quaint little affair which plied between Cork and Blarney, famed then and now for its handsome castle whose stone must be kissed to gain 'a gift of the gab', i.e., loquacity of speech. The railway track ran unprotected alongside the road. Frequently the journey was enhanced by stray animals that trespassed on to the rails and once the train was held up for a considerable period because a reclining cow refused to move.

Several times, when close to Carrigrohane, a mad old woman appeared, cursing and screaming. As the train slowed at this point due to a bend, she managed to dance alongside, using Biblical phrases interspersed with hair-raising language. Later, she used to terrorize me on the way to school. The windows of her small cottage were completely covered with holy pictures, behind which she lurked ready to ambush any stray pedestrian. Once she deeply shocked some visitors to the castle by lifting her many skirts waist-high, to advertise her shortage of underclothes.

In my childish eyes the castle resembled a fairy palace, grim but beautiful, shrouded in melancholy mystery. Due to the fact that we weren't allowed further than the dining-room, which lay off the front hall, the rest of the building appeared all the more tantalizing. From without, staring up at the rows of turreted windows, I tried vainly to visualize what those hidden rooms were like, and wondered would I ever be allowed to explore them?

Aunt Eliza and Uncle Henry had lived in the castle all their lives and were an eccentric pair. She was tall and gaunt, with a pale, cadaverous

287

face; invariably dressed in black, she wore a masculine coat with a high-crowned hat of the same sombre colour set squarely on white hair, which straggled from beneath it in all directions. She adored horses; in fact, she appeared to spend the greater part of her life in the stables.

Her brother was also tall, thin and pale. His pet passions were flowers and music. He liked to while away his time in the garden, in a quaint little octagonal hut (which he and his brothers had erected long ago) surrounded by stacks of records and his ancient gramophone.

Henry and Eliza were seldom on speaking terms. This was embarrassing, especially when they issued contradictory commands to us children; if one of them was obeyed, the other was disobeyed, so that we seemed to be always on the brink of trouble.

I knew there were dungeons beneath the castle, also it was said that a secret passage led down into the caves in the rock on which it was built. As I grew older my burning desire to explore the place increased, but all my hints to Aunt Eliza were ignored.

The lower entrance hall was dimly lit by a narrow window; the pale stone floor gave it a ghostly appearance. The dining-room was approached by a little minstrel's gallery; from it one looked down into the square room below, with its large, deepset windows and its mantelpiece heavily decorated with coats-of-arms.

The repast that Aunt Eliza served as afternoon tea did not vary greatly. A dryish shop cake, if we were lucky, some bread and butter, and always a large dish of cold boiled rice. Fortunately I liked this last item, a taste that was not shared by my sisters.

Uncle Henry never appeared at tea. I often wondered if he ever ate at all. He was so pale, frail and skinny. He slept in his little garden hut. Eliza, we suspected, dossed down often in the stables; when she decided to sleep in the castle she occupied an attic.

Why she chose a bedroom that entailed climbing five flights of stairs was a mystery. Of course, Clotilda, as already mentioned, haunted the place and had been seen most often in those lofty upper regions. The top storey must have held a strange allure for them both, just as it did for me when, eventually, we went to live there.

It was mainly due to Eliza's love of horses that she loathed all motor vehicles. If a car happened to pass the front gates when she was nearby, she rushed out towards the oncoming vehicle, waving her arms and shouting:

'Dirty roadhog! Get away from here, you dirty roadhog!'

Her voice was piercingly loud and shrill. As she yelled she danced with rage, shaking her fist. Machines travelled slowly then and many affronted countenances peered out; some inmates even shook their fists in return. The whole exhibition used to make me shriek with laughter. Mother, not unnaturally, found it extremely embarrassing. She used to call: 'Oh, *do* hush, Eliza. What *must* people think of you?'

'What do I care?' Aunt Eliza would declare, grinning triumphantly as she returned to her beloved stables. 'I'll never give up trying to stop those dirty machines coming past *my* gates, throwing up filth and dust ... Why don't they travel in a civilized way – nice and slowly, like decent, respectable people, in a pony and trap?'

It was fruitless to argue. Mother, after some further expostulations, would shrug and sigh resignedly. Eliza didn't care in the least what impression she made on passersby. But mother, conventional in some ways, felt it her duty to protest at Eliza's outbursts; no matter how frequently they occurred she always experienced the same indignant sense of outrage, which made it all the funnier for us children.

From THE ROAD TO GLENANORE

M. Jesse Hoare (1918–), author and journalist, was born in Cork, the daughter of a veterinary surgeon.

ANNE GREGORY

Literary Lunches

While there were visitors at Coole, Grandma didn't read to us, but we always went to the library or drawing room for about an hour after tea, before going on up to bed.

G.B.S. was one of the nicest visitors at Coole, and always said that he'd play a game with us. I can't really remember playing any game with him, except 'Hunt the Thimble'. He was very good at this game, and was incredibly quick at spotting where we'd hidden the thimble which infuriated Nu and me, as we could usually fox other adults, and even each other, sometimes. I'm not quite sure when or how it dawned on us, that G.B.S. was *cheating*. It started as a sort of awkward feeling that he went too directly to the place we'd hidden the thimble; he couldn't *always* be so clever? . . . and then one evening – having talked it over earlier in the day – we arranged that I would watch him through my fingers while Nu hid the thimble. (I gave Nu my solemn word that I wouldn't look at *her* at all.) To my utter horror I saw G.B.S. turn round – quite blatantly – and *look* . . . definitely look through his fingers where Nu was hiding it.

It was so *embarrassing*. A grown-up actually cheating. I had never been in a situation like this before. You couldn't accuse a grown-up of cheating, but you couldn't possibly play 'Hunt the Thimble' when you were bound to lose every time. The whole thing was unthinkable – and I did the only thing I could think of on the spur of the moment – I burst into a flood of tears. I did this fairly easily – either involuntarily or on purpose – and had found that one didn't have to explain the reason for the flood, until the noise and dampness had gone.

G.B.S. was very upset, and kept on pressing me to tell him what was wrong, and he was sure that he could make it better. But how could I tell him that I was howling because he'd been cheating for days and days. I was sent up to bed in disgrace, Nu with me, which was bad luck for her, but when she heard about G.B.S. she was shattered as I was by the

290

horror of the whole thing. Luckily G.B.S. was leaving the next day, so we were spared the awfulness of having to decide what to do about playing with him again.

In the evening we told Grandma about it, and how awful it all was. Grandma laughed till the tears fell down on to her lap.

G.B.S. wasn't *cheating*! he thought we'd seen him looking all the time and thought it was a joke, and that he was making the game more amusing. We were far from amused, secretly feeling that it might seem funny to a grown-up, but to us it was still dishonest; though we felt rather bad that we had actually accused him of such a big crime, if he really didn't think it was such a terrible thing to do.

However, at Grandma's suggestion, later we collected a lot of his favourite apples – croftons that grew on two terrifically old trees in the apple garden, and Grandma packed them up, and posted them to him 'with love from Anne and Catherine to G.B.S.' Grandma wanted us to put 'with love from Anne and Catherine to their kind playmate G.B.S.' but we definitely couldn't bring ourselves to do this.

Mr Yeats used to stay with us at Coole from as far back as I can remember.

There was a large bed of sedum in the flower garden, by the first vinery; in the summer it was alive with butterflies and I can remember Mamma once saying that sedum flowered all the year round; and while it was in flower Yeats would be at Coole.

He always seemed to be there, leaning back in his chair at table – huge, with (in our eyes) an enormous tummy. He wore a signet ring with an enormous stone in it on his little finger, and Nu and I used to giggle like mad, and say he expected everyone to kiss it, like the Pope. She and I used to copy his habit of running his fingers through the great lock of hair that fell forward over his forehead, and then hold out our hand with the imaginary ring, saying: 'This ring is a holy ring; it has been in touch with my holy halo.'

We all lunched and had tea together. Nu and I didn't dine with the grown-ups, but Richard sometimes did.

Marian always waited at table at dinner, and Richard told us that Mr Yeats always sat with his chair pushed back much farther from the table than anyone else, and every time Marian passed behind him, she used to kick the back leg of his chair, by accident on purpose, and then say, 'I'm sorry, sir, I never saw you had pulled back from the table.' Richard said Marian did it over and over again, and Mr Yeats never moved his chair in by one inch. Nu and I dared each other to kick his chair leg at tea, but we never dared.

Mr Yeats didn't speak much – while we were there anyway – and seemed sunk in thought, miles away, though he never seemed to miss any food. Grandma always seemed to be filling his cup, which he passed up the moment it was empty, without looking up and without a word.

'Manners' Nu and I used to signal to each other with a disapproving look: 'Did you see? No please or thank you.'

We had tea outside the front door on the gravel sweep every day in the summer and it never rained.

Mr Yeats sat on the garden chair that had wooden arms and a high back. Grandma sat on the green painted garden seat with curled iron arms and a back that curved over backwards, and we children had wicker stools with four legs, made by the travelling basket maker. They were made from withies and dogwood that grew on the side of the avenue. Yellow willow and red dogwood, and they had very comfortable slightly concave circular seats, and were just the right height for the tables. The tables were really just pieces of polished mahogany that folded in half. Marian and Ellen used to carry them out and put them on low trestles, and then Marian carried the enormous silver tray with the silver teapot with the acorn on the lid, and the enormous silver hot water jug, and then all the food. Masses of scones and butter and honey and strawberry jam bottled by Grandma, and lots of sponge cakes that Mary made, and which never tasted so heavenly as in the sun.

Mr Yeats actually seemed to talk more when he had tea out of doors, though he still passed his cup without a word, and anyway we often had visitors for tea in the summer.

It was great fun when people came to tea, when we were having it out of doors, because they had to drive up to the front door, virtually up to the tea table. The horses or ponies were taken down to the yard to be looked after by John Diveney, but later there were motor cars, and they merely passed the house, and parked under the enormous Ilex just beyond.

The workmen's bell was fixed in this tree, and was rung at 8.0 a.m., 12.0 noon, 1.0 p.m. and 6.0 p.m. for the starting and stopping of work. It was a lovely bell but woe betide any of us if we rang it at any other hour; though sometimes if Grandma wanted someone from the yard or garden she would tell us to go and give the bell 'two swings only', which was a thrill.

You could hear the bell nearly three miles away, and the twelve o'clock bellringing meant that however hard pressed Nu and I were, even if our camp was surrounded by Indians, we had to make a determined effort and break out within a few minutes or we'd be late for lunch.

This was one of the few unbreakable rules. We had to be back in the house in time to wash our hands and get tidy before the gong went for lunch, and I cannot remember that we were ever late.

When the Indians were becoming less dangerous – I think we had driven them off so often that they were less anxious to attack – we began to turn our minds to decorating and beautiful houses.

Near the house, on the way down to the flower garden, there was a wonderful place where old laurels had grown into an archway, making a natural entrance to a cave of dark green inside. The removal of a lot of dead wood was fairly easy, and the result was fantastic. A room big enough to carry in a bench and an enormous case that we found in the Haggart. It was easy to find an old table cloth, and we managed to slip out a bedspread for the 'sofa', and we spent several admiring hours here.

However, to have a beautiful interior is not enough. It's all right if the outside has to be disguised to prevent the enemy locating you, but *this* house was for show. It was on the edge of the direct route Grandma or any visitor took from the house to the flower garden, and therefore it must look beautiful and intriguing from the path.

I had a passion for laburnum. I could think of nothing more beautiful than waking in the morning with laburnum growing across my bedroom window in great masses, with the sun shining through the flowers on to my bed. So here was my first real chance. I picked a lot of large branches of laburnum covered in tight buds, and planted them either side of the entrance to our mansion.

Then we decided that a mansion must have an avenue – with daffodils. The daffs were out, so we dug up a great number in the woods and planted an avenue of them up to the front door. The ground was very hard and we had great difficulty in making the holes deep enough to cover the bulbs, but we propped the flowers up with sticks, certain that in the morning they would have righted themselves and be standing high and firm. This was perhaps one of the worst disappointments we had known.

It was such a wonderful thing we had planned – the whole rather dark place, glowing with yellow daffodils followed by hanging lanterns of golden laburnum.

293

Next morning we rushed down to see our lovely house. It was shocking. We could see at once that the laburnum had wilted and was collapsed on the floor – lifeless. That was bad enough, but where were the daffodils? Had they been eaten or what? They'd vanished.

Very slowly we approached, wondering if some horrible animal would rise from the ground, perhaps still chewing the final flower.

And then we saw a few pathetic yellow forms lying on the ground, their colour nearly gone, and looking so tiny and so *few*. Surely we'd planted ten times that number?

It was awful!

It was awful that it *looked* so awful, and it was awful that we had moved the daffs and they were dead, and we had killed them, and it was awful that now no one would come and admire our new house. I don't think that I have ever been so completely miserable.

Sean O'Casey was staying with us at this time, and he wandered past, gazing at the trees as he seemed to do a great deal of the time. He didn't know the names of the different trees and Grandma was teaching him. He had funny pink eyes and he saw us – or even probably heard us sobbing.

'What's up with you,' he asked us kindly enough. 'Have you hurt yourselves?'

'No,' we tried to be grown-up. 'No, we've had trouble with our avenue. The daffodils don't like being divided like this. They were all together, and we think they're *lonely*.' This was invented on the spur of the moment, but we suddenly thought it might be true.

'Ah well,' said Mr O'Casey, 'don't waste your time on lonely daffodils, there's plenty more would welcome your tears.'

We were sure he said this. It sounded very silly to us. Who would want our tears more than our poor dead daffs, killed by our own hands. Before we got too soaked with tears Grandma came along with our elevenses. Dear, dear, Grandma. One glance at the shambles.

'Goodness,' she said, 'what a wonderful idea making an avenue like that. It will be *so* beautiful next year – like a fairy road and if you are at school I'll see them coming up and I'll be able to write to you both and tell you about them, and it will make me think of you both every time I go to the flower garden.'

'But Grandma,' we wailed, 'they're dead. We've killed them.'

'Nonsense,' said Grandma, 'they're not *dead*. They may be sulking because they were having a party when you dug them up; but next year they will come up again as bright as buttons. You can never really dig up a flower when it is open and cheerful and obviously having a good time. It resents it. But when it's faded you can, because then it rather likes the idea of going somewhere new,' and Grandma came into our house with our elevenses and sat on the sofa and didn't ask where we'd got the bedspread from.

From ME AND NU

Anne Gregory (1911–   ), granddaughter of Lady Gregory, was born at Coole Park, Co. Galway.

Grannie and Grandma

A visit to Grannie Collins always promised adventure. Married to the General Manager of the Hibernian Bank, she lived in the large and rather grandiose house with immensely high rooms over the bank, which is right in the middle of the city in College Green. For a small child living in the wilds of Howth, this grandstand view of life in the big city was an excitement in itself. The frequent presence of my cousins Betty and Dorothy added spice to my visits. On one occasion, we couldn't resist the temptation of squirting soda-water from a syphon onto the bowler-hatted businessmen passing along the footpath below. Not getting sufficient reaction, since the jet was dissipated in the wind, we resorted to buckets of water. This resulted in the immense satisfaction of an outraged crowd of gesticulating victims, and we rolled about in a fit of laughter which was quite uncontrollable until a loud knocking at the hall door announced the ominous arrival of the police. We fully believed we would be sent to prison, and that Grandpa would be dismissed from his exalted position, and were greatly relieved when nothing more serious happened than banishment to our bedroom, where we discovered the delightfully pungent perfume produced by toasting orange-peel on the spiral coils of the electric heater.

Grandpa Collins would emerge from the boardroom for meals. His enormous tabby cat would sit on the table just to his right on a special mat, and with the utmost delicacy would transfix a pat of butter with one claw and lick it with the decorum necessary to pass the test for the Indian Civil Service – a standard of table manners much quoted for the benefit of us children in those days, since two of the Collins daughters had married successful candidates. The great tabby cat was called Guinness, after the immense cart-horses that used to draw the wagons of stout barrels around Dublin. He was never known to utter a sound until he fell out of the window of the first floor onto the street below. After a lengthy and anxious convalescence, he gained a healthy baritone voice and a purr like an engine.

The big drawing-room window from which Guinness fell was the scene of a more dramatic episode during 'the troubles'. Grandpa used to sit with his back to the window after breakfast, reading the paper; and his bald head was too tempting a target for the soldiers stationed on top of the Bank of Ireland across the street. Taking a pot-shot at his head, the bullet just missed it, went through the top of the *Irish Times* and the parrot's cage, and lodged in the walnut case of the piano, where it created a fascinating wiry clank on a couple of notes in the bass. Surviving this near miss, my grandfather flourished until well on in his nineties, refusing to retire until a few years before his death. He had the appealing habit of calling me over to him on quite unexpected occasions, asking whether I liked portraits. Whereupon he would produce as a tip a golden half-sovereign, pointing out the portrait of Queen Victoria or King Edward or George.

Trips to the Zoo and the Metropole cinema added to the excitement of these city visits; though a nightmarish fear of things not understood intruded upon the adventure of the journey on top of the open tram to Phoenix Park. As we passed the ruins of the Four Courts, only recently blown up, the grotesquely twisted lamp-bracket over the porch seemed somehow to distil the essence of this fear in its ominously symbolic image.

Grannie-in-the-bank was great fun. Curiously enough I was never conscious of her going to church. By contrast, Grandma was grave, and her house was like an extension of the Moravian church. Just like Queen Victoria she dressed in widow's black, with black beads all down her front, for the decade or so that she survived Grandfather Boydell. She wore a black bonnet when she ventured out to sit in the rustic summer-house under the weeping willow in the garden in Raglan Road, and when she went for drives in her carriage driven by the coachman Tye, who had a big lump on his neck and wore a top hat with a black cockade. I adored travelling in the carriage with the smell of leather, and the soothing sound of the horse's hooves and the rumble of the rubber-tyred wheels on the wooden street-sets. Pulling down the blinds and letting them flip up again was great fun – though gravely discouraged.

A special entertainment at Raglan Road was the speaking tube which enabled one to communicate from one floor to another. If you blew strongly down the tube a little yellow-stained ivory whistle would pop out and whistle a summons in the domestic quarters. The great game

297

was to make the whistle pop out into someone's mouth when they were talking into the tube. I can remember its curious taste.

Other activities when visiting Grandma were of a more serious nature. In the drawing-room, which was furnished and decorated in real Victorian style with curio cabinets and masses of photographs, was a superb Bechstein grand piano at which I would spend hours 'making up' music inspired by an old travel book of America, with engravings of Niagara Falls and other famous sights. The quite characteristic smell of a Bechstein and the sound of the bells of nearby St Bartholomew's church are vividly associated with Grandma's gravy – a culinary ideal which has never since been attained.

Besides Grandma and the lovable cook who taught me to make currant scones, the other inhabitants of the house were my maiden aunt Edie and auntie (pronounced 'anti') Hurst, the widow of my grand-mother's brother, who must have done something awful, for his name was never mentioned. As far as I was concerned auntie Hurst had no first name: in fact she was more like an item of vast black furniture than a person, though she had the horribly fascinating attribute of a large mole on her chin with very long hairs sprouting from it. I often seemed to be there on Sundays, when the only allowable entertainment was to 'play church' with Grandma and the two aunts as my personal congrega-tion. I actually enjoyed this in a curious way, though this had nothing to do with my childhood propensity for devotional fervour. Rather, my enjoyment probably centred on acting the part of a leader, imagining I had the same authority and power as Mr Hutton, the Moravian minis-ter, whom I remember commanding his flock in Kevin Street from the immense height of the pulpit, thumping the red velvet upholstery as he declared the word of God. I also enjoyed providing what I considered the appropriate music on the Bechstein, and taking up a collection from my congregation of three. I can't remember whether I was allowed to pocket the proceeds.

One Sunday in the summer it was unusually warm, and it was deemed appropriate to sit quietly in the garden. A veil must be drawn over that occasion, and the shame of it shadowed me for many years. I actually turned 'head-over-heels' on the lawn, revealing – on Sunday, remember – that even very small children possessed a part of their anatomy which, when very much older, they might refer to in naughty whispers as a 'bottom'. I fear the horror took many years off Grandma's life.

Brian Boydell (1917–   ), musician, was born in Dublin. He was Professor of Music, University of Dublin 1962–82, and has been a fellow of Trinity College since 1972. His compositions include a violin concerto, three quartets, orchestral music and symphonic music, chamber music, film music and songs. He has written extensively on music, and is a member of Aosdána.

Before the Drums

In the summer there was the Bull Island, more generally called, with prim inappropriateness, Dollymount – that gift of the sea to the people of North Dublin. The island is said to have been formed from some unwanted plants, thrown into the sea two centuries ago, by a gardener from a great estate nearby. It was a magic place, joined to the mainland by a strong wooden bridge. The smooth, golden beach, almost three miles long, was of genuine soft sand. The sand sloped up to some dunes and coarse grass and behind this people played golf in a different world. The beach and the Bull Wall, a breakwater that ran out to sea as one side of the entrance to Dublin Harbour, were ours. As soon as we could swim we dived off the rocks of the Bull Wall. The Corporation built shelters and steps at a later stage. The beach was for family parties with small children – one had to walk a long way if the tide was out. Only the first four to five hundred yards of the beach was used in those days. It was a long walk from the tram, across the bridge, along the wall and the flank of the island. Once the beach was reached, tired parents and children were content to stay at the crowded end, rather than push on still further in the soft sand, under the hot sun. The sun of childhood and of memory is always hot.

The beach had a moveable danger spot called 'Curley's Hole', named, it was said, after the first man to drown there. Some freak of the meeting tides created a deep hole in the otherwise shallow water. There was another hole, further down near St Anne's Golf Club. When the tide was out this remained full of water. We scorned the beach as a children's area with shallow water, when the tide was in. We swam in the hole when the tide was out. It was reputed to be bottomless – an immediate challenge to small boys. We used to take rocks from the Bull Wall and carry them down (sitting on bicycle crossbars) to the hole. There were no rocks any nearer to it. With the rocks in our arms we tried to plumb the depths. Down, down – sometimes for so long that we would have to drop the rocks and surface with lungs bursting. I never knew anyone to touch bottom at the deepest part.

Fairview Park was being completed in the late 1920s; it was laid over the dumped rubbish of Dublin. A wide strip of grass, similarly laid, was carried on all the way to the Bull Wall. The park became quite beautiful, with shrubs, flower-beds, a band-stand and football pitches. With what must have been quite limited resources Dublin Corporation did a great deal in those days. The main path through the park was rumoured to be half a mile long. To run it twice was to run a mile – a special feat to us, for a mile seemed a very long way then. But the 'Circle', the centre of Marino, was the main games area. There was a football team, if not two, in every class of the local school. The emphasis was on participation, before there was ever discussion on the difference between participation and spectatorship. One could find up to six games going on simultaneously on greatly shortened pitches, with jackets for goal posts, and six Christian Brothers with whistles acting as referees cum coaches. I remember them throwing hurling balls at us from all angles – we were required to hit them 'first time' in the air. The 'honours' pupils could hit a ball cleanly first time and score a point. We became proficient at this most difficult skill – able to meet or continue flying balls, striking right or left-handed, with accuracy and some power. The Brothers, with their patience and enthusiasm, could sharpen our eyes and give us accurate timing. They could not teach light-framed Dublin boys like me how to do all this and take a jostle as well. In those days, at any rate, this was an attribute of the 'country fellas' – the natural, early-starting hurlers from Cork, Tipperary and Kilkenny.

We had the most sketchy sports clothing, of course, usually just our shirt sleeves. Those were the days before the right 'gear' became half the game. Just after the Eucharistic Congress, in 1932, all the classes in Scoil Muire quite suddenly got proper football jerseys. The rumour was that an American who stayed with some relatives in the area had donated them. He can never have bought anything else half so precious in his lifetime. The thrill of donning real jerseys was memorable.

We also dug, with the same absorbed intensity we had put into shifting rocks to plumb the hole in Dollymount. The site of the present Marino Vocational School was then a piece of waste land. One boy's father had been in the Dublin Fusiliers, like many in the city at that time. The boy had a genuine British Army trenching tool, a marvellously functional piece of equipment which was, it seems, also usable as a weapon. Nancy Mitford's Uncle Matthew claimed to have killed seven

Germans with his – I had no difficulty in believing that when I read her book years afterwards. We dug trenches and holes endlessly – not, as far as I remember, in any youthful war scenario. We were, I think, as blood-thirsty as any small boys who read comics – but in the detached way by which we unconsciously separated comics from real life. We dug for the sheer joy of digging, of getting below the surface and of using the tool in turns. With its pick spike at one end and its hinged shovel-blade at the other, the tool was short, as it had to be in World War I; men could not raise their heads above the parapets, and probably used it on their knees. It was just the right size for boys. It had survived many hours of desperate work during the war; perhaps my friend's father had become attached to it. It certainly survived hours of intent digging with us – a wonderful piece of well-designed, rugged equipment from the days when British industry led the world.

All this running, digging, swimming and games must have made us fit, although we did not know it. We had healthy appetites; luxuries were few; food was plain. One could get into the cinema for fourpence and vociferously warn 'the chap' that the 'villian' (*sic*) was coming up behind him.

John Pudney's 'First Drums' had started to beat, but the sound came to us muffled, and from far away. In Europe, boys of our age were being made fit by drilling and marching; fit to kill and be killed in places they never heard of – Aandalsnes, Eben Emael, Montcornet, Tobruk, Stalingrad, El Alamein, Cassino, Kursk, Falaise, Arnhem. Hitler was a kind of uniformed Charlie Chaplin on the news reels – Goering and the generals looked more impressive. Old Father Scannell (Scanlon? – how memory dies) said that hatred was being focussed on Jews in Germany ... 'They are God's people. They have survived because his hand is over them. Persecuting a Jew is persecuting God's brother.' I cannot remember any anti-Jewish feeling or remarks. Fr Scannell was, I think, a man of wide experience – perhaps through World War I. He described hearing marching bugles in Alsace once and pointed it out on the map. He was certainly an ascetic and, as far as boys could be impressed with holiness, he came across as a holy man.

We only knew Mr Goldberg, the tailor in Haverty Road. He invisibly mended a communion suit one day when we put our pennies together to save a boy from the wrath of his parents. Mr Goldberg answered the door to our delegation, received us gravely, brought us in and sat us down. We proffered our combined resources – sevenpence, I think. He started to laugh, called in his stout little wife, and spoke to her in a foreign language. She laughed too, and, still laughing, gave us some hot cakes. It was no joking matter to us and we proffered the money again, explaining that it was a *Holy Communion* suit. He had to put down his needle, hold his rotund stomach and wipe his eyes. Mrs Goldberg gave us more cakes. So with our sevenpence intact, and a repair job not even a vigilant mother could see, we came out – still wondering what was so funny. A damaged communion suit was very serious indeed.

As the Thirties went on, or perhaps because we were growing up, the inevitability of war seemed to invade our minds and ideas. If Czechoslovakia was a faraway place to Mr Chamberlain, a European statesman, it was impossibly remote to us. All Europe seemed in uniform. In a vague, inchoate way we seemed also headed for this.

In looking back, perhaps one sees only the good things. But it was an expanding area with adequate amenities. We had two good schools, which we took for granted. We did not know that they had been partly built from the Brothers' own teaching salaries; they never spoke of this. For a hundred years these salaries had been ploughed back into schools and maintenance all over Ireland. Without this effort the effects of the penal laws would have persisted longer. The fee collection system can only seem unbelievable in our times. Envelopes were distributed for the one-pound fee. It was briefly explained that parents should make some contribution to their children's education as a matter of principle, if they could afford it. All the envelopes were to come back, even if they contained nothing. In those depressed times many envelopes were returned empty. No one ever knew who paid, or did not pay. Edmund Rice, the Order's founder, had laid down certain ideals and had said that the boys must always come first. And so they did, before the Brothers' own amenities and simple comfort. Those men had their faults, as we all have, but their *raison d'être* sustained them, and us, for a long time.

Unselfishness is hardly thinkable today, so much so that the dramatists and novelists of our materialistic times have to find some explanation for it. Exaggerating the faults of these obedient men makes good dramatic material. Giving credit to the Christian Brothers is unfashionable nowadays – but we shall not see their like again.

Colonel Edward Daly Doyle (1922–   ), soldier, was born in Dublin. He joined the Irish Army as a soldier in 1940 and retired as Director of Signals in 1984. He served with United Nations peacekeeping forces in the Congo, Cyprus and Lebanon, and commanded an Observer Group of seventeen nationalities in the Sinai Desert 1975–7. He is military correspondent for the *Irish Times*.

FERGUS ALLEN

Palmerston Park

There had been what was called The Great War. It hadn't happened in Dublin, but everyone knew about it. Seven years or so after it men in bright blue flannel hospital-uniforms could still be seen, usually in pairs, in Rathmines Road, not far from Portobello Barracks. I would spot them from the tram on the way into Grafton Street with my mother, who once told me that they were soldiers who had not yet recovered from their wounds. I could see – before averting my eyes – that some of them had empty sleeves or trouser-legs pinned up, and crutches.

The Troubles of the recent past were another matter. I doubt if at the age of five or six I had any awareness of what had gone on in my babyhood. But I recall being told of my father calling into an income tax office near Butt Bridge one evening and being held there at trembling pistol-point by a young man, whose companions drenched the building with petrol and set it ablaze. My father and everyone else was then allowed to flee, but it was said that when he got home the hair on the back of his head was found to be singed. When I was older I regarded this last detail as permissible ornamentation of a good story.

In those years just before I went to school, because my mother was apt to be exhausted by the continuous presence of a small and only child, I was taken out for a walk each weekday afternoon – weather permitting or not, if my memory can be relied on – by a young woman called Vera Bills, whom it would be pretentious to call a nursemaid but who served that purpose. Vera lived with her family in a cramped single-storey terrace house in Harold's Cross and I guess she was around twenty at the time I am writing about. Solidly built and with rounded features, she had a ready smile and a wholly sweet disposition. She may already have had trouble with her teeth, because I remember her as having a bit of a lisp. Later in life she married, and had to cope with the effects on others of TB, drink and unemployment, and then as always her Catholic faith helped her to keep going.

I think Vera and I genuinely liked each other. I probably amused her, and to me she was benign and undemanding in a way that distinguished her from most other adults. She didn't condescend. More to the point, she didn't expect me to exert myself or take initiatives or be interested in things that I didn't want to be interested in.

What held my attention at that time were railways, motor cars, machinery of all sorts and mechanical toys – none of them subjects that seemed to have any attraction for my parents. I also enjoyed observing the activities that went on in shops, and I had quite a liking for pictures – making frequent visits with my mother and father to the National Gallery and the Municipal Gallery, when the latter was still in a couple of houses on the west side of Harcourt Street. But, despite parental belief in the benefits of fresh air and exercise and rural surroundings, I was generally against Nature and the country. Green and grey, it was full of nettles, brambles, barbed wire, large and obviously dangerous animals, disagreeable smells and warnings to trespassers. It seemed to be mainly uphill and was very tiring. However, I found it expedient to keep this lack of enthusiasm to myself, and at home I co-operated in the nurture of caterpillars and water-beetles. The seaside was better than the country but was usually cold, and the salt water left one sticky. I was all in favour of sitting by the fire with a book – or with *Punch*, which I studied eagerly each week but was never known to smile at. In bed, before going to sleep, I would meditate on the higher mysteries, of which the chief was why there was no opening in the front of girls' knickers.

My walks with Vera ranged in many directions, but our most common destination was Palmerston Park. Sometimes we went by way of Upper Rathmines Road and returned by Palmerston Road and Belgrave Square, and at other times we would do the reverse. The former was preferable because of the sweet-shop in Upper Rathmines, just before Cowper Road, where one could buy ten toffees for a penny. (Sherbert was frowned on, jellies went too quickly, bulls-eyes were too strong and I hated aniseed balls.) Either way, I regretted the absence of Catholic churches on the route. As the child of unbelieving Anglicans, I liked to adventure into what I remember as dim lamplit interiors, smelling delightfully of incense and wax. Vera would genuflect and in whispers I would urge her to light a candle. But without any such religious diversion, and fuelled with toffee, we would soon reach the park (having hastily passed the corner at the top of Dartry Road where we once saw a high Johnston Mooney & O'Brien bakery van catch its wheels in the tram-lines and throw its heavy, middle-aged driver on to the cobbles, where he lay stunned, with blood oozing from his forehead).

To the left of the central gate into the park was an area of ragged grass enclosed by trees, where big rough boys used to kick a ball about with alarming energy and harsh cries. We steered sharply to the right, to the calm, municipally manicured gardens with beds of geraniums and alyssum set in tightly cut grass, which one was discouraged from walking on by spiky white wooden objects and low chains. Here smaller and more genteel children circulated and disported themselves quietly – though girlish squeals did sometimes come from the shrubberies at the western end, beyond the dripping fountain shaped like a rusty fir-cone, when hide-and-seek or tig were in progress. On the southern side of the grass was a shelter where old ladies and nursemaids sat, and behind this was an artificial mound of rocks and bushes, containing the lair of the park's custodian, Mr O'Grady. Occasionally, in the heat of some game, an excited little boy would run on to the forbidden grass, whereupon Mr O'Grady, in cap and uniform, would rush from his den, waving his stick and shouting terrible words from under his walrus moustache. Once, in a daring mood, I myself tried taking one or two small steps on the grass verge, but to my relief Mr O'Grady didn't notice.

Although I had one or two acquaintances of my own age amongst the boys who visited the park, I was not in any of the lively games-playing groups, and more often than not Vera and I would promenade around the garden, observing and commenting only to one another. Among the regulars that we saw was a pale man in tweeds – I feel I could go so far as to call him a gentleman – who sat in a wickerwork Bath chair, pushed by what we took to be a female relative. His knees were covered by a travelling rug and his hands shook continuously. A similar but less violent tremor affected his head. Vera (or it may have been my mother) told me that he had been shell-shocked in the war. Whenever we passed him on the park's tarred paths, he would give me a gentle smile – which I hope I returned. Of course he was very old – well into his thirties, perhaps even forty.

One summer afternoon, rather uncharacteristically, I decided to take my Celtic shield with me on our walk. It had been made for me by my father, who was enthusiastic about the Abbey, Lady Gregory and so on. Painted in red and green, with touches of gold leaf, he had constructed it from varnished paper with his usual artistry. Celtic mythology was not really my thing – I much preferred Sir Henry Seagrave to Cuchulain – but I daresay I had thought it would be diplomatic to give the shield an airing that day.

As I sauntered with Vera along the path by the geraniums, I caught sight of the Bath chair approaching. On reaching us it stopped, and the man eyed my shield and smiled. For the first time he spoke. 'What do you want to be when you grow up?' he asked me. This was a typically inane adult question, but the man radiated a mild benevolence and had to have a civil response. I struck an attitude, planting my left foot forward and raising the shield on my left arm. 'I want to be a hero,' I said. He looked at me, his hands shaking silently over the plaid rug.

————•◦•————

Fergus Allen (1921–   ) was born in London, son of an Irish father and an English (half-Cornish) mother, and lived in Dublin from the age of six months until, after going to school in Waterford, he completed his studies at Trinity College. Subsequently, he worked in England as a civil engineer, a director of hydraulic research, a member of the Cabinet secretariat in London, and latterly as First Civil Service Commissioner. As well as publishing technical papers, his poems have appeared in various literary journals and anthologies.

Dublin and South-Eastern Railway

I

AUGUST HOLIDAYS

We knew the names of all the stations:
Avoca, Woodenbridge, Arklow, Inch,
And, at last, Gorey.
Fortune's aged Armstrong Siddeley taxi,
The dusty high-hedged road,
Three miles, then down the linch
And, at last, the sea.
No Greeks ever shouted it so loud
THE SEA! THE SEA!

II

FOOTPLATE TRIP

Number 434 was a 2-4-2,
A high-funnelled high-domed tank;
Crammed on its footplate we went through
All stations to Bray, possessing a permit
Officially signed. The crew were given a tip;
We stood there on the platform, watching passengers exit,
Tank engine chuff off, come back on centre track,
Be coupled up, then leave with wheels aslip
Spinning wildly until they found some grip
And the train vanished off out of our view.

We waited then for the Greystones train to come,
Got chocolate from a most antique machine,
At last, heard the engine clanking up the line,
A 4-4-0, lithe and handsome,
With inside cylinders, six-foot driving wheels,
An express engine, clearly come down in the world.
She left the turntable, was coupled to the train,
Tender to the front, while the driver unfurled
A battered roll of canvas from the top of the cab,
Explaining that this would restrain the rain,
The continuous rain of drops from the tunnel tops,
And Greystones had only a thirty-two foot turntable,
And he had to take this train back to Dublin,
So the engine should face forward on the way back.

We started, swung left where the single line overtips
The surrounding roads, then a cutting, a halt unable
To justify itself at Naylor's Cove, the line risen
Above sea level, abandoned tunnel showing where the track
Was driven back by the sea's fierce eroding force.
We entered the tunnels, one bored in nineteen-seventeen,
Eleven hundred yards, light dancing from open firebox,
Loud battering noise echoing, harsh, from black rocks
Resounding till, regulator eased, we were descending
To Greystones, up platform. We took on water there
Brought the engine down the line, backed up, sea air
Whipping the smoke away as she ran light, reversed
To the carriages, and off.

                    Now we were able to peer
At Ram's Scalp Bridge, accident site where joint gave
Between the bridge rail and a new bullhead, bending
As a passenger train from Enniscorthy crashed sheer
Over the bridge that spanned the Brandy Hole
A hundred feet below; there smugglers used to run
Their cargoes where fast flowing streams lave
The rocks, racing to the sea. This fatal caracole
Left engine and tender bottom up, carriages overrun,
The last overhanging the platform of the wooden bridge

Propped by the semi-upright gutted floor of another:
Two dead, twenty-three injured in the smother
Of telescoped stock, flying debris, falling rock
On an August day in eighteen sixty-seven.

Afterwards we talked more of railway accidents,
Through the engine's hissing steam at Bray,
Discussed the spectacular one of nineteen hundred.
A goods engine's wheels locked on greasy rails;
Reversing failed to slow it, train slid like a sledge,
The fireman jumped clear, the buffer stops gave way,
The engine burst through retaining wall; hung high
Over Hatch Street but, most surprisingly, didn't fall.
The driver, William Hyland, gave evidence in hospital:
'At Ranelagh I applied the vacuum brake, reversed her
As we passed the stationmaster's office; she never stopped.'
(My mother had a photograph of the engine propped there,
Looking incongruous, cantilevered out in the air.)

Sandwiches eaten, watch examined, signal dropped,
We eased the train out of Bray, and clattered on our way;
Whistle shrilling, we crossed points at Shanganagh Junction,
Then slowed to a stop at Shankill, next at Foxrock,
Then Stillorgan and Dundrum, some conjunction
Of shared ideas leading to a fine head of steam
And a rousing sixty reached on the downhill,
On the straight to Milltown, stopped with scream
Of locked wheels, well beyond the platform,
All delighted we'd exceeded any suburban norm,
Let that gallant old lady, number 60, have her fun.
Next morning, pulling out of Milltown, she'd barely begun
To move her train, then threw her nearside connecting rod.

———•◦•———

Derry Jeffares (1920–   ), academic and writer, was born in Dublin. Until 1986 he was Professor of English Studies at Stirling University. He previously held posts in universities in Dublin, Groningen, Edinburgh, Adelaide and Leeds.

IRIS KELLETT

Pony Riding

I often think how lucky I was to have been an only child. I had enough business sense, even at an early age, to realize that had I had a number of brothers and sisters, I would have been lucky to get a share of a single family pony, instead of which I was, for a short time, the proud possessor of three.

My father was a veterinary surgeon and we lived in what was then a suburb of Dublin. Our house was the end of a row of old Regency houses on Mespil Road, the hall door being reached by a long flight of stone steps. The difference between our house and the other houses on the road was that an avenue, through a pair of old wrought-iron gates, ran from the road past the house and into our stable yard. On one side of this avenue was a shrubbery planted by my father; on the other side was a flower garden and orchard, with a field beyond. It was an oasis of trees, birds and wild flowers in the grey desert of houses and streets of the city. This was the world of my childhood – a world of horses, ponies and dogs of all breeds.

Mespil Road was dominated by the character of my father. 'T.H.', as he was known to all, was a rare personality, totally dedicated to horses, who thought nothing of sitting up all night with a sick one. Every night at eleven p.m. he checked all the horses, which for him was a labour of love. His language was colourful rather than acid; people respected rather than feared him. His sense of humour was sometimes wicked, and nicknames for his friends were legion. To me, he was a hard taskmaster, who moulded me in my early life for the discipline demanded by a career in horses. I was always in some kind of trouble: I was such a tomboy – I remember overhearing my father telling my mother that the only time he realized I was a little girl was when he saw me picking wild flowers.

The worst trouble I can remember occurred one day when my cousin Frank, who was the same age as myself, was riding with me in the field, round the outside of which ran a cinder track on which he usually rode. We were pretending to be jockeys, seeing who could ride my pony Sparklet with the shortest stirrups and gallop the fastest round the track. A hedge ran across one segment of the field, and as I galloped past, Frank jumped out from behind it, startling the pony. She shied, and I fell off. Sparklet galloped off in great delight with her tail over her back. In the field grazing was my father's best point-to-point mare, who was resting a sprained tendon, with an older horse, to keep her company. Sparklet soon had the pair of them galloping round the field after her, and for the next half-hour we exhausted ourselves trying to catch her, without success. We decided the only solution was to open the gate and let them run into the yard. This gate opened on to the avenue, which was forked at that point, one way going into the yard and the other up to the road. We were so intent on getting the horses out of the field that neither of us thought of blocking the way to the road. Instead of going into the yard, Sparklet led the two horses up the avenue, but herself stopped at the open gates. Not so the two horses, which galloped loose up Mespil Road, until somebody managed to get ahead of them on a bicycle, and eventually to turn them back on to Mespil Road and through our gates. Fortunately, the traffic in the late Thirties was not the same as it is today, or a serious accident could have occurred.

In the yard we examined both horses in fear and trepidation. They appeared none the worse for their adventure, and we thought we were safe. Everybody was sworn to secrecy, but of course my father heard about it from persons unknown. All hell broke loose. I was an irresponsible, stupid, scatterbrained twit of a child. I didn't deserve a pony and was barred not only from riding, but from setting my foot in the yard – for how long, I cannot now remember, but to a child of ten, as single-minded as I was about horses, it seemed like a lifetime. I think my mother eventually came to the rescue. I am sure she got irritated by my moping and whining round the house. My father relented and the sun shone again.

I enjoyed school, but memories of it are not etched in my mind as clearly as those of my ponies. School was only about a hundred yards from where we lived, and if I was lucky enough to have a window seat, I could see part of our field. My form mistress, however, got wise to the reason for my lack of concentration, so the privilege ceased.

Going into Dublin, though we lived in Ballsbridge, was a disagreeable chore and, before I would agree to go, I had to be bribed with a visit to Mitchell's, where buttered crumpets were a special treat. I was never a city child, though I lived on its outskirts. The only shops I was happy in were bookshops; I could easly browse in one all day. At Christmas, I always asked for books, preferably about horses. My mother always turned out my light when I went to bed, but I evolved a system of reading under the bedclothes with a torch. This guise went undiscovered for quite a long time, but eventually torch and books were confiscated from my room. Richmal Crompton, author of the William books, was my favourite for a time. We formed a William Club and made badges out of melted sealing wax. It didn't take much imagination for me to be William, for like him, I was always in some form of trouble!

I don't think I was badly spoilt, even though I was an only child. I managed, however, to get my own way, even if sometimes it took time. For instance, when I was given my first pony, my father wanted someone else to ride it in the field and also to hunt it before I did, but, because I was so keen and proved I was capable, my father allowed me to do both.

What a difference there was in those days, going to a horse show, compared to today! Now, you load up your horses or ponies into your box and leave for the show, arriving perhaps half-an-hour before the first competition begins, returning as soon as your competition is over, bedding down the horses and then seeing to your own needs. Sometimes it is even possible to do two shows in one day.

In the Thirties, there was virtually no motor transport. If you wanted to go to a show fifty miles away, in Meath, Kildare or surrounding counties, you were up before dawn, plaited and prepared the pony, hacked to the railway station, and boarded a goods train. With the pony, you were then shunted up and down the sidings and eventually attached to the train travelling to the station nearest to the show. You were again shunted up and down until eventually you reached a siding where you were unloaded. Then you got up again and hacked the last five miles or more. Goods trains usually left before dawn, so you rarely got home the same day you set out. I wonder what the youth of today would say if they had to do this. I believe we had more fun, though.

———◦◦◦———

Iris Patricia Kellett (1926–   ), President of the Association of Irish Riding Establishments and a former member of the Irish Horse Board, was born in Dublin. The youngest competitor to win the

Grand Prix at the Royal Dublin Society's Horse Show in 1948, competing against five military teams, she then twice won the Princess Elizabeth Cup at the White City, London, in 1949 and 1951, the first lady member of the Irish team. After a serious accident, she resumed competition jumping in 1956 and retired after winning the Ladies' European Championship in 1969. She and her husband John Hall, a Fellow of the British Horse Society, run the Kellett Riding School (founded by her father in 1923), the largest equestrian centre in Ireland, at which Paul Darragh, Jack Doyle and Eddie Macken began their careers.

Boarding School

Each fortnight Beefy's granny sent Swiss chocolate. And little blocks were pushed across to Balthazar in the dark. Lights out and Crunch the housemaster patrolled the dim corridors. At full moon he walked a rapid tight circle at the distant end of the hall, nervously entwining his hands and mumbling.

'We will stamp out smuttiness. We shall have straight little backs and sound bottoms. No smut here.'

October trees dripping their brown leaves on the wet grass. Chill damp dawn mornings the little boys rose shivering and clutching towels to hunch to the tub room. The still dark countryside out the window. Wintering thrushes asleep.

The screams and agonized faces as the white bodies cast themselves into the big baths of icy water. Contortions of sweating lead pipes held with shiny brass clips to the white tiled walls. The gurgling laughter, pushes and shoves. And threats of revenge.

'You just wait tonight. You'll feel something you won't like.'

Balthazar in uniform, waiting by his bed. Beefy striding back from the wash room with his morning smile. As Balthazar enquires gently as to the way in this world.

'What will happen tonight.'

'Masterdon's a big bully. He has foot rot between the toes. He'll put his larger snakes in Duffer's bed. They don't bite hard. They sometimes only give a little sting. His are only grass snakes but I am collecting adders.'

Beefy over the days steering Balthazar from the lurking harms. The priest hole where they put you in up to your neck and kicked your face. The mud bath by the river where older boys commanded young boys to wrestle. Beefy said never cry or show you are afraid, the dumbest and weakest boys get the worst and they are especially horrid to princes and lords.

And this Saturday evening at the assembly room to see a tattered film on the delights of Guatemala and splendours of Veracruz. Boys chattering at the door waiting with their pillows. While Beefy below in the basement made a raid on the kitchen and stole away to a little stray dog he sheltered in the woods and called Soandso. Sunday afternoons convened to sit and copy from the blackboard the weekly letter to parents and guardians.

Dear Mother,

Yesterday was Founder's birthday and we saw an exciting film all about Central America made by the Founder's father who explored there. On Tuesday we played golf. It was a jolly good caper. Soon we will be playing rugger. For dessert we had peaches and fresh cream. I am very happy here and very much enjoy the new friends I have made.

Balthazar

Evening prayers in a candle lit chapel this Sunday. High voices in song. Smell of wax and autumn winds bleeding through cracks of doors and windows and crevices of stone. Balthazar staring down at this hymn as the words grew faint then blurred and dimmed. Until he woke on his bed, matron bent over him, a cold compress on his forehead. Then lights out and Beefy kneeling close at his bedside.

'Are you still poorly, Balthazar.'

'No.'

'You fainted. You must be frightened and sad.'

'I want to write a letter to my nannie. And master said I can't.'

'You shall. Tomorrow after golf. And then give it to me.'

A stretch of blue in a bleak sky. Across the gently folding lawns the sun would speed. And sheltered south west, hidden by a canvas awning on the porch of the golf pavilion, Balthazar wrote his small scrawl.

Dear Nannie,

Today we are playing golf. The stick is too big for me and I cannot hit the ball. I now have a friend called Beefy. And his real name is Balthazar too. He is not afraid of anything and has gone far out of his way to protect me. On Founder's Birthday we had toast and dripping for tea. The big boys have torture chamber after lights out and they take their pleasure to bang the bottoms of the littler boys. They call it botty bashing and it hurts very much. Honourables get the worst thumping of all.

317

They are the sons of lords. Nothing else is happening here. Tonight is private dormitory feast. My friend and I eat cheese he has stolen from the kitchen. There is starvation here and I am glad my friend is good at thieving. I hope you find a nice husband for yourself soon. I am sorry the man who saw the good mend in your skirt on the boat did not make your acquaintance as he would have found you awfully nice.

Balthazar

The envelope handed across to Beefy. Who tucked it beneath his sweater and set out at a trot to disappear with a wave at the edge of the wood. The trees laying great long shadows in the reddening setting sun. And a week later a letter came for Balthazar which he opened under the smile of Beefy.

My dearest Balthazar,

I did so much appreciate your very wonderful letter. And I am so glad you have made a nice friend. He sounds quite capable. When I left you to school I came to visit my mother and father who live just outside of this town by the Grand Junction Canal. Which is not awfully grand but there is some nice countryside all round. I take long walks by the canal and I carry a bag of bread to feed the swans. I can also see the trains go by and often I think of you. I too hope I find a nice husband soon. And when he is the man in my life, you will always be the other.

It will be so nice to see you at Christmas.

Nannie

To sleep that night this letter tucked away under the pillow. And carried each day next to his flesh until the weeks went by and the writing grew faint and blurred and the paper curled and split. To open it again and again until finally it fell to pieces. And one whole line was left.

> When he
> Is the man
> In my life
> You will always
> Be
> The other.

From THE BEASTLY BEATITUDES OF BALTHAZAR B.

J. P. Donleavy (1926–   ), novelist, was born in Brooklyn, New York, of Irish parents. He was educated at Trinity College, Dublin, and has been an Irish citizen since 1967. His most famous, and bawdiest, comic novel is probably still his first, *The Ginger Man* (1955).

The Prisoner

The morning after I came in I got up and folded my blankets, and did out my cell, and ate my breakfast, and used the chamber-pot and slopped out with the rest, but was not opened up with the others when they went down to work. I thought it was something to do with being Irish and that, and in a way I was not displeased but a little bit frightened, till they came to my cell and opened the door and told me to put on my tie, for I was for the Governor.

I went down and stood with Charlie and some other fellows outside the office. The other fellows were wearing shorts and were Y.P.s the same as us, but they looked very old to me. There were three of them and all of them looked as if they shaved at least three times a week. I was hoping to God I wouldn't be left among fellows the like of that, because apart from being big, they did not look too friendly. But Charlie and I and Ginger stood together, happy enough, and listened to the whispering of the others. They were there for extra letters and one fellow was there about a visit from his wife but they said we all would have to wait till the Governor was finished with some fellows that were being had up over having snout. One fellow was a remand but had brought in a butt, a dog-end they called it, off exercise, when he was supposed to throw it in the bucket which was there for that purpose; and another fellow, a convicted prisoner, had been caught with a dog-end which this remand had brought in for him for the day before, and which the remand fellow had told about when they caught him and asked him was he bringing in the dog-ends for himself or somebody else.

When the two fellows were brought out of their cells and rushed into the Governor's office to be tried and sentenced, the other Y.P.s that were waiting with Charlie and Ginger and me just laughed and said they'd get Number One, the both of them. They whispered their laugh, but seemed really to enjoy it because they thought it was funny to be punished. For somebody else to be. They seemed to think the screws were better men than themselves, because they could do these things and get fellows put on bread and water and stand up in the circle when the Governor was gone and they were done saluting him, and bend their knees, belch, break wind, yawn, and shout at some fellow they caught talking a bit extra at his work, when he was supposed to be only asking for a loan of a scissors. The prisoners thought the screws were comedians when they caught some fellows like these two merchants and got them to inform on one another and then gave them both solitary confinement. They had a slang term for informing. 'Shopping', they called it. A nation of shoppers, and if that's the way they would treat one another, my Jesus, what would they do to me?

My name was shouted at last and I was rushed before the Governor. I was told to stand to the mat, state my registered number, name, age, and religious denomination.

I stood to attention and said, 'Behan, sir, sixteen years, Catholic.' I did not know my number, but the screw standing beside the desk shouted it for me.

'Beh-an, Bren-dan, three five oh one, sixteen years, Y.P., remand, R.C.' Then he said 'sir' to show he had finished.

The Governor was a desiccated-looking old man, in tweed clothes and wearing a cap, as befitted his rank of Englishman, and looking as if he would ride a horse if he had one. He spoke with some effort, and if you did not hear what he was saying you'd have thought, from his tone, and the sympathetic, loving, and adoring looks of the screw, P.O., and Chief, that he was stating some new philosophical truth to save the suffering world from error.

'You're—er—remanded—er—till Friday—er—I see—er. See—er—that you behave yourself—er—here and give no—er—trouble to my officers—er.' At this point the officers looked sternly, and almost reproachfully, at me, and so intense was their grateful look towards the feeble old face of the Governor that I almost expected them to raise an exultant shout of *'Viva il Papa!'* 'If you give—er—us trouble—er—we'll win—er . . . we'll win all the time.' The officers' faces set in determination with him. 'We can—er—make it—er—very—er—bad for you—er, it's—er—all the same—er—to us, and—er—it's up—er—to you, whatever—er—way you—er—want it.'

I was marched out and told to wait outside. We were to see our clergymen and I was looking forward to meeting the priest. Maybe he would be an Irishman, and it would be like water in the desert to hear a friendly Irish voice again.

But the screw put me back in my cell while the others went to see the

Protestant chaplain. The priest would not be in till Monday.

I was disappointed but thought that it would make a break in Monday morning, and this was Friday, so after tomorrow I would have Mass to look forward to on Sunday morning, and after the visit to the priest I would be well into the week till I went down to the court on Friday, and that would be that week over.

After a little while I was opened up again from my cell and brought down to the hall of the wing where we sat on our chairs in silent rows, about sixty of us, sewing mailbags. The class instructor they called the screw who went round showing the prisoners how to do the bags, and examined them or complained about the bad work when it was more or less than four stitches to the inch. That seemed to be the important thing, and most necessary for salvation.

He came over to me and sat down on a chair beside me and showed me how to wax the thread and put it through the canvas with the palm, which was a leather band with a thimble in the middle to save the skin of the palms, though sometimes even the most expert had to shove the needle through the canvas with their forefingers and thumbs, which in most of the prisoners were scarred like the hands or arms of drug addicts with the needle marks you would read about.

On Saturday afternoon we were locked up from twelve-thirty. The screw gave us a half-hour's exercise from twelve o'clock and remarked that it was handier than taking us out for exercise after dinner. It got the whole lot finished early, he said, and we could be left in our cells till morning. We all nodded our heads, and quickly, in agreement with him. It seemed the right thing to want to be locked up in your cell over the week-end, and I even felt my own head nodding when the screw said that it was better to get the exercise over with so that we would not have to be opened up again after dinner.

So locked up we were, and Charlie and I and Ginger smiled at each other, so that the others would not know that we were not used to being locked in a cell from half past twelve on Saturday morning till slop-out at seven Sunday morning, and in we went. The dinner was old potatoes, cold, and a slice of bully beef and a piece of bread. This was always the Saturday dinner and I heard a screw saying that it was like that to give the cook a chance to get off, and after all he wanted a rest, too, and when he said that we all nodded our heads, and were glad the screw was so nice and civil as to say it to us.

From Borstal Boy

322

Brendan Behan (1923–64), dramatist and journalist, was born in Dublin. He joined the IRA, was arrested in Liverpool in 1939 on explosives charges, and sentenced to Borstal. Later he served five years for shooting a policeman, and further terms for other offences. His play, *The Quare Fellow*, won him international fame.

ADÈLE CROWDER

A Proper Education

St Margaret's Hall had been a good small school run by the Badham sisters, but two had died and the school was already in a decline when I went there in 1936. Dr Edith was still headmistress, petite and upright in her eighties, with strings of pearls around her boned collars even at seven-thirty in the morning. A snuffling Pekinese followed closely behind her strapped shoes, often tripping us on the stairs. The school was still home for the ninety-year-old Miss Hensman, cycling about in a grey suit and a man's hat, a fossilized suffragette fashion from perhaps 1910. Occasionally she or Dr Badham taught a junior class when teachers were ill, in science or classics respectively, with scholarship, toughness and wit. The mixed kindergarten had produced an inordinate number of bishops and dons who came to prize-givings or garden parties for the pleasure of Miss Edith's conversation – presenting a tennis trophy to the headgirl she would say 'More brawn than brains, I'm afraid!'

The school had two gardens, at the corner of Mespil and Burlington Roads, and staring at apple blossom or the vertical grey leaves of a eucalyptus tree could fill one's mind, to the detriment of Irish verbs. I liked being in the fourth form because its windows overlooked barges on the tree-lined canal, and the lock where bargees hung out their washing and their horses lunched from nosebags. The gardens made tolerable our performances of Shakespeare, and between classes teachers and girls jogged fast round their gravel paths, skidding through the corners of sharp-angled box hedges.

The old ladies died and the school struggled on with parental help. The new headmistress was fresh from Anglican mission fields and a large Indian school. She decided we should have competitive houses, and wept when we found it absurd because the boarders all lived in a few rooms upstairs and the day girls bolted home at two-twenty. She wept again when it was discovered that the girls were circulating a book

324

on birth control, which belonged to Alma Smith's mother. The prefects were harangued for their lack of moral responsibility in allowing such a book to be read. As a prefect who had just returned, after an illness, I was much more concerned with concealing from my peers the fact that I had *not* read the book and was full of ignorance, so resigned my prefect's badge with the others, hoping no one would notice that I had been away.

The headmistress's tears baffled us. Dr Badham's reaction to the boarders' experiments with make-up had been to arrange some demonstrations by an expert, and a talk by an elegant woman on matching accessories. While there was an elaborate protocol about spilling ink and changing your shoes, we had been governed by examples of rectitude with occasional stabs of sarcasm, and were not used to appeals to our better natures.

With high principle, two Viennese refugees, Erika and Lise Fischer, were taken by the school, in 1938. They were furious at not being found jobs (they were about eighteen and fourteen), at having to play hockey in mud, and at finding themselves, a pair of sophisticated adults, living amongst badly educated children. One of Lise's few pleasures was in playing the piano at concerts: she terrified me when I had to play the bass in duets of Mussorgsky's dances, going faster and faster. Another kindness which misfired involved bringing an Irish speaker and an untrained collie from Galway to the school, where they were both miserable.

Some trouble with a lease moved St Margaret's Hall for a year to an empty diocesan boys' school. Brown varnished, with clattering iron treads on the stairs, it had an unventilated chilliness, and we were fed cocoa and doughnuts twice a day to keep us warm. The boarders lived in a flat, and lunched in a basement restaurant in Kildare Street, where every dish was buried in Bird's custard or thick gravy. They loved it! We played soccer in the concrete yard of the school, but were asked to stop disturbing the lunchtime services at St Ann's. One wall of the yard against which we banged the ball was a side of the church. Then we explored the school building, finding a space behind a cupboard in the chemistry lab which led to a staircase down to the basement. Behind the boiler was an iron ladder up to a rusty trapdoor. The two biggest of us heaved it up slowly. We found ourselves, in our conspicuous rust-red gym tunics, facing the congregation of St Ann's from the chancel floor, in the midst of an intercession service, and dropped the trapdoor down with a clang.

We discovered a skating rink, and continued to go there after it had been declared unladylike and out of bounds. We were therefore unable to tell anyone when we were bashed against the guard rails by a bunch of tough youths.

We discovered other urban games. In St Stephen's Green we would go, at lunch-time, to a little bridge beside which there were shrubberies and trees. All but one of us would hide in the bushes. The one who was 'It' put her school beret in her pocket, turned up the collar of her navy gaberdine and tightened the belt, and put on the high-heeled shoes that we brought in a bag. Then she posed in a Lili Marlene fashion on the little bridge until she was accosted. The winner was the one who was accosted most quickly or most often. If you couldn't get rid of the man you lost the point, as the whole gang would come whooping out of the bushes in their uniforms, to make him flee.

The middle of the day was secure, but we had earlier learnt to be afraid both in the early mornings and going home on dark winter afternoons. In the mornings a tramp, who wore layers of sacks and a sack on his head, often lurked in the entries off Burlington Road, and at dusk soldiers looked for tarts along the canal bank. My mother, also a Dubliner, sensibly said, 'Well, just keep riding your bicycle.'

Adèle Crowder (1926–   ), biologist, was born in Dublin and went to six schools there. She studied Natural Science at Trinity College and is now a professor in the Department of Biology at Queen's University, Kingston, Ontario, and Curator of the Fowler Herbarium. She is married to a medieval historian; they have lived in Scotland and Ulster.

RICHARD MURPHY

The Pleasure Ground

Once, when I was a child, and playing in a pleasure ground, I swallowed a poison berry. It fell into my open mouth as I watched my sister climbing among the prickly leaves of a tall Irish yew. Cure, I thought, was impossible: a pain would start, and I should soon and surely die. A terror like the one I now felt had been with me in Ceylon, in the compound with its drains full of deadly snakes. But here we were in the green and snakeless island of Ireland, where you could safely sleep without mosquito nets, and yet this foolishly had happened. It could only be a matter of minutes or perhaps hours. Prayers might prolong the time I had left for living, but as sure as anything the poison had got into my system.

I was about twelve then, and we lived with my mother at my grandfather's house in the west of Ireland, while my father worked for us abroad. Our branch of the family occupied the east wing of the house, which had once been the servants' quarters, not so many years ago when the wage on the land was sixpence a day, and no cure had been found for TB, typhus, or famine fever: dreadful diseases I had managed so far to escape, only to succumb to poison; and of all places, in what was called the pleasure ground.

We were proud of our pleasure ground: we thought it was the oldest and most beautiful in Ireland. It once had a lovers' walk marked out by cedars of Lebanon and Florence Court yews in methodical pairs, with lawns and copper beeches in the centre. The whole garden was surrounded by an Anglo-Irish wall, a great wall of pride and oppression, liberally overgrown with romantic ivy. For years the place had been neglected. Many things had improved in Ireland, but this garden of the ascendancy had declined like the family fortune. A laurel forest now covered the lawn except for a patch kept trimmed by rabbits round the trunk of the beech tree. The yew hedge, where the daughters of high sheriffs had decorously flirted, was now a dark row of trees, and the walks were impassable with briars. My mother devoted herself to restoring this pleasure ground. It had been in her family since the victories of King William of Orange, and the first thing she did was to knock down a huge stretch of the wall which had formerly imprisoned the servants, so that our house lay open to the garden. It was looking on to this pleasure ground, or sitting in the shade of the copper beech, that we did our lessons.

First an hour anxiously passed, and then a day: I had not sickened or died, and the menace of the yew-berry passed. It was the happiest time of my life. We could not be sent to schools abroad because the war was on, and travelling was then impossible. But instead of work being a difficulty, it had here become a delight. Things my mother liked were easy to learn in order to please her; things she disapproved of we grasped in a flash of revolt. One day, struggling through the tall weeds in an orchard just outside the pleasure ground, I came across a very old fig-tree, and searching under its big green leaves I found a number of small hard unripe figs. After this, the fig-tree was mine, and all through that summer I waited for the fruit to ripen; I dug the roots, manured and watered the ground, cut the weeds, sowed seeds of flowers nearby, even a row of carrots: and it was all effortless joy. Eventually I remember eating the fruit, with no fear of poison this time, though as luck would have it I was chased away by some angry wild bees at that very moment.

My mother wanted me to be a diplomat, but the lessons I learnt in that garden were not the right training for a Civil Service career. We were much too wild. Our life went from one extreme to another, from discipline to anarchy. My brother, for instance, had to pass his School Certificate. He also kept a herd of goats in the woods, and one of the kids used to lie under the piano my mother played at our morning prayers.

In the west wing lived our grandparents, in rooms grimy with portraits, especially an ugly one of Cromwell. There was a smell of tow and gun-oil and empty cartridge shells in my grandfather's study, with its racks of shot-guns he taught me to use on rabbits. There was also a Turkish rifle he had picked up on the beach at Gallipoli. Battle-axes hung on hooks, and the stairs were decorated with prints of the fighting in Rangoon, with sepoys in the act of being shot or disembowelled.

Black labrador dogs jumped up on you in the pitch-dark flagged and slippery corridors. A portable harmonium waited for Sundays in the hall under the water-glass which told the weather. My grandfather was a clergyman.

It was here in the west wing that I had been born, and my grandmother was always our ally in trouble, sickness, or romance. Here my sister was promised her future husband at cards; here ghosts were real because my grandmother frequently saw them; here were secret chambers she helped us to find – we *did* find one full of rotten muskets – and horrible practical jokes. She was fond of dogs, and I made wreaths to put on their graves at the top of the yew-walk. Moss roses grew by her well: she told me they helped a person to fall in love, and I sniffed them for hours. In her glasshouse she kept my orange tree alive.

My grandmother had been brought up on the far side of the Connemara mountains, on the harsh Atlantic coast. This was fifty miles away, and we used to motor there, from the pleasure ground, on birthdays and other family occasions. My sister used to bring her painting things, and seen through my mother's and my grandmother's eyes, this land which we entered, so stark, wild, and simple, was more beautiful than the deeply nurtured garden we had left.

It was a desperately poor part of the country. Huddled among boulders were those whose ancestors had lost the pitiless struggle for the land which ours had won. The planters of our pleasure ground had acquired an estate of 70,000 acres, which famine, revolution, and liberalism had cut down to its present size of 300 acres. But these people lived on five- or only two-and-a-half acre holdings, and we loved them better than our own relations, or the children at the rectory parties we had to attend. They were truly Irish, and that is what my brother and I wanted to be. They seemed sharper, freer, more cunning than we were. Stones, salmon-falls, rain-clouds and drownings had entered and shaped their minds, loaded with ancestral bias. They seemed most mysterious and imaginative to us. Their manners had a real charm instead of a false one, and their singing voices used tones that rasped excitingly against the hymn-tune harmonies we were used to. We wished we could talk like them. Old people among them had all the time in the world to tell us fantastic stories. It was the antidote which the poisoning in the pleasure ground needed.

Twice before, much earlier in my life, as far back as I can remember, we had lived in the Connemara hills, first by a lake and later by the sea, that greatest of all pleasure grounds. The house by the lake had a garden with a deep well which I fell into while playing with my brother. This left no mark of fear, but gave me a love and a respect for water. Near the lake was a grey Norman castle with a black stream running by the walls, and sloe hedges beside the lanes, where we walked with our pails of milk and picked wild strawberries. Even then I was terrified I might have swallowed the wrong berry.

The pleasure ground period did not last for ever. Thanks to winning a scholarship, I was sent off to boarding school in England. Death and emigration soon left my grandmother alone in the place, and the garden fell back into anarchy and decay. Chickens scratched on my mother's lupin-beds; hay was scythed on the tennis court; the laurels and the rabbits increased; the beech tree was cut down and sold for firewood; cows strayed through the rusty gates, munched yew-leaves, and died within the hour (they *were* poisonous!). Now my grandmother was mistress of a beautiful disorder, living on the last trees of a once great forest. The yew still bore a crop of berries, the fig-tree had survived; but the discipline of the garden had died. The spirit that I was looking for in the yew-berry, the fig, and the beech tree had withdrawn – that spirit which had once made poetry and music and painting, even mathematics, an effortless delight. There was no masculine energy in the place, to mend walls, plant new trees, sow and cultivate and labour, and I felt lost, and guilty.

So I went back to that older, earlier pleasure ground in the treeless hills, on the sea's edge, and rediscovered Connemara. There at the age of nineteen I abandoned myself to mountains, lakes, and waterfalls; I rolled naked in snow, and stretched without clothes on the cold ground on summer nights. I wanted to write poetry, and believed that some day, like the ripening of the figs, I should taste that fruit and it would not be poison, nor would the bees chase me from the tree. I did not dream that it would take so long and be so difficult to produce a first crop. As I grew older the garden grew wilder, losing its form as trees were felled, and its spirit as the old people died and the young left the country; so I searched more and more into the origins of that garden till I found them finally in the sea.

Effort and discipline, paths, spades, bill-hooks, walls and gates are all needed to keep a garden, which has to be cultivated, and not just reaped as in the act of fishing. Our own hands have to give the garden shape and structure. Poems are quite unlike the sea; they are like gardens in their making, in that our task is to give shape to whatever grows: to use words to control that force that shakes the berries from the branch, that throws up one fisherman drowned on the shore and another saved, that drops a poison seed into the ground.

------◆◊◆------

Richard Murphy (1927–   ), poet, was born at Milford House, Co. Galway. He was Visiting Professor of Poetry, Princeton University 1974–5.

THOMAS KINSELLA

Girl on a Swing

My touch has little force:
Her infant body falls.
Her lips lightly purse
With panic and delight
And fly up to kiss
The years' brimming glass;
To drink; to sag sweetly
When I drop from sight.

Thomas Kinsella (1928–   ), poet, academic and publisher, was born in Dublin. He was a civil servant 1946–65.

PETER CONNOLLY

Damson Wine

Every time I recall it now I am tickled and teased afresh by the appalling portent of disaster it must have presented to our hapless elders. For only in recent times have I come across the key to their experience of that childhood episode and only since then indeed has the memory tumbled clear and entire from the shadows in which it had been buried. About five years ago quite by chance an old man in our neighbourhood, rambling on about our family, let drop two facts which, he said, he had always associated with tales of my grandfather. ... Apparently he had had a passion for swimming (rare enough in rural parts) and spent much of his free time tracking up and down and over and back across the waters of our local lake of Ballyhoe. Then in his latter years, according to report, he had taken to passing his evenings drinking at length with labouring men and idlers in a shebeen with a dubious reputation which overlooked the lake. On one such night he had to be carried from there – dying of a heart attack – home to his wife in the teacher's residence on the Hill. At that moment I suddenly realized there had been all along some kind of family skeleton in the cupboard – or what passed for one in the aspiring bourgeois but insecure minds of our various aunts and uncles. An unsavoury shadow had fallen on the last days of 'The Master' – he who had been the local schoolteacher, model citizen and patriarch for thirty years or so. Over that period he had also bought up three farms and established Clan Connolly in three houses strung out at intervals along 'our' road; but somehow he had let them all down in the end, falling away without heed from a few of the careful codes of respectable middle-class living. ...

With this piece of news from the folk a number of things in our childhood began to fall into place in my mind: how very little – or next to nothing – we had heard of our paternal grandparents in the talk of any of our adult relatives; how my father – who was the only one of that generation to drink whiskey – took his occasional sup at fairs or with visitors in the house, wearing a certain air of false bravado; how our two maiden aunts – Kate and Ellen – took it on themselves to impress on us, the young brood, standards of 'the shocking' and of 'nice manners' which were far tighter than anything prevailing in our own home. Living as they did in that high narrow house over the Chapel yard they supervised our goings and comings to school and Sunday Mass and presided over our First Communions with gifts of new suits and keep-sake photos. When Confirmation Days arrived and each of us in turn was administered the Pledge against Strong Drink (an extra rite in which we had no choice at all), it was they who lent all the solemnity of initiation to that moment.

Looking back on it now I see how inevitable it was that The Event should occur at the *other* house. That was the home of our youngest married uncle – lying on the other side of ours – and it was there we used to hive off to as often as we could for unthinking games and forays with our younger cousins. Its presiding spirit was Aunt Lena, one of those women who love to indulge children with exotic 'treats' of the kind they would not or could not be given in their own homes. She had come from West Clare to marry into our clan and she loved to organize huge party-spreads for our birthdays and for feastdays of all kinds at which we gorged ourselves on lashings of ham and mince-pie, cream-jellies and trifles, fruit-cake and puddings, syrups and cordials – things we fantasized about long before and after each orgy.

In addition to being one of nature's mother-figures and a culinary genius Lena was a real specialist at making the local wine – an expert and prize-winner acknowledged by all the neighbourhood. Home brew-ing of wine was not all that common, I fancy, in the Ireland of those days but our area was a designated 'fruit-district', being dotted with orchards of apple, plum and pear and especially fertile in a fruit called the Damson. Lines of damson-trees enclosing the fields ran north without a break through Monaghan into south Armagh and through winter and spring the dark ruby-coloured liquid stood gently fizzing and maturing in small barrels and vats in the cool back rooms and pantries of Aunt Lena's place. . . .

That year a bumper vintage was surely coming along. It must have been about 1938 – for the five of us ranged in age from thirteen to seven. I am certain it could only have been Lena's pride in her special wine and her local fame that allowed her to get by at all with the unheard-of suggestion that the children should be allowed to sample one small glass each of this year's produce with their dessert. The experiment passed off

334

decorously if a little stiffly but then, as we flocked outside to play, a bottle of the stuff standing on the floor in a corner, open and nearly full, caught my eye and, using my brother as cover, I scooped it up and smuggled it out. I don't know still what got into me – the eldest of them – but in my experience all major lapses from rectitude have this appearance of suddenness.... In the safety of the haybarn, inhaling the musty scent of silage, we passed the bottle around between us, sipping at it awkwardly and gingerly with much giggling and high jinks. We knew of course that we were crossing a line into taboo country but, like all victims of the brew, we never knew at what point we had crossed the physical line of no return. All of a sudden we found there was no stopping us. Singing and cavorting out into the fields we trooped through a gap in the hedge of yellow furze which lined the brow of the hill on which the house was built. There some one of us (I forget which it was this time) lay sideways to the grassy slope and began to roll over and over downwards propelled by the gentle curves of the terraced sod – down twenty yards or so to the flat shelf over a stream which checked the roller. Soon all five of us were caught up in the act, imitating and vying with one another as we rolled down faster and faster, turned and then scrambled and crawled back up to the top on all fours. Singing ... laughing ... screaming ... faster ... and faster. Everything in our familiar world cart-wheeled around us – the line of yellow furze – Ballyhoe lake in its socket of hills to the left – the woods and church spire over towards Carrick – the distant blue humpbacks of Slieve Gullion and the Mournes....

How long we kept that up I cannot say but if we were mildly tipsy when we began the state we soon arrived at can only be described in terms of hallucination and ecstasy. When we were discovered and the interrogation began we were not only drunk by any standard but stoned out of our wits! We stood before our judges stunned and, literally, wordless. Nothing could be done about it; we were packed off to bed; the incident was never referred to again.

Well, as things turned out in later years, not a single alcoholic emerged from that bunch of young bacchanals. Without exception they silently dropped the code of their elders but in favour of an equable and moderate love of the divine liquor. But this sequel, edifying as it is, can have little to do with the electric glow that surrounds this episode in my memory. It tugs at muy imagination now partly because it seems to have been one of those very rare moments when siblings of that number really felt and acted as one. Mostly we were a group of solitary and fairly

335

jealous individuals – but for that magic interlude we had been performing something in perfect unison, as if swayed by a common impulse or driven by a shared instinct. Perhaps too one or two among us were already giving their hearts, unwittingly, to the sensuous joys of life rather than to their greyer counterparts. Whether or no, I like to think that on that day the censored grandfather moved in our blood – and laughed aloud.

Father Peter Connolly (1927–87) was born at Drumconrath, Co. Meath. He was Professor of English at St Patrick's College, Maynooth, a constituent college of the National University of Ireland 1955–85, retiring early owing to ill-health. He edited *Literature in a Changing Ireland* (1982) and contributed widely to Irish and American journals on such subjects as Censorship, Obscenity, and problems of Law and Morality.

The Cage

My father, the least happy
man I have known. His face
retained the pallor
of those who work underground:
the lost years in Brooklyn
listening to a subway
shudder the earth.

But a traditional Irishman
who (released from his grille
in the Clark Street I.R.T.)
drank neat whiskey until
he reached the only element
he felt at home in
any longer: brute oblivion.

And yet picked himself
up, most mornings,
to march down the street
extending his smile
to all sides of the good
(non negro) neighbourhood
belled by St Teresa's church.

When he came back
we walked together
across fields of Garvaghey
to see hawthorn on the summer
hedges, as though
he had never left;
a bend of the road

which still sheltered
primroses. But we
did not smile in
the shared complicity
of a dream, for when
weary Odysseus returns
Telemachus must leave.

Often as I descend
into subway or underground
I see his bald head behind
the bars of the small booth;
the mark of an old car
accident beating on his
ghostly forehead.

———◦◦◦———

John Montague (1929–   ), academic, poet and writer of short stories, was born in Brooklyn, New York, spent his childhood in Co. Tyrone and was educated at University College, Dublin. He is Associate Professor of English, University College, Cork.

Going Back

The first thing I remember is an iron gate leading into a jungle that had bees and butterflies in it. I remember a tap in a back-yard, beneath a window-sill, and black limestone steps. The gate is immense, the jungle endless, the window-sill protrudes as an overhanging cliff.

These images belong in three small towns in Co. Cork: in Mitchelstown tucked away beneath the Galtee mountains, and Youghal by the sea, and Skibbereen which people said was at the back of beyond. I look, in Mitchelstown, for the iron gate but the gate has been replaced and the jungle is a patch of docks and nettles now. No butterfly hovers, and the long, wearying journey from the gate to the back door of the house has become a matter of yards. The house itself, once spaciously rambling, is modest in its terrace, opposite the garda station.

Mitchelstown itself, once a bustling universe, sleeps peacefully through a June afternoon, looking as though someone has sat on it. It has a beaten look that memory has failed to register, its pubs and shops economically squat, its skyline humble beneath the mountains. On a telegraph pole Councillor Joe Sherlock is billed as your best bet in the local elections; Paul Roche is keen to supply you with bottled gas.

A man opens a window and asks me what I want. I tell him I was born in this house in 1928. I'm looking for some black limestone steps, I tell him, and a tap in a back-yard, beneath a window-sill. A frown gathers slowly on the man's face. He stares at me, not speaking. The house has no back-yard, he finally reveals, and no steps that you could describe as black. 'They must be in Youghal,' I murmur, and the man continues to stare at me, frowning a little more. He nods eventually and agrees that the steps I'm looking for are sure to be in Youghal. Youghal has most things, he suggests with an effort, being a seaside resort.

He's right. The steps belong to a narrow house, cocked up high among fuchsia shrubs, staring out to sea. This house has a derelict look; it's a rooming house of some kind now, and the steps have a pile of rubbish on them, an old mattress and two wet cardboard boxes, and the springs of a pram. I look for the tap beneath the window-sill but it isn't there any more. I look at the halldoor and remember being able to reach the Yale lock for the first time.

I remember the wooden breakwaters and the lighthouse and a ferry that cost a penny. Sir Walter Raleigh lived here and in my time a neat old woman called Miss Goff, who drove around in a wickerwork trap, throwing ginger biscuits to children if she liked the look of them. Is that true? Did she really do that? And that family who were born without fingers: did their father really, in the First World War, hack at the praying hands of the Virgins in Belgian churches just because he was an Orange mason? No one in Youghal remembers.

In the narrow house among the fuchsia the rain crept in beneath the windows. From the kitchen a red door led down to the coal cellar, where I hid after I'd eaten a packet of Chiver's raspberry jelly. Out on the sea there were trawlers and rowing boats, and often in storms it was dangerous for fishermen. A man called Tommy Atkins saved the life of a summer visitor, a woman who afterwards lay plump and unconscious on the sand in a blue bathing dress and a white rubber cap. Years later I twice created a nuisance by almost drowning myself.

Youghal, so smartly elegant in my memory, is tatty on a wet after-noon. A carful of German tourists crawls along the seafront, the misty beach is empty. Once, people pointed here, and remarked; I listened but didn't understand. A taste of that bewilderment returns, with the mys-terious eavesdroppings that took years to make sense. The eavesdrop-pings tell of an afternoon love affair conducted on that brief promenade, he a married doctor, she a girl dressed in the fashions of the 1930s. He strides along the promenade with a walking stick and a small black dog, she waits for him on a seat. Now, on their wet promenade they stroll again and I see them as I made them in my fascination: she is thin, and dressed in red, laughing, with pale long hair; he is Ronald Coleman with a greyer moustache. They smile at one another; defiantly he touches her hand. They are breathtaking in their sinning, and all their conversation is beautiful; they are the world's most exciting people.

I walk away from their romance, not wanting to tell myself that they were not like that. On the sands where old seaside artists sprinkled garish colours the rain is chilly. The Pierrots performed here, and the man and woman who rode the Wall of Death for a fortnight every year sunned themselves at midday. From the Loreto Convent we trooped down here to run the end-of-term races, Sister Tracy in charge. The sands haven't changed, nor have the concrete façades of the holiday boarding-houses, nor the Protestant church with its holes for lepers to peer through. But Horgan's Picture House is not at all as it was. It has two screens and a different name, and there are sexual fantasies instead of Jack Hulbert in *Round the Washtub*.

In Youghal there was a man who shot himself in a henhouse. Unlike the sea-front love affair, I understood that perfectly. Life had been hell for this man, voices whispered, and the henhouse, quite near the back of our garden, developed an eeriness that the clatter of birds made even more sinister. The henhouse isn't there any more, but even so as I stand where it was I shudder, and remember other deaths.

The King of England died, that old bearded face in the *Daily Sketch*. The funeral service was on our new Philips wireless, and a man kept coughing during the service: a few weeks later the wireless announced that this man had died himself. Then another man died, a man who used to come quite often to our house, who had the habit of very finely chopping up his salad. And a woman we bought fish from died. But all that death seemed quite in order at the time, except for the violence in the henhouse.

Youghal itself died in a way, for yellow furniture vans – Nat Ross of Cork – carted our possessions off, through Cork itself, westward through the town that people call Clonakilty God Help Us, to Skibbereen, the back of beyond

Memory focuses here, the images are clearer. Horses and carts pass slowly through the narrow streets, with milk churns for the creamery. On fair-days you push through cattle on your way to school, gingerly moving on pavements slithery with dung. Farmers with sticks stand by their animals, their shirts clean for the occasion, without collar or tie. There's a smell of whiskey, and sawdust and stout and dung. Pots of geraniums nestle among chops and ribs in the small windows of butchers' shops, and in other windows there is nothing at all except a sunburnt poster maybe, advertising the arrival of Duffy's Circus a year ago.

It was a mile and a half, the journey to school through the town, past Driscoll's sweetshop and Murphy's Medical Hall and Power's drapery, where you could buy oilcloth as well as dresses. You made the journey home again at three. By three on fair-days the buying and selling was over, the publicans' takings safely banked, the dung sliding towards the gutters. If you had money you spent it on liquorice pipes or stuff for making lemonade which was delicious if you ate it just as it was. The daughters of Power's drapery sometimes had money. But they were always well ahead, on bicycles because they were well-to-do. On fair-days their mother drove them in her Hillman because of the dung.

In the town's approximate centre, where four streets meet, a grey woman still stands, a statue of the Maid of Erin. E. O'Donovan, undertaker, still sells ice-cream and chocolate. The brass plate of Redmond O'Regan, solicitor, once awkwardly high, is now below eye-level. In the grocers' shops the big-jawed West Cork women buy bread and sausages and tins of plums, but no longer wear the heavy black cloaks that made them seem like figures from another century. They still speak in the same West Cork lisp, a lingering careful voice, never in a hurry. I ask one if she could tell me the way to a house I half remember. 'Ah, I could tell you grand,' she replies. 'It's dead and buried, sir.'

The door beside the Methodist church, once green, is purple. The church, small and red-brick, stands behind high iron railings and gates, with gravel in front of it. Beyond the door that used to be green is the dank passage that leads to Miss Willoughby's schoolroom, where first I learnt that the world is not an easy-going place. Miss Willoughby was stern and young, in love with the cashier from the Provincial Bank. Like the church beside her schoolroom, she was Methodist and there burnt in her breast an evangelical spirit which stated that we, her pupils, except for her chosen few, must somehow be made less wicked than we were. Her chosen few were angels of a kind, their handwriting blessed, their compositions a gift from God. I was not among them.

On the gravel in front of the red-brick church I vividly recall Miss Willoughby. Terribly, she appears. Severe and beautiful, she pedals against the wind on her huge black bicycle. 'Someone laughed during prayers,' her stern voice accuses, and you feel at once that it was you, although you know it wasn't. *V. poor* she writes in your headline book when you've done your best to reproduce, four times, perfectly, *Pride goeth before destruction*.

As I stand on the gravel, her evangelical eyes seem again to dart over me without pleasure. Once I took the valves out of the tyres of her bicycle. Once I looked in her answer book. 'Typical,' her spectre says. 'Typical, to come prying.' I am late, I am stupid. I cannot write twenty sentences on A Day in the Life of an Old Shoe, I cannot do simple arithmetic or geography. I am always fighting with Jasper Swanton. I move swiftly on the gravel, out on to the street and into the bar of Eldon's Hotel: in spectral form or otherwise, Miss Willoughby will not be there.

In Shannon's grocery there is a man who breeds smooth-haired fox-

342

terriers. He gave us one, a strange animal, infatuated by our cat. The man was tall and thin, and behind the counter now he's only different because he's old. Other faces, forgotten and now remembered, are different in that way too. But Barbara, the belle of Miss Willoughby's schoolroom, eldest daughter of Power's drapery, is nowhere to be found.

She runs a café in the main street, I'd heard, with an exotic African name, where every morning at coffee-time she presides. Perhaps I dreamed it, for the café in the main street has no name at all, and trades mundanely in lunchtime fare of stewed meat and vegetables. I peer through the window, and through the diners seated at chromium-legged tables, but the soft-haired Barbara is not there. No figure stands there as gracious as the Lady of Shalott, no face recalls the nine-year-old beauty of Class III. Can she really be one of those hurrying women with trays? A man consuming turnips wags his head at me. A message in the window says someone has found a purse.

Illusions fall fast in the narrow streets of Skibbereen, as elsewhere they have fallen. Yet for me, once, there was something else, nicest thing of all. Going to Cork it was called, fifty-two miles in the old Renault, thirty miles an hour because my mother wouldn't permit speed. On St Stephen's Day to the pantomime in the Opera House, and on some other occasion to the White Horse Inn, which my father had heard was good. In Cork my appendix was removed because Cork's surgical skill was second to none. In Cork my tongue was cut to rid me of my incoherent manner of speaking. To Cork, every day of my childhood, I planned to run away.

Twice a year perhaps, on Saturday afternoons, there was going to Cork to the pictures. *Snow White and the Seven Dwarfs* is the only film I remember seeing that had been specially made for children. Otherwise, it was Clark Gable and Myrna Loy in *Too Hot to Handle*, or *Fast and Loose*, or *Mr Deeds Goes to Town*. No experience in my whole childhood, and no memory, has remained as deeply etched as these escapes to the paradise that was Cork. Nothing was more lovely or more wondrous than Cork itself, with its magnificent array of cinemas, the Pavilion, the Savoy, the Palace, the Ritz, the Lee, and Hadji Bey's Turkish Delight factory. Tea in the Pavilion or the Savoy, the waitresses with silver-plated tea-pots and buttered bread and cakes, and other people eating fried eggs with rashers and chipped potatoes at half-past four in the afternoon. The sheer sophistication of the Pavilion or the Savoy could never be adequately conveyed to a friend in Skibbereen who had never had the good fortune to experience it. The Gentlemen's

343

lavatory in the Victoria Hotel had to be seen to be believed, the Munster Arcade left you gasping. For ever and for ever you could sit in the middle stalls of the Pavilion watching Claudette Colbert, or Spencer Tracy as a priest, and the earthquake in San Francisco. And for ever afterwards you could sit while a green-clad waitress carried the silver-plated tea-pot to you, with cakes and buttered bread. All around you was the clatter of life and of the city, and men of the world conversing, and girls' laughter tinkling. Happiness was everywhere.

William Trevor (1928–   ), novelist and writer of short stories, was born in Mitchelstown, Co. Cork, and spent his childhood in provincial Ireland. Among his books are *The Old Boys* (1964; Hawthornden Prize), *Angels at the Ritz* (1975; Royal Society of Literature Award), *The Children of Dynmouth* (1976; Whitbread Award), *Fools of Fortune* (1983; Whitbread Award). His latest collection of short stories is *The News from Ireland* (1986). He is a member of the Irish Academy of Letters, and was awarded an honorary CBE in 1977.

Light

When I was born, a long time ago,
(Or so my parents said)
I'd a tree in one hand and a glass in the other
And the hat of death on my head;
But when I was only a little child
I found out first where I was bound:
I met him walking in the golden bread,
And the thunder of singing twisted my heart right round.

The problem of possibility troubled me at twelve,
The blow of doubt nearly took away my breath:
Crying, gripping the pillow, I felt the dark disaster
As the world slowly prepared itself for death.
I was better at questions than at answering,
When he came back suddenly one night:
I was astounded by gratitude and fright,
My knees bent double and my mouth cried Master.

The nature of humanity concerned me at nineteen:
Millions of wandering skulls came into sight;
The bogs of ignorance and the seas of suffering
Hardly seemed right.
But reading at evening I felt him across the table,
Light beyond bearing, love without price:
My bones were burning and my hair stood up like corn
When I heard the cheering in Paradise.

Soon after I went from home to the pagan nations,
I watched what was shown to me, and listened to what
  was said:
Chewing ideas with the disintegrators
Until the sun was dead.
Yet also here I was shaken by his power,
The dark words crumbled in the descending flame;
Ice-thaw, white avalanche, dry earth drank deep where
  the steep floods tumbled,
And a miracle of tears sang to his name.

He breaks me like a stick and sets me on fire,
He strings me up like a sail to catch the sky,
He is the one reply that I require,
The sole reason I trouble myself or try.
And told me this, that, as the pain grows worse,
Walk in its darkening quiet and unafraid:
Love is the answer to the universe,
Given, not made.

Seán Lucy (1931–), academic and poet, was born in Bombay and
came to Ireland in 1935. He has been Professor of Modern English
at University College, Cork, since 1967.

346

CHRISTY BROWN

A Look of Pity

Thirteen – and still very much the boy artist who hadn't yet discovered himself or come to know his own abilities sufficiently to make use of them. Painting became everything to me. By it I learnt to express myself in many subtle ways. Through it I made articulate all that I saw and felt, all that went on inside the mind that was housed within my useless body like a prisoner in a cell looking out on a world that hadn't yet become a reality to me.

I saw more with my mind than with my eyes. I'd sit for hours sometimes, alone in my bedroom, not painting or doing anything else, but just sitting and staring into a world of my own, away and beyond everything that made up my ordinary life. When I went into one of those day-dreams I forgot everything else: the loud voices in the stuffy little kitchen below. . . . Peter trying to play the mouth organ on the doorstep. . . . The sound of jazz music coming from the wireless down-stairs. . . . The high shrill voice of the ragman in the street outside. . . . They all melted and faded into one confused blurring noise, and then gradually I'd hear nothing more or see nothing more. I'd just sit there, thinking. . . .

I didn't go out at all now. I had stopped going out a long time ago. I didn't even play in the house with my brothers any more. This puzzled them at first, but they slowly began to accept the new kind of relation-ship that had come between us. I didn't become a stranger to the rest of the family, of course, because with so many of us all living together in the same house that was impossible; we all formed part of one another, so to speak. But I had come to live more within myself. I lived *with* the others, but at the same time I lived *apart* from them, apart from all the things that meant most to them. I was happy by myself, but I didn't know then how far I really was from being self-sufficient.

And yet, withdrawn as I was from the ordinary life of a boy, the life of the streets and back alleys, I found that my heart was still miles ahead of my body in growth and development. I lost it again, good and truly this time. Another 'dream-girl' had come into my vision, not as tall and beautiful as my old one, but more my own age. She was called Jenny. She lived a few doors away from my house. She was small, energetic, gay, with a mass of brown curls framing her pretty elfin face with its lively green eyes and pouting lips. Unfortunately Jenny was a coquette; she could start a riot among all the boys on our street by just using those lovely eyes of hers in the right way. They were all crazy about her and there were many fights when they started arguing about who would marry her when they grew up into men.

I didn't go out any more, but that didn't stop me from seeing Jenny. I worshipped her from afar, that is from my bedroom window. It made me lazy in my painting, for whenever I heard Jenny's voice in the street below I'd crawl over to the window and sit on the bed, gazing out at her as she ran and skipped about with the other girls, whom I didn't notice at all. One day she looked up at me as I sat gazing down on her. I felt my face grow hot and made to draw back, but at that moment she smiled. I managed to smile back, and then she threw me a kiss. I could hardly believe my eyes when she did this, but she did it again before running away down the street, her dark curls flying and her white dress blowing in the wind.

That night I tore a page from an old jotter and, holding the pencil in my shaking toes, I wrote a passionate little note to Jenny, which I got one of my younger brothers to deliver, threatening him with my foot if he didn't give it to Jenny herself. I told her in the note that I thought she was the prettiest kid on our street and that I'd paint her lots of pictures if she'd let me. Then, in a hurried postscript, I told her that I loved her 'lots and lots of times'.

I waited for my brother to come back in excitement and fear, not daring to hope that Jenny would reply. In a half an hour's time he returned – with a note from her tucked up his jersey!

I took the note and read it eagerly, quite forgetful of my brother, who stood by staring at me in a funny way as if he thought I'd gone mad or something. I read Jenny's little letter over and over again, especially the part where she said she'd come and see me in my back yard the next day if I wanted her to. There was a queer fluttering inside me and a lightness in my head. I felt myself go hot and cold in turn. After a while I looked up. My brother was still standing with his hands behind his back and his mouth open, a look of bewilderment in his big blue eyes as he fixed them on my face. I yelled at him to 'scram', and he scuttled from the room like a startled rabbit. Then I threw myself back on the pillow and sighed, my heart jumping crazily.

I kept the appointment next day, all spruce and 'done up' with Tony's de luxe hair grease actually dripping down my forehead. Little Jenny was very sweet. We sat and looked over some of my paintings, and she gave a little gasp of admiration at each one I showed her. I was shy and awkward at first because of my slurred speech and the way I used my foot instead of my hands. But Jenny was either a very innocent person or a very tactful one, for she didn't seem to notice anything queer about me, but talked on gaily to me about games and parties and the boy next door the same as if I had been Peter or Paddy. I liked her for that.

We became great pals, Jenny and I. We never said a great deal to each other, but we exchanged innumerable little notes each week and she'd steal over to see me every Saturday night, bringing me little books and magazines which I never read but which I treasured very much, storing them all away in the old worm-eaten cupboard in my bedroom.

I was secretly proud that I, a cripple, had made friends with the prettiest and most sought-after girl in our neighbourhood. I often heard Peter saying fervently that Jenny was a 'peach' and that he'd do anything to be her favourite 'beau'. Every time I heard this I felt very proud of myself and enormously vain, thinking myself quite a conqueror, because it was not I who went to Jenny, but Jenny who came to me!

Peter became suspicious and one Saturday he came upon Jenny and me as we sat together in the back yard, our heads very close to one another, although we were only looking at some old story book that Jenny had brought along. I got red in the face, but Jenny didn't move. She just lifted her head, smiled at my brother briefly, and bent over the book again. Peter gave me a murderous look and went into the house, banging the door after him.

That evening, before she left, Jenny sat very quietly, toying idly with the book, a little frown creasing her forehead and her lower lip pushed out, as she always looked when she wanted to say something difficult. After a little while she got up, hesitated, then suddenly knelt down on the grass beside me and kissed me very tenderly on the forehead. I drew back, surprised, bewildered, for she had never kissed me before.

I opened my mouth to try and say something, but at that moment Jenny sprang to her feet, her face flushed and her eyes wet with tears, and rushed from the garden, her small black shoes clattering noisily as she ran down the stone path and disappeared into the street.

She didn't come for weeks after this, and I didn't hear from her although I fairly bombarded her with notes. In the meantime Peter tried to discourage me by telling me many wicked tales about poor little Jenny, but I didn't believe him a bit, not even when he told me that she made every one of the boys pay her a penny for every kiss she gave them.

'That's why I'm always broke!' he said mournfully, his hands stuck in his empty pockets.

I often sat up in my bed at night, thinking of Jenny and the way she kissed me that day in the back garden. I felt very melancholy and alone. Why doesn't she come, I asked myself, as I tossed restlessly in the dark, hearing Peter snoring comfortably at my side.

My fourteenth birthday came along, and among the other birthday cards I got that morning there was one written in a small childish hand which was Jenny's: but still she never came to see me. I often saw her from my bedroom window playing in the streets below, but she kept her eyes away from my house and never looked up once. I'd sit at the window for hours, hoping she'd glance up at me, until the twilight came and everything grew dark and I could see nothing more save the dim whiteness of her frock as she ran along the street with the other girls, while a laughing crowd of boys chased after them.

To hide my disappointment I painted furiously for the whole of every day, painting crazy little pictures that had neither pattern or theme. They were just haphazard slices of my boiling mind dashed on to the paper wildly and recklessly.

Then one day as I sat disconsolately in the back yard with my back against a soapbox I heard a step close by. I looked up wearily. . . . It was *Jenny*! She stood a few feet away, at the entrance to the yard, her slim, childish figure outlined against the white wall behind her, vividly bright in the June sunshine, her shadow falling crookedly on the warm concrete ground. She was looking across at me, but – it was with a *look of pity*.

I knew then, as I came to know many times later, how bitter and crushing a simple look of pity can be to someone like myself who needs something other than sympathy – the strength that only genuine human affection can give to the weakest heart.

I lowered my head under her pitying gaze and without a word being said on either side Jenny turned slowly and left me to myself in the yard.

From MY LEFT FOOT

———•◦•———

Christy Brown (1932–81), poet, novelist and painter, was born in Dublin, almost totally paralysed. *My Left Foot*, his first book, was typed out with a toe of that foot.

The Convent

The convent was forty miles away and situated at the foot of a lake into which, legend said, a former hedonist city had been plunged and swallowed up. The town was grey and somewhat seedy and time seemed to pass slowly and without event. To go through the gateway and then hear the hasp being shut by the stooped gatekeeper was to take a step from which one could not retreat for five long years. The parents lingered in the reception hall talking to a nun and certain mechanical courtesies were exchanged. Then you were handed over, and the snivelling was dismissed by the nun with brusque and off-putting optimism.

Big spaces from now on – recreation hall, classrooms and refectory, rules for everything and nametapes on all one's belongings. The only escape came at dawn three mornings a week when we went to attend Mass in the Augustinian church and there one sometimes caught sight of the 'lovely priest', lost to us in his beautiful vestments and his mysterious Latin. Otherwise it was a world of women – nuns, lay nuns and little postulants and one was always seeing veils and starched headgear that framed the face and out of which eyes and nose peered as if out of a burrow. To see a nun's eyebrow was as wicked and as bewitching as Keats felt when he saw the ungloved hand of the woman he loved as she walked over Vauxhall Bridge.

Sins got committed by the hour, sins of thought, word, deed and omission, the sin of eating, nay devouring an illicit jam tart snatched from the cookery kitchen, the sin of smiling at a nun and having bad 'thoughts' about her such as brushing against her hand, the sin of sprinkling caster sugar onto the palm of one's hand and licking it to one's heart's content, the dreaded sin of consulting the mirror and then hawing on it to give oneself a dreamier look.

Once a year we were allowed out to the local show but there was about it a sort of unexpressed lethargy and disappointment, what with the muddied field, the winds (it was always October when the winds were said to lament), the men in their great coats, the women in their felt hats, the fillies and mares whinnying and rearing, the precarious showjumps and the spartan amusements (it was wartime) so that nothing quite lived up to anyone's expectations.

One of the vexations of later life is how carelessly we treat our elders. There is no regaining that time. There was the couple who had had a made match, who still kept the top tier of the wedding cake for the offspring that was not forthcoming. The wife was a distance away under an umbrella with a group of ladies, murmuring. He winked at me and said I was growing into a fine woman, then winked with the other eye, then nothing more. Standing there sucking the fibres of her scarf was a 'peculiar' lady who at times would burst into laughter and at other times accused people of laddering her viyella stockings with their diamond engagement rings. Except that there was not a diamond ring in sight, only the brown felt hats, the flecked tweed costumes, and brooches with lifelike similarity to beetles or spiders, brooches that were in vogue that year. The peculiar lady was just back from Lourdes and complained how everyone had to bathe in the same water, how it was not hygienic. Then she buried her face like a little girl in her fur collar, basked in it. I saw her twenty years later in a mental hospital, whereupon she asked me for a 'ciggy' and was playful as she had not been that day on the hill, when a horse bolted and the women became as hysterical as the children they were trying to protect. The odd toff had binoculars or a walking stick and one man with a black beard distinguished himself by wearing a faded green cape.

For refreshments we had lemonade, apples, and coffee-flavoured biscuits with a coffee icing. These biscuits required the accompaniment of hot tea to melt the icing slightly in the mouth so that the two extractions of coffee could be properly sampled and united. The apples smelt of nothing in particular out of doors, but back in the convent and just prior to Hallowe'en the parcels would pour in, be kept in the nun's little parlour, and to walk by there was to see them dimly through the frosted glass of the door and at once to imagine oneself in the ripest of orchards. Every girl's parcel contained a barmback and apples regardless of other treats and for a few days the convent acquired another smell and hence another atmosphere, whereby prayer and discipline and wax polish took mere second place and gorging was lauded.

Once after a nosebleed, when I had been laid on the red tiled floor and had keys and bunches of keys put all over my person, I was subsequently brought into that little parlour and told that I was a good girl, and given

352

as reward a glass of lukewarm milk, which I hated. When the nun hurried out of the room to stop someone playing the piano in the recreation hall, I repaired to the vicinity of the three potted plants – a castor oil, a maiden hair and a bizzie lizzie, and doused each of them with the lukewarm stuff. I was still toying with the contents in the end of the glass when out of the corner of my eye I saw the milky liquid seep through the bottom of the terra cotta pots to the little saucers provided. Would she notice it?

'Have you thought of what you are going to be?' she asked with a certain coyness. Almost flirtatious was she. Oh to please her and win one's way into her hard heart and be invited to do little favours for her, like carrying her books, or opening or closing a window or cleaning the blackboards, oh oh to be her slave!

'A nun,' I said, quicker and more soulfully than I had ever said aught. The thought of a vocation danced before me; like a banner, the word waved and with it the vision of a young postulant with a see-through veil, one foot in the world and the other sinking deeper and deeper into the mists of spirituality, towards the 'never to be forgotten day' when one would take final vows and be cut off from the world outside, from family, from pleasure, from men, from earthly love, from buses and shops and cafeterias, from life.

'A nun,' she said, swollen with pride. Meanwhile I was brimming with tears that were as thick as glycerine, though not so nourishing.

From then on there was a subtle understanding I would become a nun and thus devolved on me extra duties such as to walk softly, to talk softly, to stay in the chapel after the others – the motley – had trooped out, to deny myself jam on Sunday, to drag my hair back severely from the forehead and therefore give no reign to quiffs or prettiness, to drink the senna tea without making a face, to read no delectable love story in the magazine that some day-girls brought in, to write a letter home only when one was permitted and to keep one's mind on such things as the visions of St Margaret Mary and the mortifications of the saints.

Parents seemed to exist no longer, or rather they had receded into being people who had given birth to one and about whom one had certain fossilized feelings, just as one day these nuns – the next instalment of parents – would recede and be replaced by another authority and yet another.

On Saturday night the head nun would read out to us something of moral, religious or political import. We would hear how St Bridget of Opaco achieved her destiny by going to join her dying brother in

Tuscany, but not going as an ordinary traveller, rather in the middle of eating a meal of herbs and small fishes was transported across the sea by an angel. There and then she was told that she would have to set aside all earthly life and retire to a cave to live in austerity and penance. Or we would be told how bombs fell near Jaffa, that ancient city of the Bible, and how those bombs shattered the windows of a Franciscan monastery near which 'St Peter once so wondrously sojourned in the house of Simon the Tanner'. The next item might be that when the fishermen in Newfoundland felt their sight going they cooked and ate a cod's liver, or that poor Poland, the sister of dear Ireland, was in tears, suffering for faith and fatherland. And all over Europe that there was a bacon shortage. Then we were warned about literature, told how new writers were arch hands at depicting immodesty, in flaming imagery, relating the most obscene details, describing the worst carnal vices with subtle analysis and adorning them with all the brilliance and allurements of style so that nothing was left inviolate. Now that I was her favourite, I would carry her books and the weekly newspaper back to her desk, to the little parlour and there clandestinely I read a shocking letter discussing the favourability of studies from the nude, of sun baths, air baths and gymnastic exercises in which both sexes took part. The categoric answer was that the modern statuary of the nude or scarcely veiled statuary or photographs were all highly dangerous and that protracted gazing at such things without any just reason was usually a grievous sin indeed. If a painting had to be done on such a theme, then it was advised that all precautions should be taken, including the veiling of the sexual parts, the avoidance of mixed classes and the checking of ribaldry. Sun baths, and air baths taken by members of both sexes without costumes were fertile sources of sin it said, and gymnastics an offence against modesty.

I read it despite myself, then continued up the stairs to bed with legs sealed, hands clenched, armpits so close that not even a little flea could crawl in there. The same routine – shoes off outside the dormitory door, strategic undressing under the shelter of one's dressing gown and under the same awning washing in a basin of cold water, getting into one's nightgown and uttering further night prayers.

Most of the beds used to creak and some of the coarser girls would bounce up and down, the better to draw attention to this need for hilarity. Sometimes slices of cake, a biscuit or a cherry might be covertly passed to one in the dark, and the pleasure of eating it was not a little mitigated by the realization of the sin that was being committed, the sin

354

that on some Cemetery Sunday in the distant future some soul would have to pray for in that communion of souls between living and dead.

There used to be the cups of hot senna on Sunday mornings and subsequently a great rush allied with a great anxiety for one of the four lavatories, that were situated on each of the four landings. Queues everywhere, girls holding their middles and swearing that they were not able to hold it, so that they could be let in next, fierce bangs on the door while they were having difficulty with the faulty chain. In her flounder one girl flushed a pink ten-shilling note away and when by coincidence the head nun said there was a great flush of money everyone burst out laughing, but no one could explain why in spite of repeated and stringent enquiries. She sensed some foul unseemly plot and as a punishment we had to stand all next day for study, and those who coughed were singled out and put to stand near the rostrum facing the bulk of the pupils.

From MOTHER IRELAND

————◦◦————

Edna O'Brien (1932–   ), novelist and dramatist, was born in Tuamgraney, Co. Clare. Among her works are *The Country Girls* and *August is a Wicked Month*.

Poem from Love Cry

Religion class. Mulcahy taught us God
While he heated his arse to a winter fire
Testing with his fingers the supple sallyrod.
'Explain the Immaculate Conception, Maguire,
And tell us then about the Mystical Blood.'
Maguire failed. Mulcahy covered the boy's head
With his satchel, shoved him stumbling among
The desks, lashed his bare legs until they bled.

'Who goes to hell, Dineen? Kane, what's a saint?
Doolin, what constitutes a mortal sin?
Flynn, what of the man who calls his brother a fool?'
Years killed raving questions. Kane stomped around Dublin
In policeman's boots. Flynn was afraid of himself.
Maguire did well out of whores in Liverpool.

———•◦•———

Brendan Kennelly (1936–), academic, poet and novelist, was born in Ballylongford, Co. Kerry. He is Professor of Modern Literature, Trinity College, Dublin.

Life and Death in the Dublin Tenements

'My father and mother were both from the Coombe area, the Liberties – an area in Dublin that was immediately outside the city walls and was exempt from the taxes within the city and got its name from this. We had tenement rooms. . . . It was a very nomadic existence living in tenements in Dublin, one of the reasons was that people would be constantly seeking better and bigger rooms, ones with more light, better situations – maybe you'd have water on the stairs. . . . If you had water, it was on the landing, literally a trough with running water in it and where you'd go up and get it – there'd be no such thing as the refinement of having it in a room. . . . I often hear people now talking about these deprived people say in America who have running water in their flats etcetera, complaining of the cockroaches, but we not only had the cockroaches but we had rats as well. . . .

'In the tenements there was an awful lot of typhus and typhoid and all the rest, kids' rickets and malnutrition, bad hygiene and squashed conditions, so many people living in the one area, just one tap in the yard and one toilet, maybe two dozen families using one toilet, and, hygiene what it was, people weren't conscious of washing their hands after using the toilet even, and disease spread very rapidly.

'Poverty is always comparative – to yourself, to your time and to the place you are in. But the great thing about it was there was a great cameraderie in the tenements and if one person had a surplus of any given thing, they'd share it with their neighbours and they wouldn't share because it was a big thing to do but because it *was* the thing to do. For instance, if someone was down the country and brought back a sack of apples (maybe they'd be welders doing a job or whatever) it was taken as automatic you shared with the neighbours. Maybe some fella might get a job on a fishing boat or something for a couple of days or know someone working on one and maybe come back with a sack or a half-sack or a half-box of herrings. Then immediately everyone'd get a share of them; and again these were all perishable things anyway, which you couldn't very well store. But it really stemmed from the thing that in the country, for instance, if someone killed a pig, well immediately the neighbours would all get a share of it. You know, they'd give some the liver, some the heart, and you'd get ribs and you'd get the various parts; the pig's blood would be made into black puddings which would be shared. There was this genuine sharing thing with people, literally sharing. . . . They were part of the greater community and this was the thing about the tenements. . . . The tenements were great places for stories – the wakes and the weddings, now everybody went to them; like you weren't invited to a wake or a wedding, you were there. . . . You came automatically.

'There was Devereux's dairy, or Devericks as we used to call it, which was a huge big yard. They had a milk herd there, their own herd of milk cows . . . they had their own dairy, an oldfashioned dairy, just the bare dairy, nothing fancy in it, but just the old utensils – you'd have the churns, you'd also have the big ceramic dishes where they had the cream and the milk and even the buttermilk – you'd get the buttermilk as well; the buttermilk was great! And the butter was from a big chunk of butter: it'd be just muslin-covered, you know, home-made butter, and they'd give that to you with the two butter-pats, two little lads'd tap the butter on the scale and weigh it up for you. And the whole thing was a kind of ritual: it was like going into church in a way, because it was very clean, very solemn; and even if you went in for a quarter of butter and half a pint of milk you were treated with the same respect as if you were getting ten pounds of butter and a ton of milk. . . . So the old world courtesy was beautiful literally, and I loved the place, I loved to go into it.

'My father reared and bred greyhounds and he worked for a bookie. One of the bad things about it, one of the worst things about it, was later on he never got his cards stamped, so he worked for your man and just without any cards or anything else, which wasn't a great idea, as it turned out. But we always had – when he was working – plenty; there was always full and plenty, we'd always plenty of food, we were relatively well off in regard to people of equal position in the tenements beside us. The thing was either Ma'd send me or some of the others in – she'd have someone next door whose husband mightn't be working and she'd say, 'Give Mrs So-and-so that. Tell her I have too much; would she mind using that?" The thing was that largesse was never presented as if you were doing a favour. It was always, "Would you *mind* using that, Mrs, because it'll only go off," that sort of thing. This was it, and it was the way it was presented was as important as the presentation of the thing itself. And I remember that later when things'd be bad my old ma'd a great sense of pride and she was a great one. She'd have the fire going with a pot on the hob with just water in it and someone'd come in and say, "God, you have your dinner on very early, Mrs Weldon," and she might have nothing in it at all. But it was a sense of pride, she wasn't going to admit that they had nothing – this would be after my father died, but up to that things would be very good and I often remember going out with my da.

'Da had the greyhounds out at places like Cabinteely. . . . I've spent a week or two out there coming up to a greyhound derby or something like that. Now I remember I was out there for the week or ten days – it was school holidays – and the Da said "Do you mind if he comes out with me?" "Ah," she says, "glad to get rid of him!" because I was a nuisance round the house, I was always getting into trouble. I was a terrible active kid, jumping and running about.

'But we were out there and we slept three days, three days in a row before this greyhound derby, in the stables, in the kennels. . . . In the kennels we were sleeping because it was very prevalent at that time nobbling dogs and horses – rival gangs of the racecourses would get in and dope other people's horses and dogs. The old man and meself slept down in the kennels for three nights in a row and he'd this bloody baseball bat under his pillow and I said to him one night, I said, "What's that?" And another fella had an alarm rigged up from the kennels up to the house, something like a hundred and fifty yards up, you know what I mean? So that if anything was suspicious or anything went wrong, he just pulled the switch and set off a buzzer, an electric buzzer, and there was two other fellas sleeping in the house and they'd be down immediately. But then as it happened nothing came, but they had a sort of warning on the grape-vine that there was going to be an attempt so I must admit the boys who were going to do it may have heard the word that it'd have been a tough proposition, so they may have thought better of it.

'But the Da'd bring me sometimes to the meetings themselves when he had to be there. Now there was such a big build up on this, they were all quite convinced this dog was a real cert for a winner. Now the thing about it was that this particular dog was not the favourite; it was fairly fancied, you see, but they had kind of kept it back. He was good, there was no chicanery about it, but what they had done was brought it along very quietly – but they knew, they knew its actual potential where, like, they had run it a couple of times and it was beaten by a short head by the other dogs, and these other dogs would be in the same race. But they knew themselves – these were fellas of years of experience – that the way they had this dog was in a pink condition where he was going to win – nothing is certain, you know, but they were so convinced that *they all bet like hell*. These be the fellas that'd be working for the group, like my da and a few of his immediate friends, the bookie himself and his friends, all being twenty or thirty people in the know who had a good idea that this dog was going to win. And, bedad, we went to the races and it *did* win by a short head, it just pipped by at the post. A great race, and it was really a near thing. I'd been with the dog for weeks, and you know what a child is like, roaring my head off. Apart from winning the prize – they won the prize, a big silver cup, and a couple of hundred each; two hundred and fifty pounds was the prize money – going back that night, going home now, they were up and down to the bar getting gargle. And I was sick drinking orange and the fellas giving me bars of chocolate and packets of biscuits – my pockets were bulging out.

'But anyway going back in the cab I was lucky with a big fat gentleman smelling of the whiskey shoving half-dollars at me – and a half-crown's a lot of money – and I'd a pocket full of half-dollars and two bob bits going back. My father gave me the money for my ma in a brown bag or something. "That's for your mother," he said. "Tell her there's an extra few quid there, we had a good night, etcetera whatever." So I went home and of course my mother was delighted with the extra few quid, and she heard me chinking and she asked me how much, and I had about six pounds – an enormous amount of money for a kid then, I'm talking of the forties. I think she gave me about two pounds ten out of it and she said, "I won't give it to you altogether because you'll only squander it." She said, "I'll give you this now and you can bring your pals to the pictures or whatever." It was only fourpence into the pictures then you must remember. So not only was I able to bring them to the pictures but I was able to buy sweets and toffee-apples and all the rest of it and ice-cream on the way home and I still had a pound and the change of a pound, and for a couple of weeks I was king of the street. . . .

'Things like that are the happy memories for me. The unhappy things would have been, by the same token, in the same tenement room. . . . Listening to my father dying for maybe a week or ten days. He had a very bad chest and he got bronchial pneumonia. They hadn't got a great

360

many drugs then. He was a pretty strong bloke in his time; he was a footballer, but he preferred to go after the dogs and that, horses, etcetera – he was pretty hefty.

'Da was a great man for listening to a yarn; he could tell a yarn himself. But when he got this bronchial pneumonia – you can imagine in a tenement room. There were eight of us – the thing was we had two big double-beds and Da'd be lying in one and the Head Murphy (a neighbour) sitting on the other side talking to him, keeping him going and making him cups of tea. He'd come up in the evening now. . . . The Ma'd be there all day and this'd give her a bit of a break, and she'd go up to her sister's or something in the tenements down in Stephen Street. . . . And when the Da got delirious which he did for the last week before he died, he'd got into delirium and he'd be singing things like "The Rocky Road to Dublin". I think I was the only one of the kids – I was the oldest and I'd be about twelve – to realize that he was actually dying because the doctor had been in and out and I heard all the chit-chat, the bits and pieces. The strange thing about it that always stuck in my head was adults, then particularly, didn't think of kids; and they didn;t think kids had any real intelligence in that sense, and they would talk over your head, and I was taking everything in. I knew exactly what was happening, the whole of it, so it was a rather scaring experience for me. . . .'

Liam Weldon (1933–   ), folksinger and raconteur, was born in Dublin.

Death of a Naturalist

All year the flax-dam festered in the heart
Of the townland; green and heavy headed
Flax had rotted there, weighted down by huge sods.
Daily it sweltered in the punishing sun.
Bubbles gargled delicately, bluebottles
Wove a strong gauze of sound around the smell.
There were dragon-flies, spotted butterflies,
But best of all was the warm thick slobber
Of frogspawn that grew like clotted water
In the shade of the banks. Here, every spring
I would fill jampotfuls of the jellied
Specks to range on window-sills at home,
On shelves at school, and wait and watch until
The fattening dots burst into nimble-
Swimming tadpoles. Miss Walls would tell us how
The daddy frog was called a bullfrog
And how he croaked and how the mammy frog
Laid hundreds of little eggs and this was
Frogspawn. You could tell the weather by frogs too
For they were yellow in the sun and brown
In rain.

Then one hot day when fields were rank
With cowdung in the grass the angry frogs
Invaded the flax-dam; I ducked through hedges
To a coarse croaking that I had not heard
Before. The air was thick with a bass chorus.
Right down the dam gross-bellied frogs were cocked
On sods; their loose necks pulsed like sails. Some hopped:
The slap and plop were obscene threats. Some sat

Poised like mud grenades, their blunt heads farting.
I sickened, turned, and ran. The great slime kings
Were gathered there for vengeance and I knew
That if I dipped my hand the spawn would clutch it.

Seamus Heaney (1939–   ), poet and critic, was born in Co. Derry.
He is at present a professor at Harvard University.

The Library Boxes

The two-teacher school in which my parents taught side by side for thirty-eight years had been built in the 1840s (and condemned as an unsuitable building not long afterwards). My father bore the title of Principal, and in theory, therefore, held sway over his Assistant Teacher in matters of discipline, punctuality, and faith and morals in general. She was his wife, my mother, and I suspect that in his quiet shrewdness my father understood the realities of life; in his own essays and books he always referred to her as 'the Competent Authority'.

This small, dark-eyed, pretty woman had answered the school authority's advertisement in 1924; Miss Burke was retiring. When Miss O'Sullivan arrived by bus from the city of Limerick thirty miles away, she did not realize that she was about to renew an acquaintance she had made with my father a year earlier, at a summer camp set up by the newly formed Government of the South in order that teachers should learn Gaelic. They married in 1925.

All these histories come from hazy hearsay. I do not know the definitive version: my upbringing still resonated with Victorian aloofness. We, my seven brothers and sisters, never enquired too closely into such frivolous matters as parental romance – or, indeed, emotions of any description. My memory, though, of seeing and hearing my parents together is one of much laughter between them, banter, harmless argument, long quiet talks and walks.

It is a de-romanticized memory, with no colours in it, just factual and daily, with predictable undercurrents of anxiety and tension. These latter are a business which I believe I have only observed through hindsight, and I do not quite know whether I project them upon my parents through my own psyche. The record of the times, though, seems to support my impression. When I was born, in 1942, the war was at a zenith, the 'rations' at a nadir, brothers and sisters had to be sustained at boarding school and then I arrived, the youngest of eight. Although Ireland remained neutral, my father had a right, it seems to me, to be anxious – and my mother too, although the actual practice of ensuring health, comfort and kitchen welfare, as well as teaching school all day, kept her occupied in a practical way which was not as freely available to my father.

Life, consequently, had sharp hidden edges. I have a recurring dream now, of great thumbs marching across the landscape towards me, benign in their intent, provided I never challenge them. But I can distinguish the magnified Scotland-Yard whorls and features of each one, and I know that I must be careful lest any of these soft, personal monsters overwhelm me, fall on me. Rightly or wrongly, my interpretation of this dream tells me that this was what childhood felt like, awareness of great forces which could at any moment topple upon us all, despite the strength, authority and protection of my father, the softness of his blue Viyella shirts and tweed jackets, the sturdiness of his brown brogue, or black, toe-capped shoes, the respect amounting to fear that he inspired.

In the midst of the slowly accumulating anxieties and the deserts of utter lonesomeness that children know, I had an oasis, full of sweet freshness and renewal. Every month, from Clonmel, the county town twenty miles away, a van delivered two boxes of library books to all primary schools in the parishes of the South Riding. (Incidentally, a Riding, from the old Icelandic, means an administrative division into three, a territorial thirding: exquisitely, Tipperary possesses only two, a North and South Riding.)

Each of these library boxes had a couple of shiny, fresh padlocks, holding down a pair of long narrowed hasps, gleaming black. Each box stood about four feet long by three feet wide by two feet deep, wooden, stout, undistinguished, and with no other use that one could possibly contemplate. And each box gave off an odour, musty and brown and quiet and privileged.

The books bore initialled classifications in the lower spine, in neat but emphatic white, or even gold, lettering. I immediately drove towards the label JF – and, rare indulgence, was never held back. Junior Fiction meant everything, much Stevenson, some Ransome and Ballantyne, Richmal Crompton, Enid Blyton, Irish writers such as Aodh de Blacam, and the various books published by a New York house I have never since been able to find, called, I believe, Cupple & Leon.

Thirty-five years on, I can now understand that the main function of the library boxes was to provide an Introduction – and rather a grand, cosmopolitan one. The state called Southern Ireland had only been in existence for twenty years, since the signing of the Anglo-Irish Treaty. The society, which had formed among what can most easily be described as a rural middle- and working-class, had not developed an access to culture in the same way that English or European children could expect music, drama, painting classes as an educational norm.

The poverty of our parish was such that keeping the bodies and souls of many of the schoolchildren together was often as much as my parents could do. Where my four brothers and three sisters were concerned, we received a secondary education – perhaps the first entire family in our locality to do so – and above that my mother attempted some piano lessons, with limited time and success; only a few of my siblings prevailed and graduated to classes with other music teachers.

Culture dwelt in a balladry, local, national, still largely rebel, an awareness of popular song, which linked into a strong ancient oral tradition. And over all of these hovered the crude brutal hand of repressive Roman Catholicism, ready to censor, and, if necessary, destroy anything which challenged the Faith. Local priests had awesome powers; the national hierarchy was omnipotent. Neither level possessed much cultural or artistic sensitivity. In the main, any such intake was controlled by ignorant men with narrow vision, who saw only sin in anything which had the glimmer of an idea. The intellectual charm of the Jesuits scarcely ever penetrated this far. I believe that even they came under suspicion.

Therefore, the first glimmer of culture, the first hints of outside experience, came out of those library boxes. When Junior Fiction had been exhausted, all others were devoured. In this small schoolroom, whose wooden floors had just been sprinkled with water to keep the dust down while sweeping, Thomas Hardy came into view. He was ideal: one could identify to some degree with his characters in their rural setting. The short stories seemed most compatible with my experience; perhaps the attention span had something to do with it, although I now feel certain that the scale of operations was a clearer reason. Ireland provides the ideal vehicle for the short story, inner rather than outer space.

Dickens and Jane Austen joined up, inevitably. Slightly later, from the same boxes, Lawrence – a surprising choice, did he get in under the

366

wire, or over the heads? – gave me a most valuable insight. He proved to me that a provincial boy has rights to the world, too. The steeply sloping street of a black, grim town in Nottinghamshire existed worlds away from the lushness of Tipperary fields, but ideologically they had much in common – an awareness of natural sensuality, a wariness of the small closed attitudes and an appreciation of being alone. (Obviously *Lady Chatterley* did not make it through the barbed wire entanglements. Later I read it in school, through the traditional channels, and for years afterwards I could hardly read any novel without at first receiving it page by torn-out page under a desk or table.)

All the writers rolled up in attendance. Tolstoy, Dostoevsky, Chekhov, Balzac, Thackeray, whose poor wife went mad on the steamer to Cork, Swift, who had stayed in the castle across the fields. Sterne was born where Anthony Trollope had lived, in Clonmel; de Maupassant, Defoe, Henty, God bless the Imperial mark!, Antony Hope's Ruritania, Hazlitt, who had walked nearby, Galsworthy – I was provided with an unending supply of good good books, and good bad books. Some proved unreadable: Turgenev, the novels of Mrs Gaskell, Fielding, but accessible if one skipped large portions.

Modern novelists, of whom one was not supposed to get hold, were read surreptitiously, such as Howard Spring. How *My Son My Son* got past the eagle eyes I shall never know: that Libations of Hebe scene, where a bare-breasted lover sits up in bed to have breakfast with the narrator, must have been passed in the interest of classical reference. An occasional John O'Hara came through, Bruce Graeme's *Blackshirt* novels, with the hero Richard Verrell, upper-class gent by day, cracksman by night, and of Leslie Charteris I read every single word.

Outside the schoolroom window the lack of riches in the countryside was mirrored in the shortage of broad cultural intake. Occasionally, a touring theatrical company of considerable if eccentric merit, such as Lord Longford or Anew MacMaster would come by, but dare they put on anything more adventurous than a 'safe' interpretation of Shakespeare? They would be 'read from the pulpit' and their box-office would starve. Once in a while, with, I am certain, a degree of mischief, they would offer a vehement version of, say, *Oedipus Rex*, in an interpretation obscure enough to impress and fool everybody, clergy included.

Much though I enjoyed all of these performances, my internal cast of characters remained more colourful and satisfying. As did their presentation: the feel and handling and texture of books, acquired a long time ago in that small smoky schoolroom, will continue to be an unsentimental pleasure, which sustained me through much darkness – and still does, through all the times of being, in Joyce's words, 'yung and easily freudened'.

———•◦•———

Frank Delaney (1942–   ) was born in Tipperary and worked as a bank clerk before becoming a writer and broadcaster. He was Chairman of the National Book League 1984–6.

KATE CRUISE O'BRIEN

The Missing Ingredient

I didn't have an Irish childhood, I invented one. I decided at an early age that my own family – whom I loved very much – wasn't Irish enough for me so I adopted a family to supply the missing Irish ingredient. Being Irish, as I understood it then, meant being Catholic and going to Mass on Sundays. It meant having a coal fire in the living-room and eating dinner at four o'clock and having tea in the evening. It meant home-made cakes and the smell of baking. It meant not much meat but plenty of soda bread, it meant pelmets in a parlour that was very rarely used.

The Greenes (as I shall call them), from the moment I met them, seemed to me to epitomize Irishness. I met Mary Greene at Amiens Street Station one rainy evening when I was searching for my train. Mary was carrying a music case which I coveted because it looked so professional and I asked her where my train might be because I wanted to talk to her. Mary, miraculously, came from Howth too and we travelled home together by train and by tram and became friends for ever on the open top of the Howth tram as we searched the starry sky for the Sputnik.

We stayed together in each other's houses. Mary thought that my home was the height of sophistication. 'Steak for dinner and dinner in the evening' she crooned. 'And your *mother*! She's so beautiful, your mother, so beautiful and young. I could look at her for ever and all her wonderful clothes.' Mary thought my father was hilarious. I'd never seen my father in quite that light. His moments of exuberance embarrassed the priggish little girl I used to be. But Mary was enchanted by him: 'I love it when he bangs the table and goes "Boom! Boom! Boom!"' she'd say, 'Conor, will you read that noisy poem again?'

I forget which poem that was, but I will always remember that Mary's enthusiasm made me realize how lucky I was to have such a family – even if they weren't very Irish. And her family entranced me.

On Sundays Mr Greene played golf and Mrs Greene and Tom and

369

Mary and Patricia went for a walk. After a while, I came too. We walked through the rhododendron bushes in the grounds of Howth Castle and we walked up over the golf course for a glimpse of Mr Greene. We walked along the cliff path and we walked over Howth headland where the grass was thick and close and spongy. One day we went to the lighthouse and Mrs Greene persuaded the lighthouse keeper to show us around inside.

In summer we went to beaches. We went to Red Rock where there were little pools with sea anemones and crabs, or to the Hole in the Wall where a boy had drowned so we had to be very careful, or to the Claremont Strand where there was a high wall dividing the railway line from the beach. Mary used to climb on that wall when her mother wasn't looking. But that wasn't very often for Mrs Greene, placid, firm and kind, was nearly always looking. She never swam or I can never remember her swimming. She sat on the beach with her towel and her book while we raced off to enjoy ourselves. I don't think she minded. She was a busy lady, a national schoolteacher and a housewife with no home help. She didn't often get an opportunity to sit still in the sun.

After the beach or the walk, we went home to a fire and Mrs Greene's boiled cake while Mr Greene read his paper in the old leather chair with its peeling arms. After tea Mrs Greene did the ironing. The nuns in Talbot Street did her washing for her but the clothes had to be ironed, and she baked cakes and taught me how to make soda bread in a plastic basin.

Mary was sent off to boarding school, a convent in Monaghan, but I wasn't forgotten. I still went to tea with the Greenes and played with Patricia and when the convent gave a concert I was invited along. But while the school orchestra struck up with an ear-splitting wail, I read the programme and wondered what had happened to Mary. Mary had a glorious voice but Mary wasn't amongst the soloists. Mrs Greene was wondering too: 'I don't see Mary's name here anywhere,' she whispered unhappily. I turned the page and understood. 'Mrs Greene,' I whispered a few minutes later. 'Mrs Greene, it says here that Mary is the last of the passers-by.' Mrs Greene never forgave the nuns for that. She was fiercely proud of her children and was determined that they could and should shine. The last of the passers-by was no place for a daughter of hers.

Inevitably, my association with a family as naturally devout as the Greenes raised questions in my mind. They were Catholic, I was not. They had rules and I did not and it began to worry me that I had no religion which would tell me what to do when I was an adult. Adulthood and sex had become inextricably linked in my mind since I had discovered the facts of life. How was I going to be good? I wondered. The Greenes were taught that adultery was wrong, their church told them so, but there was nothing to prevent me from becoming an adulterous woman when I was older – no rule and no church. I didn't want to become a woman like that but adults seemed to find passion addictive, according to the books I'd read, and when the time came, who or what was to keep me from temptation?

Through one long and dreadful summer I pondered the problem. It nagged at me and haunted me and kept me from sleeping. I think I thought that if I stayed awake adulthood and its temptations couldn't sneak up on me unawares. I was really frightened and truly miserable and I couldn't ask my mother about it. It might seem rude since she wasn't a Catholic either. I knew of course that my mother was an adult and a non-believer and a virtuous woman but I suspected that that was because she had a better character than I had. It was natural for her to be good. She wouldn't even be tempted to go astray.

So I worried and wondered and eventually I decided to ask Mrs Greene about it, Mrs Greene who didn't mind that I wasn't a Catholic, Mrs Greene who laughed at nuns.

I arrived in her garden one sunny afternoon when she was resting in a basket chair with her feet up on a stool. I poured out my problem in a vehement rush because I was frightened that if I stopped at all I'd never be able to tell her of my fears. She listened quietly and then she said, 'You're a child now so you don't have to worry about it for at least three years. If I were you I wouldn't think about it at all till then. Just leave it alone and remember that as your body grows up, your mind will be growing too. So when you're old enough to be tempted, your mind will be old enough to cope with temptation.'

She didn't laugh and she didn't tell me it was nonsense. She just returned me firmly to the childhood I should have been enjoying. She gave me time and space to grow in.

Kate Cruise O'Brien (1948–), journalist and writer of short stories, is the daughter of Conor Cruise O'Brien. She won the Hennessy Award for New Irish Writing in 1971, and the Rooney Prize for Irish Literature in 1979.

Cleansing with Pain

The corridors of Blackrock, oppressive to me as a day boy, were positively claustrophobic as a boarder. I noticed then, for the first time, just how cold the place was. The cold began in the dormitory, a long spartan room with metal pillars, high ceilings and eight-foot tall windows which were always kept open. At first light the prefect, who slept in a little panelled room partitioned from the rest of the dorm, would walk between the rows of beds clapping his hands and shouting for the twenty-six boys to rise. Then under the life-size crucifix hung on one wall which dominated the room he would say morning prayers as the inmates stood by their beds in shivering oblation. Then there was a rush to the washroom where at a huge marble trough more than twenty feet long we would splash ourselves with icy water from its twenty-five taps. It was a perfunctory operation which was more than could be said of the weekly shower, for which we would have to troop down to the games block. We were required to shower in our shorts to preserve us from the impure sight of an alien scrotum. It was so cold there that we would take the blankets from our beds to wrap ourselves in after we were dried and dressed. On the way to morning mass I would sometimes see fog creeping up the main corridor outside the chapel, obscuring the stained glass window at the end of the corridor. For the rest of the school day, in which we were joined for lessons by the day boys, you would never really warm through.

After the day boys had gone at 4 p.m. there would be a break and then an afternoon tea of bread and butter and tinned fruit. The bread was ancient, its ends curled up from where it had been dipped in water to soften and the tea sometimes had a golden scum floating on the top of it because the serving youths, whom we called 'skivs', would occasionally put an old dishcloth in the teapot as a form of revenge.

A boarding school is designed to distort its pupils' perspective. There are no outside concerns or demands to dilute the intensity of the school experience so everything which happens in it assumes an exaggerated importance. At tea there would be fierce fights over who would get the extra peach from the can.

Thought I still saw all my old day boy friends like Foley and Cully I found that, increasingly, I had less in common with them. Their interests were focused entirely outside Blackrock and I could no longer go with them down to Murray's, to Stella House or simply round to their homes to drink tea and watch TV. But I also carried with me a residual antipathy to the boarder's claustral world with its bathroom gropings and dormitory faggotry. I began to feel as if I belonged in neither world. If I looked out of the window I could see my home. It was only a few minutes away. But there was no respite in my monthly visits home. I felt like a stranger there too.

At school the ideology of the church became more dominant too. Every day there was mass before breakfast in the school chapel, its gaudy baroque splendour made sinister by the misty morning half-light. To me it had always been an empty ritual, lacking even the theatre of Benediction, with its rich sensual scent of incense and its dark magical music. Besides, Benediction only lasted ten minutes. Mass bored me. I wasn't sure what I believed, but it wasn't this. I had nothing against religion, in fact I like to see people praying. I felt about the mass like the men who you can see attend every Irish Church every Sunday. They hover about the entrance and stub out their cigarettes before the consecration, then they hitch up their trousers and drop to one knee in reverential habit. Then the 'stabber' is re-ignited and the dash to the pub begins.

I actively disliked the church and its institutionalized morality, which I felt bedevilled Ireland. The bishops were the doddering old creeps who imposed it and the priests the ones who implemented it. They were not the same as the men I met later in Africa and elsewhere who were giants in comparison: great, pragmatic men driven by a sense of responsibility towards others. I felt humbled by them; they had given up everything and saw God in the suffering of others. This is something I cannot see. I see there a negation of God.

It is one of those unctuous Irish Catholic assumptions that 'pain is cleansing'. It is probably the reason they resorted to so much pain as punishment at Blackrock.

'Why did the Church use a fish as a symbol, Father?'
'Because Peter was a fisherman.'
'What sort of fish is it?'

373

'What do you mean?'

'Is it cod or mullet or gurnet, or what?'

'Sit down, Geldof.'

'Father, is God in everything or *is* he everything?'

'That's a good question, Geldof.'

'Thank you, Father.'

'God is *in* everything, because he *is* everything.'

'So, um, God is an ant.'

'No, God is all ants.'

'Then you could have an ant as a symbol, Father.'

'That's enough, Geldof.'

'If God is in everything, Father, then I'm God.'

'Yes, God is even in you, Geldof,' he said wearily.

'But you said he's *in* me, Father, because he *is* me. So I must be God.'

'That's blasphemy, Geldof. Perhaps God passed you by,' he smirked.

'Surely *that's* blasphemy, Father.'

'Right, Geldof, get out.'

Pain is cleansing – I got beaten. The priests could also be tormented by the Church's less than fabulous political history. The Spanish bishops' support of the fascist state was always a good one to get them floundering. So, too, was their hesitant denunciation of violence in the North, less than a hundred miles away. I also felt them responsible for many of the horrendous social evils of our country. They were insular, self-protective, powerful, omnipresent and faceless. They were almost my natural enemies. But as I, to use a very apt expression in this case, kicked against the pricks, I could not shirk off my fifteen years of training. Intellectually I resisted, but though logic stripped away the cant and ceremony I still could not rid myself of the voodoo.

From IS THAT IT?

———•◦•———

Bob Geldof K.B.E. (1952–   ), pop singer and song writer, was born in Dublin. He was the originator and organizer of Band Aid, Live Aid and Sport Aid, to raise funds for famine relief in Africa.

CARAGH DEVLIN

The Cat Sat on the Hat

I was born in Belfast on 31 July 1969. I was much admired by aunts who came to the Belfast City Hospital to poke and prod me, and by uncles who arrived with them to smoke cigars and to look for a celebratory 'jar'. The night before I left the Jubilee Maternity Unit, fires blazed in several parts of the city and casualties were brought in to the Accident and Emergency Unit. I knew nothing at all about this, and for many years when my mum said, 'The troubles began the day I left hospital,' I thought she meant me. Maybe she did.

Some people collect stamps. I collect aunts. They are reference marks on my map of Ireland. My mother came from Cork in the extreme south. She was one of a large and close family. With soft Irish names like Mary, Kitty, Betty, Anne, Brid, Deirdre, Philomena, Pauline and so on, Noreen and her sisters were the country girls who went to Dublin with Edna O'Brien to seek employment and adventure, or stayed at home to seek love in some Ballroom of Romance. What they found were husbands, children, nephews and nieces. My father came from Derry, in the extreme north. He was one of a small family of three. Their names – Catherine, Alexander, Frederick – had an altogether more stern, northern sound about them; come to think of it, like a family of Russian Tsars, which resulted from grandparents who perhaps read too many Russian novels. What's in a name? I sometimes wonder about this. It is usual in Ireland to be named after a saint or to inherit a name. Not me. I cannot trace any family ancestry for my first name, although in County Kerry I did come across a Caragh Lake, a Caragh River and a Caragh Bridge. So here am I, born in Belfast of a southern mother and a northern father, an only child called after a bridge in County Kerry.

I live in east Belfast, within sight of the Stormont Parliament Buildings and within sound of Harland and Wolff's shipyard and Short's aircraft factory at Sydenham. I belong to the parish of St Colmcille and attended the primary school attached to the chapel. Now I am a pupil at

Sullivan Upper School, a co-educational, non-sectarian grammar school, founded in 1877 and situated in Holywood on the shores of Belfast Lough. I am studying for 'A' levels, but already I am getting ready for the day I will leave school. There is a new seriousness about my school friends. We talk as much about what we hope to do or become and about keeping in touch, as we do about what is happening in school. We say, 'Imagine this will be our last Speech Day, our last Sports' Day, our last School Play,' as if only we had discovered that fact. We exult about the things we will not have to do any more: no more hockey, no more school dinners and no more sensible black shoes. We spur each other on, because we know we are going to miss Sullivan. It's that kind of school. We will become past pupils and think that our year was in some way a special year, but behind some classroom window as we board the school bus for the last time, I would not be surprised to find some tired teacher saying, 'Well, that's another lot through. Roll on Majorca.'

What of life outside school? There's always the television, except that I do not see much of that. In our house it is simply too much trouble to set about watching it. We keep the TV in a small cloakroom under the stairs, and to bring it out means pushing out the hoover, removing coats, shoes and sporting gear, and disturbing the cat, who sleeps on top of it. The cat can get very annoyed and spiteful about this. With tail waving angrily, she will walk out after the TV and off-handedly jump up to sleep on top of it again, as if this were the most natural thing in the world for a cat to do. My father defends her behaviour. He explains to anyone who happens to be in the room that she thinks she is a Royal Doulton cat and that, for the moment, we are tolerating her whim in the hope that she will grow out of it. It is not possible to take television seriously with a cat like ours. JR looks positively 'wet' with a cat on top of his stetson. We first put the set in the cloakroom when my father replaced his student days' record player with a stereo system on wheels. My mother took one look at the room and said that if it held anything more on wheels, it would look like a parking lot for supermarket trollies. So out to the cloakroom went the TV.

Then there's music. One way or another, it takes up a large part of my time. It began with my father. 'Listen to your father, he could stand in for James Galway any day of the week. And to think he hadn't a note in his head until he met me!' That's my mother speaking again. It's true, too, for my father whistles complete concertos and symphonies. He also conducts the stereo system. The cat watches in amazement. She has seen many things in her life, but never the like of this. I think she hopes that one day he is going to make her laugh. He has me as daft about music as he is. He first took me to piano lessons when I was six. Now I also play the violin. I practise the piano before I go to school in the morning, and the violin when I come home in the evening. I go out to the City of Belfast School of Music three nights a week for lessons, and play in the Youth Orchestra. We meet for three hours every Saturday morning. There are about ninety of us and we come from all over the city. In between playing, we exchange vital information with each other about the latest arrivals in Dorothy Perkins and Top Shop, haircuts and where to go for a good meal.

Saturday is also the day I go swimming. I was taught by Aaron Currie, a man from east Belfast, who devoted his life to teaching swimming. It was then that my father decided that he, too, would learn to swim. Mr Currie put him into the toddlers' class. My mother sat on the bench with their mothers. My father was so enthusiastic that he nearly drowned himself and the toddlers, because he could not wait to learn the strokes. The other mothers protested, but my mother encouraged him. I sometimes wonder why. When he swam his first width of the pool, she cooed her praises to him. He dismissed them, saying that he hadn't swum but had 'got across in a series of convulsions'. When I swam my first quarter-mile, she just said, 'Okay, why don't you try half a mile!' In the end we both became strong swimmers, and now we keep up the Belfast tradition of going to the baths on a Saturday night.

Sunday is a day of rest, but nobody told this to my mother. To her, Sunday means exercise: exercising me. She believes in exercising me as other people do their dogs. 'If it's the last thing I'll do,' she says, 'I'm going to make you enjoy your Sundays.' This would be fine if they all fell in summer and it meant sunbathing in a bikini or swimming in the sea at Portrush. Most Irish Sundays, however, are wet and windy, and it's Mum in her Adidas track-suit and Nike training shoes, Dad in his woollen hat and 'nature trekkers', and everybody crushed into the car and off to the Mourne Mountains for the good of my health.

I am also a member of the Irish Youth Orchestra, the national youth orchestra, which draws its members from both north and south of Ireland. Twice a year we come together for a residential course and to give concerts under the conductor, that illustrious Irish musician, Hugh Maguire. Through this orchestra I have become friends with a girl from Enniscorthy, County Wexford, called Clare. We look forward to seeing each other when the orchestra meets. It is wonderful that young musicians can be given the opportunity to come together to play, and to reflect on the part music should play in their future. When the time comes to go home, tears of farewell are shed, promises are made to keep in touch, and secret prayers offered to our supporters and sponsors who make it all possible.

What of the future? I am now seventeen, which means that the Troubles have now also been going on for seventeen years. I love the city of my birth. Its motto, *Pro Tanto Quid Retribuamus*, is always there to remind young people especially that they are expected to make some return to Belfast for the opportunities that the city has given them. I also love Ireland and feel at home in it, both north and south. I feel this way about Scotland, too, to which I go on holiday every year. I like the Scottish road sign that says, 'Heed your Speed', and repeat this to myself when I feel my life is rushing ahead too quickly. I look forward to 'A' levels and leaving school. That's when I think my future will really begin. This morning I heard Dolly Parton sing a very pretty little song called 'Love is Like a Butterfly'. What love is for Dolly Parton, my future seems at the moment to be for me. Something tantalizing and beckoning and just out of reach. I feel that I dare not stop to think about it or try just yet to catch it in the net. It is still just something for me, a Belfast girl, to dream about.

———•◦•———

Caragh Devlin (1969–   ), daughter of a civil servant, was born and brought up in Belfast.

Acknowledgements

We are particularly grateful to Fergus Allen, Brian Boydell, Peter Connolly, Adèle Crowder, Frank Delaney, Caragh Devlin, E. D. Doyle, Iris Kellett, Kate Cruise O'Brien, William Trevor and Liam Weldon for responding to our requests for contributions to this book.

Thanks are also due to the following for permission to reproduce copyright material – Samuel Beckett and John Calder (Publishers) Ltd for the extract from *How It Is*; Century Hutchinson Publishing Group Ltd for the extract from *Borstal Boy* by Brendan Behan; Bridget Boland and the Bodley Head Ltd for the extract from *At My Mother's Knee*; Virago Press for the extract from *Bowen's Court*, copyright © 1964 by Elizabeth Bowen, first published in Great Britain by Longmans, Green and Co. Ltd in 1942, and by Virago Press in 1984; Martin Secker and Warburg Ltd for the extract from *My Left Foot* by Christy Brown; Muller, Blond and White Ltd for the extract from *My Life and Easy Times* by Patrick Campbell; Curtis Brown Ltd, London, for the extract from *A House of Children*, copyright Joyce Cary 1941; Associated Book Publishers (UK) Ltd for the extract from *Twice Round the Black Church* by Austin Clarke, published by Routledge and Kegan Paul Ltd; Andre Deutsch Ltd for the extract from *Enemies of Promise* by Cyril Connolly; Gill and Macmillan Ltd for the extract from *Under the Receding Wave* by C. P. Curran; Dolmen Press Ltd for the rhyme from *Out She Goes*, compiled by Leslie Daiken; Curtis Brown Ltd, London, for the extract from *Eamon de Valera*, © 1978 The Earl of Longford and Thomas P. O'Neill; Penguin Books Ltd for the extract from *The Beastly Beatitudes of Balthazar B.*, © 1968 J. P. Donleavy, published by Penguin Books 1970; Curtis Brown Ltd, London, on behalf of John Child Villiers and Valentine Lamb as Literary Executors of Lord Dunsany for the extract from *Patches of Sunlight*, copyright estate of Lord Dunsany; Century Hutchinson Publishing Group Ltd for the extract from *Thy Tears Might Cease* by Michael Farrell; Bob Geldof and Sidgwick and Jackson Ltd for the extract from *Is That It?*; Oliver D. Gogarty for the poem by Oliver St John Gogarty; Anne Gregory and Colin Smythe Ltd for the extract from *Me and Nu*; Colin Smythe Ltd for the extract from *Seventy Years* by Lady Gregory; Seamus Heaney and Faber and Faber Ltd for the poem from *Death of a Naturalist*; Colin Smythe Ltd for the extract from *Five Arches* by T. R. Henn; M. Jesse Hoare and Howard Baker Press Ltd for the extract from *The Road to Glenanore*; Valentin Iremonger; Derry Jeffares and Colin Smythe Ltd for poems from *Brought up in Dublin* and *Brought up to Leave*; Jonathan Cape Ltd for the extract from *A Portrait of the*

379

Index

381